THE HAWTHORN
DICTIONARY OF PSEUDONYMS

THE HAWTHORN DICTIONARY OF PSEUDONYMS

Compiled by Andrew Bauer

Hawthorn Books, Inc.   *Publishers*   New York

PREFACE

This dictionary of pseudonyms is meant to serve as a handy reference book giving the pseudonymous names of writers and artists most likely to arouse the interest of the general reader. Past writers who have made no significant impression on the history of literature are generally excluded whereas contemporary writers are generally included, irrespective of critical opinion of their work. The artists who have been included have been so for the sake of simple curiosity; the concentration is on those of the Renaissance and the post-Renaissance period. The most recent biographical reference books were used in compiling this dictionary. The names were collected from large standard works as well as from articles in newspapers and magazines. Some of the reference books used were:

Canadian Authors
The Century Cyclopedia of Names
Current Biography
Dictionary of American Biography
Dictionary of National Biography
Dictionnaire Biographique des Auteurs de Tous les Temps et de Tous les Pays
Dizionario Universale della Letteratura Contemporanea
Encyclopædia Britannica
Facts on File
International Who's Who
Kindlers Literatur Lexikon
Lexikon der Weltliteratur
Moderne Encyclopedie de Wereldliteratur
Webster's Biographical Dictionary
Who's Who (British)
Who's Who in America (and supplements)

The compiler cannot pretend that the dictionary is flawless; omissions and even errors are inevitable. In compiling this dictionary clarity has been the guideline rather than strict uniformity of style. In most cases the main entry appears under the pseudonym. This is especially true if the pseudonym is the better known of the names used by the artist or writer. In many cases, however, the main entry appears under the real name, particularly if the person in question used two or more pseudonymous names. For the most part, Oriental and Welsh names are listed under the first name. There are exceptions to this: This usually occurs with the names of later Japanese and Chinese writers who have adopted the custom of putting their family name last. Thus "Takayama Chogyu" appears as is, whereas the entry for "Adet Jusu Lin" appears "Lin, Adet Jusu." In cases such as "Daniele da Volterra" the main entry is at "Volterra, Daniele da" unless the whole name is translated as a cognomen. Some pseudonyms that begin "Cousin" or "Father," such as "Father Abraham," appear as such, whereas when the word is used as a title, standard style is used: e.g., "Louis, Father M.," "Seuss, Dr.," "Bonaventura, Saint," "Mary Frances, Mother," "Dooley, Mr.," "Angelico, Fra." For names containing connective elements the connective has usually been placed first and determines the alphabetical order: Examples are "Le Corbusier" and "Van der Kulk, Willem." There are exceptions to this, of course, especially with the "van" and "von" connectives. Another exception would be "Vecchio, Il."

Russian names are spelled with much inconsistency in English reference works. The dictionary editor has attempted to unify spellings, especially variations introduced into English from French, German, and other languages, except in the case where the usage has become so widespread as to demand universal recognition. Birth and death dates are given in full wherever possible. Where there is uncertainty, appropriate question marks are fixed beside the date in doubt. Circa dates are indicated, or only the death date is given if that is all that is available. When there are no dates available, the general era is indicated. When there are no dates available and the writer is a contemporary writer, this is also indicated.

It is devoutly hoped by the editor that any difficulties caused by the stylistic peculiarities and idiosyncracies imposed by him upon this little reference book will be overcome by use and consequent familiarity.

A. B.

THE HAWTHORN
DICTIONARY OF PSEUDONYMS

"A"

A.A. of *Punch.* See WILLIS, ANTHONY ARMSTRONG.

æ (or Æ). Pseudonym of George William Russell (1867–1935), Irish poet and essayist.

A.L.F. Pseudonym of Theodor van Snakenburg (d. 1750), Dutch poet and translator.

A.L.O.E. (i.e., A Lady of England). Pseudonym of Charlotte Maria Tucker (1821–1893), English writer and missionary.

Aarons, Edward Sidney (1916–   ). Mystery writer, whose pseudonyms are *Paul Ayres* and *Edward Ronns.*

Ab'a. See SHAPIRO, KONSTANTIN.

Abag. See GOTTLOBER, ABRAHAM BAER.

Abarbanel, Judah León (1460–before 1535). Italian philosopher and Hebrew poet, also known as *Leone Ebreo* and *Leo Judaeus.*

Abbas Effendi. See ABDU'L-BAHA.

Abbattutis, Gian Alesio. Anagrammatic pseudonym of Gianbattista Basile (c1575–1632), Italian poet and short-story writer.

Abbing, Justine. Pseudonym of Carolina Lea (Carry) Van De Haan Bruggen (1881–1932), Dutch novelist and essayist.

Abbot, Anthony. Pseudonym of Charles Fulton Oursler (1893–1952), American journalist, playwright, and fiction writer, used for his detective stories.

Abbott, A. A. Pseudonym of Samuel Spewack (1899–   ), mystery writer and playwright.

Abbott, Bruce. See REACH, JAMES.

Abbott, Manager Henry. See STRATEMEYER, EDWARD L.

Abby, Kieran. Pseudonym of Helen Kieran Reilly (1890?–1962), mystery writer.

Abdu'l-Baha (1844–1921). Persian writer, also known as *Abbas Effendi.*
He helped to establish the Bahai faith in Europe and America.

Abel, Alan. See BRISTOL, JULIUS.

Abel, Jeanne. See BRONSTEIN, YETTA.

Abellio, Raymond. Pseudonym of Jean Georges Soulès (1907–   ),
French writer.

Abelson, Ann. Pseudonym of Ann Abelson Cavallaro (1918–   ),
American author.

Abeozen. Pseudonym of Yann-Fañch Eliès (1896–   ), Breton poet.

Ab-o'-th'-Yate. Pseudonym of Benjamin Brierley (1825–1896), English
writer of short stories and verse in Lancashire dialect.

Abraham a Sancta Clara. Religious name of Johann Ulrich Megerle
(1644–1709), German preacher and pamphleteer.

Abrahams, Doris Caroline (1901–   ). Mystery writer, whose pseudonyms are *Caryl Brahms* and *Oliver Linden.*

Abrahamsohn, Otto. Pseudonym of Otto Brahm (1856–1912), German
journalist and short-story writer.

Abramanti. See BRAMANTE, DONATO.

Abramovich, Sholem Jacob. See MENDELE MOCHER SFORIM.

Abu-L-Atahiya. Pseudonym of Abu Ishak Ismail ben al-Kasim ben Su-
wayd ben Kaysan (748–c825/26), Arabic author. His pseudonym
means "The Father of Madness."

Abu'l-Najm, Ahmad. See MANUCHIHRI.

Academic Investor. Pseudonym of W. Brian Reddaway (1913–   ),
English writer on economics.

Accolti, Bernardo (1465–1536). Italian poet, also known as *L'Unico
Aretino.* He was the brother of Piero Accolti.

Acernus. Pseudonym of Sebastian Klonowic (1545?–1602), Polish satirical poet.

Achad Haam (or **Ahad Ha-am**). Pseudonym of Asher Ginzberg (1856–
1927), Jewish-Ukrainian philosopher, essayist, and editor.

Achyut. Pseudonym of Lakshminiwas Birla (1909–   ), Indian writer.

Acken. See BOSCH, HIERONYMUS.

Ackermann, Alexander. See AGRICOLA, ALEXANDER.

Acosta, Gabriel (c1591–1647?). Portuguese philosopher, also called
Uriel da Costa.

Acre, Stephen. See GRUBER, FRANK.

Actius Syncerus. Pseudonym of Jacopo Sannazzaro (1456/58–1530),
Italian humanist and poet.

Adair, Cecil. Pseudonym of Evelyn Everett-Green (1856–1932), mystery writer.

Adair, Dennis. See CRONIN, BERNARD.

Adalisa, Anne. See RAINE, ALLEN.

Adam. Pseudonym of Abraham Dov Lebenson (1789/94–1878), Hebrew poet and scholar. He has been called the father of modern Hebrew poetry.

Adam, Cornel. Pseudonym of Cornel Adam Lengyel (1915–   ), American writer.

Adam, Juliette (1836–1936). French writer, whose pseudonyms are *Juliette Lamber, La Messine*, and *Compte Paul Vasili.*

Adam de la Halle. See ADAM LE BOSSU.

Adam le Bossu ("Adam the Hunchback"). Cognomen of Adam de la Halle (1235?–1285), French musician and playwright.

Adams, A. Don. See CLEVELAND, PHILIP JEROME.

Adams, Betsy. See PITCHER, GLADYS.

Adams, Christopher. See HOPKINS, KENNETH.

Adams, Cleve Franklin (1895–1950). Mystery writer, whose pseudonyms are *Franklin Charles* and *John Spain.*

Adams, Clifton (1919–   ). American free-lance writer, whose pseudonyms are *Jonathan Gant, Matt Kinkaid*, and *Clay Randall.*

Adams, Franklin Pierce. See F.P.A.

Adams, Harriet. See KEENE, CAROLYN.

Adams, Harrison. See STRATEMEYER, EDWARD L.

Adams, Henry T. Pseudonym of Jay Ellis Ransom (1914–   ), American writer.

Adams, Herbert. See GRAY, JONATHAN.

Adams, Lowell. Pseudonym of James Herz Joseph (1924–   ), American writer.

Adams, Moses. Pseudonym of George William Bagby (1828–1883), American humorist and lecturer. He was also known as *Mozis Addums.*

Adams, Robert Martin. See KRAPP, R. M.

Adams, Samuel Hopkins. See FABIAN, WARNER.

Adams, William Taylor. See OPTIC, OLIVER.

Adamson, Graham. See GROOM, ARTHUR WILLIAM.

Addis, Eric Erlington. See DRAX, PETER.

Addiscombe, John. See HUNTER, JOHN.

Addison, Carol. See CLARKE, J. CALVITT.

Addison, Hugh. Pseudonym of Harry Collinson Owen (1882–), mystery writer.

Addums, Mozis. See ADAMS, MOSES.

Adib al-Mamalik (1860/61–1917). Persian poet, satirist, and journalist, also known as *Sadiq Amiri.*

Adine, France. Pseudonym of Cécile Van Drome (1890–), Belgian writer.

Adler, Irene. See STORR, CATHERINE.

Adler, Irving. See IRVING, ROBERT.

Adler, Kaspar. See AQUILA, KASPAR.

Adonim ha-Levi. See DUNASH BEN LABRAT.

Adret (or ibn-Adret), Solomon (c1235–c1310). Spanish-Hebrew religious writer, also known as *Rashba.*

Adrian, Mary. Pseudonym of Mary Venn Jorgensen, contemporary American wildlife and mystery writer.

Aeken. See BOSCH, HIERONYMUS.

Aelian. See AELIANUS, CLAUDIUS.

Aelianus, Claudius. Roman name of Aelian, 3rd-century Greek writer in Latin, who lived near Rome.

Afterwit, Anthony. See FRANKLIN, BENJAMIN.

Agalstein, Mieczysław. See JASTRUN, MIECZYSŁAW.

Agapida, Friar Antonio. See IRVING, WASHINGTON.

Agar, Brian. See BALLARD, TODHUNTER.

Agnew, Edith J. See MARCELINO.

Agnon, Shemuel Joseph (1888–). Galician-Hebrew novelist and short-story writer, whose original name was Shmuel Yoseph Tchatsky.

Agoult, Marie Catherine Sophie de Flavigny, Comtesse d'. See STERN, DANIEL.

Agricola, Alexander. Pseudonym of Alexander Ackermann (1446?–1506), German composer.

Agricola, Georg. Pseudonym of George Bauer (1494–1555), Saxon legal writer.

Agricola, Johannes. Cognomen of Johannes Schnitter (1494?–1566), German Protestant reformer, whose original surname was Sneider. He was also called *Magister Islebius.*

Agricola, Martin. Pseudonym of Martin Sohr (1486–1556), German musician and composer.

Agricola, Rodolphus. Latinized name of Roelof Huysman (1443–1485), Dutch scholar and painter.

Ahad Ha-am. See ACHAD HAAM.

Ahern, Margaret McCrohan. See O'CONNELL, PEG.

Aherne, Owen. See CASSILL, RONALD VERLIN.

Ahlgren, Ernst. Pseudonym of Victoria Maria Benedictsson (1850–1888), Swedish novelist and playwright.

Ahlqvist, Carl August Engelbreckt. See OKSANEN.

Ahmedi. Pseudonym of Taceddin Ibrahim (1334–1413), Turkish epic poet.

Aho, Juhani. Pseudonym of Juhani Brofeldt (1861–1921), Finnish writer.

Aiguillette. Pseudonym of Reginald Charles Hargreaves (1888–   ), English writer.

Aiken, Conrad Potter. See JEAKE, SAMUEL, JR.

Aikio, Matti. See ISAKSEN, MATHIS.

Aikman, Ann. Pseudonym of Ann Aikman McQuade (1928–   ), American writer.

Aimard, Gustave. Pseudonym of Olivier Gloux (1818–1883), French traveler and writer.

Ainsworth, Norma. See RUEDI, NORMA PAUL.

Ainsworth, Ruth. Pseudonym of Ruth Gallard Ainsworth Gilbert (1908–   ), English writer.

Aintree. See WALLACE, JOHN.

Airlie, Catherine. Pseudonym of Jean Sutherland Macleod (1908–   ), Scottish-English novelist.

Akers, Floyd. See BAUM, LYMAN FRANK.

Akhmatova, Anna (1888–1966). Russian poet, also known as *Anna Andreyevna Gorenko.*

Alain. Pseudonym of Emile Auguste Chartier (1868–1951), French philosopher and essayist.

Alain-Fournier. Pseudonym of Henri Alban Fournier (1886–?1914), French novelist.

Alan, A. J. Pseudonym of Leslie Harrison Lambert, contemporary mystery writer.

Alan, Marjorie. Pseudonym of Doris Marjorie Bumpus (1905–   ), mystery writer.

Alas, Leopoldo. See CLARÍN.

Alas y Ureña, Leopoldo. See CLARÍN.
Alberdingk Thijm, Karel Jan Lodewijk. See DEYSSEL, LODEWIJK VAN.
Albert, Marvin H. See ROME, ANTHONY.
Alberti, Konrad. Pseudonym of Konrad Sittenfeld (1862–1918), German actor and journalist.
Albert i Paradís, Catarina. See CATALÀ, VICTOR.
Albrand, Martha (1914–). German-American writer, whose pseudonyms are *Katrin Holland* and *Christine Lambert.*
Alcayaga, Lucila Godoy de. See MISTRAL, GABRIELA.
Alcon, R. See BRONTË, EMILY JANE.
Alcott, Louisa May. See FAIRFIELD, FLORA.
Alcuin (735–804). Poet and ecclesiastic, adviser to Charlemagne. His Anglo-Saxon name was Ealhwine.
Alcuinus. See CALVIN, JOHN.
Alda, Frances (1883–1952). New Zealand operatic soprano and author. Her original name was Frances Davis.
Aldanov, Mark. Pseudonym of Mark Alexandrovitch Landau (1886–1957), Russian emigré novelist.
Aldiss, Brian Wilson. See SHACKLETON, C. C.
Aldon, Adair. Pseudonym of Cornelia Lynde Meigs (1884–), American writer.
Aldrich, Earl Augustus. See LEONARD, A. B.
Aleichem, Shalom (or **Sholem**). Pseudonym of Solomon Rabinowitz (or Rabinovitz) (1859–1916), Russian-American-Yiddish humorist.
Alekseyev, Konstantin Sergeyevich. See STANISLAVSKI.
Alepudelis, Odisséus. See ELITIS, ODISSÉUS.
Aleramo, Sibilla. Pseudonym of Rina Facciò (1876–1960), Italian poet.
Alexander, Charles. See HADFIELD, ELLIS CHARLES RAYMOND.
Alexander, Colin James. See JAY, SIMON.
Alexander, Jocelyn Anne Arundel. See ARUNDEL, JOCELYN.
Alexander, John. See VLASTO, JOHN ALEXANDER.
Alexander, Mrs. Pseudonym of Annie Hector (1825–1902), British novelist.
Alexander, Ruth. Pseudonym of Ruth Rogers (1890–), mystery writer.
Alexeyev, Sergey Alexandrovich. See NAYDENOV, S.
Alexis, Willibald. Pseudonym of George Wilhelm Häring (1798–1871), German novelist.

Ali Gier-Ber. See GIER-BER, ALI.

Aliki. Pseudonym of Aliki Liacouras Brandenberg (1929–   ), American illustrator and writer.

Alington, Cyril Argentine. See WESTERHAM, S. C.

Allan, Dennis. See DENNISTON, ELINORE.

Allan, George. See KREMNITZ, MITE.

Allan, Luke. Pseudonym of Lacey Amy, contemporary mystery writer.

Allan, Mabel Esther (1915–   ). English-born author, whose pseudonyms are *Jean Estoril* and *Anne Pilgrim.*

Allardyce, Paula. See TORDAY, URSULA.

Allegri, Antonio. See CORREGGIO.

Allen, Adam. See EPSTEIN, BERYL WILLIAMS, and EPSTEIN, SAMUEL.

Allen, Allyn. See EBERLE, IRMENGARDE.

Allen, Barbara. See STUART, VIVIAN.

Allen, Betsy. See CAVANNA, ELIZABETH ALLEN.

Allen, Elizabeth. See PERCY, FLORENCE.

Allen, Grant (1848–1899). British writer, whose pseudonyms are *Cecil Power, Olive Pratt Rayner, Martin Leach Warborough,* and *J. Arbuthnot Wilson.*

Allen, Marion C. See ALLEN, SAM.

Allen, Sam. Pseudonym of Marion C. Allen (1914–   ), American author.

Allerton, Mark. Pseudonym of William Ernest Cameron, contemporary mystery writer.

Allerton, Mary. See GOVAN, CHRISTINE NOBLE.

Allison, Clay. See KEEVIL, HENRY JOHN.

Allison, Marian. Pseudonym of Frances Pugh Reid (1910–   ), American writer.

Allison, Rand. See MCCORMICK, WILFRED.

Allison, Sam. See LOOMIS, NOEL MILLER.

Allyn, Paul. Pseudonym of Paul Allyn Schosberg (1938–   ), American writer.

Almafuerte. Pseudonym of Pedro Bonifacio Palacios (1854–1917), Argentinian poet.

Alman, David. See DAVID, EMILY.

Alman, Emily. See DAVID, EMILY.

Almedingen, E. M. Pseudonym of Martha Edith Von Almedingen (1898–   ), Russian-English author.

Alpert, Hollis. See CARROLL, ROBERT.

Alsop, Mary O'Hara. See O'HARA, MARY.

Altenberg, Peter. Pseudonym of Richard Engländer (1862?–1919), Austrian writer.

Alter, Moshe Jacob. See ROSENFELD, MORRIS.

Alter, Robert Edmond (1925–1965). American writer, whose pseudonyms are *Robert Raymond* and *Robert Retla.*

Alun. Pseudonym of John Blackwell (1797–1840), Welsh poet, who began life as a shoemaker and became a cleric.

Alvarez, Alejandro Rodríguez. See CASONA, ALEJANDRO.

Alzey, Konrad von. Pseudonym of Konrad Nies (1861–1921), German-American poet.

Amalie Marie Friederike Auguste, Duchess of Saxony. See HEITER, AMALIE.

Amamoo, Joseph Godson. See KAMBU, JOSEPH.

Amarcius (fl. 1040). Satirist and monk from the Rhineland, whose full pseudonym was *Sextus Amarcius Gallus Pisistratus.*

Amatora, Sister Mary. See FLEURY, DELPHINE.

Ambler, Eric. See REED, ELIOT.

Ambrogini, Angiolo. See POLIZIANO, ANGELO.

Ambrose of Camaldoli, Saint. Religious name of Ambrogio Traversari (1386–1439), Italian scholar.

Ambrose, Eric (1908–   ). English architectural critic and writer, whose pseudonyms are *Esor B. MacIre, Christopher Rennie,* and *Edgar Vance.*

Ames, Francis H. See WATSON, FRANK.

Ames, Jennifer. See GREIG, MAYSIE.

Amiri, Sadiq. See ADIB AL-MAMALIK.

Amis, Breton. Pseudonym of Rayleigh Breton Amis Best (1905–   ), English free-lance writer.

Amis, Kingsley. See MARKHAM, ROBERT.

Amos, Alan. Pseudonym of Kathleen Moore Knight, contemporary mystery writer.

Amundsen, Johan Fredrik. See PAASCHE, JOHAN FREDRIK.

Amy, Lacey. See ALLAN, LUKE.

Amyntor, Gerhard von. Pseudonym of Dagobert von Gerhardt (1831–1910), German soldier and writer.

Ancona, Ciricco de (1391–1452). Italian epigraphist, also known as *Ciriaco de Pizzicolli.*

Anczyc, Władysław Ludwik. See GÓRALCZYK, KOZIMIERZ.

Anders, Edith Mary England. See ENGLAND, E. M.

Andersen, Hans Christian. See WALTER, VILLIAM CHRISTIAN.

Anderson, Alexander. See SURFACEMAN.

Anderson, Betty. See CANYON, CLAUDIA.

Anderson, George. See GROOM, ARTHUR WILLIAM.

Anderson, George. Pseudonym of Jack Weissman (1921–   ), American writer.

Anderson, Madeleine Paltenghi. See PALTENGHI, MADELEINE.

Anderson, Paul William. See SANDERS, WINSTON P.

Ando Hachizaemon. See ANDO JISHO.

Ando Jisho. Pseudonym of Ando Hachizaemon (1658–1745), Japanese novelist.

Andom, R. Pseudonym of Alfred Walter Barrett (1869–?), mystery writer.

Ando Tokitaro. See HIROSHIGE.

Andrade, Oswald de. Pseudonym of José Oswald de Sousa (1890–1954), Brazilian poet.

Andreus, Hans. Pseudonym of Johan Wilhelm van der Zant (1926–   ), Dutch writer.

Andrews, Charles Robert Douglas Hardy (1908–   ). American writer, whose pseudonyms are *Robert Douglas* and *Douglas Hardy.*

Andrews, Wayne. See O'REILLY, MONTAGU.

Andrews, William Linton. See SETTLE, EDITH.

Andreyevich. Pseudonym of Evgeny Andreyevich Solovyëv (1863–1905), Russian critic and literary historian.

Andrézel, Pierre. See BLIXEN-FINECKE, BARONESS KAREN CHRISTENTZE.

Anet, Claude. Pseudonym of Jean Schopfer (1868–1931), French novelist and essayist.

Angeli, Pietro Angelo (1517–1596). Italian poet, also known as *Pier Angelo Bargeo.*

Angelico, Fra (1387–1455). Italian painter and Dominican friar, whose full name was *Il Beato Fra Giovanni Angelico da Fiesole.* His original name was Guido di Pietro.

Anghiera, Pietro Martire d'. See MARTYR, PETER.

Anglerius. See MARTYR, PETER.

Anglesey, The Marquess of. See MARQUESS OF ANGLESEY, THE.

Anglus, Alexander. See CARPENTER, ALEXANDER.

Angoff, Charles. See HINTON, RICHARD W.

Aniante, Antonio. Pseudonym of Antonio Rapisarda (1909–   ), Italian writer.

Anmar, Frank. See NOLAN, WILLIAM FRANCIS.

Annett, Cora. Pseudonym of Cora Annett Scott (1931–   ), American writer.

Ansel, Franz. Pseudonym of Franz Folie (1874–1939), Belgian writer.

An-Ski, Sh. A. Pseudonym of Solomon Samuel Rappaport (1863–1920), Russian-Yiddish writer.

Anstey, F. Pseudonym of Thomas Anstey Guthrie (1856–1934), English writer.

Antal, Adèle Sophia Cornelia von. See WALLIS, A. S. C.

Anthony, C. L. Pseudonym (until 1935) of Dodie Smith (1896–   ), English playwright.

Anthony, Evelyn. See WARD THOMAS, EVELYN BRIDGET PATRICIA STEPHENS.

Anthony, John. Pseudonym of Ronald Brymer Beckett (1891–   ), British author.

Anthony, John. Pseudonym of John Anthony Sabini (1921–   ), American-Lebanese writer.

Anthony, Peter. Joint pseudonym of Anthony Shaffer (1926–   ) and Peter Shaffer (1926–   ), mystery writers.

Anti-Climacus. See KIERKEGAARD, SØREN AABYE.

Antonio the Elder. See SANGALLO.

Antonio the Younger. See SANGALLO.

Antschel, Paul. See CELAN, PAUL.

Aoibhinn, An Craoibhín. Gaelic name of Douglas Hyde (1860–1949), Irish poet and scholar.

Apeltern, H. van. See ENGELEN, ADRIAAN.

Apianus, Petrus. Latinized name of Peter Bienewitz (or Bennewitz) (1501?–1552), German astronomer, mathematician, and geographer.

Apollinaire, Guillaume. Pseudonym of Wilhelm Apollinaris de Kostrowitski (1880–1918), French poet.

Apperley, Charles James. See NIMROD.

Appleton, Victor. Collective pseudonym for the "Don Sturdy" series. See STRATEMEYER, EDWARD L.

Appleton, Victor, II. Collective pseudonym for the "Tom Swift, Jr." series. See STRATEMEYER, EDWARD L.

Appley, Mortimer Herbert. See APPLEZWEIG, M. H.

Applezweig, M. H. Pseudonym of Mortimer Herbert Appley (1921–), American-Canadian scholar.

Applin, Arthur. See SWIFT, JULIAN.

Apulia, Nicholas (Pietri) de. See PISANO, NICOLA.

Aquarian. Pseudonym of Joel Lester Oppenheimer (1930–), American writer.

Aquen. See BOSCH, HIERONYMUS.

Aquila, Kaspar (1488–1560). German Protestant theologian, whose original name was Kaspar Adler.

Arai Hakuseki. Pseudonym of Arai Kimiyoshi (1657–1725), Japanese historian.

Arai Kimiyoshi. See ARAI HAKUSEKI.

Araujo, Joachim Aurelio Barreto Nabuco de. See NABUCO, JOAQUIM.

Arbuthnot, John. See SCRIBLERUS, MARTINUS.

Arcagnuolo. See ORCAGNA, ANDREA.

Archer, A. A. See JOSCELYN, ARCHIE L.

Archer, Lane. See HAUCK, LOUISE.

Ard, William Thomas (1922–). American free-lance writer, whose pseudonyms are *Ben Kerr, Mike Moran, Jonas Ward,* and *Thomas Wills.*

Arden, Barbie. See STOUTENBURG, ADRIEN PEARL.

Arden, J. E. M. Pseudonym of Robert Conquest (1917–), English writer.

Ardenne, Jean d'. Pseudonym of Léon Dommartin (1839–1919), Belgian journalist.

Ardutiel ben Isaac, Sem Tob ibn-. See SANTOB DE CARRIÓN DE LOS CONDES.

Aresbys, The. See BAMBERGER, HELEN R.

Aretino, L'Unico. See ACCOLTI, BERNARDO.

Aretius Felinus. Pseudonym of Martin Bucer (or Butzer) (1491–1551), German Protestant reformer and theologian, whose original surname was Kuhhorn.

Arghezi, Tudor. Pseudonym of Ion Theodorescu (1880–), Hungarian poet and pamphleteer.

Argus. See PHILLIPS-BIRT, DOUGLAS.

Arid, Ben. Pseudonym of Melville Clemens Barnard, contemporary mystery writer.

Ariel. Pseudonym of Frank Robert Moraes (1907–), Indian writer.

Aristotile. See SANGALLO.

Arkel, Frank Floriszoon van. Pseudonym of Maurits Cornelis van Hall (1768–1858), Dutch poet and writer.

Arlen, Michael (1895–1956). British novelist and playwright, whose original name was Dikran Kouyoumdjian.

Armand. See STRUBBERG, FRIEDRICH ARMAND.

Armstrong, Anthony. See WILLIS, ANTHONY ARMSTRONG.

Armstrong, Douglas Albert (1920–). British writer, whose pseudonyms are *Albert Douglas, Tribune,* and *Rex Windsor.*

Armstrong, John Byron (1917–). American writer, whose pseudonyms are *John Byron* and *Charles Willard.*

Armstrong, Raymond. See LEE, NORMAN.

Armstrong, Terence Ian Fytton. See GAWSWORTH, JOHN.

Armstrong, William Alexander. See HAZELTON, ALEXANDER.

Arnarson, Ørn. Pseudonym of Magnús Stefánsson (1884–1942), Icelandic poet.

Arnold, Joseph H. Pseudonym of Joseph Hayes (1918–), American playwright and novelist.

Arnold, L. J. See CAMERON, LOU.

Arnold, Richards. See COCH-Y-BONDDHU.

Arouet, François Marie. See VOLTAIRE.

Arp, Bill. Pseudonym of Charles Henry Smith (1826–1903), American humorist and writer.

Arp, Hans. See ARP, JEAN.

Arp, Jean (1887–). French poet, sculptor, and pioneer of abstract art, also known as *Hans Arp.*

Ar-Raihant, Amin. See REEHANY, AMIN.

Arre, Helen. See ROSS, ZOLA HELEN.

Arrighi, Cletto. Pseudonym of Carlo Righetti (1830–1906), Italian writer.

Arrom, Cecilia Francisca Josefa de. See CABALLERO, FERNÁN.

Arthur, Frank. Pseudonym of Arthur Frank Ebert (1902–), mystery writer.

Arthur, H. Preston. See HANKINS, ARTHUR PRESTON.

Arthur, Harry. Pseudonym of Harry Arthur Bates, contemporary mystery writer.

Arthur, William. See NEUBAUER, WILLIAM ARTHUR.

Arundel, Jocelyn. Pseudonym of Jocelyn Anne Arundel Alexander (1930–), American writer.

Ary, Sheila Mary Littleboy. See LITTLEBOY, SHEILA M.
Ascoli, Cecco d'. Cognomen of Francesco degli Stabili (c1257–1327), Italian poet and philosopher.
Asenjo Barbieri, Francisco. See BARBIERI, FRANCISCO ASENJO.
Ash, Peter. See HAUCK, LOUISE.
Ashbrook, Harriette. See SHANE, SUSANNAH.
Ashe, Gordon. See CREASEY, JOHN.
Asher. See SHAPIRO, KONSTANTIN.
Asher (or Asheri) ben Yehiel (c1250–1327). Spanish-Hebrew religious writer, also known as *Rosh.*
Asher ha-Levi, Elijah ben. See LEVITA, ELIJAH.
Ashkenazi, Elijah. See LEVITA, ELIJAH.
Ashley, Ernest. See VIVIAN, FRANCIS.
Ashley, Graham. See ORGAN, JOHN.
Ashlin, John. Pseudonym of John Ashlin Cutforth (1911–   ), English writer.
Ashton, Winifred. See DANE, CLEMENCE.
Asimov, Isaac. See FRENCH, PAUL.
Askari, Hussaini Muhammad. See PEREIRA, HAROLD BERTRAM.
Askham, Francis. Pseudonym of Julia Eileen Courtney Greenwood (1910–   ), English writer.
Asnyk, Adam. See EL-Y.
Aspazia. Pseudonym of Elsa Rosenberg (1868–1943), Latvian writer.
Asselbergs, Willem Jan Marie Anton. See VAN DUINKERKEN, ANTON.
Assiac. See FRAENKEL, HEINRICH.
Asterisk. Pseudonym of Robert James Fletcher (1877–   ), mystery writer.
Aswin. Pseudonym of Prema Nandakumar (1939–   ), Indian writer.
Atchison, Sandra Dallas. See DALLAS, SANDRA.
Atheling, William. See POUND, EZRA LOOMIS.
Athos. See WALKERLY, RODNEY LEWIS.
Atrachovich, Kandrat. See KRAPIVA, KANDRAT.
Aubrey-Fletcher, Sir Henry Lancelot. See WADE, HENRY.
Auchincloss, Louis Stanton. See LEE, Andrew.
Audemars, Pierre. See HODEMART, PETER.
Aung, Maung Htin. See FOURTH BROTHER, THE.
Aurispa, Giovanni (1375?–1459). Italian humanist. His original name was Giovanni Pichumerio.
Auskelis. Pseudonym of Mikus Krogzemju (1850–1879), Latvian writer.

Austin, Brett. See FLOREN, LEE.

Austin, Hugh. Pseudonym of Hugh Austin Evans, contemporary mystery writer.

Austwick, John. See LEE, AUSTIN.

Auty, Phyllis. See RICHARDS, PHYLLIS.

Avallone, Michael Angelo, Jr. (1924–   ). American free-lance writer, whose pseudonyms are *Mark Dane* and *Steve Michaels.*

Avellaneda y Arteaga, Gertrudis Gómez de. See PEREGRINA, LA.

Avempace (d. 1138). Spanish-Arabian philosopher, whose Arabic name was abu-Bakr Muhammad ibn-Yahya ibn-Bajjah. He was also known simply as *ibn-Bajjah* and *ibn-al-Sa'igh.*

Aventinus, Johannes. Latinized name of Johann Turmair (1477–1534), German humanist and historian.

Averill, H. C. See SNOW, CHARLES HORACE.

Averlino (or Averulino), Antonio di Pietro. See FILARETE.

Averroës (1126–1198). Spanish-Arabian philosopher, whose Arabic name was abu-al-Walid Muhammad ibn-Ahmad ibn-Rushd. He was also known simply as *ibn-Rushd.*

Avery, Al. See MONTGOMERY, RUTHERFORD GEORGE.

Avery, Lynn. See COLE, LOIS DWIGHT.

Avicebrón. Pseudonym of Solomon ben Judah ibn-Gabirol (c1020–c1057), Hebrew poet and Arabian philosopher, also known simply as *Gabirol.*

Avicenna (980–1035). Arabian philosopher, whose Arabic name was abu-'Ali al-Husayn ibn-Sina. He was also known simply as *ibn-Sina.*

Avinoam. Pseudonym of Reuben Grossmann (1905–   ), Hebrew poet.

Aylmer, Felix. Pseudonym of Felix Edward Aylmer Jones (1889–   ), English writer.

Ayres, Paul. See AARONS, EDWARD SIDNEY.

Ayrton, Michael. See GOULD, MICHAEL.

Ayscough, John. Pseudonym of Monsignor Count Francis Browning Drew Bickerstaffe-Drew (1858–1928), English Roman Catholic clergyman and novelist.

Azorín. Pseudonym of José Martínez Ruíz (1874–1967), Spanish essayist, critic, and playwright.

"B"

B.B. See WATKINS-PITCHFORD, DENYS JAMES.

B.V. (i.e., Bysshe Vanolis). Pseudonym of James Thomson (1834–1882), Scottish poet. The name is derived from Shelley's middle name and an anagram of Novalis.

Ba'al ha-Turim. See JACOB BEN ASHER.

Baal Shem-Tov. See ISRAEL BEN ELIEZER.

Baastad, Babbis Friis. See FRIIS-BAASTAD, BABBIS ELLINOR.

Baba Tahir-i Hamadani. See URYAN.

Babbis, Eleanor. See FRIIS-BAASTAD, BABBIS ELLINOR.

Babbler. See LLOYD, J. IVESTER.

Babcock, Frederic. See MARK, MATTHEW.

Babcock, Winnifred. See WATANNA, ONOTO.

Babic, Ljuba. See GJALSKI, KSAVER SANDOR.

Babjuk, Andrey. See IRCHAN, MYROSLAV.

Babli, Hillel. Pseudonym of Hillel Raschgolski (1893–   ), Hebrew poet.

Baccio della Porta. See BARTOLOMMEO, FRA.

Bach, Paul. Pseudonym of Rudolf Baumbach (1840–1905), German lyric and narrative poet.

Bachi, Amurath-Effendi Hekim. Pseudonym of Pieter van Woensel (1747–1808), Dutch physician and satirical writer.

Bachiacca, Il. Cognomen of Francesco Ubertini (1494?–1557), Italian painter.

Bachur, Elijah. See LEVITA, ELIJAH.

Baciccio, Il. Cognomen of Giovanni Battista Gaulli (1639–1709), Italian painter.

Backx, Pieter. See VAN DUINKERKEN, ANTON.

Bacon, Josephine Dodge Daskam. See LOVELL, INGRAHAM.

Bacovia, George. Pseudonym of George Vasiliu (1881–1947), Rumanian poet.

Badchen, Eliakim. See ZUNSER, ELIAKIM.

Badi' al-Zaman ("Wonder of the Age"). Cognomen of al-Hamadhani (969–1007), Moslem poet.

Baertmaeker, Jan de. See SMEKEN, JAN.

Bagarag, Shibli. See LAWLOR, PATRICK ANTHONY.

Bagby, George. See STEIN, AARON MARC.

Bagby, George William. See ADAMS, MOSES.

Bagnacavallo, Il. Cognomen of Bartolommeo Ramenghi (1484–1542), Italian painter.

Bagnold, Enid. See LADY OF QUALITY, A.

Bagritsky, Eduard. Pseudonym of E. Dzyubin (1897–1934), Russian poet.

Bagrjana, Elisaveta. Pseudonym of Elisaveta Belcheva (1893–   ), Bulgarian poet.

Bagrynowski, K. See SIEROSZEWSKI, WACLAW.

Bagster, Hubert. Pseudonym of Hubert Bagster Trumper (1902–   ), English writer.

Bahar, Malik al-Shu'ara. Pseudonym of Muhammad Taqi Bahar (1886–1951), Persian poet.

Bahar, Muhammad Taqi. See BAHAR, MALIK AL-SHU'ARA.

Bahithat al-Badiyah ("Searcher of the Desert"). Pseudonym of Malak Hifni Nasif (1886–1918), Egyptian-Arab poet, essayist, and feminist.

Bahur, Elijah. See LEVITA, ELIJAH.

Bahya ben Joseph. See BAHYA IBN-PAQUDA.

Bahya ibn-Paquda (eleventh century). Spanish-Hebrew poet and Arabic philosopher, also known as *Bahya ben Joseph.*

Bailey, Frederick Augustus Washington. See DOUGLASS, FREDERICK.

Bailey, Hilea. Pseudonym of Ruth Lenore Marting (1907–   ), mystery writer.

Bailey, Matilda. See RADFORD, RUBY LORRAINE.

Bajjah, ibn-. See AVEMPACE.

Bakalov. Pseudonym of Tsanko Tserkovski (1869–1926), Bulgarian writer.

Baker, Asa. See DRESSER, DAVIS.

Baker, Betty D. See RENIER, ELIZABETH.

Baker, Marceil Genée Kolstad. See MILLER, MARC.

Baker, Mary Gladys. See STUART, SHEILA.

Baker, Ray Stannard. See GRAYSON, DAVID.

Bakin (or **Kyokutei Bakin**). Pseudonym of Takizawa Okikuni (1767–1848), one of the greatest Japanese novelists, who produced over 300 works. He was also known as *Takizawa Tokuru.*

Bakst, Léon Nikolayevich (1886–1924). Russian painter, whose original surname was Rosenberg.

Balázs, Béla. Pseudonym of Herbert Bauer (1886–   ), Hungarian-Austrian journalist, poet, and editor.

Balbulus the Stammerer. Cognomen of Notker (c840–912), Germanic writer and monk of the Abbey of St. Gaul.

Balbus. Occasional pseudonym of Julian Sorell Huxley (1887–   ), English scholar.

Balduc, Fiamengo (or Bosco) di. See BOSCH, HIERONYMUS.

Baldung, Hans (1476?–1545). German painter, also called *Hans Grien* (or *Grün*).

Baldwin, Bates. See JENNINGS, JOHN E., JR.

Baldwin, Gordo. See BALDWIN, GORDON C.

Baldwin, Gordon C. (1908–   ), American archeologist and writer, whose pseudonyms are *Gordo Baldwin* and *Lew Gordon.*

Baldwin, Michael. See JESSE, MICHAEL.

Balfour, Eva. See BALFOUR, HEARNDEN.

Balfour, Hearnden. Joint pseudonym of Eva Balfour and Beryl Hearnden, contemporary mystery writers.

Balfour, Patrick. Pseudonym of Patrick Lord Kinross (1904–   ), English free-lance journalist and writer.

Baline, Israel. See BERLIN, IRVING.

Ball, Doris Bell. See BELL, JOSEPHINE.

Ball, Zachary. Pseudonym of Kelly R. Masters (1897–   ), American writer.

Ballagi, Mór (1818–1891). Hungarian theologian and grammarian, whose original name was Moritz Bloch.

Ballard, Dean. See WILKES-HUNTER, RICHARD.

Ballard, K. G. See ROTH, HOLLY.

Ballard, P. D. See BALLARD, TODHUNTER.

Ballard, Todhunter (1903–   ). American writer, whose pseudonyms are *Brian Agar, P. D. Ballard, W. T. Ballard, Parker Bonner, Sam Bowie, Hunter D'Allard, Harrison Hunt, John Hunter, Neil Mac-Neil,* and *John Shepherd.*

Ballard, W. T. See BALLARD, TODHUNTER.

Ballew, Charles. See SNOW, CHARLES HORACE.

Ballinger, William Sanborn (1912–   ). American writer, whose pseudonyms are *Bill S. Ballinger, Frederic Freyer,* and *B. X. Sanborn.*

Balucki, Michal. See ELPIDON.

Balzano, Jeanne Koppel (1912–   ). American author, whose pseudonyms are *Gina Bell* and *Gina Bell-Zano.*

Bamberger, Helen R. (1888–   ). Mystery writer, whose pseudonyms are *Helen Berger* and, with Raymond S. Bamberger, *The Aresbys.*

Bamberger, Raymond S. See BAMBERGER, HELEN R.

Bamboccio, Il. Cognomen of Pieter van Laar (or Laer) (1592?–1642), Dutch landscape painter and etcher.

Bancroft, F. Pseudonym of Frances Charlotte Slater (d. 1947), South African novelist.

Bang-Hasen, Odd (1908–   ). Norwegian scholar, whose pseudonyms are *Paol Furu* and *Lars Lund.*

Banjo, The. Pseudonym of Andrew Barton Paterson (1864–1941), Australian poet.

Bank-Jensen. Pseudonym of Thea Tauber Ottesen (1913–   ), Danish author.

Bankoff, George Alexis (1903–   ). Mystery writer, whose pseudonyms are *George Borodin, George Braddon, Peter Conway,* and *George Sava.*

Banner, Hubert Stewart. See VEXILLUM.

Bannon, Peter. Pseudonym of Paul Durst (1921–   ), mystery writer.

Banti, Anna. Pseudonym of Lucia Longhi Lopresti (1895–   ), Italian writer.

Banzan. See KUMAZAWA BANZAN.

Baptist, R. Hernekin. Pseudonym of Ethelreda Lewis (d. 1946), South African novelist.

Bapu. Pseudonym of Narayan Bhaskar Khare (1882–   ), Indian author.

Baranauskas, Antanas (1835–1902). Lithuanian poet, also known as *Antanas Baronas.*

Barba, Harry (1922–   ). American professor of literature and writer, whose pseudonyms are *Baron Mikan* and *Ohon.*

Barba-Jacob, Porfirio. Pseudonym of Miguel Ángel Osorio (1883–1942), Colombian poet.

Barbanti. See BRAMANTE, DONATO.

Barbarelli, Giorgio. See GIORGIONE, IL.

Barbari, Jacopo de'. See WALCH, JAKOB.

Barbatelli, Bernardino (or **Bernardo**). See POCCETTI, BERNARDINO.

Barbellion, W. N. P. Pseudonym of Bruce Frederick Cummings (1889–1919), Welsh biologist and diarist.

Barber Poet, The. See JASMIN, JACQUES.

Barbette, Jay. Pseudonym of Bart Spicer (1918–   ), mystery writer.

Barbiere, Domenico del. See FIORENTINO, DOMENICO.

Barbieri, Francisco (1823–1894). Spanish composer and writer, also known as *Francisco Asenjo Barbieri.*

Barbieri, Giovanni Francesco. See GUERCINO.

Barbilian, Dan. See BARBU, ION.

Barbour, Ralph Henry. See POWELL, RICHARD STILLMAN.

Barbu, Ion. Pseudonym of Dan Barbilian (1895–   ), Rumanian poet.

Barclay, Ann. See GREIG, MAYSIE.

Barclay, Isabel. Pseudonym of I. M. B. Dobell (1909–   ), Canadian-American author of children's books.

Barcynska, Countess. See EVANS, MARGUERITE FLORENCE HÉLÈNE.

Bardemeyer, Geert. See BRUNCLAIR, VICTOR J.

Bardens, Dennis Conrad (1911–   ). English writer, whose pseudonyms are *Conrad Farel* and *Julian Roberts.*

Bardi, Donato di Niccolò di Betto di. See DONATELLO.

Bar Dora. See LIEBERMANN, AHRON SAMUEL.

Baretti, Giuseppe Marc' Antonio. See SCANNABUE, ARISTARCO.

Barfield, Owen. See BURGEON, G. A. L.

Bargeo, Pier Angelo. See ANGELI, PIETRO ANGELO.

Bargonne, Charles. See FARRÈRE, CLAUDE.

Barham, Richard Harris. See INGOLDSBY, THOMAS.

Barisini, Tommaso da. See MODENA, TOMMASO DA.

Barker, Arthur James. See MUSKETEER.

Barker, Leonard Noel. See NOEL, L.

Barker, Ronald Ernest. See RONALD, E. B.

Barker, S. Omar (1894–   ). American writer, whose pseudonyms are *Jose Canusi, Dan Scott,* and *Phil Squires.*

Barker, Will. See DEMAREST, DOUG.

Barlay, Bennett. See CROSSEN, KENDELL.

Barling, Charles. See BARLING, MURIEL VERE MANT.

Barling, Muriel Vere Mant (1904–   ). English mystery writer, whose pseudonyms are *Charles Barling, Pamela Barrington,* and *P. V. Barrington.*

Barlow, Roger. See LECKIE, ROBERT.

Barnard, Melville Clemens. See ARID, BEN.

Barnard, Wilhelmus. See GRAFT, GUILLAUME VAN DER.

Barnes, Clara Ernst. See ERNST, CLARA.

Barnes, Djuna. See STEPTOE, LYDIA.

Barnett, L. David. Pseudonym of Barnett D. Laschever (1924–   ), American journalist and writer.

Barnsley, Alan Gabriel. See FIELDING, GABRIEL.

Barnum, Richard. See STRATEMEYER, EDWARD L.

Barocchio, Giacomo. See VIGNOLA, GIACOMO DA.

Baron, Peter. Pseudonym of Leonard Worswick Clyde (1906–   ), mystery writer.

Baronas. See BARANAUSKAS, ANTANAS.

Barondess, Sue Kaufman. See KAUFMAN, SUE.

Barozzi, Giacomo. See VIGNOLA, GIACOMO DA.

Barr, Robert. See SHARP, LUKE.

Barren, Charles. See RAINHAM, THOMAS.

Barrett, Alfred Walter. See ANDOM, R.

Barrington, E. See BECK, LILY ADAMS.

Barrington, George. Pseudonym of George Waldron (1755–c1840), Irish writer who lived in New South Wales.

Barrington, Howard. See STONE, SIMON.

Barrington, P. V. See BARLING, MURIEL VERE MANT.

Barrington, Pamela. See BARLING, MURIEL VERE MANT.

Barrios, Miguel de (1625?–1701?). Spanish poet, also known as *Daniel Leví de Barrios.*

Barry, Charles. Pseudonym of Charles Bryson (1877–   ), mystery writer.

Barry, Joe. Pseudonym of Joe Barry Lake, contemporary mystery writer.

Barry, Lord (1580–1629). English dramatist, also known as *Lord David, Lodowich,* and *Lording.*

Bart, Jakub. Pseudonym of Jakub Cizinski (1856–1909), Polish poet.

Barth, Lois. Pseudonym of Lois Diane Freihofer (1933–   ), American writer.

Barthélemy, Nicolas. See BARTHOLOMAEUS.

Bartholomaeus. Latinized name of Nicolas Barthélemy (1478–c1540),

French Benedictine humanist and poetry writer.

Bartimeus. Pseudonym of Lewis Ritchie (1886–   ), British naval paymaster and writer.

Bartlett, David. See MASON, MADELINE.

Bartlett, Philip A. Collective pseudonym for the "Roy Stover Mystery" series. See STRATEMEYER, EDWARD L.

Bartlett, Vernon. See OLDFELD, PETER.

Bartolomé Cossío, Manuel. See COSSÍO.

Bartolommeo, Fra. Religious name of Bartolommeo (or Baccio) della Porta (1475–1517), Dominican monk and Florentine painter.

Bartolommeo, Michelozzo di. See MICHELOZZO.

Barton, Eustace. See RAWLINS, EUSTACE.

Barton, May Hollis. Collective pseudonym for the "Barton Books for Girls" series. See STRATEMEYER, EDWARD L.

Baruch. Löb. See BÖRNE, LUDWIG.

Basho. Pseudonym of Matsuo Munefusa (1644–1694), Japanese poet and writer of haiku.

Basile, Gianbattista. See ABBATTUTIS, GIAN ALESIO.

Basket-Maker, The. Cognomen of Thomas Miller (1807–1874), English poet and novelist.

Bason, Frederick Thomas. See GALLERITE, THE.

Bass, Eduard. Pseudonym of Eduard Schmidt (1888–1946), Czech novelist and essayist.

Bassett, John Keith. See KEATING, LAWRENCE A.

Bassett, William B. K. See DARIEN, PETER.

Bates, Barbara S. (1919–   ). American writer, whose pseudonyms are *Stephen Cuyler* and *Jim Roberts.*

Bates, Harry Arthur. See ARTHUR, HARRY.

Batten, Joyce Mortimer. Pseudonym of Joyce Kells Batten Mankowska (1919–   ), British writer.

Battiscombe, E. Georgina Harwood. See HARWOOD, GINA.

Bauer, Erwin A. (1919–   ). American free-lance writer, specializing in outdoor travel and adventure, whose pseudonyms are *Ken Bourbon, Tom Hardin,* and *Charles W. North.*

Bauer, George. See AGRICOLA, GEORG.

Bauer, Herbert. See BALÁZS, BÉLA.

Baum, Lyman Frank (1856–1919). American juvenile writer, whose pseudonyms are *Floyd Akers, Schuyler Stanton,* and *Edith Van Dyne.*

Baumbach, Rudolf. See BACH, PAUL.

Baumrin, Bernard H. (1934–   ). American scholar, whose pseudonyms are *Stefan Baumrin* and *Stefan Bernard.*

Baumrin, Stefan. See BAUMRIN, BERNARD H.

Bawden, Nina. Pseudonym of Nina Mary Kark (1925–   ), English writer.

Bawn, Mary. Pseudonym of Mary Pamela Godwin Wright (1917–   ), English writer.

Bax, Roger. See WINTERTON, PAUL.

Baxter, Gregory. Joint pseudonym of Eric De Banzie (1894–   ) and John Ressich (1877–   ), mystery writers.

Baxter, Olive. Pseudonym of Helen Baker Eastwood (1892–   ), mystery writer.

Baxter, Valerie. See MEYNELL, LAURENCE WALTER.

Baxter, Young. Pseudonym of W. I. James, contemporary mystery writer.

Bayer, Eleanor Rosenfeld. See BAYER, OLIVER WELD.

Bayer, Karl Robert Emmerich von. See BYR, ROBERT.

Bayer, Leo G. See BAYER, OLIVER WELD.

Bayer, Oliver Weld. Joint pseudonym of Eleanor Rosenfeld Bayer and Leo G. Bayer, contemporary mystery writers.

Bayliss, John Clifford. See CLIFFORD, JOHN.

Bayly, Ada Ellen. See LYALL, EDNA.

Bazzi, Giovanni Antonio. See SODOMA, IL.

Beach, Charles Amory. Collective pseudonym for the "Air Service Boys" series. See STRATEMEYER, EDWARD L.

Beach, Thomas Miller. See LE CARON, HENRY.

Beamish, Annie O'Meara de Vic. See BEAMISH, NOEL DE VIC.

Beamish, Noel de Vic. Pseudonym of Annie O'Meara de Vic Beamish (1883–   ), Irish-French novelist.

Bean, Keith F. (1911–   ). Australian-English writer, whose pseudonyms are *Kay Fenwick* and *K. Harrington.*

Beaton, Anne. See WASHINGTON, MARGUERITE BEAUCHAMP.

Beaton, George. Pseudonym of Gerald Brenan (1894–   ), British writer.

Beatty, Elizabeth. See HOLLOWAY, TERESA.

Beatty, Jerome, Jr. See STOOKEY, AARON W.

Beatus Rhenanus. Pseudonym of Theodor Birt (1852–1933), German classical philologist and writer.

Beatus Rhenanus. Latinized name of Bild aus Rheinau (1485–1547), Alsatian humanist.

Beauchamp, Kathleen Mansfield. See MANSFIELD, KATHERINE.

Beauchamp, Pat. See WASHINGTON, MARGUERITE BEAUCHAMP.

Beaumarchais, Pierre-Augustin Caron de (1732–1799). French playwright, whose original name was Pierre-Augustin Caron.

Beaumont, Charles (1929–   ). American free-lance writer, whose pseudonyms are *Keith Grantland, C. B. Lovehill,* and *S. M. Tenneshaw.*

Beaumont, Edgar. See HALIFAX, CLIFFORD.

Beauvoir, Roger de. Pseudonym of Édouard Roger de Bully (1809–1866), French poet, playwright, and novelist.

Beccadelli, Antonio (1349–1471). Italian humanist, founder of the Neapolitan Academy. He was also known as *Panormita.*

Beccafumi, Domenico (1486–1551). Italian painter, whose original name was Domenico di Pace. He was also called *Il Meccherino.*

Beccari, Antonio. See FERRARA, ANTONIO DA.

Beck, Lily Adams (d. 1931). English novelist, whose pseudonyms are *E. Barrington* and *Louis Moresby.*

Becker, Florence. Pseudonym of Florence Becker Lennon (1895–   ), American author.

Becker, Stephen David. See DODGE, STEVE.

Beckers, Frans (1905–   ). Dutch playwright, whose pseudonyms are *Frans Demers* and *J. M. Elsing.*

Beckett, Mark. Pseudonym of Marcus George Truman (1890–   ), mystery writer.

Beckett, Ronald Brymer. See ANTHONY, JOHN.

Beckwith, Lillian. Pseudonym of Lillian Comber (1916–   ), English writer.

Bede, Andrew. See BEHA, ERNEST.

Bede, Cuthbert. Pseudonym of Edward Bradley (1827–1899), English clergyman and humorist.

Bedford, Annie North. See WATSON, JANE WERNER.

Bedford, John. See HASTINGS, PHYLLIS DORA HODGE.

Bedny, Demyan. Pseudonym of Efim Alexeyevich Pridvorov (1883–1945), Russian poet and propagandist.

Beech, Webb. See BUTTERWORTH, WILLIAM EDMUND, III.

Beeding, Francis. See PALMER, JOHN LESLIE, and SAUNDERS, HILARY AIDAN ST. GEORGE.

Beer, Eloise C. S. (1903–   ). American free-lance writer, whose pseudonyms are *Lisl Beer* and *Lisl Drake.*

Beer, Johann (1655–1700). German novelist and composer, whose best-known pseudonyms are *Jan Rebhu, Wolfgang von Willenhag,* and *Zendorius a Zendoriis.*

Beer, Lisl. See BEER, ELOISE C. S.

Beets, Nikolaas. See HILDEBRAND.

Beffroy de Reigny, Louis Abel. See COUSIN JACQUES.

Beg, Toran. Pseudonym of Norman McKillop (1892–   ), Scottish writer.

Beha, Ernest (1908–   ). English writer, whose pseudonyms are *Andrew Bede* and *Drake Elvin.*

Beith, John Hay. See HAY, IAN.

Bejła, J. Pseudonym of Count Henryk Rzewuski (1791–1866), Polish novelist.

Bekker, Jay de. See WINCHELL, PRENTICE.

Beklemishev, Yuri Solomonovich. See KRYMOV, YURI.

Belaney, George Stanfeld. See GREY OWL.

Belcampo. Pseudonym of Herman P. Schönfeld Wichers (1902–   ), Dutch writer.

Belcheva, Elisaveta. See BAGRJANA, ELISAVETA.

Bell, Acton. See BRONTË, ANNE.

Bell, Currer. See BRONTË, CHARLOTTE.

Bell, Ellis. See BRONTË, EMILY JANE.

Bell, Emily Mary. Pseudonym of Mabel Earp Cason (1892–   ), American author and illustrator.

Bell, Gina. See BALZANO, JEANNE KOPPEL.

Bell, John Keble. See HOWARD, KEBLE.

Bell, Josephine. Pseudonym of Doris Bell Ball (1897–   ), English physician and writer.

Bell, Neil. See SOUTHWOLD, STEPHEN.

Belle Cordière, La ("The Beautiful Ropemaker"). Pseudonym of

Louise Labé (1526–1566), French poet.

Bellefroid, Martha. See GRONON, ROSE.

Bellemare, Eugène Louis Gabriel de. See FERRY, GABRIEL.

Bellemare, Gabriel de. See FERRY, GABRIEL.

Bellew, John Chippendall Montesquieu (1823–1874). English clergyman and writer, whose original surname was Higgen.

Bello, Francesco. See CIECO DI FERRARA, IL.

Belloc, Hilaire. Pseudonym of Joseph Hilary Pierre Belloc (1870–1953), English writer.

Belloc, Marie Adelaide. See LOWNDES, BELLOC.

Bellocq, Louise. Pseudonym of Marie-Louise Boudat (1909–   ), French writer.

Belloy, Dormont de. Pseudonym of Pierre Laurent Buyrette (1727–1775), French actor and playwright.

Bell-Zano, Gina. See BALZANO, JEANNE KOPPEL.

Bely, Andrey. Pseudonym of Boris Nikolayevich Bugayev (1880–1934), Russian novelist and poet.

Ben Ami. Pseudonym of M. Rabinovitch (1858–1932), Russian-Yiddish writer.

Benarria, Allan. Pseudonym of Allan Benarria Goldenthal (1920–   ), American writer.

Ben-Avigdor. Pseudonym of Arieh Leib Shalkovitz (1866–1921), Hebrew novelist.

Benci, Antonio and **Piero.** See POLLAIUOLO, ANTONIO and PIERO.

Bencur, Matej. See KUKUCHIN, MARTIN.

Bender, Jay. See DEINDORFER, ROBERT GREENE.

Bendit, Gladys Williams. See PRESLAND, JOHN.

Bendonski, Szymon. See SZYMONOWICZ, SZYMON.

Benedict, Joseph. Pseudonym of Charles Joseph Dollen (1926–   ), American writer.

Benedict, Leopold. See WINCHEVSKY, MORRIS.

Benedictsson, Victoria Maria. See AHLGREN, ERNST.

Benedictus. Religious name of Jacob van Haeften (1588–1648), Dutch spiritual writer.

Benes, Vaclav. See TREBIZSKY, VACLAV BENES.

Benet, Edouard. See EDWARDS, WILLIAM BENNETT.

Benetević, Martin (d. 1607). Dalmatian poet and playwright, also known as *Martin Benetti*.

Benetti, Martin. See BENETEVIĆ, MARTIN.
Beniuseviciute-Zimantiene, Julija. See ZEMAITE.
Benjamin, Claude (1911–   ). American writer, whose pseudonyms
    are *Max Edwards* and *Marion E. George.*
Bennett, Christine. See NEUBAUER, WILLIAM ARTHUR.
Bennett, Dorothea. Pseudonym of Dorothea Bennett Young (1924–
    ), Swiss author.
Bennett, Dwight. See NEWTON, DWIGHT BENNETT.
Bennett, Geoffrey. See SEA-LION.
Bennett, Hall. See HALL, BENNIE CAROLINE.
Bennett, Rachel. See HILL, MARGARET.
Bennewitz, Peter. See APIANUS, PETRUS.
Ben-Nez. See WINCHEVSKY, MORRIS.
Benson, Thérèse. Pseudonym of Emilie Benson Knipe (1870–1958),
    mystery writer.
Ben Yehuda. Pseudonym of Eliezer Perelmann (1858–1922), Hebrew
    scholar, essayist, and novelist.
Ben-Zion, Sh. Pseudonym of Simcha Alter Gutmann (1870–1932), He-
    brew novelist.
Beolco, Angelo. See RUZZANTE, IL.
Berch, William O. Pseudonym of Joseph E. Coyne (1918–   ), Ameri-
    can writer.
Berckman, Evelyn Domenica. See WADE, JOANNA.
Berdiczevsky, Micha Yoseph. See BIN GORION, M. Y.
Berend, Alice. Pseudonym of Alice Berend Breinlinger (1878–   ),
    German novelist and playwright.
Berent, Wacław. See RAWICZ, WACŁAW.
Beresford, Leslie. See PAN.
Beresford, Marcus. See BRANDEL, MARC.
Bergamo, Andrea da. Pseudonym of Pietro Nelli (1511?–?), Italian poet
    and satirist.
Berge, Carol. See KEEL, LAURA.
Berger, Helen. See BAMBERGER, HELEN R.
Berger, Josef. See DIGGES, JEREMIAH.
Berghe, Jan van den (d. 1559). Dutch poet, also known as *Jan van Diest.*
Bergmann, Anton. See TONY.
Bergstedt, Harald Alfred (1877–   ). Danish poet and novelist, whose
    original surname was Petersen.
Berkebile, Fred Donovan (1900–   ). American author, whose pseudo-

nyms are *William Donovan, William Ernest,* and *Don Stauffer.*

Berkeley, Anthony. See COX, ANTHONY BERKELEY.

Berlin, Irving (1888–). American songwriter, whose original name was Israel Baline.

Bernai, Alexandre de. 12th-century French poet, also known as *Alexandre de Paris.*

Bernard, Robert. Pseudonym of Robert Bernard Martin (1918–), American scholar and mystery writer.

Bernard, Stefan. See BAUMRIN, BERNARD H.

Bernarn, Terrave. See BURNETT, DAVID.

Bernasek, Antonin. See TOMAN, KAREL.

Bernays, Anne. Pseudonym of Anne Bernays Kaplan (1930–), American writer.

Bernhard, Karl. Pseudonym of Andreas Nicolai de Saint-Aubain (1798–1865), Danish novelist.

Béroalde de Verville, François Vatable. Pseudonym of François Vatable Brouart (1556–?1629), French writer and poet.

Berrettini, Pietro. See CORTONA, PIETRO DA.

Berrien, Edith Heal (1903–). American writer, whose pseudonyms are *Edith Heal, Eileen Page,* and *Margaret Powers.*

Berry, Le Héraut (1386–1455?). French chronicler, herald to the Dauphin (later Charles VII). His real name was Gilles Le Bouvier.

Berschadsky, Isaiah. Pseudonym of Isaiah Domaschevitsky (1872–1910), Russian-Hebrew novelist.

Bertelli, Luigi. See VAMBA.

Berton, Guy. Joint pseudonym of Eadfrid A. Bingham and Guy Robert La Coste, contemporary mystery writers.

Bertou, Gwilherm. See KERVERZHIOU.

Bertrand, Aloysius (1807–1841). French poet, whose original name was Jacques-Louis-Napoléon Bertrand.

Bertrand, Jacques-Louis-Napoléon. See BERTRAND, ALOYSIUS.

Berwick, Mary. Pseudonym of Adelaide Anne Procter (1825–1864), English poet, daughter of Bryan Waller Procter.

Bessarian, Basil (1395–1472). Byzantine humanist, whose original given name was John.

Bessarian, John. See BESSARIAN, BASIL.

Best, Rayleigh Breton Amis. See AMIS, BRETON.

Bestuzhev, Alexander Alexandrovich. See MARLINSKI, COSSACK.

Bethell, Mary Ursula. See HAYES, EVELYN.

Betschla, Andrea. See BEZZOLA, ANDREA.

Betschla, Eduard. See SPIGNA, N. U.

Betteridge, Anne. Pseudonym of Margaret Potter (1926–   ), English novelist.

Betteridge, Don. Pseudonym of Bernard Newman (1897–   ), mystery writer.

Betti (or **di Betto**) **di Biagio, Bernardino.** See PINTURICCHIO.

Bettina. Pseudonym of Bettina Bauer Erlich (1903–   ), Austrian-English writer for children.

Betto di Bardi, Donato di Niccolò di. See DONATELLO.

Betz, Eva Kelly. See PETERS, CAROLINE.

Bevans, Torre. See CHANSLOR, MARJORIE TORREY HOOD.

Bevk, France. Pseudonym of Pavle Sedmak (1890–   ), Slovak writer.

Beyle, Marie Henri. See STENDHAL.

Beynon, Jane. See LEWIS, LANGE.

Beynon, John. See HARRIS, JOHN BEYNON.

Bezruc, Petr. See Vasek, VLADIMIR.

Bezzola, Andrea (1840–1897). Swiss poet, also known as *Andrea Betschla.*

Bezzola, Eduard. See SPIGNA, N. U.

Bialk, Elisa. Pseudonym of Elisa Bialk Krautter, contemporary American writer.

Bianchi-Ferrari, Francesco. See FRARE, IL.

Bibbiena, Il. Cognomen of Bernardo Dovizi (1470–1520), Italian playwright and cardinal.

Bibliander. Grecized surname of Theodor Buchmann (1500?–1564), Swiss Protestant theologian and oriental scholar.

Bibliophile Jacob. See LACROIX, PAUL.

Bickerstaff, Isaac. Pseudonym adopted by the following: Richard Steele (1672–1729), British essayist and dramatist, when he wrote in the *Tatler;* Benjamin West (1730–1813), American mathematician; and Jonathan Swift (1667–1745), English satirist, when he wrote a pamphlet lampooning John Partridge.

Bickerstaffe-Drew, Monsignor Count Francis Browning Drew. See AYSCOUGH, JOHN.

Bickham, Jack Miles (1930–   ). American writer, whose pseudonyms are *Jeff Clinton* and *John Miles.*

Bickle, Judith Brundrett. See TWEEDALE, J.

Biedermann, Felix. See Dörmann, FELIX.
Bielski, Marcin (1495?–1575). Polish poet, also called *Marcin Wolski.*
Bienewitz, Peter. See APIANUS, PETRUS.
Bierce, Ambrose. See GRILE, DOD.
Bigi, Francesco di Cristofano. See FRANCIABIGIO.
Biglow, Hosea. Occasional pseudonym of James Russell Lowell (1819–
    1891), American poet and essayist.
Bigordi, Domenico di Tommaso. See GHIRLANDAJO.
Billings, Josh. See SHAW, HENRY WHEELER.
Bimyo. See YAMADA BIMYO.
Binder, Otto Oscar (1911–   ). American science-fiction writer,
    whose pseudonyms are *Eando Binder, John Coleridge, Gordon A.
    Giles,* and *Dean D. O'Brien.*
Binder, Eando. See BINDER, OTTO OSCAR.
Binet, Satané. Pseudonym of Francisque Sarcey (1827–1899), French
    journalist and drama critic.
Bingham, Carson. See CASSIDAY, BRUCE BINGHAM.
Bingham, Eadfrid A. See BERTON, GUY.
Bingham, Madeleine. See MANNERING, JULIA.
Bin Gorion, M. Y. Pseudonym of Micha Yoseph Berdiczevsky (1865–
    1921), Hebrew novelist, essayist, and philosopher.
Binns, Ottwell. See BOLT, BEN.
Bird, Brandon. See EVANS, GEORGE BIRD, and EVANS, KAY HARRIS.
Bird, Kenneth. See FOUGASSE.
Birkley, Dolan. See HITCHENS, DOLORES BIRK OLSEN.
Birla, Lakshminiwas. See ACHYUT.
Birmingham, George A. Pseudonym of James Owen Hannay (1865–
    1950), Irish writer.
Birney, Hoffman. See KENT, DAVID.
Birren, Faber (1900–   ). American writer, whose pseudonyms are
    Gregor Lang and *Martin Lang.*
Birt, Theodor. See BEATUS RHENANUS.
Bishop, Curtis Kent (1912–   ). American free-lance writer, whose
    pseudonyms are *Curt Brandon* and *Curt Carroll.*
Bishop, E. (or Evelyn) Morchard. See STONOR, OLIVER.
Bishop, Jack. Pseudonym of Michael Dorman (1932–   ), American
    free-lance writer on political and civil-rights topics.
Bishop, Morris. See JOHNSON, W. BOLINGBROKE.

Bisinzo, Alberic von (c1120). Franco-Provençal writer, also known as *Briançon* and *Pisançon*.

Bisque, Anatole. Pseudonym of Alain Bosquet (1919–   ), Russian-American writer.

Bite, Ben. See SCHNECK, STEPHEN.

Bitzius, Albert. See GOTTHELF, JEREMIAS.

Bivar, Rodrigo (or **Ruy**) **Díaz de.** See CID, EL.

Bixby, Jerome Lewis (1923–   ). American writer for films and for science-fiction, adventure, and western magazines, whose pseudonyms are *Jay B. Drexel, Emerson Jans, D. B. Lewis, Harry Neal, Albert Russell, J. Russell,* and *M. St. Vivant.*

Bjarklind, Unnur Benediktsdóttir. See HULDA.

Bjarme, Brynjolf. Pseudonym of Henrik Ibsen (1828–1906), Norwegian playwright and poet, used for his unsuccessful tragedy *Catilina.*

Bjerke, André. See BORGE, BERNHARD.

Black, Gavin. Pseudonym of Oswald Wynd (1913–   ), mystery writer.

Black, M. Dana. Pseudonym of H. M. Butler, contemporary mystery writer.

Black, Mansell. See TREVOR, ELLESTON.

Blackstock, Charity. See TORDAY, PAULA.

Blackstock, Lee. See TORDAY, PAULA.

Blackwell, John. See ALUN.

Blaiklock, Edward Musgrave. See GRAMMATICUS.

Blaine, John. See GOODWIN, HAROLD LELAND.

Blair, Dorothy. See SCARLETT, ROGER.

Blair, Eric Arthur. See ORWELL, GEORGE.

Blaisdell, Anne. See LININGTON, ELIZABETH.

Blake, Andrew. See JANIFER, LAURENCE MARK.

Blake, E. A. (also **Eleanor**). See PRATT, ELEANOR BLAKE ATKINSON.

Blake, Katherine (also **Kay**). See WALTER, DOROTHY BLAKE.

Blake, Monica. See MUIR, MARIE.

Blake, Nicholas. Pseudonym of Cecil (or C.) Day Lewis (1904–   ), English poet, used for his detective fiction.

Blake, Sally Mirliss. See SARA.

Blake, Walker E. See BUTTERWORTH, WILLIAM EDMUND, III.

Blakeston, Oswell. See BURFORD, ROGER D'ESTE.

Blaman, Anna. Pseudonym of Johanna Petronella Vrugt (1905–1960), Dutch writer.

Blanco Crespo, José María (1775–1841). Spanish writer and poet, who fled to England, where he was known as *Joseph Blanco White.*

Blanco White, Joseph. See BLANCO CRESPO, JOSÉ MARÍA.

Blasco, José Ruiz. See PICASSO, PABLO.

Blatty, William Peter. See CLYNE, TERENCE.

Bledlow, John. Pseudonym of Henry Edmund Theodoric Vale (1888–), British author.

Blenkinsop, Vicesimus. See HOOK, THEODORE EDWARD.

Bligh, Norman. See NEUBAUER, WILLIAM ARTHUR.

Bliss, Adam. See BURKHARDT, EVE, and BURKHARDT, ROBERT FERDINAND.

Bliss, Reginald. Occasional pseudonym of Herbert George Wells (1866–1946), English novelist, sociological writer, and historian.

Blixen-Finecke, Baroness Karen Christentze (1885–1962). Danish novelist, whose principal pseudonym is *Isak Dinesen.* She also used the pseudonyms *Pierre Andrézel* and *Osceola.*

Bloch, Moritz. See BALLAGI, MÓR.

Blom, Eric Walter. See FARR, SEBASTIAN.

Blondel de Nesle (twelfth century). French lyric poet. Blondel is thought to be the cognomen of Jean II, Lord of Nesle.

Blood, Matthew. See DRESSER, DAVIS.

Blooman, Percy A. See PAB.

Bloomfield, Robert. See EDGLEY, LESLIE.

Bloomgarten, Shloime. See YEHOASH.

Blouet, Paul. See O'RELL, MAX.

Blue, Wallace. Pseudonym of Margaret Kraenzel (1899–), American writer.

Blumer, Henry Kenneth (1921–). English writer, whose pseudonyms are *Ernest Corley, Philip Kent, Karl Maras,* and, with John Newman, *Kenneth Johns.*

Blundell, Peter. Pseudonym of Frank Nestle Butterworth, contemporary mystery writer.

Blunt, Don. See BOOTH, EDWIN.

Bluphocks, Lucien. See SELDES, GILBERT VIVIAN.

Blutig, Eduard. See GOREY, EDWARD ST. JOHN.

Bly, Nellie. Pseudonym of Elizabeth Seaman (1867–1922), American journalist.

Bobillier, Marie. See BRENET, MICHEL.

Bocage (or **Boccage**), **Manuel Maria Barbosa du.** See SADINO, ELMANO.

Bocca, Al. See WINTER, BEVIS.

Bochenski, Joseph M. See MICHE, JOSEF.

Bodell, Mary. Pseudonym of Mary Bodell Pecsok (1919–), American writer.

Boden, Hilda. See BODENHAM, HILDA MORRIS.

Bodenham, Hilda Morris (1901–). English writer, whose pseudonyms are *Hilda Boden* and *Pauline Welch*.

Bodenstedt, Friedrich von (1819–1882). German poet known for his pseudo-Oriental poems, which he passed off as those of Mirza Schaffy, his Tartar teacher.

Bodington, Nancy. See SMITH, SHELLEY.

Bodkin, Matthias McDonnell. See CROM A BOO.

Boe, Jacques. See JASMIN, JACQUES.

Boece, Hector (c1465–1536). Scottish historian, also known as *Hector Boethius.*

Boerneef. Pseudonym of Izak Willem van der Merwe (1897–), Afrikaans writer.

Boethius, Hector. See BOECE, HECTOR.

Boëx, Joseph-Henri. See ROSNY, J. H.

Boëx, Justin. See ROSNY, J. H.

Bofill i Mates, Jaume. See GUERAN DE LIOST.

Boganis. Pseudonym of Wilhelm Dinesen (1845–1895), Danish writer, father of Isak Dinesen.

Bogar, Jeff. See THOMAS, RONALD WILLS.

Bogbinder, Hilarius. See KIERKEGAARD, SØREN AABYE.

Bogdanov, Alexander Alexandrovich. Pseudonym of Alexander Alexandrovich Malinovsky (1873–1928), Russian writer and philosopher.

Bogoraz, Vladimir Germanovich. See TAN.

Bohlman, Edna McCaull. See McCAULL, M. E.

Bois-Hébert, Marquise Guy de. See BOVET, MARIE ANNE DE.

Boissard, Maurice. Pseudonym of Paul Léataud (1872–1956), French writer.

Boito, Arrigo. See GORRIO, TOBIA.

Boldrewood, Rolf. Pseudonym of Thomas Alexander Browne (1826–1915), Australian novelist.

Bolesławita. Pseudonym of Józef Ignacy Kraszewski (1812–1887), Polish novelist.

Bolintineanu, Dimitrie. Pseudonym of Dimitrie Cosmad (1819–1872), Rumanian poet and playwright.

Bolitho, William. Pseudonym of William Bolitho Ryall (1891–1930), British journalist and author.

Bologna, Giovanni. See GIAMBOLOGNA.

Bologna, Pellegrino da. See TIBALDI, PELLEGRINO.

Bologna, Vitale da (c1309–c1369). Italian painter and wood sculptor, also known as *Vitale d'Aimo de' Cavalli.*

Bolognese, Il. Cognomen of Giovanni Francesco Grimaldi (1606–1680), Italian painter.

Bolstad, Øivind (1905–   ). Norwegian writer and critic, whose pseudonyms are *Martin Eden* and *Theo Eikan.*

Bolt, Ben. Pseudonym of Ottwell Binns (1872–   ), mystery writer.

Bolton, Maisie Sharman (1915–   ). British free-lance writer, whose pseudonyms are *Stratford Davis* and *Maisie Sharman.*

Bólu-Hjálmar. See JÓNSSON, HJÁLMAR.

Bomba, Gerwazy. See SZTYRMER, LUDWIK.

Bonaventura. Pseudonym of Friedrich Gottlob Wetzel (1799–1819), German writer.

Bonaventura, Saint. Religious name of Giovanni di Fidanza (1221–1274), cardinal and devotional writer.

Boncourt, Louis Charles Adélaïde Chamisso de. See CHAMISSO, ADELBERT VON.

Bond, Florence Demarest Foos. See DEMAREST, ANN.

Bond, Gladys Baker. See MENDEL, JO.

Bond, Ian. See WILLETT, BROTHER FRANCISCUS.

Bonehill, Captain Ralph. See STRATEMEYER, EDWARD L.

Bonett, Emery. Pseudonym of Felicity Carter Coulson (1907–   ), English author.

Bonett, John. Pseudonym of John Hubert Arthur Coulson (1906–   ), English writer.

Bonichi, Gino. See SCIPIONE.

Boniface (c675–764). British grammarian, versifier, and preacher, whose original name was Wynfrith.

Boniface, Joseph Xavier. See SAINTINE, XAVIER.

Bonifazio Veronese (1487–1553). Venetian painter, whose real name was Bonifazio di Pitati.

Bonnamy, Francis. Pseudonym of Audrey Walz, contemporary mystery writer.

Bonner, Geraldine. See HARD PAN.

Bonner, Michael. Pseudonym of Anne Bonner Glasscock (1924–   ), American writer of Western fiction.

Bonner, Parker. See BALLARD, TODHUNTER.

Bonner, Sherwood. Pseudonym of Katherine Sherwood MacDowell (1849–1883), American writer.

Bonnette, Victor. See ROY, EWELL PAUL.

Bonney, Bill. See KEEVIL, HENRY JOHN.

Bontemps, Roger. Pseudonym of Roger de Collerye (1470–1540), French poet, used for his organization of a society of *bon vivants*.

Bonvicino, Alessandro. See MORETTO, IL.

Boone, Pat (1934–   ). American entertainer and writer, whose real name is Charles Eugene Boone.

Booth, Edwin. Contemporary American writer, whose pseudonyms are *Don Blunt* and *Jack Hazard*.

Bor, Matej. Pseudonym of Vladimir Pavshich (1913–   ), Slovak poet and playwright.

Borch, Ted. Pseudonym of A. Morten Lund (1926–   ), American free-lance writer, editor, and film producer.

Borchard, Ruth (1910–   ). German-English writer, whose pseudonyms are *Iqua* and *Anne Medley*.

Borden, Lee. Pseudonym of Borden Deal (1922–   ), American writer.

Borden, M. See SAXON, GLADYS RELYEA.

Borden, Mary. See MACLAGAN, BRIDGET.

Borel, Petrus. Pseudonym of Joseph Pierre Borel (1809–1859), French poet.

Borge, Bernhard. Pseudonym of André Bjerke (1918–   ), Norwegian poet.

Borgmann, Dmitri. See UQSOR, EL.

Borgognone, Ambrogio (fl. 1473–1524). Italian painter, whose real name was Ambrogio Stefani (or di Stefano or da Fossano).

Borgognone, Il. See COURTOIS, JACQUES.

Borland, Harold Glen. See WEST, WARD.

Borland, William Armstrong. See DIXON, BINGHAM.

Borne, Dorothy. See RICE, DOROTHY MARY.

Börne, Ludwig (1786–1837). German political writer and satirist, whose original name was Löb Baruch.

Borneman, Ernest. See MCCABE, CAMERON.

Borodin, George. See BANKOFF, GEORGE ALEXIS.

Borodin, Levasiov. Pseudonym of Piotr Alexeyevich Kropotkin (1842–1921), Russian novelist and anarchist.

Borodin, Sergey Petrovich. Pseudonym of Amir Sargidzhan (1902–), Soviet Russian novelist.

Borovsky, Havel. Pseudonym of Karel Havlícek (1821–1856), Czech journalist.

Borromini, Francesco (1599–1667). Italian master stonecutter, sculptor, and architect, whose original name was Francesco Castelli.

Borth, Willan G. See BOSWORTH, WILLAN GEORGE.

Bos. See BOSCH, HIERONYMUS.

Bosch, Girolamo. See BOSCH, HIERONYMUS.

Bosch, Hieronymus (1450?–1516). Flemish painter whose real name was Jeroen van Aken (or Aeken or Aquen or Acken). In the sixteenth and seventeenth centuries he was known in Spain as *Geronimo Bosco* and *El Bosco*. In Italy he was called *Girolamo Bosch* and *Fiamengo* (or *Bosco*) *di Balduc;* in Flanders the form *Bos* prevailed.

Bosco, El. See BOSCH, HIERONYMUS.

Bosco, Geronimo. See BOSCH, HIERONYMUS.

Bosquet, Alain. See BISQUE, ANATOLE.

Boss, Meinart. See VAN EERBEEK, J. K.

Boston, Charles K. See GRUBER, FRANK.

Bosworth, Willan George (1904–). Mystery writer, whose pseudonyms are *Willan G. Borth* and *Leonid.*

Both, L. W. Pseudonym of Louis Schneider (1805–1878), German actor and writer.

Botticelli, Sandro (1445–1510). Florentine painter, whose original name was Alessandro di Mariano dei Filipepi. The name was derived from that of his brother, Giovanni, who was called Il Botticello ("The Little Barrel").

Botto, Ján. See KRASKO, IVAN.

Boucher, Anthony (1911–1968). American writer and editor, whose pseudonyms are *H. H. Holmes* and *Herman W. Mudgett.* His original name was William Anthony Parker White.

Boudat, Marie-Louise. See BELLOCQ, LOUISE.

Bouhélier, Saint-Georges de. Pseudonym of Georges de Bouhélier-Lepelletier (1876–   ), French poet and playwright.

Boularan, Jacques. See DEVAL, JACQUES.

Boulting. See COTES, PETER.

Bourbon, Ken. See BAUER, ERWIN A.

Bourguignon, Le. See COURTOIS, JACQUES.

Bourillon, Pierre. See HAMP, PIERRE.

Bourne, Lesley. See MARSHALL, EVELYN.

Bourne, Peter. See JEFFRIES, GRAHAM MONTAGUE.

Boutelleau, Jacques. See CHARDONNE, JACQUES.

Bovet, Marie Anne de. Pseudonym of Marquise Guy de Bois-Hébert (1860–   ), French novelist and translator.

Bowden, Jean (1920–   ). Mystery writer, whose pseudonyms are *Avon Curry* and *Belinda Dell.*

Bowen, Betty Morgan. Pseudonym of Betty West (1921–   ), American writer.

Bowen, Marjorie. See LONG, GABRIELLE MARGARET VERE.

Bowen-Judd, Sara Hutton. See WOODS, SARA.

Bowers, Santha Rama Rau. See RAU, SANTHA RAMA.

Bowie, Jim. See STRATEMEYER, EDWARD L.

Bowie, Sam. See BALLARD, TODHUNTER.

Bowood, Richard. See DANIELL, ALBERT SCOTT.

Box, Edgar. Occasional pseudonym of Gore Vidal (1925–   ), American writer.

Boy. Pseudonym of Tadeusz Żeleński (1874–1942), Polish author, and translator of many French authors.

Boyd, Frank. Pseudonym of Frank Kane (1912–   ), American writer.

Boyd, Nancy. Pseudonym of Edna St. Vincent Millay (1892–1950), American poet and writer, used for her light fiction.

Boyer, Columbia. Pseudonym of Nell Columbia Boyer Martin (1890–   ), mystery writer.

Boyer, Jean Auguste. See BOYER D' AGEN.

Boyer d'Agen (1857–1943/46). French writer, whose original name was Jean Auguste Boyer.

Boyles, Clarence Scott. See BROWN, WILL C.

Boylesve, René. Pseudonym of René Tardivaux (1867–1926), French novelist.

Boysen, Johann Wilhelm (1834–1870). German poet, also known as *Boysen van Nienkarken.*

Boz. See DICKENS, CHARLES JOHN HUFFAM.

Brabander, Gerard Den. Pseudonym of Jan Gerardus Jofriet (1900–), Dutch poet.

Braccatone, Il. See VOLTERRA, DANIELE DA.

Braccesi, Alessandro (1445–1503). Italian poet, also known as *Alessandro Bracci.*

Bracci, Alessandro. See BRACCESI, ALESSANDRO.

Brace, Timothy. Pseudonym of Theodore Pratt (1901–), mystery writer.

Bradbury, Ray Douglas. See SPAULDING, LEONARD.

Braddon, George. See BANKOFF, GEORGE ALEXIS.

Bradford, Adam, M.D. Pseudonym of Joseph D. Wassersug (1912–), American medical writer.

Bradley, Edward. See BEDE, CUTHBERT.

Bradley, Katharine Harris. See FIELD, MICHAEL.

Bradly, Mr. See BURROUGHS, WILLIAM SEWARD.

Brady, Nicholas. See TURNER, JOHN VICTOR.

Braeme, Charlotte Monica. See CARTER, NICK.

Bragaglia, Anton Giulio. Pseudonym of Giovanni Miracola (1890–), Italian writer.

Bragdon, Elspeth MacDuffie. See ELSPETH.

Braha, George. See ROBINSON, LEWIS GEORGE.

Brahm, Otto. See ABRAHAMSOHN, OTTO.

Brahms, Caryl. See ABRAHAMS, DORIS CAROLINE.

Brainerd, Chauncey Corey. See RATH, E. J.

Brainerd, Edith Rathbone Jacobs. See RATH, E. J.

Braly, Malcolm. See LORNING, RAY.

Bramah, Ernest. Pseudonym of Ernest Bramah Smith (1869?–1942), English mystery writer.

Bramante, Donato (1444–1514). Italian painter and architect, whose real name was Donato de Pascuccio d'Agnolo (or d'Angelo). His family name has appeared mistakenly as Abramanti, Barbanti, and Lazzari.

Bramantino, Il. Cognomen of Bartolommeo Suardi (c1460–c1536), Italian painter and architect. He was a follower of Bramante.

Brambeus, Baron. Pseudonym of Osip Ivanovich Senkovsky (1800–1859), Russian journalist.

Bramer, Jennie Perkins. See PERKINS, FAITH.

Bramwell, James Guy. See BYRON, JAMES.

Brand, Charles Neville. See LORNE, CHARLES.

Brand, Christianna. See LEWIS, MARY CHRISTIANNA MILNE.

Brand, Peter. Pseudonym of Erling Larsen (1909–   ), American writer.

Brand, Willem Simon. See BRANDT, WILLEM.

Brandel, Marc. Pseudonym of Marcus Beresford (1919–   ), British writer.

Brandenberg, Aliki Liacouras. See ALIKI.

Brandon, Curt. See BISHOP, CURTIS KENT.

Brandon, Joe. Pseudonym of Robert P. Davis (1929–   ), American free-lance writer.

Brandt, Adolf. See STILLFRIED, FELIX.

Brandt, Harvey. See EDWARDS, WILLIAM BENNETT.

Brandt, Kaspar. Pseudonym of Jacob Winkler Prins (1849–1906), Dutch poet.

Brandt, Tom. See DEWEY, THOMAS BLANCHARD.

Brandt, Willem. Pseudonym of Willem Simon Brand (1905–   ), Dutch poet.

Brannon, William T. (1906–   ). American free-lance fiction, nonfiction, and feature writer, mainly on crime subjects, whose pseudonyms are *Lawrence Gardner, Jack Hamilton, Peter Hermanns, Dwight McGlinn, Peter Oberholtzer, S. T. Peters,* and *William Tibbetts.*

Braxatoris, Ondrey. See SLADKOVICH, ANDREY.

Braza, Jacque. See McKEAG, ERNEST L.

Brebner, Percy James. See LYS, CHRISTIAN.

Breck, Vivian. Pseudonym of Vivian Gurney Breckenfeld (1895–   ), American author.

Breckenfeld, Vivian Gurney. See BRECK, VIVIAN.

Breda, Tjalmar. Pseudonym of David Cornel DeJong (1905–1967), American author.

Breden, Christiane von. See CHRISTEN, ADA.

Bredow, Miriam. Pseudonym of Miriam Bredow Wolf (1895–   ), American writer.

Breetveld, Jim Patrick. See MANN, AVERY.

Breinlinger, Alice Berend. See BEREND, ALICE.

Brekke, Paal Emanuel. See RHODE, ARVID.

Bremer, Ward. See REACH, JAMES.

Brenan, Gerald. See BEATON, GEORGE.

Brenet, Michel. Pseudonym of Marie Bobillier (1858–1918), French writer on music.

Brennan, Joseph Lomas. See LOMAS, STEVE.

Brennan, Tim. See CONROY, JOHN WESLEY.

Brennand, Frank. See LAMBERT, ERIC.

Brenner, Arvid. Pseudonym of Helge Heerberger (1907–   ), Swedish writer.

Brennglas, Adolf. Pseudonym of Adolf Glassbrenner (1810–1876), German writer.

Brenning, L. H. See HUNTER, JOHN.

Brent, Loring. Pseudonym of George Frank Worts (1892–   ), mystery writer.

Brent, Nigel. Pseudonym of Cecil Gordon Wimchurst, contemporary mystery writer.

Brescia, Moretto da. See MORETTO, IL.

Brescianino. See MUZIANO, GIROLAMO.

Bressano, Girolamo. See MUZIANO, GIROLAMO.

Breton de Nijs, E. Pseudonym of Robert Nieuwenhuys (1908–   ), Dutch writer.

Brett, David. Pseudonym of Will Davis Campbell (1924–   ), American author.

Brett, Martin. See SANDERSON, DOUGLAS.

Brett, Mary Elizabeth. See BRETT, MOLLY.

Brett, Michael. Pseudonym of Miles Tripp (1923–   ), English freelance writer.

Brett, Molly. Pseudonym of Mary Elizabeth Brett, contemporary English author of children's stories.

Brewer, Fred. See WYNN, ALFRED.

Brewster, Benjamin. See FOLSOM, FRANKLIN BREWSTER.

Březina, Otakar. Pseudonym of Václav Ignac Jebavý (1868–1929), Czech poet.

Briançon. See BISINZO, ALBERIC VON.

Brice, Germain (1500?–1538). French ecclesiastic and neo-Latin poet, also known as *Brixius.*

Bridie, James. Pseudonym of Osborne Henry Mavor (1888–1951), Scottish playwright.

Brierley, Benjamin. See AB-O'-TH'-YATE.

Brinitzer, Carl. See USIKOTA.

Brinton, Henry. See FRASER, ALEX.

Briosco, Andrea. See RICCIO, ANDREA.

Brisebarre, Jean (b. 1340?). French poet, also known as *Jean Le Court.*

Brister, Richard (1915–   ). American writer, whose pseudonyms are *Will O. Grove, C. L. Lewin,* and *George Richmond.*

Bristol, Julius. Pseudonym of Alan Abel (1928–   ), American writer.

Britt, Sappho Henderson. See WOOLFOLK, JOSIAH PITTS.

Britton, Mattie Lula Cooper. See PATTERSON, JANE.

Brixius. See BRICE, GERMAIN.

Broadbottom, Geffery. Pseudonym of Philip Dormer Stanhope, 4th Earl of Chesterfield (1694–1773), English statesman and man of letters, used for signing letters attacking the ministry under George III.

Brock, Alan St. Hill. See DEWDNEY, PETER.

Brock, Gavin. Pseudonym of John Maurice Lindsay (1918–   ), Scottish-English writer.

Brock, Lynn. See MCALLISTER, ALISTER.

Brock, Stuart. See TRIMBLE, LOUIS P.

Brodie, John. See GUTHRIE, JOHN.

Brodie, Julian Paul. See DENBIE, ROGER.

Brody, Marc. See WILKES-HUNTER, RICHARD.

Broemel, Rose. See EVELYN, ROSE D'.

Brofeldt, Juhani. See AHO, JUHANI.

Broncense, El. Cognomen of Francisco Sánchez de las Bronzas (1523–1601), Spanish essayist.

Bronson, Lynn. Pseudonym of Evelyn Sibley Lampman (1907–   ), American author of juvenile books.

Bronstein, Leib Davydovich. See TROTSKY, LEON.

Bronstein, Yetta. Pseudonym of Jeanne Abel (1937–   ), American writer.

Brontë, Anne (1820–1849). English poet and novelist, whose pseudonyms are *Acton Bell, Lady Geralda, Olivia Vernon,* and *Alexandria Zenobia.*

Brontë, Charlotte (1816–1855). English poet and novelist, whose principal pseudonym is *Currer Bell.* In some of her earlier writings she used the pseudonyms *Genius, C. B., The Marquis of Douro,* and *Lord Charles Wellesley.*

Brontë, Emily Jane (1818–1848). English poet and novelist, whose principal pseudonym is *Ellis Bell.* Some of her earlier pieces were signed *R. Alcon.*

Bronzas, Sánchez de las. See BRONCENSE, EL.

Bronzino, Il. Cognomen of Agnolo (or Angiolo) di Cosimo di Mariano (1502-1572), Florentine painter.

Brook, Barnaby. Pseudonym of Collin Brooks (1893–   ), mystery writer.

Brooke, A. B. See JENNINGS, LESLIE NELSON.

Brooke, Carole. Pseudonym of Valerie Patricia Roskams Ramskill, contemporary English author.

Brooker, Bertram (1888–1955). Mystery writer, whose pseudonyms are *Huxley Herne* and *Richard Surrey.*

Brooks, Anne Tedlock (1905–   ). American writer, whose pseudonyms are *Anne Carter* and *Cynthia Millburn.*

Brooks, Collin. See BROOK, BARNABY.

Brooks, Edwy Searles (1889–   ). Mystery writer, whose pseudonyms are *Robert W. Comrade* and *Berkeley Gray.*

Brooks, Jeremy. See MEIKLE, CLIVE.

Brooks, Maria. See OCCIDENTE, MARÍA DEL.

Brooks, Vivian Collin. See MILLS, OSMINGTON.

Broome, Adam. Pseudonym of Godfrey Warden James (1888–   ), mystery writer.

Brosbøll, Johan Carl Christian. See ETLAR, CARIT.

Brother Antoninus. Pseudonym of William Oliver Everson (1912–   ), American writer.

Brother Flavius. Pseudonym of James E. Ellison (1927–   ), American writer of juvenile books.

Brouart, François Vatable. See BÉROALDE DE VERVILLE, FRANÇOIS VATABLE.

Brouwer, A. Pseudonym of Jacobus van Looy (1855–1925), Dutch painter and writer.

Broward, Donn. See HALLERAN, EUGENE EDWARD.

Browin, Frances Williams. See WILLIAMS, FRANCIS B.

Brown, Alice. See REDFIELD, MARTIN.

Brown, Emily. See STERNE, EMMA GELDERS.

Brown, John J. See SHERASHEVSKI, BORIS.

Brown, Margaret Wise. See SAGE, JUNIPER.

Brown, Morna Doris (1907–   ). English professional detective writer, whose pseudonyms are *Elizabeth Ferrars* and *E. X. Ferrars.*

Brown, Mr. See THACKERAY, WILLIAM MAKEPEACE.

Brown, Rosalie Gertrude Moore. See MOORE, ROSALIE.

Brown, Thomas, the younger. See MOORE, THOMAS.

Brown, Will C. Pseudonym of Clarence Scott Boyles (1905–   ), American writer.

Brown, Zenith (1898–   ). American mystery writer, whose pseudonyms are *Leslie Ford* and *David Frome.* Her original name was Zenith Jones.

Browne, Charles Farrar. See WARD, ARTEMUS.

Browne, Howard. See EVANS, JOHN.

Browne, Sam. See SMITH, RONALD GREGOR.

Browne, Thomas Alexander. See BOLDREWOOD, ROLF.

Browning, Sterry. See GRIBBLE, LEONARD REGINALD.

Bruce, Arthur Loring. Pseudonym of Francis Welch Crowninshield (1872–1947), American editor.

Bruce, Leo. See CROFT-COOKE, RUPERT.

Bruce, Monica. Pseudonym of Constance L. Melaro (1929–   ), American writer.

Bruckner, Ferdinand. Pseudonym of Theodor Tagger (1891–1958), German writer.

Bruff, Nancy. Pseudonym of Nancy Bruff Gardner (1915–   ), American novelist and poet.

Bruggen, Carolina Lea Van De Haan. See ABBING, JUSTINE.

Brühl, Gustav. See KARA, GIORG.

Brulin, Tone. Pseudonym of Antoon van den Eynde (1926–   ), Dutch playwright.

Bruller, Jean. See VERCORS.

Brunclair, Victor J. (1899–1944). Dutch poet, critic, essayist, and novelist, whose pseudonyms are *Geert Bardemeyer, J. Fikkens,* and *Lirio.*

Brunne, Robert of. See MANNYNG, ROBERT.
Brunner, Constantin. Pseudonym of Leo Wertheimer (1862–1937), German philosopher.
Brunner, John Kilian Houston. See WOODCOTT, KEITH.
Brusasorci, Il. Cognomen of Domenico Riccio (1494–1567), Italian painter.
Bryans, Robert Harbinson (1928–   ). Irish writer, whose pseudonyms are *Robin Bryans* and *Robert Harbinson.*
Bryans, Robin. See BRYANS, ROBERT HARBINSON.
Bryce, Ronald. See ROCKEY, HOWARD.
Bryson, Charles. See BARRY, CHARLES.
Bryson, Leigh. Pseudonym of Nancy Rutledge, contemporary mystery writer.
Brzechwa, Jan. Pseudonym of Jan Wiktor Lesman (1900–   ), Polish poet.
Brzozowski, Leopold Stanisław Leon. See CZEPIEL, ADAM.
Bucer, Martin. See ARETIUS FELINUS.
Buchanan, B. J. See SHEPHERD, JOAN.
Buchanan, William. Joint pseudonym of William Ray Buck (1930–   ) and Russell Thorndike (no dates available), American writers.
Buchinskaya, Nadezhda Alexeyevna. See TEFFY.
Buchmann, Theodor. See BIBLIANDER.
Buck, Pearl. See SEDGES, JOHN.
Buck, William Ray. See BUCHANAN, WILLIAM.
Buckingham, Bruce. Joint pseudonym of Peter Lilley and Anthony Stansfeld, contemporary mystery writers.
Budd, Jackson. See BUDD, WILLIAM JOHN.
Budd, William John (1898–   ). Mystery writer, whose pseudonyms are *Jackson Budd* and *Wallace Jackson.*
Bugayev, Boris Nikolayevich. See BELY, ANDREY.
Bugbee, Ruth Carson. See CARSON, RUTH.
Bugenhagen, Johann (1485–1558). German Protestant reformer, who was called *Pomeranus* and *Dr. Pommer.* The names were derived from his birthplace, Pomerania.
Bukki ben Yogli. Pseudonym of Yehuda Loeb Katznelson (1847–1917), Hebrew writer.
Bull, Lois (1900–   ). Mystery writer, whose pseudonyms are *Melville Burt* and *Judith Grovner Wright.*

Bullard, Arthur. See EDWARDS, ALBERT.

Bulleid, H. A. V. See COLLINS, D.

Bullett, Gerald William. See FOX, SEBASTIAN.

Bullingham, Rodney. See SLADEN, NORMAN ST. BARBE.

Bullock, Michael. See HALE, MICHAEL.

Bully, Édouard Roger de. See BEAUVOIR, ROGER DE.

Bulwer Lytton, Edward Robert, 1st Earl of Lytton. See MEREDITH, OWEN.

Bumpus, Doris Marjorie. See ALAN, MARJORIE.

Buntline, Ned. Pseudonym of Edward Zane Carroll Judson (1823–1886), American adventurer and writer of dime novels.

Bunya no Yasuhide. See FUNYA NO YASUHIDE.

Buonaccorsi, Pietro. See VAGA, PERINO DEL.

Buontalenti, Bernardo (1536–1608). Florentine architect, painter, and sculptor, whose original name was Bernardo dalla Girandole.

Buonvicino, Alessandro. See MORETTO, IL.

Burchiello, Domenico (1404–1449). Florentine barber poet, whose original name was Domenico di Giovanni.

Burford, Eleanor. See HIBBERT, ELEANOR BURFORD.

Burford, Roger d'Este (1904–   ). British mystery writer, whose pseudonyms are *Roger East* and, with Oswell Blakeston, (1907–   ), *Simon.*

Burg, Paul. Pseudonym of Paul Schaumberg (1884–   ), German historical novelist.

Burge, Milward Rodon Kennedy (1894–   ). Mystery writer, whose pseudonyms are *Milward Kennedy* and *Robert Milward Kennedy.*

Burgeon, G. A. L. Pseudonym of Owen Barfield (1898–   ), English writer.

Bürger, Hugo. Pseudonym of Hugo Lubliner (1846–1911), German playwright.

Burger, John. Pseudonym of Leopold Marquard (1897–   ), South African writer.

Bürger, Lucian. Pseudonym of Charlotte Niese (b. 1854), German writer.

Burgess, Anthony. Pseudonym of John Burgess Wilson (1917–   ), English writer. He also writes under the name of *Joseph Kell.*

Burgess, Trevor. See TREVOR, ELLESTON.

Burghardt, Oswald. See JURIJ, KLEN.

Burgoyne, Elizabeth. Pseudonym of M. Elizabeth Pickles (1902–   ), English author.

Burguillos, El Licenciado Tomé de. See VEGA, LOPE DE.

Burke, Fielding. Pseudonym of Olive Dargan, contemporary American poet and novelist.

Burke, John Frederick (1922–   ). English writer, whose pseudonyms are *Jonathan Burke* and *Sara Morris.*

Burke, Jonathan. See BURKE, JOHN FREDERICK.

Burke, Noel. See HITCHENS, DOLORES BIRK OLSEN.

Burkhardt, Eve (1899–   ). Mystery writer, whose pseudonyms, with Robert Ferdinand Burkhardt, are *Adam Bliss, Rob Eden,* and *Rex Jardin.*

Burkhardt, Robert Ferdinand (1892–1947). Mystery writer, whose pseudonyms, with Eve Burkhardt, are *Adam Bliss, Rob Eden,* and *Rex Jardin.*

Burnaby, Nigel. Pseudonym of Harold Pincton Ellett (1882–   ), mystery writer.

Burne, Glen. Joint pseudonym of Alan Baer Green (1906–   ) and Gladys Elizabeth Blun Green (1908–   ), mystery writers.

Burnett, David (1931–   ). Austrian-American writer, whose pseudonyms are *Terrave Bernarn* and *Peter Pace.*

Burney, Anton. See HOPKINS, KENNETH.

Burnham, Clara Louise. See DOUGLAS, EDITH.

Burns, Eedson Louis Millard. See CONWAY, ARLINGTON.

Burroughs, William Seward (1914–   ). American writer, whose pseudonyms are *Mr. Bradly, William Lee,* and *Mr. Martin.*

Bürstenbinder, Elisabeth. See WERNER, E.

Burt, Melville. See BULL, LOIS.

Burte, Hermann. Pseudonym of Hermann Strübe (1879–   ), German writer.

Burton, Miles. See STREET, CECIL JOHN CHARLES.

Burton, Robert. See DEMOCRITUS JUNIOR.

Burton, Thomas. See LONGSTREET, STEPHEN.

Bury, Jan (1885–1953). Polish author, whose real name was Stanisław Wasylewski. He has been called the "Polish Goncourt."

Bush, Christopher. See HOME, MICHAEL.

Buson. Pseudonym of Taniguchi Tora (1716–1784), Japanese poet and painter, also known as *Yosa Buson.*

Busta, Christine. Pseudonym of Christine Dimt (1915–   ), Austrian poet.

Bustamante, Carlos. See CONCOLORCORVO.

Busybody, The. See FRANKLIN, BENJAMIN.

Butler, H. M. See BLACK, M. DANA.

Butters, Dorothy Gilman. See GILMAN, DOROTHY.

Butterworth, Frank Nestle. See BLUNDELL, PETER.

Butterworth, William Edmund, III (1929–   ). American writer, whose pseudonyms are *Webb Beech, Walker E. Blake,* and *Edmund O. Scholefield.*

Butzer, Martin. See ARETIUS FELINUS.

Buxbaum, Martin. See NOLL, MARTIN.

Buyle, Hubert. See HELDERENBERG, GERY.

Buyrette, Pierre Laurent. See BELLOY, DORMONT DE.

Bynner, Witter (1881–1968). American poet who became widely known through a hoax perpetrated by him and Arthur Davison Ficke. They published a book under the respective pseudonyms of *Emanuel Morgan* and *Anne Knish.*

Byr, Robert. Pseudonym of Karl Robert Emmerich von Bayer (1835–1902), Austrian novelist and writer on military subjects.

Byron, James. Pseudonym of James Guy Bramwell (1911–   ), English-French writer.

Byron, John. See ARMSTRONG, JOHN BYRON.

"C"

Caballero, Fernán. Pseudonym of Cecilia Francisca Josefa de Arrom (1797?–1877), Spanish novelist.

Cabasilas, Nicholas (d. 1371). Byzantine theologian, also called *Chameatus.*

Cadell, James. See THOMAS, RONALD WILLS.

Cadlubco. See KADŁUBEC, WINCENTY.

Caeiro, Alberto. See PESSOA, FERNANDO.

Caesar, Eugene Lee (1927–   ). American writer, whose pseudonyms are *Johnny Laredo* and *Anthony Sterling.*

Caesar, R. D. See JAMES, DYNELY.

Cagney, Peter. See WINTER, BEVIS.

Cain, Christopher. See FLEMING, THOMAS JAMES.

Caire, Edwin de. Pseudonym of Edwin Alfred Williams, contemporary
   mystery writer.

Caissa. See FRAENKEL, HEINRICH.

Çajupi. Pseudonym of Andon Zako (1866–1930), Albanian poet.

Cala, Antonio Martínez de. See NEBRIJA, ELIO ANTONIO DE.

Calamy, Edmund. See SMECTYMNUUS.

Caldara, Polidoro. See CARAVAGGIO, POLIDORO DA.

Caldarelli, Nazareno. See CARDARELLI, VINCENZO.

Caldwell, Janet Miriam Taylor Holland (1900–   ). American novelist, whose principal pseudonym is *Taylor Caldwell.* She also uses the
   pseudonym *Max Reiner.*

Caldwell, Taylor. See CALDWELL, JANET MIRIAM TAYLOR HOLLAND.

Caliari, Paolo. See VERONESE, PAOLO.

Caliban. Pseudonym of Richard Nordhausen (1868–   ), German
   writer.

Calkins, Franklin. See STRATEMEYER, EDWARD L.

Callahan, Claire Wallis (1890–   ). American free-lance writer, whose
   pseudonyms are *Ann Kilborn Cole* and *Nancy Hartwell.*

Callard, Thomas Henry. See ROSS, SUTHERLAND.

Callas, Theo. See MCCARTHY, SHAUN.

Callender, Julian. See LEE, AUSTIN.

Calvin, John (1509–1564). French theologian and reformer, whose original name was Jean Chauvin. He was also known as *Alcuinus,*
   Lucanius, and *Lucianus.*

Calvin, Henry. Pseudonym of Clifford Hanley (1922–   ), Scottish
   writer.

Cámara, Juan de la. See RODRÍGUEZ DEL PADRÓN, JUAN.

Cameron, Elizabeth. See ROBINSON, ELIZABETH CAMERON.

Cameron, Elizabeth Jane. See DUNCAN, JANE.

Cameron, Ian. See PAYNE, DONALD GORDON.

Cameron, John. See MACDONELL, ARCHIBALD GORDON.

Cameron, Kenneth Neill. See MADDEN, WARREN.

Cameron, Lou (1924–   ). American writer, whose pseudonyms are *L.
   J. Arnold, Steve Cartier,* and *W. R. Marvin.*

Cameron, Margaret. See LINDSAY, KATHLEEN.

Cameron, William Ernest. See ALLERTON, MARK.

Camino y Galicia, Léon-Felipe. See LÉON-FELIPE.

Campbell, Blanche. See FISH, JULIAN.

Campbell, Bruce. See EPSTEIN, SAMUEL.

Campbell, Clive. Pseudonym of Donald G. MacRae (1921–   ), Scottish-English scholar.

Campbell, Colin. See CHRISTIE, DOUGLAS.

Campbell, Donald. See GILFORD, C. B.

Campbell, Francis Stuart. See KUEHNELT LEDDIHN, ERIK RITTER VON.

Campbell, Hannah. See FRANKLIN, ELIZABETH.

Campbell, Jane. Pseudonym of Jane Campbell Edwards (1932–   ), American writer for young people.

Campbell, Joseph (1879–1944). Irish poet, who published under his Gaelic name *Seosamh Mac Cathmhaoil.*

Campbell, Joseph. See ULTACH.

Campbell, Judith. Pseudonym of Marion Pares (1914–   ), English writer.

Campbell, Keith. Pseudonym of Keith Campbell West-Watson, contemporary mystery writer.

Campbell, Scott. Pseudonym of Frederick William Davis (1858–1933), mystery writer.

Campbell, Walter Stanley. See VESTAL, STANLEY.

Campbell, Will Davis. See BRETT, DAVID.

Campbell, William Edward March. See MARCH, WILLIAM.

Camper, Shirley. Pseudonym of Shirley Soman (1922–   ), American writer.

Campion, Sidney Ronald. See SWAYNE, GEOFFREY.

Campos, Alvaro de. See PESSOA, FERNANDO.

Canaday, John E. See HEAD, MATTHEW.

Canale, Antonio. See CANALETTO, ANTONIO.

Canaletto, Antonio (1697–1768). Venetian painter, whose real name was Antonio Canale (or Canal).

Candid, Peter. See CANDIDO, PIETRO.

Candido, Pietro. Italianized name of Peter Candid (1548?–1628), Flemish painter, whose original name was Pieter de Wit (or de Witte).

Candy, Edward. Pseudonym of Barbara Alison Boodson Neville (1925–   ), English novelist.

Canisius, Peter. Religious name of Pieter De Hondt (1521–1597), German Catholic theologian.

Cannell, Charles. Pseudonym of Evelyn Charles H. Vivian, contemporary mystery writer.

Canning, Effie. Pseudonym of Effie Carlton (1857–1940), American actress, who wrote the lullaby *Rock-a-Bye Baby.*

Cano, Alonso. See GRANADINO, EL.

Cantarini,. Simone. See PESARESE, IL.

Canusi, Jose. See BARKER, S. OMAR.

Canyon, Claudia. Pseudonym of Betty Anderson, contemporary mystery writer.

Capel, Roger. Pseudonym of Lancelot Capel Sheppard (1906–   ), English writer.

Capon, Peter. See OAKLEY, ERIC GILBERT.

Capstan. Pseudonym of Rex Hardinge (1904–   ), mystery writer.

Capuccino, Il. See STROZZI, BERNARDO.

Caradon, Lord. Pseudonym of Hugh Mackintosh Foot (1907–   ), English author.

Caravaggio, Michelangelo da (c1565–1610). Italian painter, whose real name was Michelangelo Merisi. The name was derived from his birthplace, Caravaggio.

Caravaggio, Polidoro da (c1495–1543). Italian painter, whose real name was Polidoro Caldara. The name was derived from his birthplace, Caravaggio.

Carbery, Eithne. Pseudonym of Anna Johnston (1886–   ), Irish poet.

Carco, Francis. Pseudonym of François Carcopino-Tusoli (1886–1958), French novelist and critic.

Carcopino-Tusoli, François. See CARCO, FRANCIS.

Cardarelli, Vincenzo. Pseudonym of Nazareno Caldarelli (1887–1959), Italian poet and writer.

Cardozo, Lois Steinmetz (1934–   ). American writer, whose pseudonyms are *Lois Duncan* and *Lois Kerry.*

Carducci, Giosuè. See ROMANO, ENOTRIO.

Cardwell, Ann. Pseudonym of Jean Powley, contemporary mystery writer.

Čarenc, Egiše. Pseudonym of Egiše Sohomonjàn (1897–1937), Armenian poet.

Carew, Jean. See CORBY, JANE.

Carew, John Mohun. See CAREW, TIM.

Carew, Tim. Pseudonym of John Mohun Carew (1921–   ), English writer.

Carey, Charles. Pseudonym of Charles Carey Waddel (1868–1930), mystery writer.

Carey, Elisabeth. See MAGOON, CAREY.

Carfagne, Cyril. See JENNINGS, LESLIE NELSON.

Carhart, Arthur Hawthorne (1892–   ). American writer, whose pseudonyms are *Hart Thorne* and *V. A. Van Sickle.*

Carle, C. E. See MORGAN, MICHAEL.

Carleton, S. Pseudonym of Susan Carleton Jones (1869–   ), mystery writer.

Carlton, Effie. See CANNING, EFFIE.

Carlyle, Anthony. Pseudonym of Gladys Alexandra Milton, contemporary mystery writer.

Carman, Dulce. Pseudonym of Edith Marie Dulce Carman Drummond (1883–   ), British writer.

Carmi, T. Pseudonym of Carmi Charny (1925–   ), American writer.

Carmichael, Ann. Pseudonym of Margaret H. MacAlpine (1907–   ), Scottish writer.

Carmichael, Harry. See OGNALL, LEOPOLD HORACE.

Carmontelle, Louis. Professional name of Louis Carrogis (1717–1806), French painter, engraver, and writer.

Carnac, Carol. See RIVETT, EDITH CAROLINE.

Carol, Bill J. Pseudonym of William Cecil Knott, Jr. (1927–   ), American author.

Caron, Pierre-Augustin. See BEAUMARCHAIS, PIERRE-AUGUSTIN CARON DE.

Carpenter, Alexander (fl. 1429). Popular preacher and religious writer, whose pseudonyms are *Alexander Angelus* and *Fabricius.*

Carpi, Girolamo da (1501–1556). Italian painter, whose original name was Girolamo de' Sellari.

Carr, A. H. Z. Pseudonym of Albert Zolotkoff Carr (1902–   ), American writer.

Carr, Albert Zolotkoff. See CARR, A. H. Z.

Carr, Catharine. Pseudonym of Rosalind Herschel Wade (1909–   ), English novelist.

Carr, Dorothy Stevenson Laird. See LAIRD, DOROTHY.

Carr, Glyn. Pseudonym of Showell Styles (1908–   ), mystery writer.

Carr, John Dickson (1905–   ). American-English mystery writer, whose pseudonyms are *Carter Dickson* and *Carr Dickson.*

Carr, Roberta. See ROBERTS, IRENE.

Carrick, Edward. Pseudonym of Edward A. Craig (1905–   ), English writer.

Carrick, John. Pseudonym of Hugh Provan Crosbie (1912–   ), Scottish-English writer.

Carrington, Charles Edmund. See EDMUNDS, CHARLES.

Carrogis, Louis. See CARMONTELLE, LOUIS.

Carroll, Curt. See BISHOP, CURTIS KENT.

Carroll, Lewis. Pseudonym of Charles Lutwidge Dodgson (1832–1898), English mathematician and story writer.

Carroll, Robert. Pseudonym of Hollis Alpert (1916–   ), American novelist. He adopted his mother's maiden name.

Carrucci, Jacopo. See PONTORMO, JACOPO DA.

Carson, Captain James. See STRATEMEYER, EDWARD L.

Carson, Ruth. Pseudonym of Ruth Carson Bugbee (1903–   ), American writer.

Carter, Anne. See BROOKS, ANNE TEDLOCK.

Carter, Bruce. Pseudonym of Richard Hough (1922–   ), English author.

Carter, John Franklin (1897–1967). Mystery writer, whose pseudonyms are *Diplomat, Jay Franklin,* and *Unofficial Observer.*

Carter, Nick. Pseudonym of author or authors (c1870) of early detective and adventure stories. The character was reputedly invented by John R. Coryell (1848–1924). Later writers were Thomas Chalmers Harbaugh (1849–1924) and Frederick Van Rensselaer Dey (1861–1922). These writers are also supposed to have written novels under the pseudonym *Bertha M. Clay,* which was originated by Charlotte Monica Braeme (1836–1884). Other known authors of the Carter series were Frederick William Davis (1858–1933), George Charles Jenks (1850–1929), and Eugene T. Sawyer (1846–1924).

Carter, Phyllis Ann. See EBERLE, IRMENGARDE.

Carter, Ralph. See NEUBAUER, WILLIAM ARTHUR.

Carteromaco. Pseudonym of Niccolò Forteguerri (or Fortiguerra) (1674–1735), Italian prelate and poet.

Cartier, Steve. See CAMERON, LOU.

Cartland, Barbara. See MCCORQUODALE, BARBARA.

Carton, Richard Claude. Pseudonym of Richard Claude Critchett (1856–1928), English actor and playwright.

Cartwright, James McGregor. See JENNINGS, LESLIE NELSON.

Carus, Sterne. Pseudonym of Ernst Ludwig Krause (1837–1903), German science writer.

Casalandra, Estelle. Pseudonym of Sister Mary Estelle (1907–   ), American author.

Case, Justin. Pseudonym of Rupert Seeley Gleadow (1909–   ), English writer.

Case, L. L. Pseudonym of Leonard C. Lewin (1916–   ), American writer and editor.

Case, Michael. Pseudonym of Robert West Howard (1908–   ), American writer.

Caseleyr, Camille. See DANVERS, JACK.

Casewit, Curtis (1922–   ). German-American free-lance writer, whose pseudonyms are *D. Green, D. Vernor,* and *K. Werner.*

Cash, Sebastian. Pseudonym of Roger Smithells (1905–   ), English writer.

Caskoden, Sir Edwin. Pseudonym of Charles Major (1856–1913), American novelist.

Cason, Mabel Earp. See BELL, EMILY MARY.

Casona, Alejandro. Pseudonym of Alejandro Rodríguez Alvarez (1903–   ), Spanish playwright.

Casque, Sammy. Pseudonym of Sydney Charles Houghton Davis (1887–   ), English writer.

Cassells, John. See DUNCAN, W. MURDOCH.

Cassiday, Bruce Bingham (1920–   ). American writer, whose pseudonyms are *Carson Bingham* and *Max Day.*

Cassill, Ronald Verlin (1919–   ). American free-lance writer, whose pseudonyms are *Owen Aherne* and *Jesse Webster.*

Castelfranco, Giorgione da. See GIORGIONE, IL.

Castelli, Francesco. See BORROMINI, FRANCESCO.

Castelnuovo, Leo di. Pseudonym of Leopoldo Pullè (1835–1917), Italian playwright.

Castlemon, Harry. Pseudonym of Charles Austin Fosdick (1842–1915), American writer of juveniles.

Caswell, Anne. See DENHAM, MARY ORR.

Català, Victor. Pseudonym of Catarina Albert i Paradís (1873–1952), Catalan novelist.

Cathal O Dubh. Pseudonym of Charles St. Lawrence Duff (1894–   ), Irish-English writer and translator.

Catlow, Joanna. Pseudonym of Joan Catlow Lowry (1911–   ), English novelist.

Cato. Joint pseudonym of Peter D. Howard (1908–1965), Michael Foote, and Frank Owen, English writers.

Catz, Max. Pseudonym of Milton Glaser (1929–   ), American writer.

Caudwell, Christopher. Pseudonym of Christopher St. John Sprigg (1907–1937), English poet.

Cauldwell, Frank. Occasional pseudonym of Francis Henry King (1923–   ), English writer.

Cauley, Terry. Pseudonym of Troy Jesse Cauley (1902–   ), American writer.

Cauley, Troy Jesse. See CAULEY, TERRY.

Cauliflower, Sebastian. See SELDES, GILBERT VIVIAN.

Cavallaro, Ann Abelson. See ABELSON, ANN.

Cavalli, Vitale d'Aimo de'. See BOLOGNA, VITALE DA.

Cavanna, Elizabeth (or **Betty**) **Allen** (1909–   ). American writer, whose pseudonyms are *Betsy Allen* and *Elizabeth Headley.*

Cave, Edward. See URBAN, SYLVANUS, GENT.

Cave, Roderick George James Munroe. See MUNROE, JAMES.

Cavendish, Peter. See HORLER, SIDNEY.

Caverhill, William Melville. See MELVILLE, ALAN.

Cayado, Henrique. See CAIADUS, HERMICUS.

Cazimir, Ottilia. Pseudonym of Alexandrina Gavrilescu, contemporary Rumanian poet.

Cecil, Henry. Pseudonym of Henry Cecil Leon, contemporary mystery writer.

Ceder, Georgiana Dorcas. See DOR, ANA.

Ceiriog. Pseudonym of John Ceiriog Hughes (1832–1887), Welsh poet.

Celan, Paul. Pseudonym of Paul Antschel (1920–   ), German writer.

Celebi, Mustafa. See NAILI.

Céline, Louis-Ferdinand. Pseudonym of Louis Fuch Destouches (1894–1961), French novelist.

Celoistre. See SLUTER, CLAUS.

Celtis (or **Celtes**), **Conradus.** Latinized name of Konrad Pickel (1459–1508), German-Latin humanist and poet.

Celuister (or **Celustre**). See SLUTER, CLAUS.

Cepeda y Ahumada, Teresa Sánchez de. See TERESA OF JESUS, SAINT.

Ceram, C. W. Pseudonym of Kurt W. Marek (1915–   ), German-American writer.

Cerano, Il. Cognomen of Giovanni Battista Crespi (1557–1663), Italian painter.

Cerclaria, Thomasin de. See THOMASIN VON ZERCLAERE.

Cerna, Panait. Pseudonym of Panait Stancioff (1881–1913), Rumanian poet.

Chaber, M. E. See CROSSEN, KENDELL.

Chadwick, Lester. Collective pseudonym for the "Baseball Joe" and "College Sports" series. See STRATEMEYER, EDWARD L.

Chagas, António das. Religious name of António da Fonseca Soares (1631–1682), Portuguese novelist.

Chamberlain, Theodore. Joint pseudonym of Ronald Johnson (1935–   ) and Jonathan Chamberlain Williams (1929–   ), American writers.

Chambers, Dana. See LEFFINGWELL, ALBERT.

Chambers, Peter. See PHILLIPS, D. J.

Chameatus, Nicholas. See CABASILAS, NICHOLAS.

Chamisso, Adelbert von (1781–1838). French-German poet, whose original name was Louis Charles Adélaïde Chamisso de Boncourt.

Champfleury. Pseudonym of Jules François Felix (Fleury-) Husson (1821–1889), French novelist.

Chamson, André Jules Louis. See LAUTER.

Chamudot, Danial Yish. See LIEBERMANN, AHRON SAMUEL.

Chanakya. See KAUTILYA.

Chancellor, John. Pseudonym of Charles de Balzac Rideaux (1900–   ), mystery writer.

Chandos, Fay. See TEMPEST, JAN.

Ch'ang Ch'un. Monastic name of Ch'iu Ch'u-chi (1148–1227), Chinese Taoist writer.

Chang Wen-ming. See I-CHING.

Chanslor, Marjorie Torrey Hood (1899–   ). Mystery writer, whose pseudonyms are *Torre Bevans* and *Marjorie Torrey.*

Chapman, Allen. Collective pseudonym for the "Boys of Business," "Darwell Chums," "Radio Boys," and "Railroad" series. See STRATEMEYER, EDWARD L.

Chapman, George Warren Vernon. See WARREN, VERNON.

Chapman, John Stanton Higham. See CHAPMAN, MARISTAN.

Chapman, Maristan. Joint pseudonym of John Stanton Higham Chapman (1891–   ) and Mary Hamilton Chapman (1895–   ), English writers.

Chapman, Mary Hamilton. See CHAPMAN, MARISTAN.

Chapman, Raymond. See NASH, SIMON.

Chapman-Mortimer, William Charles. See MORTIMER, CHAPMAN.

Chardonne, Jacques. Pseudonym of Jacques Boutelleau (1884–   ), French novelist.

Charivarius. Pseudonym of Gijsbert Johannes Nolst Trénité (1870–1946), Dutch critic and scholar.

Charles, Franklin. See ADAMS, CLEVE FRANKLIN.

Charles, J. B. Pseudonym of Willen Hendrik Nagel (1910–   ), Dutch poet and essayist.

Charles, Louis. See STRATEMEYER, EDWARD L.

Charles, Theresa. Joint pseudonym of Charles Swatridge and his wife, Irene Swatridge, contemporary English authors.

Charlier, Jean. See GERSON, JEAN CHARLIER DE.

Charlson, David. Pseudonym of David Charles Holmes (1919–   ), American writer.

Charni, Shmuel. See NIGER, SHMUEL.

Charny, Carmi. See CARMI, T.

Chartier, Émile Auguste. See ALAIN.

Chase, James Hadley. See RAYMOND, RENÉ.

Chastellain de Couci, Le (d. 1203). French lyric poet, referred to by this title in the medieval manuscripts that contain his work. He was probably Gui de Thurotte, who was chastelain of Couci from 1186 to 1203 and who died at sea during the fourth crusade. It is also possible that he was Renaut de Magny, chastelain from 1207–1218.

Chastellain, Pierre (1408–1475). French minstrel, also known as *Vaillant.*

Chatrian, Alexandre. See ERCKMANN-CHATRIAN.

Chatzopulos, Kostas. See VASILIKOS, PETROS.

Chauvin, Jean. See CALVIN, JOHN.

Cheixaou, Elisabeth. Pseudonym of Bonny L. E. de Graaf-Boukema (1907–   ), Dutch poet.

Chenault, Nell. Pseudonym of Linell Nash Smith (1932–   ), American writer and illustrator.

Chenevière, Jacques. Pseudonym of Alexandre Guérin (1886–   ), French-Swiss poet.

Cheng Chu-yuan. See CHENG TEK-CHEUNG.

Cheng Tek-cheung. Pseudonym of Cheng Chu-yuan (1927–   ), Chinese-American scholar.

Chen Hwei. Pseudonym of William Stevenson (1925–   ), English writer.

Chénin, Émile. See MOSELLY, ÉMILE.

Chennevière, Georges. See DEBILLE, GEORGE.

Cherbonnel, Alice. See DE LA BRÈTE, JEAN.

Chërmy, Sasha. Pseudonym of Alexander Mikhaylovich Glikberg (1880–   ), Russian poet.

Chesney, Weatherby. Pseudonym of Charles John Cutcliffe Wright Hyne (1865–1944), mystery writer.

Chester, Peter. See PHILLIPS, D. J.

Chestor, Rui. Pseudonym of Sidney Hobson Courtier, contemporary mystery writer.

Chetham-Strode, Warren. See HAMILTON, MICHAEL.

Chevalier, Sulpice Guillaume. See GAVARNI.

Chiang Ping-chih. See TING-LING.

Chichester, Jane. Pseudonym of Jane Chichester Longrigg (1929–   ), English writer.

Chietek, Jan. Pseudonym of Jan Smrek (1898–   ), Slovak poet.

Chievre, La. Cognomen of Robert de Reims, 13th-century French lyric poet.

Chignon, Niles. See LINGEMAN, RICHARD R.

Chikamatsu Monzaemon. Pseudonym of Sigimori Nobumori (1653–1725), Japan's most famous playwright.

Childs, C. Sand. Pseudonym of Maryanna Childs (1910–   ), American writer.

Childs, Maryanna. See CHILDS, C. SAND.

Chimenti, Piero. See COSIMO, PIERO DI.

Chipperfield, Joseph Eugene. See CRAIG, JOHN ELAND.

Chipperfield, Robert Orr. See OSTRANDER, ISABEL EGENTON.

Chitty, Sir Thomas Wills. See HINDE, THOMAS.

Ch'iu Ch'u-chi. See CH'ANG CH'UN.

Chiyojo. See FUKUZOYA CHIYO.

Chiyoni. See FUKUZOYA CHIYO.

Chlebnikov, Velemir. Pseudonym of Victor Viktorovich Chlebnikov (1885–1922), Russian poet.

Chlebnikov, Victor Viktorovich. See CHLEBNIKOV, VELEMIR.

Choate, Gwen Peterson. See CHOATE, R. G.

Choate, R. G. Pseudonym of Gwen Peterson Choate (1922–   ), American writer.

Chogyu. See TAKAYAMA CHOGYU.

Chomette, René. See CLAIR, RENÉ.

Chorny, Fedya. See KOJUHAROV, TUDOR.

Chorny, Kuzma. Pseudonym of N. K. Romanousky (1900–1944), Russian writer.

Chou Shu-jen. See LUSIN.

Chrétien de Troyes. See CHRETIEN LI GOIS.

Chretien li Gois. Twelfth-century French poet. He may be Chrétien de Troyes, who is credited with many medieval romances.

Christen, Ada. Pseudonym of Christiane Frideriks von Breden (1844–1901), Austrian poet and novelist.

Christiaens, Andre G. Pseudonym of N. A. Drojine (1905–   ), Dutch poet.

Christian, Frederick. See GEHMAN, RICHARD BOYD.

Christian, Kit. Joint pseudonym of Delos Russell Thorson (1906–   ) and Sara Winfree Thorson (1906–   ), mystery writers.

Christiansen, Synnøve. Pseudonym of Mai Lindegard (1919–   ), Norwegian writer.

Christie, Agatha. See WESTMACOTT, MARY.

Christie, Douglas (1894–   ). Mystery writer, whose pseudonyms are *Colin Campbell* and *Lynn Durie.*

Christie, Keith. Pseudonym of Alfred Henry Haynes (1910–   ), English writer.

Christopher, Louise. See HALE, ARLENE.

Christophersen, Solveig. See CHRISTOV, S.

Christophus. Pseudonym of George Essex Evans (1863–1909), Australian poet.

Christov, S. Pseudonym of Solveig Christophersen (1918–   ), Norwegian writer.

Chrysoloras, Manuel. See CRISOLORA, MANUELE.

Church, Granville. Pseudonym of Granville Church People, contemporary mystery writer.

Church, Jeffrey. Pseudonym of Richard Kirk (1931–   ), American writer.

Chu Ta. See PA-TA-SHAN-JEN.

Chute, Rupert. See CLEVELAND, PHILIP JEROME.

Cialente, Fausta. Pseudonym of Fausta Cialente Terni (1900–   ), Italian writer.

Cid, El. Cognomen of Rodrigo (or Ruy) Díaz de Bivar (1040?–1099), Spanish soldier and hero of the oldest extant Spanish epic. He was properly called *El Cid Campeador* ("The Lord Champion").

Cidiè. See SARFATTI, MARGHERITA.

Cieco di Ferrara, I ("The Blind One of Ferrara"). Cognomen of Francesco Bello (d. 1505), Italian poet.

Cihlar, Milutin. See NEHAJEV, MILUTIN.

Cima da Conegliano (c1459–c1517). Venetian painter, whose real name was Giovanni Battista Cima.

Cinna. See FRAENKEL, HEINRICH.

Cinthio. See GIRALDI, GIOVANNI BATTISTA CINZIO.

Cione, Andrea di. See ORCAGNA, ANDREA.

Cione, Andrea di Michele. See VERROCCHIO, ANDREA DEL.

Cizinski, Jakub. See BART, JAKUB.

Claassen, Harold. See POMEROY, HUB.

Clain, Samuil. Pseudonym of Miculu Maniu (1745–1806), Transylvanian historian and philologist. He was also known as *Samuilu, the monk.*

Clair, René. Professional name of René Chomette (1898–   ), French journalist and motion-picture director and producer.

Clairville, Louis François. Pseudonym of Louis François Nicolaie (1811–1879), French playwright.

Clandon, Henrietta. See VAHEY, JOHN GEORGE HASLETTE.

Clare, Francis D. Pseudonym of Mother Mary Francis (1921–   ), American nun and writer.

Clare, Margaret. Pseudonym of Margaret M. Maison (1920–   ), English writer.

Clarín. Pseudonym of Leopoldo Alas y Ureña (1852–1901), Spanish novelist and critic, also known as *Leopoldo Alas.*

Clark, Alfred Alexander Gordon. See HARE, CYRIL.

Clark, Dale. Pseudonym of Ronal Kayser, contemporary mystery writer.

Clark, Dorothy Park. See McMEEKIN, CLARK.

Clark, Howard. Pseudonym of Dorothy Clark Haskin (1905–   ), American writer.

Clark, Winifred. See FINLEY, SCOTT.

Clarke, Captain Jafer. Pseudonym of Robert I. Nesmith (1891–   ), American authority on sunken treasure ships.

Clarke, David Waldo. See WALDO, DAVID.

Clarke, J. Calvitt (1888–   ). Mystery writer, whose pseudonyms are *Carol Addison* and *Richard Grant.*

Clarke, John. See LAUGHLIN, VIRGINIA CARLI.

Clarke, John (1913–   ). English writer, whose pseudonyms are *Hugh Cleland* and *Robert Kingsley.*

Clarke, Josephine Fitzgerald. See FITZGERALD, ERROLL.

Clarke, Rebecca Sophia. See MAY, SOPHIE.

Clarke, William James. See MONKSHOOD, G. F.

Claud(e). See LORRAIN, CLAUDE.

Claudio. See LORRAIN, CLAUDE.

Clauvot-Geer, Ursina. See GIRUN, GIAN.

Clay, Bertha M. See CARTER, NICK.

Clay, Duncan. Pseudonym of W. W. Diehl (1916–   ), American writer.

Claymore, Tod. Pseudonym of Hugh Clevely, contemporary mystery writer.

Clayton, Barbara. Pseudonym of Barbara Littlefield Pluff (1926–   ), American writer.

Clayton, Richard Henry Michael. See HAGGARD, WILLIAM.

Clear, Claudius. Pseudonym of Sir William Robertson Nicoll (1851–1923), Scottish clergyman and editor.

Cleaver, Nancy. Pseudonym of Evelyn Craw Mathews (1906–   ), Canadian writer.

Cleland, Hugh. See CLARKE, JOHN.

Cleland, Mabel. See WIDDEMER, MABEL CLELAND.

Cleland, Morton. See RENNIE, JAMES ALAN.

Clemens, Samuel Langhorne. See TWAIN, MARK.

Clement, Hal. Pseudonym of Harry C. Stubbs (1922–   ), American writer, used for his science fiction.

Clemons, Elizabeth. See ROBINSON, ELIZABETH CAMERON.

Clerk, N. W. See LEWIS, CLIVE STAPLES.

Cleveland, John. See MCELFRESH, ELIZABETH ADELINE.

Cleveland, Philip Jerome (1903–   ). American religious writer, whose pseudonyms are *A. Don Adams* and *Rupert Chute.*

Clevely, Hugh. See CLAYMORE, TOD.

Clifford, Harold B. See FARNHAM, BURT.

Clifford, John. Pseudonym of John Clifford Bayliss (1919–   ), English writer.

Climacus, Johannes. See KIERKEGAARD, SØREN AABYE.

Climacus, John. See SCHOLASTICUS.

Clinton, Iris A. Corbin. See CORBIN, IRIS.

Clinton, Jeff. See BICKHAM, JACK MILES.

Clodion (1738–1814). French sculptor, whose real name was Claude Michel.

Cloots, Anacharsis. See GIER-BER, ALI.

Cloots, Jean Baptiste du Val-de-Grâce, Baron de. See GIER-BER, ALI.

Close, Upton. Pseudonym of Josef Washington Hall (1894–1960), American writer.

Clowes, Sir William Laird. See NAUTICUS.

Clutha, Janet Paterson Frame. See FRAME, JANET.

Clyde, Leonard Worswick. See BARON, PETER.

Clynder, Monica. See MUIR, MARIE.

Clyne, Terence. Pseudonym of William Peter Blatty (1928–   ), American writer.

Cobbett. See LUDOVICI, ANTHONY M.

Cobbett, William. See PORCUPINE, PETER.

Coccio, Marcantonio. See SABELLICO, MARCANTONIO.

Cochrane de Alencar, Gertrude E. L. See SCHWARZENFELD, GERTRUDE VON.

Coch-y-Bonddhu. Pseudonym of Richards Arnold (1912–   ), British writer.

Cockin, Joan. Pseudonym of Edith Joan Burbridge Macintosh (1919–   ), mystery writer.

Cody, Al. See JOSCELYN, ARCHIE L.

Cody, C. S. Pseudonym of Leslie Waller (1923–   ), mystery writer.

Coe, Douglas. See EPSTEIN, BERYL WILLIAMS, and EPSTEIN, SAMUEL.

Coelho, J. G. Gomes. See DINIS, JÚLIO.

Coenraads, Edward. Pseudonym of Pieter Endt (1883–1936), Dutch scholar and writer.

Coffin, Geoffrey. See MASON, FRANCIS VAN WYCK.

Coffman, Ramon Peyton. See UNCLE RAY.

Cogswell, Coralie. See HOWARD, CORALIE.

Cohen, Mike. Pseudonym of Morris Cohen (1912–   ), American author.

Cohen, Morris. See COHEN, MIKE.

Cohen, Morton Norton. See MORETON, JOHN.

Cohen, Rosalyn. Pseudonym of Rosalyn Cohen Higgins (1937–   ), English political writer.

Cohn, Emil. See LUDWIG, EMIL.

Colbron, Grace Isabel. See MARCHANT, ROMANO ISABEL.

Cole, Ann Kilborn. See CALLAHAN, CLAIRE WALLIS.

Cole, Davis. See ELTING, MARY.

Cole, Jackson. See SCHISGALL, OSCAR.

Cole, Lois Dwight. Contemporary American writer, whose pseudonyms are *Lynn Avery, Nancy Dudley, Allan Dwight,* and *Anne Eliot.*

Cole, Margaret Alice. Contemporary English writer, whose pseudonyms are *Rosemary Manning, Julia Renton,* and *Ione Saunders.*

Cole, Stephen. Pseudonym of Gale Dudley Webbe (1909–   ), American author.

Coleman, Robert William Alfred. See INSIGHT, JAMES.

Coleridge, John. See BINDER, OTTO OSCAR.

Coleridge, Samuel Taylor. See COMBERBACK, SILAS TOMKYN.

Coles, Cyril Henry (1898–   ). English writer, whose pseudonyms, with Adelaide Frances Oke Manning, are *Manning Coles* and *Francis Gaite.*

Coles, Manning. See COLES, CYRIL HENRY, and MANNING, ADELAIDE FRANCES OKE.

Collans, Dev. See WINCHELL, PRENTICE.

Collen, Neil. Pseudonym of Lincoln Lee (1922–   ), English writer.

Collerye, Roger de. See BONTEMPS, ROGER.

Collier, Douglas. See FELLOWES-GORDON, IAN DOUGLAS.

Collins, D. Pseudonym of H. A. V. Bulleid (1912–   ), English writer.

Collins, Hunt. See HUNTER, EVAN.

Collins, Tom. Pseudonym of Joseph Furphy (1843–1912), Australian novelist.

Collinson, Peter. Pseudonym of Dashiell Hammet (1894–1961), mystery writer.

Collison, Wilson. See KENT, WILLIS.

Collodi, Carlo. Pseudonym of Carlo Lorenzini (1824–1890), Italian writer, creator of the character Pinocchio.

Colombo, Dale. See MONROE, KEITH.

Colorado, Antonio J. Pseudonym of Antonio Julio Colorado Capella (1903–   ), Puerto Rican writer.

Colorado Capella, Antonio Julio. See COLORADO, ANTONIO J.

Colt, Clem. See NYE, NELSON CORAL.

Colt, Martin. See EPSTEIN, SAMUEL.

Coltman, Ernest Vivian. Pseudonym of Ernest Dudley (1908–   ), English writer.

Colton, A. J. Pseudonym of Alfred Samuel Hook, contemporary mystery writer.

Colton, Mel. See TRASK, MERRILL.

Columba, Saint (521–597). Irish scribe, who devoted his life to the conversion of the Picts. He was also called *Colum* and *Colum-cille* ("Dove of the Church").

Colum-cille. See COLUMBA, SAINT.

Colver, Anne. See HARRIS, COLVER.

Comber, Lillian. See BECKWITH, LILLIAN.

Comberback, Silas Tomkyn. Pseudonym of Samuel Taylor Coleridge (1772–1834), English poet, used during his brief enlistment in the Light Dragoons.

Combs, Robert. Pseudonym of John Murray (1923–   ), American free-lance writer.

Comendador Griego, El ("The Greek Commentator"). Cognomen of Hermán Núñez de Guzmán (1485?–1553), Spanish humanist.

Comenius, Johannes Amos. Latinized name of Jan Amos Komenský (1592–1670), Czech philosopher.

Compassione. Pseudonym of George Frans Haspels (1864–1916), Dutch writer.

Compere, Mickie. Pseudonym of Mickie Compere Davidson (1936–   ), American author of juvenile books.

Compton, Ann. See PREBBLE, MARJORIE MARY CURTIS.

Comrade, Robert W. See BROOKS, EDWY SEARLES.

Concolorcorvo. Eighteenth-century Peruvian writer, whose real name is thought to be Carlos Bustamante.

Condor, Gladyn. Pseudonym of Gladys Patton Davison (1905–   ), American free-lance writer.

Conegliano, Emanuele. See PONTE, LORENZO DA.

Conger, Lesley. Pseudonym of Shirley Suttles (1922–   ), American free-lance writer.

Connell, Norreys. Pseudonym of Conal O'Connell O'Riordan (1874–1948), Irish novelist and playwright.

Conner, Patrick Reardon. See MALIN, PETER.

Connett, Eugene Virginius. See VIRGINIUS.

Connington, J. J. See STEWART, ALFRED WALTER.

Connington, John Jervis. See STEWART, ALFRED WALTER.

Connolly, Cyril Vernon. See PALINURUS.

Connor, John Anthony (1930–   ). English poet, whose pseudonyms are *Tony Connor* and *Adam Hardwick.*

Connor, Ralph. Pseudonym of Charles William Gordon (1860–1937), Canadian clergyman and novelist.

Connor, Tony. See CONNOR, JOHN ANTHONY.

Conquest, Robert. See ARDEN, J. E. M.

Conrad, Clive. Pseudonym of Frank King (1892–1958), mystery writer.

Conrad, Georg. Pseudonym of Prince George of Prussia (1826–1914), German playwright.

Conrad, Joseph (1857–1924). Polish-English novelist, whose original name was Theodor Józef Konrad Korzeniowski.

Conrad, Kenneth. Pseudonym of Kenneth V. Lottich (1904–   ), American scholar.

Conrad, Tod. See WILKES-HUNTER, RICHARD.

Conroy, John Wesley (1899–   ). American author, whose pseudonyms are *Tim Brennan* and *John Norcross.*

Conscience, Hendrik. See GEWEETEN, HENDRIK.

Constant, W. Pseudonym of Constant Wurzbach (1818–1893), Austrian writer.

Contucci, Andrea. See SANSOVINO, ANDREA.

Conway, Arlington. Pseudonym of Eedson Louis Millard Burns (1897–   ), Canadian author.

Conway, Denise. See PREBBLE, MARJORIE MARY CURTIS.

Conway, Peter. See BANKOFF, GEORGE ALEXIS.

Cook, Ramona Graham. See GRAHAM, RAMONA.

Cookson, Catherine. See MARCHANT, CATHERINE.

Coole, W. W. See KULSKI, WŁADYSŁAW WSZEBOR.

Coolidge, Susan. Pseudonym of Sarah Chauncey Woolsey (1835–1905), American writer of stories for girls.

Coolus, Romain. Pseudonym of René Weill (1868–1952), French playwright.

Coombs, Murdo. See DAVIS, FREDERICK CLYDE.

Cooper, Alfred Morton. See COOPER, MORLEY.

Cooper, Charles. Pseudonym of Arnold Charles Cooper Lock, contemporary mystery writer.

Cooper, Edith Emma. See FIELD, MICHAEL.

Cooper, Esther. Pseudonym of Esther Kellner, contemporary American writer.

Cooper, James R. See STRATEMEYER, EDWARD L.

Cooper, Jefferson. See FOX, GARDNER FRANCIS.

Cooper, John Murray. See SUTHERLAND, WILLIAM.

Cooper, John R. Collective pseudonym for the "Mel Martin Baseball Stories" series. See STRATEMEYER, EDWARD L.

Cooper, Mae Klein. Contemporary American writer, whose pseudonyms are *Nina Farewell* and, with Grace Klein, *Nina Cooper-Klein.*

Cooper, Morley. Pseudonym of Alfred Morton Cooper (1890–   ), American writer.

Cooper, William. Pseudonym of Harry Summerfield Hoff (1910–   ), English writer.

Cooper-Klein, Nina. Joint pseudonym of Mae Klein Cooper and Grace Klein, contemporary American writers.

Cooplandt, A. Pseudonym of Ary Prins (1860–1922), Dutch writer.

Cope, Jack. Pseudonym of Robert Knox Cope (1913–   ), South African writer.

Cope, Robert Knox. See COPE, JACK.

Cope, Vincent Zachary. See ZETA.

Copplestone, Bennet. Pseudonym of Frederick Harcourt Kitchin (1867–1932), mystery writer.

Corbière, Édouard Joachim. See TRISTAN.

Corbin, Iris. Pseudonym of Iris A. Corbin Clinton (1901–   ), English-Rhodesian writer.

Corby, Jane (1899–   ). Mystery writer, whose pseudonyms are *Jean Carew* and *Joanne Holden.*

Cordell, Alexander. Pseudonym of Alexander Graber (1914–   ), Welsh-English writer.

Cordiani, Antonio. See SANGALLO.

Cordiani, Battista. See SANGALLO.

Corelli, Marie. Pseudonym of Mary Mackay (1855–1924), English writer of melodramatic novels.

Corley, Ernest. See BLUMER, HENRY KENNETH.

Cormon. Pseudonym of Fernand Anne Piestre (1845–1924), French painter.

Cormon, Eugène. Pseudonym of Pierre Étienne Piestre (1811–1903), French playwright.

Cornwall, Barry. Pseudonym of Bryan Waller Procter (1787–1874), English playwright, father of Adelaide Anne Procter.

Cornwall, Jim. See RIKHOFF, JAMES C.

Cornwell, David John Moore. See LE CARRÉ, JOHN.

Corominas, Pere. See MERCADER, ENRIQUE.

Corra, Bruno. Pseudonym of Bruno Corradini (1892–   ), Italian writer.

Corradini, Bruno. See CORRA, BRUNO.

Corrall, Alice Enid. See GLASS, JUSTINE.

Correggio (1489–1534). Italian painter, whose real name was Antonio Allegri. His name was derived from his birthplace, Correggio.

Corrigan, Mark. See LEE, NORMAN.

Corsari, Willy. Pseudonym of Wilhelmina Angela Schmidt (1897–   ), Dutch novelist and cabaret artist.

Corson, Geoffrey. Pseudonym of Anna McClure Sholl, contemporary mystery writer.

Cortona, Pietro da (1596–1669). Italian painter and architect, whose father's name was Giovanni di Luca Berrettini. His name was derived from his birthplace, Cortona.

Corvinus, Jakob. Pseudonym of Wilhelm Raabe (1831–1910), German poet and novelist.

Corvo, Frederick Baron. Pseudonym of Frederick William Rolfe (1860–1913), English writer.

Cory, Desmond. See MCCARTHY, SHAUN.

Cory, William (1823–1892). English poet, whose original name was William Johnson.

Coryell, John R. See CARTER, NICK.

Cotes, Peter (1912–   ). English writer, whose pseudonyms are *Boulting* and *Northcote.*

Cosimo, Piero di (1462–1521). Florentine painter, whose family name was Chimenti. The name was derived from that of his teacher, Cosimo Rosselli.

Cosmad, Dimitrie. See BOLINTINEANU, DIMITRIE.

Cossío. Pseudonym of Manuel Bartolomé Cossío (1857–1935), Spanish art critic and educator.

Costa, Uriel da. See ACOSTA, GABRIEL.

Costere, Jan de. See STROOSNYDER, JAN.

Couch, Helen Fox. See FOX, V. HELEN.

Coulson, Felicity Carter. See BONETT, EMERY.

Coulson, John Hubert Arthur. See BONETT, JOHN.

Countess of Romanones. Pseudonym of Maria Aline Griffith y Dexter, Condesa de Quintanilla (1921–   ), American-Spanish writer.

Coupling, J. J. Pseudonym of John Robinson Pierce (1910–   ), American author of books on electronics and science fiction.

Courage, John. Pseudonym of Richard Goyne, contemporary mystery writer.

Cournos, John (1881–1966). Russian-American writer, whose pseudonyms were *John Courtney* and *Mark Gault.*

Courteline, Georges. Pseudonym of Georges Moineaux (1860–1929), French humorist and writer.

Courtier, Sidney Hobson. See CHESTOR, RUI.

Courtland, Roberta. See DERN, PEGGY GADDIS.

Courtney, John. See COURNOS, JOHN; JUDD, FREDERICK CHARLES.

Courtney, Robert. Pseudonym of Charles Daly King (1895–   ), mystery writer.

Courtois, Jacques (1621–1676). French-Italian painter, also known as *Le Bourguignon* and *Il Borgognone.*

Cousin Jacques. Pseudonym of Louis Abel Beffroy de Reigny (1757–1811), French writer of farces.

Cousins, Margaret (1905–   ). American writer, whose pseudonyms are *Avery Johns, William Masters,* and *Mary Parrish.*

Coverack, Gilbert. Pseudonym of John Russell Warren (1886–   ), mystery writer.

Coward, Noel. See WHITTLEBOT, HERNIA.

Cowen, Frances. Pseudonym of Frances Munthe (1915–   ), English writer.

Cowlin, Dorothy. Pseudonym of Dorothy Whalley (1911–   ), English writer.

Cowlishaw, Ranson. See WOODROOK, R. A.

Cox, Anthony Berkeley (1893–   ). Mystery writer, whose pseudonyms are *Anthony Berkeley* and *Francis Iles.*

Cox, William R. See REEVE, JOEL.

Coxe, Kathleen Buddington. See LONG, AMELIA REYNOLDS.

Coyne, Joseph E. See BERCH, WILLIAM O.

Craddock, Charles Egbert. Pseudonym of Mary Noailles Murfree (1850–1922), American short-story writer.

Craig, Alexander George. See CRAIK, ARTHUR.

Craig, Denys. Pseudonym of Dennis G. Stoll (1912–   ), English composer and writer on musical subjects.

Craig, Edward A. See CARRICK, EDWARD.

Craig, Georgia. See DERN, PEGGY GADDIS.

Craig, John Eland. Pseudonym of Joseph Eugene Chipperfield (1912–   ), British writer.

Craig, Lee. See SANDS, LEO G.

Craig, Mary Francis. See SHURA, MARY FRANCIS.

Craig, Peter. Pseudonym of Victor MacClure (1887–   ), mystery writer.

Craigie, Pearl Mary Teresa. See HOBBES, JOHN OLIVER.

Craik, Arthur. Pseudonym of Alexander George Craig (1897–   ), English writer.

Crainic, Nichifor (1889–   ). Pseudonym of Ion Dobre, Rumanian poet and essayist.

Cranbrook, James L. See EDWARDS, WILLIAM BENNETT.

Crane, Alex. See WILKES-HUNTER, RICHARD.

Crane, Edna Temple. See EICHER, ELIZABETH.

Crane, Robert. See ROBERTSON, FRANK CHESTER.

Crawfurd, Oswald John Frederick (1834–1909). Mystery writer, whose pseudonyms are *John Daingerfield* and *John Latouche.*

Crayon, Geoffrey. See IRVING, WASHINGTON.

Creasey, John (1908–   ). English mystery writer, whose pseudonyms are *Gordon Ashe, Norman Deane, Michael Halliday, Kyle Hunt, Peter Manton, J. J. Marric, Richard Martin, Anthony Morton, Ken Ranger, William K. Reilly, Tex Riley,* and *Jeremy York.*

Crébillon. Pseudonym of Prosper Jolyot, Sieur de Crais-Billon (1674–1762), French tragic poet.

Crespi, Giovanni Battista. See CERANO, IL.

Créspigny, Capt. Charles de. See WILLIAMSON, ALICE MURIEL LIVINGSTON, and WILLIAMSON, CHARLES NORRIS.

Crèvecoeur, Michel Guillaume Jean de. See ST. JOHN, J. HECTOR.

Creyton, Paul. Pseudonym of John Townsend Trowbridge (1827–1916), American writer.

Crisolora, Manuele (1350?–1415). Byzantine grammarian, also known as *Manuel Chrysoloras.*

Crispin, Edmunds. Pseudonym of Robert Bruce Montgomery (1921–), mystery writer.

Critchett, Richard Claude. See CARTON, RICHARD CLAUDE.

Critic. Pseudonym of Basil Kingsley Martin (1897–1969), English writer.

Criticus. Pseudonym of Melville Harcourt (1909–), English writer.

Criticus. See ROE, F. GORDON.

Crnjanski, Milos. See MILL, C. R.

Crockett, James. Joint pseudonym of James A. MacPhail and Cornelia Warriner, contemporary mystery writers.

Croft, Taylor. See CROFT-COOKE, RUPERT.

Croft-Cooke, Rupert (1903–). British mystery writer, whose pseudonyms are *Leo Bruce* and *Taylor Croft.*

Croise, Jacques. Pseudonym of Princess Zinaida Schakovskoy (1906–), Russian-French writer and poet.

Croisilles, Chardon de (fl. c1235). French lyric poet, also known as *Chardon de Reims.*

Croisset, Francis de. Pseudonym of Franz Wiener (1877–1937), French novelist and playwright.

Croly, Jane. See JUNE, JENNIE.

Crom a Boo. Pseudonym of Matthias McDonnell Bodkin (1850–1933), mystery writer.

Cromie, Alice Hamilton (1914–). American writer, whose pseudonyms are *Alice Hamilton* and *Vivian Mort.*

Crompton, John. Pseudonym of John Battersby Crompton Lamburn (1893–), English writer.

Crompton, Margaret Norah Mair. See MAIR, MARGARET.

Crompton, Richmal. Pseudonym of Richmal Crompton Lamburn (1890–), English writer.

Cronin, Bernard (1884–). Mystery writer, whose pseudonyms are *Dennis Adair, Wallace Dixon,* and *Eric North.*

Cronin, Brendon Leo. See CRONIN, MICHAEL.

Cronin, Michael. Pseudonym of Brendon Leo Cronin, contemporary mystery writer.

Cronus, Diodorus. Pseudonym of Richard Taylor (1919–), American scholar.

Crosbie, Hugh Provan. See CARRICK, JOHN.

Crosby, Lee. Pseudonym of Ware Torrey (1905–), mystery writer.

Cross, Colin John. See WEIR, JOHN.

Cross, Henri Edmond. See DELACROIX, HENRI EDMOND.

Cross, James. Pseudonym of Hugh J. Parry (1916–), English-American writer.

Cross, John Keir. See MACFARLANE, STEPHEN.

Cross, Mark. See PECHEY, ARCHIBALD THOMAS.

Crossen, Ken. See CROSSEN, KENDELL.

Crossen, Kendell (1910–). American writer, whose pseudonyms are *Bennett Barlay, M. E. Chaber, Ken Crossen, Richard Foster, Christopher Monig,* and *Clay Richards.*

Crowe, Bettina Lum. See LUM, PETER.

Crowfield, Christopher. Occasional pseudonym of Harriet Elizabeth Beecher Stowe (1811–1896), American writer.

Crowninshield, Francis Welch. See BRUCE, ARTHUR LORING.

Crowquill, Alfred. Joint pseudonym of Alfred Henry Forrester (1804–1872) and his brother, Charles Robert Forrester (1803–1850), English novelists.

Crowther, Wilma. See GEORGE, WILMA.

Crozier, Kathleen Muriel Eyles (1913–). Mystery writer, whose pseudonyms are *Merle Eyles* and *Catherine Tennant.*

Cruse, Heloise. See HELOISE.

Csezmiczey, János. See PANNONIUS, JANUS.

Cuevas, Ramon de las. See HARRINGTON, MARK RAYMOND.

Cullingford, Guy. Pseudonym of Constance Lindsay Taylor (1907–), mystery writer.

Culver, Kathryn. See DRESSER, DAVIS.

Cumberland, Marten (1892–). English writer, whose pseudonyms are *R. Laugier* and *Kevin O'Hara.*

Cummings, Bruce Frederick. See BARBELLION, W. N. P.

Cunningham, Albert Benjamin. See HALE, GARTH.

Cunningham, E. V. See FAST, HOWARD.

Curran, Mona Elisa. Contemporary English writer, whose pseudonyms are *Giles Merton, Adrian Murray,* and *Mervyn Thomas.*

Currie, Baroness Mary Montgomerie. See FANE, VIOLET.

Currier, Jay L. Pseudonym of James Leal Henderson (1913–), mystery writer.

Curry, Avon. See BOWDEN, JEAN.

Curtis, John. Pseudonym of John Edwards Curtis Prebble (1915–), English writer.

Curtis, Marjorie. See PREBBLE, MARJORIE MARY CURTIS.

Curtis, Peter. Pseudonym of Norah Robinson Lofts (1904–), British-American writer.

Curtis, Tom. See PENDOWER, JACQUES.

Curtis, Will. See NUNN, WILLIAM CURTIS.

Curzon, Sam. Pseudonym of Samuel A. Krasney (1922–), American writer.

Curzon, Virginia. Pseudonym of Hector Hawton (1901–), English writer.

Cutforth, John Ashlin. See ASHLIN, JOHN.

Cutler, Ivor. See KNIFESMITH.

Cutler, Samuel. See FOLSOM, FRANKLIN BREWSTER.

Cuyler, Stephen. See BATES, BARBARA S.

Cynan. Pseudonym of Albert Evans-Jones (1895–), British scholar.

Cynthius. See GIRALDI, GIAMBATTISTA.

Czaska, Tomasz. Pseudonym of Tadeusz Rittner (1873–1921), Polish novelist and playwright.

Czepiel, Adam. Pseudonym of Leopold Stanisław Leon Brzozowski (1878–1911), Polish critic and novelist.

"D"

Daalberg, Bruno (1758–1818). Dutch novelist and essayist, whose real name was Petrus de Wakker van Zon.

Daeten, Pieter. See DATHENUS, PETRUS.

Dagonet. Pseudonym of George Robert Sims (1847–1922), English novelist and playwright.

Dahl, Vladimir Ivanovich. See LUGANSKY, KAZAK.

Daingerfield, John. See CRAWFURD, OSWALD JOHN FREDERICK.

Daini no Sammi (1000–c1050). Japanese poet, whose real name was Fujiwara no Katako.

Daisne, Johan. See THIERY, HERMAN.

Dakhow. Pseudonym of Ali Akbar Dihkhoda (1880–   ), Russian poet and scholar.

Dale, Margaret Jessy Miller. See MILLER, MARGARET J.

D'Allard, Hunter. See BALLARD, TODHUNTER.

Dallas, Sandra. Pseudonym of Sandra Dallas Atchison (1939–   ), American writer.

Dally, Ann Mullins. See MULLINS, ANN.

Daly, Jim. See STRATEMEYER, EDWARD L.

Daly, Martin. Pseudonym of Stephen MacKenna (1872–1934), Irish journalist and translator of Plotinus.

Daly, Maureen. Pseudonym of Maureen Daly McGivern, contemporary Irish-American writer.

Dalzel, Jon Patrick. See DALZEL, PETER.

Dalzel, Peter. Pseudonym of Jon Patrick Dalzel (1913–   ), English-Scottish writer.

Dame, Lawrence. See POMFRET, BARON.

Dana, Rose. See ROSS, DON.

Danby, Frank. Pseudonym of Julia Davis Frankau (1864–1916), mystery writer.

Dane, Clemence. Pseudonym of Winifred Ashton (1888–1965), English novelist. The name is derived from the church of St. Clements Dane, in London.

Dane, Joel Y. Pseudonym of Joseph Francis Delany (1905–   ), mystery writer.

Dane, Mark. See AVALLONE, MICHAEL ANGELO, JR.

Dane, Mary. See MORLAND, Nigel.

Dangerfield, Balfour. Pseudonym of Robert McCloskey (1914–   ), American writer.

Daniel, Glyn Edmund. See REES, DILWYN.

Daniell, Albert Scott (1906–   ). English author, whose pseudonyms are *Richard Bowood* and *David Scott Daniell.*

Daniell, David Scott. See DANIELL, ALBERT SCOTT.

Daniel-Rops, Henri. Pseudonym of Henri Petiot (1901–   ), French novelist and historian.

Daniels, John S. See OVERHOLSER, WAYNE D.

Daniłowski, Gustaw. Pseudonym of Władysław Orwid (1872–1927), Polish novelist.

Dannay, Frederic (1905–   ). American mystery writer, whose pseudonyms, with Manfred B. Lee, are *Daniel Nathan, Ellery Queen, Ellery Queen, Jr.,* and *Barnaby Ross.*

Danning, Melrod. Pseudonym of Sinclair Gluck (1887–   ), mystery writer.

D'Annunzio, Gabriele. See DUCA MINIMO.

Dantiscus, Joannes de Curiis (1485–1548). Polish Latin poet, whose real name was Flachsbinder.

Danvers, Jack. Pseudonym of Camille Caseleyr (1909–   ), Belgian-Australian writer.

Danzai Shundai. Pseudonym of Dunzai Jun (1680–1747), Japanese scholar.

D'Apery, Helen. See HARPER, OLIVE.

Darby, J. N. See GOVAN, CHRISTINE NOBLE.

Dare, Alan. See GOODCHILD, GEORGE.

D'Arfey, William. See PLOMER, WILLIAM CHARLES FRANKLIN.

Dargan, Olive. See BURKE, FIELDING.

Darien, Peter. Pseudonym of William B. K. Bassett (1908–   ), American writer.

Darío, Rubén. Pseudonym of Félix Rubén García-Sarmiento (1867–1916), Nicaraguan writer.

Dashwood, Edmée Elizabeth Monica de la Pasture. See DELAFIELD, E. M.

Dashwood, Robert Julian. See HILLAS, JULIAN.

Dathenus, Petrus. Latinized name of Pieter Daeten (or Daets) (1531/32–1588), Dutch poet and writer.

Daurat (or **Dorat**), **Jean.** Pseudonym of Jean Disnemandi (1508–1588), French poet.

Davenport, Spencer. See STRATEMEYER, EDWARD L.

Davey, Jocelyn. Pseudonym of Chaim Raphael (1908–   ), mystery writer.

David, Emily. Joint pseudonym of David Alman (1919–   ) and his wife, Emily Alman, American writers.

David, Lord. See BARRY, LORD.

David, Nicholas. See MORGAN, THOMAS BRUCE.

Davidson, Hilda Roderick Ellis. See ELLIS, HILDA RODERICK.

Davidson, Mickie Compere. See COMPERE, MICKIE.

Davies, Betty Evelyn. See WARWICK, PAULINE.

Davies, David Margerison. See MARGERSON, DAVID.

Davies, Eileen Winifred. See ELIAS, EILEEN.

Davies, Ernest. See MARTIN, OLIVER.

Daviot, Gordon. See MACKINTOSH, ELIZABETH.

Davis, Arthur Hoey. See RUDD, STEELE.

Davis, Burton. See SAUNDERS, LAWRENCE.

Davis, Claire Ogden. See SAUNDERS, LAWRENCE.

Davis, Don. See DRESSER, DAVIS.

Davis, Frances. See ALDA, FRANCES.

Davis, Frederick Clyde (1902–   ). Mystery writer, whose pseudonyms are *Murdo Coombs* and *Stephen Ransome.*

Davis, Frederick William. See CAMPBELL, SCOTT, and CARTER, NICK.

Davis, Gordon. Pseudonym of Robert Salisbury Dietrich (1928–   ), American writer.

Davis, Gwen. See FINK, BRAT.

Davis, Harry. Pseudonym of Roberta Hill, contemporary mystery writer.

Davis, Lavinia Riker. See FARMER, WENDELL.

Davis, Maralee G. Pseudonym of Maralee G. Thibault (1924–   ), American poet and writer.

Davis, Martha Wirt. See VAN ARSDALE, WIRT.

Davis, Robert P. See BRANDON, JOE.

Davis, Stratford. See BOLTON, MAISIE SHARMAN.

Davis, Sydney Charles Houghton. See CASQUE, SAMMY.

Davison, Gladys Patton. See CONDOR, GLADYN.

Dawson, Elmer A. Collective pseudonym for the "Buck & Larry Stories" and "Gray Grayson Football Stories" series. See STRATEMEYER, EDWARD L.

Dax, Anthony. See HUNTER, JOHN.

Day, Beth Feagles. See FEAGLES, ELIZABETH.

Day, George Harold. See QUINCE, PETER.

Day, Max. See CASSIDAY, BRUCE BINGHAM.

Day, Michael. See DEMPEWOLFF, RICHARD FREDERIC.

Deal, Borden. See BORDEN, LEE.

Deal, Mason. Pseudonym of Henry Ware Eliot (1879–   ), mystery writer.

Deale, Kenneth Edwin Lee. See MARTIN, PAUL.

Dean, Gregory. Pseudonym of Jacob D. Posner (1883–   ), mystery writer.

Dean, Robert George. See GRISWOLD, GEORGE.

Dean, Spencer. See WINCHELL, PRENTICE.

Deane, Lorna. Pseudonym of Lorna Hilda Kathleen Wilkinson (1909–   ), English author.

Deane, Norman. See CREASEY, JOHN.

Deauville, Max. Pseudonym of Maurice Duwez (1881–   ), Belgian playwright.

De Banzie, Eric. See BAXTER, GREGORY.

Debeljak, Tine. See KALIN, JEREMIJA.

Debille, George. Pseudonym of Georges Chennevière (1884–1927), French poet.

Debrett, Hal. See DRESSER, DAVIS.

Debuchi, Jirokichi. See ENCHO.

DeCamp, Lyon Sprague (1807–   ). American science-fiction writer, whose pseudonyms are *Lyman R. Lyon* and *J. Wellington Wells.*

Dechet, Hippolyte Louis Alexandre. See JENNEVAL.

De Chirico, Andrea. See SAVINIO, ALBERTO.

Decker, Frank. See DUVENECK, FRANK.

Dee, Henry. See TORBETT, HARVEY DOUGLAS LOUIS.

Defoe, Daniel (c1660–1731). English novelist, journalist, and pamphleteer, whose original surname was Foe.

De Forbes. See FORBES, DELORIS STANTON.

DeFrees, Madeline. Secular name of Sister Mary Gilbert (1919–   ), American writer.

De Frenzi, Giulio. Pseudonym of Luigi Federzoni (1878–   ), Italian writer.

Degée, Olivier. See TOUSSEUL, JEAN.

Deghy, Guy (1912–   ). Hungarian-English writer, whose pseudonyms, with Keith Waterhouse, are *Hearld Froy* and *Lee Gibb.*

De Hamel, Felix John. See HEXHAM, LIONEL J. F.

Dehan, Richard. Pseudonym of Clotilde Inez Mary Graves (1863–1932), Irish novelist.

De Hondt, Pieter. See CANISIUS, PETER.

Deindorfer, Robert Greene (1922–   ). American free-lance magazine writer and author, whose pseudonyms are *Jay Bender, Jay Dender,* and *Robert Greene.*

DeJong, David Cornel. See BREDA, TJALMAR.

Dekker, Eduard Douwes. See MULTATULI.

Dekker, Maurits Rudolph Jöell. See PROBAZKI, BORIS.

Dekobra, Maurice. Pseudonym of Ernest-Maurice Tessier (1885–   ), French writer.

De la Brète, Jean. Pseudonym of Alice Cherbonnel (1858–?), French writer.

Delacroix, Henri Edmond (1856–1910). French painter, also known as *Henri Edmond Cross.*

Delafield, E. M. Pseudonym of Edmée Elizabeth Monica de la Pasture Dashwood (1890–1943), English writer.

De La Mare, Walter. See RAMEL, WALTER.

Delaney, Denis. Pseudonym of Peter Morris Green (1924–   ), British scholar.

Delany, Joseph Francis. See DANE, JOEL Y.

Delaporte, Théophile. Pseudonym of Julian Green (1900–   ), French-American novelist and essayist.

Delavrancea, Barbu. Pseudonym of Barbu Stefanescu (1858–1918), Rumanian novelist and playwright.

De Leeuw, Cateau (1903–   ). American writer and artist, whose pseudonyms are *Kay Hamilton* and *Jessica Lyon.*

Delf, Thomas. See MARTEL, CHARLES.

Delgado, Francisco. See DELICÀDO, FRANCISCO.

Delicàdo, Francisco. 16th-century Spanish novelist and cleric, who lived in Rome and Venice. He was also known as *Francisco Delgado.*

Dell, Belinda. See BOWDEN, JEAN.

Della Porta, Bartolommeo (or **Baccio**). See BARTOLOMMEO, FRA.

Dell'arco, Mario. Pseudonym of Mario Fagiolo (1905–   ), Italian poet and architect.

Dellaurana, Luciano. See LAURANA, LUCIANO.

Dellbridge, John. See PLUMMY.

Delorme (or **de l'Orme, deLorme, De L'Orme**), **Philibert** (1510–1570). French cleric and architect, also known as Monsieur de Saint-Serge and Monsieur d'Ivry as he became head of these abbeys. The name was derived from the location of the family house, which stood near an elm tree.

Delrue, Emiel. See STRAETEN, EMIEL VAN DER.

Delta. See DENNETT, HERBERT VICTOR.

Delta. Pseudonym of David Macbeth Moir (1798–1851), Scottish poet.

Delta. See TURNBULL, DORA AMY DILLON.

Demaine, Don. Pseudonym of Gordon Don Drinkall (1927–   ), English writer.

De Mar, Paul. Pseudonym of Pearl Foley, contemporary American mystery writer.

Demarest, Ann. Pseudonym of Florence Demarest Foos Bond, contemporary mystery writer.

Demarest, Doug. Pseudonym of Will Barker (1913–   ), American writer.

Demers, Frans. See BECKERS, FRANS.

Deming, Richard. See FRANKLIN, MAX.

Demme, Hermann Christoph Gottfried. See STILLE, KARL.

Democritus Junior. Pseudonym of Robert Burton (1577–1640), English clergyman and writer.

De Mol. See GHISTELE, CORNELIS VON.

Dempewolff, Richard Frederic (1914–   ). American writer, whose pseudonyms are *Michael Day, Dick Frederick*, and *Frederick Wolf.*

Denbie, Roger. Joint pseudonym of Julian Paul Brodie and Alan Baer Green (1906–   ), mystery writers.

Dender, Jay. See DEINDORFER, ROBERT GREENE.

Dendermonde, Max. Pseudonym of Hendrik Hazelhoff (1919–   ), Dutch poet.

Denham, Mary Orr. Contemporary American actress and writer, whose pseudonyms are *Anne Caswell* and *Mary Orr.*

Denholm, Terese Mary Zita White. See WHITE, ZITA.

D'Ennery, Adolphe Philippe (1811–1899). French playwright, whose original surname was Dennery.

Dennett, Herbert Victor (1893–   ). English writer, whose pseudonyms are *Delta, John Syntax*, and *Ned Tent.*

Dennis, Patrick. See TANNER, EDWARD EVERETT, III.

Denniston, Elinore (1900–   ). Mystery writer, whose pseudonyms are *Dennis Allan* and *Rae Foley.*

Denver, Boone. See RENNIE, JAMES ALAN.

Denver, Drake C. See NYE, NELSON CORAL.

Derby, George Horatio (1823–1861). American humorist, whose pseudonyms are *John Phoenix* and *Squibob.*

Derby, Mark. Pseudonym of Harry Wilcox, contemporary mystery writer.

Derème, Tristan. Pseudonym of Philippe Huc (1889–1941), French poet.

De Reneville, Mary Margaret Motley Sheridan. See MOTLEY, MARY.

Derin, P. L. See LANSEL, PEIDER.

Derleth, August William. See MASON, TALLY.

Dern, Peggy Gaddis (1895–1966). American writer, whose pseudonyms are *Roberta Courtland, Georgia Craig, Peggy Gaddis, Gail Jordan, Carolina Lee, Perry Lindsay,* and *Joan Sherman.*

Desbordes-Valmore, Marceline. Pseudonym of Marceline Félicité Josèphe Desbordes (1786–1859), French poet.

Desjardins, Marie Catherine. See VILLEDIEU, MME. DE.

de Sluter. See SLUTER, CLAUS.

Despard, Leslie. See HOWITT, JOHN LESLIE DESPARD.

Desplaines, Baroness Julie. See JENNINGS, LESLIE NELSON.

Destouches, Louis Fuch. See CÉLINE, LOUIS-FERDINAND.

Deus, João de. See RAMOS, JOÃO DE DEUS.

Deutsch, Nikolaus. See MANUEL, NIKOLAUS.

Deutscher, Isaac. See PEREGRINE.

Deval, Jacques. Pseudonym of Jacques Boularan (1894–   ), French dramatist.

Dewall, Johannes van. Pseudonym of August Kühne (1829–1883), German novelist and army officer.

Dewdney, Peter. Pseudonym of Alan St. Hill Brock (1886–   ), mystery writer.

Dewes, Simon. See MURIEL, JOHN SAINT CLAIR.

Dewey, Thomas Blanchard (1915–   ). American mystery writer, whose pseudonyms are *Tom Brandt* and *Cord Wainer.*

De Witt, James. Pseudonym of Mildred D. Lewis (1912–   ), American writer for young people.

Dey, Frederick Van Rensselaer. See CARTER, NICK.

Deyssel, Lodewijk van. Pseudonym of Karel Jan Lodewijk Alberdingk Thijm (1864–1952), Dutch critic and prose writer.

Dibdin, Thomas Frognall. See WOLFE, REGINALD.

Dick, Alexandra. See ERIKSON, SIBYL ALEXANDRA.

Dickens, Charles John Huffam (1812–1870). English novelist. He was first published in periodicals under the pseudonym *Boz,* a contraction of "Boses" (a child's pronunciation of Moses, a name given to Dickens's younger brother because of Charles's love for *The Vicar of Wakefield*). He also used the pseudonyms *Tibbs* and *Timothy Sparks.*

Dickson, Carr. See CARR, JOHN DICKSON.

Dickson, Carter. See CARR, JOHN DICKSON.

Dickson, Helen. See REYNOLDS, HELEN MARY CAMPBELL.

Diehl, W. W. See CLAY, DUNCAN.

Diest, Jan van. See BERGHE, JAN VAN DEN.

Dietrich, Robert Salisbury. See DAVIS, GORDON.

Dietzenschmidt. Professional name of Anton Franz Schmidt (1893–1955), German playwright, novelist, and critic.

Digges, Jeremiah. Pseudonym of Josef Berger (1903–   ), American writer.

Di Giacomo, Giovanni Antonio. See VANN'ANTO.

Dihati, Muhammad-i Mas'ud (?–1947). Persian author, also known simply as *Muhammad-i Mas'ud.*

Dihkhoda, Ali Akbar. See DAKHOW.

Dil, Zakhmi. Pseudonym of Richard Hilton (1894–   ), English writer.

Dimt, Christine. See BUSTA, CHRISTINE.

Dinesen, Isak. See BLIXEN-FINECKE, BARONESS KAREN CHRISTENTZE.

Dinesen, Wilhelm. See BOGANIS.

Dingwall, Peter. Pseudonym of Robin Forsythe (1879–   ), mystery writer.

Dinis, Júlio. Pseudonym of J. G. Gomes Coelho (1839–1871), Portuguese poet.

Dion, Sister Raymond de Jesus. See JESUS, MOTHER RAYMOND DE.

Diplomat. See CARTER, JOHN FRANKLIN.

Dirceu. Pseudonym of Tomaz Antônio Gonzaga (1744–1807), Portuguese poet.

Diricksens, Joos-Joseph. See ZETTERNAM, EUGEEN.

Disnemandi, Jean. See DAURAT, JEAN.

Dito und Idem. See ELIZABETH, QUEEN OF RUMANIA, and KREMNITZ, MITE.

Ditzen, Rudolf. See FALLADA, HANS.

Divine, Arthur Durham. See RAME, DAVID.

Dix, Dorothy. Pseudonym of Elizabeth Gilmer (1870–1951), American advice columnist.

Dixon, Bingham. Pseudonym of William Armstrong Borland (1893–   ), mystery writer.

Dixon, Franklin W. Collective pseudonym for the "Hardy Boys" and "Ted Scott Flying Stories" series. See STRATEMEYER, EDWARD L.

Dixon, Henry Hall. See DRUID, THE.

Dixon, Wallace. See CRONIN, BERNARD.

Długosz, Jan. See LONGINUS, JOHANNES.

Dniprova, Chaika. Pseudonym of Ludmyla Vasilevska (1861–1927), Soviet Ukrainian writer.

Doane, Marion S. Pseudonym of Grace Steele Woodward (1899–), American author of historical books.

Dobell, I. M. B. See BARCLAY, ISABEL.

Dobell, Sydney Thompson. See YENDYS, SYDNEY.

Döblin, Alfred. See POOT, LINKE.

Dobraczynski, Jan (1910–). Polish author, whose pseudonyms are *Hozjusz* and *Eugeniusz Kurowski.*

Dobre, Ion. See CRAINIC, NICHIFOR.

Dobrogeanu-Gherea, Ion (1855–1920). Rumanian literary critic, also known as *Ion Gherea.*

Dobson, E. Philip. See SPRING, PHILIP.

Docherty, James. See RAYMOND, RENÉ.

Dodge, Langdon. Pseudonym of Victor Wolfson (1910–), mystery writer.

Dodge, Mary Abigail. See HAMILTON, GAIL.

Dodge, Steve. Pseudonym of Stephen David Becker (1927–), American free-lance writer.

Dodgson, Charles Lutwidge. See CARROLL, LEWIS.

Doe, John. See THAYER, TIFFANY.

Doerffler, Alfred (1884–). American religious writer, whose pseudonyms are *Harris Dunn, Fred Ford,* and *Carl H. Thomas.*

Doesticks, Q. K. Philander, P.B. Pseudonym of Mortimer Neal Thomson (1831–1875), American humorist.

Dogwood, Mrs. Silence. See FRANKLIN, BENJAMIN.

Dollen, Charles Joseph. See BENEDICT, JOSEPH.

Domaschevitsky, Isaiah. See BERSCHADSKY, ISAIAH.

Domenichino, Il. Cognomen of Domenico Zampieri (1581–1641), Italian painter of the Bolognese school.

Dommartin, Léon. See ARDENNE, JEAN D'.

Donald, Vivian. See MACKINNON, CHARLES ROY.

Donalds, Gordon. See SHIRREFFS, GORDON D.

Donalitius, Christian (1714–1780). Lithuanian poet, whose real name was Kristijonas Duonelaitis.

Donatello (1386?–1466). Italian sculptor, whose real name was Donato di Niccolò di Betto Bardi.

Donavan, John. See MORLAND, NIGEL.

Donker, Anthonie. Pseudonym of Nicolaas Anthonie Donkersloot (1902–   ), Dutch poet and essayist.

Donkersloot, Nicolaas Anthonie. See DONKER, ANTHONIE.

Dono, Paolo di. See UCCELLO, PAOLO.

Donovan, Dick. Pseudonym of Joyce Emmerson Preston Muddock (1843–1934), mystery writer.

Donovan, William. See BERKEBILE, FRED DONOVAN.

Doog, K. Caj. Pseudonym of Irving John Good (1916–   ), British scholar.

Doolaard, A. Den. Pseudonym of Cornelis Spoelstra (1901–   ), Dutch poet.

Dooley, Mr. Pseudonym of Finley Peter Dunne (1867–1936), American satirist.

Doolittle, Hilda. See H.D.

Doone, Jice. Pseudonym of James Vance Marshall, contemporary Australian writer.

Dor, Ana. Pseudonym of Georgiana Dorcas Ceder, contemporary American writer.

Dora d'Istria. Pseudonym of Princess Helene Ghica (1828–1888), Rumanian writer.

Dorant, Gene. Pseudonym of Dora Geneva Lent (1904–   ), Canadian writer.

Dore, Claire Morin (1934–   ). Canadian writer, whose pseudonyms are *Claire France* and *Claire Morin.*

Dorgan, Thomas Aloysius. See TAD.

Dorgelès, Roland. Pseudonym of Roland Lécavelé (1886–   ), French novelist.

Dorlandus, Petrus. Latinized name of Pieter Dorlant (1454–1507), Dutch mystical writer.

Dorlant, Pieter. See DORLANDUS, PETRUS.

Dorman, Michael. See BISHOP, JACK.

Dörmann, Felix. Pseudonym of Felix Biedermann (1876–1928), Austrian writer.

Dorn, Dean M. See MORGAN, MICHAEL.

Dorst, Jean Pierre. See URSTELLE, PIERRE D'.

D'Ors y Rovira, Eugenio. See XENIUS.

Doshun. See HAYASHI RAZAN.

Dossi, Battista. See LUTERO, BATTISTA DI.

Dossi, Dosso (1479?–1542). Italian painter, whose real name was Giovanni di Lutero. He was the brother of Battista Dossi.

Doubleday, Roman. Pseudonym of Lily Augusta Long (d. 1927), American mystery writer.

Dougherty, Joanna Foster. Pseudonym of Joanna Foster (1928–   ), American author.

Douglas, Albert. See ARMSTRONG, DOUGLAS ALBERT.

Douglas, Edith. Pseudonym of Clara Louise Burnham (1854–1927), mystery writer.

Douglas, Ellen. Pseudonym of Ellen Douglas Williamson, contemporary American writer.

Douglas, Malcolm. See SANDERSON, DOUGLAS.

Douglas, Robert. See ANDREWS, CHARLES ROBERT DOUGLAS HARDY.

Douglas, Shane. See WILKES-HUNTER, RICHARD.

Douglas-Scott-Montagu, Edward John Barrington. See MONTAGU OF BEAULIEU, THIRD BARON.

Douglass, Frederick. Assumed name of Frederick Augustus Washington Bailey (1817–1895), American diplomat, editor, and runaway slave. He took the name in admiration of the character in Walter Scott's *Lady of the Lake.*

Dovizi, Bernardo. See BIBBIENA, IL.

Dowdy, Mrs. Regera. See GOREY, EDWARD ST. JOHN.

Dowen, Anne Ophelia Todd. See TODD, ANNE OPHELIA.

Dowers, Penn. See PENDOWER, JACQUES.

Downes, Quentin. Pseudonym of Michael Harrison (1907–   ), mystery writer.

Downing, Major Jack. Pseudonym of Seba Smith (1792–1868), American satirist.

Doyle, Lynn. Pseudonym of Leslie Alexander Montgomery (1873–1961), Irish playwright and novelist.

Drackett, Philip. See KING, PAUL.

Drake, Lisl. See BEER, ELOISE C. S.

Drax, Peter. Pseudonym of Eric Erlington Addis, contemporary mystery writer.

Dresser, Davis (1904–   ). Mystery writer, whose pseudonyms are *Asa Baker, Matthew Blood, Kathryn Culver, Don Davis, Brett Halliday, Anthony Scott, Peter Shelley, Anderson Wayne,* and, with Kathleen Rollins, *Hal Debrett.*

Drexel, Jay B. See BIXBY, JEROME LEWIS.

Drinan, Adam. Pseudonym of Joseph MacLeod (1903–   ), Scottish poet.

Drinkall, Gordon Don. See DEMAINE, DON.

Drojine, N. A. See CHRISTIAENS, ANDRE G.

Droogenbroeck, Jan van. See FERGUUT, JAN.

Drower, Ethel Stefana May. See STEVENS, E. S.

Druce, Christopher. Pseudonym of Christopher Robert Druce Pulling (1893–   ), English writer.

Druid, The. Pseudonym of Henry Hall Dixon (1822–1870), English writer.

Drummond, Anthony. See HUNTER, JOHN.

Drummond, Edith Marie Dulce Carman. See CARMAN, DULCE.

Druyanov, Alter. See HAEDREYI, ABGAD.

Dryander. See ENZINAS, FRANCISCO DE.

Duane, Jim. See HURLEY, VIC.

du Blane, Daphne. See GROOM, ARTHUR WILLIAM.

Duboc, Édouard. See WALDMÜLLER, ROBERT.

Dubois, Alan. Pseudonym of Clement Wood (1888–1950), mystery writer.

DuBose, Louise Jones. See TELFAIR, NANCY.

Duca Minimo. Occasional pseudonym of Gabriele D'Annunzio (1863–1938), Italian writer and poet.

Ducasse, Isidore-Lucien. See LAUTRÉAMONT, LE COMTE DE.

Duchamp, Gaston. See VILLON, JACQUES.

Duchamp, Marcel (1887–1968). French painter, one of the founders of Dadaism. In 1917 he signed a piece *R. Mutt.* He has also signed some with the name *Rose Sélavy,* a pun on *c'est la vie.* He was the brother of both Gaston Duchamp *(Jacques Villon),* cubist painter, and Raymond Duchamp *(Duchamp-Villon),* sculptor.

Duchamp, Raymond. See DUCHAMP-VILLON, RAYMOND.

Duchamp-Villon, Raymond (1876–1918). French sculptor, whose real name was Raymond Duchamp. He was the brother of both Gaston Duchamp *(Jacques Villon),* cubist painter, and Marcel Duchamp, one of the founders of Dadaism.

DuChesne. See ENZINAS, FRANCISCO DE.

Duchesne, Jacques. Pseudonym of Michel Jacques Saint-Denis (1897–   ), French-English author and adapter of plays.

Duchess, The. Pseudonym of Margaret Wolfe Hungerford (1855?–1897), Irish novelist.

Dudevant, Aurore. See SAND, GEORGE.

Dudley, Ernest. See COLTMAN, ERNEST VIVIAN.

Dudley, Frank. Pseudonym of Ward Greene (1892–1956), mystery writer.

Dudley, Nancy. See COLE, LOIS DWIGHT.

Duff, Charles St. Lawrence. See CATHAL O DUBH.

Dufour, Pierre. See LACROIX, PAUL.

Dughet, Gaspard (1613–1675). French-Italian painter, known as *Le Guaspre* and *Dughet Gaspard-Poussin.*

Duguid, Robert. Pseudonym of Robert D. F. Pring-Mill (1924–   ), English scholar.

Duhamel, Georges. See THÉVENIN, DENIS.

Duke, Donald Norman. See VALENTINE, ROGER.

Dumarchais, Pierre. See MACORLAN, PIERRE.

Dumas, Alexandre (père). Pseudonym of Alexandre Davy de la Pailleterie (1803–1870), French writer.

Dunash ben Labrat (c920–980?). Hebrew poet and grammarian, also known as *Adonim ha-Levi.*

Duncan, Actea. See THOMAS, CAROLYN.

Duncan, Gregory. See MCCLINTOCK, MARSHALL.

Duncan, Jane. Pseudonym of Elizabeth Jane Cameron (1910–   ), Scottish writer.

Duncan, Julia K. Collective pseudonym for the "Doris Force" series. See STRATEMEYER, EDWARD L.

Duncan, Lois. See CARDOZO, LOIS STEINMETZ.

Duncan, W. Murdoch (1909–   ). Scottish writer of detective novels, whose pseudonyms are *John Cassells, Neill Graham, Martin Locke, Peter Malloch,* and *Lovat Marshall.*

Dunkerley, William Arthur. See OXENHAM, JOHN.

Dunlap, Lon. See MCCORMICK, WILFRED.

Dunlop, Agnes M. R. Contemporary Scottish novelist and author of children's books, whose pseudonyms are *Elisabeth Kyle* and *Jan Ralston.*

Dunn, Harris. See DOERFFLER, ALFRED.

Dunn, James. See WILKES-HUNTER, RICHARD.

Dunne, Finley Peter. See DOOLEY, MR.

Dunne, Mary Chavelita. See EGERTON, GEORGE.

Dunstan, Guy Mainwaring. See MORTON, GUY MAINWARING.

Dunzai Jun. See DUNZAI SHUNDAI.

Duonelaitis, Kristijonas. See DONALITIUS, CHRISTIAN.

Dupin, Amandine Aurore Lucie. See SAND, GEORGE.

Duplessis, Yves. Pseudonym of Yvonne Jaurand (1912–   ), French writer.

Dupont, Paul. Pseudonym of Leslie Ronald Frewin (1917–   ), English writer.

Dupres, Henri. See FAWCETT, FRANK DUBREZ.

Duquesnoy, François. See FLAMAND, FRANÇOIS.

Duran, Carolus. Professional name of Charles Auguste Émile Durand (1837–1917), French painter.

Durand, Alice. See GRÉVILLE, HENRY.

Durand, Charles Auguste Émile. See DURAN, CAROLUS.

Durgnat, Raymond. See GREEN, O. O.

Duribreux, Gaston. See VAN WIEREN, JAN.

Durie, Lynn. See CHRISTIE, DOUGLAS.

Durrell, Lawrence George (1912–   ). British writer, whose pseudonyms are *Charles Norden* and *Gaffer Peeslake.*

Durst, Paul. See BANNON, PETER.

Durtain, Luc. Pseudonym of André Nepveu (1881–1959), French writer.

Du Toit, J. D. See TOTIUS.

Duval, Paul. See LORRAIN, JEAN.

Duveneck, Frank (1848–1919). American painter, sculptor, and etcher, whose original name was Frank Decker.

Duvernois, Henri. Pseudonym of Simon Schabacher (1875–1937), French poet and writer.

Duveyrier, Anne Honoré Joseph. See MÉLESVILLE.

Duwez, Maurice. See DEAUVILLE, MAX.

Dwight, Allan. See COLE, LOIS DWIGHT.

Dyce, Gilbert. Pseudonym of Percy Hetherington Fitzgerald (1834–1925), mystery writer.

Dygas. Pseudonym of Tomasz Adolf Dygasiński (1839–1902), Polish writer.

Dygasiński, Tomasz Adolf. See DYGAS.

Dymov, Osip Isidorovich. Pseudonym of Joseph Perelman (1878–
    ), Russian-Yiddish writer.
Dzyubin, E. See BAGRITSKY, EDUARD.

"E"

Eagle, Solomon. Early pseudonym of Sir John Collings Squire (1884–
    1958), English writer.
Ealhwine. See ALCUIN.
East, Michael. Occasional pseudonym of Morris Langlo West (1916–
    ), Australian writer.
East, Roger. See BURFORD, ROGER D'ESTE.
Eastaway, Edward. Pseudonym of Philip Edward Thomas (1878–1917),
    British poet and critic.
Easterling, Narena. See EASTERLING, RENÉ.
Easterling, René. Pseudonym of Narena Easterling, contemporary mys-
    tery writer.
Eastwood, Helen Baker. See BAXTER, OLIVE.
Eaton, George L. Pseudonym of Charles Spain Verral, contemporary
    Canadian-American free-lance writer.
Eberle, Irmengarde (1898–   ). American writer of children's books,
    whose pseudonyms are *Allyn Allen* and *Phyllis Ann Carter.*
Ebert, Arthur Frank. See ARTHUR, FRANK.
Ebreo, Leone. See ABARBANEL, JUDAH LEÓN.
Echo, Proteus, Esq. See FRANKLIN, BENJAMIN.
Ecke, Betty Tseng Yu-ho. See TSENG YU-HO.
Eden, Martin. See BOLSTAD, ØIVIND.
Eden, Rob. See BURKHARDT, EVE, and ROBERT FERDINAND.
Edgley, Leslie (1912–   ). Mystery writer, whose pseudonyms are
    Robert Bloomfield and, with Mary Edgley, *Brook Hastings.*
Edgley, Mary. See EDGLEY, LESLIE.
Edgren, A. C. Married name and occasional pseudonym of Anne Char-
    lotte Leffler (1849–1892), Swedish playwright and novelist.
Edmiston, Helen Jean Mary. See ROBERTSON, HELEN.
Edmunds, Charles. Pseudonym of Charles Edmund Carrington (1897–
    ), English author.

Edschmid, Kasimir. Pseudonym of Eduard Schmidt (1890–1966), German writer.

Eduardi, Guillermo. See EDWARDS, WILLIAM BENNETT.

Edward, Frederik. See FRANCKEN, FRITZ.

Edwards, Al. Pseudonym of Alan Edward Norse (1928–   ), American physician and writer.

Edwards, Albert. Pseudonym of Arthur Bullard (1879–1929), American writer and journalist.

Edwards, Bertram. Pseudonym of Herbert Charles Edwards (1912–   ), English writer.

Edwards, Charman. See EDWARDS, FREDERICK ANTHONY.

Edwards, Eli. Pseudonym of Claude McKay (1890–1948), American poet.

Edwards, F. E. See NOLAN, WILLIAM FRANCIS.

Edwards, Frederick Anthony (1896–   ). Mystery writer, whose pseudonyms are *Charman Edwards* and *J. Van Dyke.*

Edwards, Herbert Charles. See EDWARDS, BERTRAM.

Edwards, James G. See MACQUEEN, JAMES WILLIAM.

Edwards, Jane Campbell. See CAMPBELL, JANE.

Edwards, Julie. See STRATEMEYER, EDWARD L.

Edwards, Max. See BENJAMIN, CLAUDE.

Edwards, Stephen. See PALESTRANT, SIMON S.

Edwards, Thomas. See TWM O'R NANT.

Edwards, William Bennett (1927–   ). American writer, whose pseudonyms are *Edouard Benet, Harvey Brandt, James L. Cranbrook, Guillermo Eduardi, Charles S. Johnson, Capt. Wilbur Jones,* and *William C. L. Thompson.*

Eeden, Frederick van. See PARADIJS, CORNELIS.

Een Geabonneerde. See HUET, CONRAD BUSKEN.

Eftaliotis, Arjyris. Pseudonym of Kleanthis Michaildis (1849–1923), neo-Hellenic writer.

Egan, Lesley. See LININGTON, ELIZABETH.

Egerton, George. Pseudonym of Mary Chavelita Dunne (1859–1945), Australian writer.

Egestorff, Georg. Pseudonym of Baron Georg von Ompteda (1863–1931), German writer and translator.

Églantine, Fabre d'. See FABRE D'ÉGLANTINE.

Eglinton, John. Pseudonym of William Kirkpatrick Magee (1868–), Irish essayist and poet.

Ehrenkranz, Benjamin Wolf. See ZBARSHER, VELVEL.

Ehrlich, Bettina Bauer. See BETTINA.

Eicher, Elizabeth. Contemporary American writer, whose pseudonyms are *Edna Temple Crane* and, for magazines, *Emily Paul* and *William Paul.* She also uses the house name of Dell.

Eichrodt, Ludwig. See RODT, RUDOLF.

Eifion Wyn. Pseudonym of Eliseus Williams (1867–1926), Welsh poet.

Eikan, Theo. See BOLSTAD, ØIVIND.

Eiker, Mathilde. See EVERMAY, MARCH.

Eisenstat, Jane Sperry. See SPERRY, JANE.

Eitemal. Pseudonym of Willem Jacobus du Plooy Erlank (1901–   ), South African writer.

Ejima Ichiroemon. See EJIMA KISEKI.

Ejima Kiseki (1667–1736). Japanese novelist, whose real name was Ejima Shigetomo. He was also known as *Ejima Ichiroemon.*

Ejima Shigetomo. See EJIMA KISEKI.

Elder, Marc. Pseudonym of Marcel Tendron (1884–   ), French novelist.

Eleuter. Pseudonym of Jarosław Iwaszkiewicz (1894–   ), Polish poet and novelist.

Eleutero. Pseudonym of Antonio Luca Pagnini (1737–1814), Italian writer.

Eleutherophilos. Pseudonym of Paulus Hubert Adriann Jan Strick van Linschoten (1769–1819), Dutch poet.

Elfed. Pseudonym of Howel Elvet Lewis (1860–   ), Welsh poet and translator.

Elia. Pseudonym of Charles Lamb (1775–1834), English writer and critic.

Elias, Eileen. Pseudonym of Eileen Winifred Davies (1910–   ), English free-lance journalist.

Elias, Willem. See VRANCX, WILLEM.

Eliashiv, Isadore. See MACHSHOVES BAAL.

Eliès, Yann-Fañch. See ABEOZEN.

Elín-Pelín. See JOTOV, DIMITĂR IVANOV.

Eliot, Anne. See COLE, LOIS DWIGHT.

Eliot, George. Pseudonym of Mary Ann (or Marian) Evans (1819–1880), English novelist.

Eliot, Henry Ware. See DEAL, MASON.

Elisheva. Pseudonym of Lisabetta Girkova (1888–1949), Russian poet.

Elitis, Odisséus. Pseudonym of Odisséus Alepudelis (1912–   ), neo-Hellenic poet.

Eliza, Godfried. See HUEL, FRITS.

Elizabeth, Queen of Rumania (1843–1916). Poet, novelist, and playwright, whose pseudonyms are *Carmen Sylva* and, with Mite Kremnitz, *Dito und Idem.*

Ellett, Harold Pincton. See BURNABY, NIGEL.

Ellis, Hilda Roderick. Pseudonym of Hilda Roderick Ellis Davidson (1914–   ), English scholar.

Ellison, James E. See BROTHER FLAVIUS.

Elliston, Valerie Mae Watkinson. See WATKINSON, VALERIE.

Elloposcleros, Huldrich. Pseudonym of Johann Fischart (1546?–1590), Protestant humorist and satirist. He was also known as *Mentzer* and *Mainzer.*

Ellsworth, Elmer, Jr. See THAYER, TIFFANY.

Ellsworth, Paul. Pseudonym of Paul Ellsworth Triem (1882–   ), American mystery writer.

Elman, Richard M. See PEARL, ERIC.

Elola y Guliérrez, José de. See IGNOTUS.

Elpidon. Pseudonym of Michal Balucki (1837–1901), Polish playwright, novelist, and short-story writer.

Elro, H. van. Occasional pseudonym of Roel Houwink (1899–   ), Dutch poet, writer, and essayist.

Elsheimer, Adam. See TEDESCO, IL.

Elsing, J. M. See BECKERS, FRANS.

Elspet. Pseudonym of Cornelis Jacob Langenhoven (1878–1932), Afrikaans writer.

Elspeth. Pseudonym of Elspeth MacDuffie Bragdon (1897–   ), American writer.

Elsschot, Willem. Pseudonym of Alfons Joseph de Ridder (1882–1960), Flemish writer.

Elting, Mary (1906–   ). American writer, whose pseudonyms are *Davis Cole* and *Campbell Tatham.*

Elton, John. see MARSH, JOHN.

Éluard, Paul. Pseudonym of Eugène Grindel (1895–1952), French poet.

Elvestad, Sven. See RIVERTON, STEIN.

Elvin, Drake. See BEHA, ERNEST.

El-y. Pseudonym of Adam Asnyk (1838–1897), Polish poet and drama-tist.

Ely, Frederick. Pseudonym of Jascha Kessler (1929–   ), American scholar.

Elysio, Filinto. Pseudonym of Francisco Manoel do Nascimento (1734–1819), Portuguese poet.

Embey, Philip. See PHILIPP, ELLIOT ELIAS.

Emerson, Alice B. Collective pseudonym for the "Betty Gordon Stories" and "Ruth Fielding Stories" series. See STRATEMEYER, EDWARD L.

Emerson, Edward. See SIMMONS, EDWARD.

Eminescu, Mihail. Pseudonym of Mihail Eminovici (1850–1889), Rumanian poet.

Eminovici, Mihail. See EMINESCU, MIHAIL.

Emmanuel, Pierre. Pseudonym of Noël Mathieu (1916–   ), French writer.

Emrys ap Iwan. Pseudonym of Robert Ambrose Jones (1851–1906), Welsh minister, critic, and advocate of home rule.

E'nami Kiemon. See KI NO KAION.

Encho (1839–1900). Japanese storyteller, whose real name was Debuchi Jirokichi.

Endt, Pieter. See COENRAADS, EDWARD.

Engelen, Adriaan (1804–1890). Dutch writer, whose real name was H. van Apeltern.

England, E. M. Pseudonym of Edith Mary England Anders (1899–   ), Australian free-lance writer.

Engländer, Richard. See ALTENBERG, PETER.

Enzinas, Francisco de (1520?–1552). Spanish humanist, known as *Dryander, DuChesne,* and *Van-Eick.*

Epernay, Mark. Pseudonym of John Kenneth Galbraith (1908–   ), Canadian-born historian.

Ephesian. Pseudonym of Carl Eric Bechhofer Roberts (1894–1949), American mystery writer.

Epp, Margaret A. See GOOSSEN, AGNES.

Epstein, Beryl Williams (1910–   ). American free-lance writer, whose pseudonyms are *Beryl Williams* and, with her husband, Samuel Epstein, *Adam Allen* and *Douglas Coe.*

Epstein, Michail Semënovich. See GOLODNYJ, MICHAIL.

Epstein, Samuel (1909–). American author, whose pseudonyms are *Bruce Campbell, Martin Colt, Charles Strong,* and, with his wife, Beryl Williams Epstein, *Adam Allen* and *Douglas Coe.*

Erasmus, M. Nott. Pseudonym of Stanley I. Stuber (1903–), American writer.

Erceldoune, Thomas of (fl. 1220–1297). Legendary Scottish prophet and poet, also known as *Thomas Learmont* and *Thomas the Rhymer.*

Erckmann, Émile. See ERCKMANN-CHATRIAN.

Erckmann-Chatrian. Joint pseudonym of Émile Erckmann (1822–1899) and Alexandre Chatrian (1826–1890), Alsatian novelists.

Eremita, Victor. See KIERKEGAARD, SØREN AABYE.

Erickson, Sabra Rollins. See HOLBROOK, SABRA.

Ericson, Walter. See FAST, HOWARD.

Eriksen, Andreas. Pseudonym of Pelle Vigg (1915–), Norwegian writer.

Erikson, Charlotte. See ERIKSON, SIBYL ALEXANDRA.

Erikson, Sibyl Alexandra. Contemporary mystery writer, whose pseudonyms are *Alexandra Dick, Charlotte Erikson,* and *Frances Hay.*

Erlank, Willem Jacobus du Plooy. See EITEMAL.

Ermengem, Frédéric van. See HELLENS, FRANZ.

Ernest, William. See BERKEBILE, FRED DONOVAN.

Ernst, Clara. Pseudonym of Clara Ernst Barnes (1895–), American author.

Ernst, Otto. Pseudonym of Otto Ernst Schmidt (1862–1926), German playwright.

Erskine, Firth. Joint pseudonym of Gladys Shaw Erskine (1895–) and Ivan Eustace Firth (1891–), American mystery writers.

Erskine, Gladys Shaw. See ERSKINE, FIRTH.

Erskine, Margaret. Pseudonym of Margaret Wetherby Williams, contemporary mystery writer.

Erskine, Rosalind. Pseudonym of Roger Erskine Longrigg (1929–), American writer.

Erythraeus, Ianus Nicius. Pseudonym of Gian Vittorio Rossi (1577–1647), Italian scholar and novelist.

Esad, Mehmed. See GALIB, SEYH.

Escherich, Elsa Falk. See FALK, ELSA.

Esclavo, El ("The Slave"). Cognomen of Juan de Pareja (1606?–1670), West Indian–Spanish painter. He had been the slave of Velázquez.

Esser, Maurits. See VAN ECKEREN, GERARD.

Essex, Richard. Pseudonym of Richard Harry Starr (1878–   ), mystery writer.

Estella, Frate Diego de. Religious name of Diego de San Cristóbal (1524–1578), Spanish religious writer.

Esteven, John. See SHELLABARGER, SAMUEL.

Estoril, Jean. See ALLAN, MABEL ESTHER.

Estúñiga, Lope de. Sixteenth-century Spanish poet, also called *Stúñiga.* He was the son of the Marshal of Navarre.

Etienne. Pseudonym of William Stephen Richard King-Hall (1893–   ), English writer.

Etlar, Carit. Pseudonym of Johan Carl Christian Brosbøll (1816–1900), Danish writer.

Eton, Robert. See MEYNELL, LAURENCE WALTER.

Ettinghausen, Maurice. See SACHS, MAURICE.

Euchaita, John of. See MAUROPOUS, JOHN.

Eustace, Robert. See RAWLINS, EUSTACE.

Evans, Caradoc. Pseudonym of David Evans (1878–1933), Anglo-Welsh writer.

Evans, Constance May (1890–   ). Canadian-English author, whose pseudonyms are *Jane Gray* and *Mairi O'Nair.*

Evans, David. See EVANS, CARADOC.

Evans, Evan. See IEUAN GLAN GEIRIONYDD.

Evans, George Bird (1906–   ). American writer, whose pseudonyms, with his wife, Kay Harris Evans, are *Brandon Bird* and *Harris Evans.*

Evans, George Essex. See CHRISTOPHUS.

Evans, Harris. See EVANS, GEORGE BIRD, and EVANS, KAY HARRIS.

Evans, Hugh Austin. See AUSTIN, HUGH.

Evans, John. Pseudonym of Howard Browne (1908–   ), mystery writer.

Evans, Julia. See HOBSON, POLLY.

Evans, Kay Harris (1906–   ). American writer, whose pseudonyms with her husband, George Bird Evans, are *Brandon Bird* and *Harris Evans.*

Evans, Marguerite Florence Hélène (1894–1964). British writer, whose pseudonyms are *Countess Barcynska* and *Oliver Sandys.*

Evans, Mary Ann. See ELIOT, GEORGE.

Evans-Jones, Albert. See CYNAN.

Evelyn, Anthony. See WARD-THOMAS, EVELYN BRIDGET PATRICIA STEPHENS.

Evelyn, John Michael. See UNDERWOOD, MICHAEL.

Evelyn, Rose d'. Pseudonym of Rose Broemel, contemporary mystery writer.

Evens, Glyn Kinnaird. See RAQ.

Everardi, Joannes. See SECUNDUS, JANUS.

Everett, Gail. See HALE, ARLENE.

Everett-Green, Evelyn. See ADAIR, CECIL.

Everly, Jeannette Hyde. See GRIFFITH, JEANNETTE.

Eversley, David Edward Charles. See SMALL, WILLIAM.

Everson, William Oliver. See BROTHER ANTONINUS.

Everton, Francis. Pseudonym of Francis William Stokes (1883–   ), American mystery writer.

Everymay, March. Pseudonym of Mathilde Eiker (1893–   ), American mystery writer.

Evoe. Pseudonym of Edmund George Valpy Knox (1881–   ), English humorist and editor of *Punch.*

Exall, Barry. Pseudonym of John Peter Nugent (1930–   ), American writer.

Eyles, Merle. See CROZIER, KATHLEEN MURIEL EYLES.

Eynde, Antoon van den. See BRULIN, TONE.

"F"

F.O.O. See STREET, CECIL JOHN CHARLES.

F.P.A. Pseudonym of Franklin Pierce Adams (1881–1960), American journalist.

Fabian, Warner. Pseudonym of Samuel Hopkins Adams (1871–1958), mystery writer.

Fabre, Philippe François Nazaire. See FABRE D'ÉGLANTINE.

Fabre d'Églantine. Pseudonym of Philippe François Nazaire Fabre (1750–1794), French playwright and revolutionary politician.

Fabriano, Gentile da (c1370–1427). Italian painter, whose real name was Gentile di Nicolò di Massio.

Fabricius. See CARPENTER, ALEXANDER.

Fabricius, Sara. See SANDEL, CORA.

Facciò, Rina. See ALERAMO, SIBILLA.

Fa-ch'ang. See MU-CH'I.

Fagiolo, Mario. See DELL'ARCO, MARIO.

Fagus. Pseudonym of Georges Eugène Faillet (1872–1933), French poet and critic.

Fahrenkopf, Anne. See IRVING, ALEXANDER.

Fa-hsien. Religious name of Kung (d. 420), Chinese monk and travel writer.

Faillet, Georges Eugène. See FAGUS.

Fair, A. A. See GARDNER, ERLE STANLEY.

Fairbairn, Helen. Pseudonym of Helen Fairbairn Southard (1906–), American scholar.

Fairfield, Cicily Isabel. See WEST, REBECCA.

Fairfield, Flora. One-time pseudonym of Louisa May Alcott (1832–1888), American author.

Faizilber, Illia Arnoldovitsky. See ILF, ILLIA.

Falca, Pietro. See LONGHI, PIETRO.

Falconer, James. See KIRKUP, JAMES.

Faleński, Felicjan Medard. See FELICJAN.

Falk, Elsa. Pseudonym of Elsa Falk Escherich (1888–), American author.

Falke, Konrad. See FREY, KARL.

Falkland, Samuel. See HEIJERMANS, HERMAN.

Fallada, Hans. Pseudonym of Rudolf Ditzen (1893–1947), German novelist.

Fallon, Martin. See PATTERSON, HENRY.

Falstaff Fakir. Pseudonym of Axel Wallengren (1865–1896), Swedish humorist.

Fane, Violet. Pseudonym of Baroness Mary Montgomerie Currie (1843–1905), English writer.

Fantasio. See HUET, CONRAD BUSKEN.

Fantazy. Pseudonym of Wiktor Gomulicki (1851–1919), Polish poet and writer.

Fa Presto. Cognomen of Luca Giordano (1632–1705), Neapolitan painter, derived from his swiftness of execution.

Farazdaq, al-. Pseudonym of Hammam ben Ghalib ben Sacsaca (d. 728), Arabic writer.

Farel, Conrad. See BARDENS, DENNIS CONRAD.

Farewell, Nina. See COOPER, MAE KLEIN.

Fargo, Joe. See RIKHOFF, JAMES C.

Farigoule, Louis. See ROMAINS, JULES.

Farjeon, Eleanor. See TOMFOOL.

Farjeon, Joseph Jefferson. See SWIFT, ANTHONY.

Farkas, Aladar A. See RAY, OSCAR.

Farmacevten. Pseudonym of Sven A. Holm (1902–   ), Danish free-lance writer.

Farmer, Bernard James. See FOX, OWEN.

Farmer, Peter. See LLOYD, J. IVESTER.

Farmer, Wendell. Pseudonym of Lavinia Riker Davis (1909–1961), American mystery writer.

Farnash, Hugh. Pseudonym of Stanley George Anthony Luff (1921–   ), Anglo-Italian writer.

Farndale, John. Pseudonym of John Wilfred Harvey, contemporary mystery writer.

Farnham, Burt. Pseudonym of Harold B. Clifford (1893–   ), American writer.

Farnwald. See STRUBBERG, FRIEDRICH ARMAND.

Farr, Diana Pullein-Thompson. See PULLEIN-THOMPSON, DIANA.

Farr, Douglas. See GILFORD, C. B.

Farr, John. See WEBB, JACK.

Farr, Sebastian. Pseudonym of Eric Walter Blom, contemporary mystery writer.

Farra, Madame E. See FAWCETT, FRANK DUBREZ.

Farrell, Catharine. Pseudonym of Sister Mary Catharine O'Connor, contemporary American writer.

Farrell, David. Pseudonym of Frederick Escreet Smith (1922–   ), English writer.

Farrell, Desmond. See ORGAN, JOHN.

Farrell, James Thomas. See FOGARTY, JONATHAN TITULESCU, ESQ.

Farrell, M. J. Pseudonym of Mary Nesta Skrine (1905–   ), Irish writer.

Farren, Robert. See O'FARACHAIN, ROIBEARD.

Farrère, Claude. Pseudonym of Charles Bargonne (1876–1957), French naval officer and writer.

Fast, Howard (1914–   ). American novelist and playwright, whose pseudonyms are *E. V. Cunningham* and *Walter Ericson.*

Father Abraham. See FRANKLIN, BENJAMIN.

Father Acunha. See WU LI.

Father Caedmon. Pseudonym of Caedmon Thomas Wahl (1931–　), American writer of religious works.

Father Prout. Pseudonym of Francis Sylvester Mahony (1804–1866), Irish essayist and priest.

Fattore, Il. Cognomen of Gianfrancesco Penni (1488?–1528), Italian painter.

Faulkner, Anne Irvin. See FAULKNER, NANCY.

Faulkner, Nancy. Pseudonym of Anne Irvin Faulkner (1906–　), American writer.

Faulknor, Cliff. See WILLIAMS, PETE.

Fawcett, Frank Dubrez (1891–　). English free-lance writer, whose pseudonyms are *Henri Dupres, Madame E. Farra, Eugene Glen, Griff, Coolidge McCann, Elmer Eliot Saks, Ben Sarto,* and *Simpson Stokes.*

Fay, Dorothy. Pseudonym of Anna Chandler Lindholm (1870–　), mystery writer.

Fazzano, Joseph E. See FITZGERALD, JOHN.

Feagles, Anita MacRae. See MACRAE, TRAVIS.

Feagles, Elizabeth. Pseudonym of Beth Feagles Day (1924–　), American free-lance writer.

Featherstonehaugh, Francis. Pseudonym of Alasdair Alpin MacGregor (1899–　), English author, photographer, and illustrator.

Febronius, Justinus. Pseudonym of Johann Nikolaus von Hontheim (1701–1790), German Roman Catholic priest and theologian.

Federzoni, Luigi. See DE FRENZI, GIULIO.

Feikema, Feike. Pseudonym of Frederick Feikema Manfred (1912–　), American novelist.

Feilding, Dorothy. See FIELDING, A.

Fei of Han, Prince. See HAN-FEI-TZU.

Felicjan. Pseudonym of Felicjan Medard Faleński (1825–1910), Polish playwright, poet, and novelist.

Fellowes, Anne. See MANTLE, WINIFRED LANGFORD.

Fellowes-Gordon, Ian Douglas (1921–　). American free-lance journalist, whose pseudonyms are *Douglas Collier* and *Ian Gordon.*

Felsen, Henry Gregor. See VICKER, ANGUS.

Felton, Ronald Oliver. See WELCH, RONALD.

Feltre, Vittorino da (1378?–1446). Italian humanist, whose real name was Vittorino de' Ramboldoni.

Fel'zen, Yuri. Pseudonym of Nikolay Bernardovich Freidenstein (?–1943), Russian writer.

Feng Meng-lung. See MO-HAN CHAI.

Fenn, Caroline K. See MCGREW, FENN.

Fenwick, Kay. See BEAN, KEITH F.

Ferguson, Charles W. See GREGORY, HILTON.

Ferguson, Lady Hannay. See LESLIE, DORIS.

Ferguson, William Blair Morton. See MORTON, WILLIAM.

Ferguut, Jan. Pseudonym of Jan van Droogenbroeck (1835–1902), Flemish poet.

Ferling. Pseudonym of Lawrence Ferlinghetti (1919–   ), American writer.

Ferlinghetti, Lawrence. See FERLING.

Fern, Edna. Pseudonym of Fernande Richter (1861–1941), German-American novelist.

Fernández de Lizardi, José Joaquín. See PENSADOR MEXICANO, EL.

Ferrara, Antonio da. Pseudonym of Antonio Beccari (1315–1370?), Italian poet.

Ferrara, Il Cieco di. See CIECO DI FERRARA, IL.

Ferrars, E. X. See BROWN, MORNA DORIS.

Ferrars, Elizabeth. See BROWN, MORNA DORIS.

Ferris, James Cody. Collective pseudonym for the "X Bar X Boys" series. See STRATEMEYER, EDWARD L.

Ferry, Gabriel. Pseudonym of Eugène Louis Gabriel de Bellemare (1809–1852), Mexican writer. His son, Gabriel de Bellemare (1846–?), novelist and playwright, also used the name.

Fetter, Elizabeth Head. See LEES, HANNAH.

Feylbrief, J. K. See OUDSHOORN, J. VAN.

Fiamengo, Girolamo Boschi. See BOSCH, HIERONYMUS.

Ficke, Arthur Davison. See BYNNER, WITTER.

Fickling, G. G. Pseudonym of Skip Forrest Fickling (1925–   ), American mystery writer.

Fickling, Skip Forrest. See FICKLING, G. G.

Fidanza, Giovanni di. See BONAVENTURA, SAINT.

Fidelio. Pseudonym of Edgar Hubert Hunt (1909–   ), English writer.

Field, Frank Chester. See ROBERTSON, FRANK CHESTER.

Field, Joanna. Pseudonym of Marion Milner (1900–   ), English author.

Field, Julian Osgood. See X.L.

Field, Michael. Joint pseudonym of Katharine Harris Bradley (1846–1914) and her niece, Edith Emma Cooper (1862–1913), English authors of lyric poetry and poetic dramas.

Fielden, Thomas Perceval (1882–   ). English scholar, whose pseudonyms are *P. de Fletin* and *E. de P. Flint.*

Fielding, A. Pseudonym of Dorothy Feilding (1884–   ), American mystery writer, whose works were erroneously attributed to Archibald E. Fielding (1900–   ).

Fielding, Archibald E. See FIELDING, A.

Fielding, Gabriel. Pseudonym of Alan Gabriel Barnsley (1916–   ), English writer.

Fielding, Howard. Pseudonym of Charles Witherle Hooke (1861–1929), mystery writer.

Fiesole, Giovanni da. See ANGELICO, FRA.

Fiesole, Mino da (1431?–1484). Florentine sculptor, also known as *Mino da Poppi,* from his birthplace, Poppa. The name is derived from the Fiesole Cathedral, where he worked.

Figaro. Pseudonym of Mariano José de Larra (1807–1837), Spanish satirist.

Figgis, Darrell. See IRELAND, MICHAEL.

Fikkens, J. See BRUNCLAIR, VICTOR J.

Fikso, Eunice Cleland. See GRIFFIN, C. F.

Filarete. Pseudonym of Antonio di Pietro Averlino (or Averulino) (1400?–1470?), Florentine architect and sculptor.

Filipepi, Alessandro di Mariano dei. See BOTTICELLI, SANDRO.

Finch, Matthew. Pseudonym of Merton Fink (1921–   ), English writer.

Findley, Ferguson. Pseudonym of Charles Weiser Frey (1910–   ), mystery writer.

Fineman, Irving. See JOSEPH, JONATHAN.

Fini, Tommaso di Cristoforo. See MASOLINO DA PANICALE.

Fink, Brat. Nickname of Gwen Davis (1936–   ), American writer.

Fink, Merton. See FINCH, MATTHEW.

Finlay, Finona. See STUART, VIVIAN.

Finley, Glenna. Pseudonym of Glenna Finley Witte (1925–   ), American free-lance writer.

Finley, Scott. Pseudonym of Winifred Clark (1909–   ), mystery writer.

Finnegan, Robert. See RYAN, PAUL WILLIAM.

Finney, Mark. Pseudonym of Kenneth Arthur Muir (1907–   ), English writer.

Fiore della Neve. Pseudonym of Martinus Gesinus Lambert van Loghem (1849–1934), Dutch poet and fiction writer.

Fiorentino, Domenico (1501–1565). Italian painter, sculptor, and engraver, whose real name was Domenico del Barbiere.

Firth, Ivan Eustace. See ERSKINE, FIRTH.

Fischart, Johann. See ELLOPOSCLEROS, HULDRICH.

Fish, Julian. Pseudonym of Blanche Campbell (1902–   ), American writer.

Fish, Robert L. See PIKE, ROBERT L.

Fisher, Laine. Pseudonym of James A. Howard (1922–   ), American author.

Fisher, Lois Jeannette. See JARRETT, JEANNETTE.

Fisher, Stephen Gould (1912–   ). American mystery writer, whose pseudonyms are *Stephen Gould* and *Grant Lane.*

Fisk, John. See FISKE, JOHN.

Fiske, John. Assumed name of John Fisk (1842–1901), American philosopher and historian, whose original name, changed in 1855, was Edmund Fisk Green.

Fitch, Clarke. See SINCLAIR, UPTON BEALL.

Fite, Mack. See SCHNECK, STEPHEN.

Fitt, Mary. Pseudonym of Kathleen Freeman (1897–   ), mystery writer.

Fitzboodle, George Savage. See THACKERAY, WILLIAM MAKEPEACE.

Fitzgerald, Erroll. Pseudonym of Josephine Fitzgerald Clarke, contemporary mystery writer.

Fitzgerald, Jack. Pseudonym of John Gerald Shea (1906–   ), American writer.

Fitzgerald, John. Pseudonym of Joseph E. Fazzano (1920–   ), American writer.

Fitzgerald, Lawrence Pennybaker. See LAWRENCE, JACK.

Fitzgerald, Percy Hetherington. See DYCE, GILBERT.

Fitzhardinge, Joan Margaret. See PHIPSON, JOAN.

Flachsbinder, Jan. See DANTISCUS, JOANNES DE CURIIS.

Flacius Illyricus, Matthias (1520–1575). Protestant Church historian, whose original name was Matthias Vlačič.

Flake, Otto. Pseudonym of Leo F. Kotta (1880–1963), German writer and essayist.

Flamand, François (1594?–1642). Belgian sculptor, whose real name was François Duquesnoy.

Flekser, A. L. See VOLYNSKY, AKIM L'NOVICH.

Fleming, George. Pseudonym of Constance Fletcher (1858–1938), American novelist and playwright.

Fleming, Oliver. See MACDONALD, PHILIP.

Fleming, Peter (1907–   ). Mystery writer, whose pseudonyms are *Moth* and *Strix.*

Fleming, Thomas James (1927–   ). American writer, whose pseudonyms are *Christopher Cain, T. F. James,* and *J. F. Thomas.*

Fletcher, Adam. See FLEXNER, STUART BERG.

Fletcher, Adele. See ORMISTON, ROBERTA.

Fletcher, Charlie May Hogue. See SIMON, CHARLIE MAY.

Fletcher, Constance. See FLEMING, GEORGE.

Fletcher, Harry Luft Verne (1902–   ). English-Welsh author, whose pseudonyms are *John Garden* and *John Hereford.*

Fletcher, Helen Jill (1911–   ). American writer, whose pseudonyms are *Carol Lee* and *Charles Morey.*

Fletcher, Lucille. Pseudonym of Lucille Fletcher Wallop (1912–   ), American author.

Fletcher, Robert James. See ASTERISK.

Fletin, P. de. See FIELDEN, THOMAS PERCEVAL.

Fleuridas, Ellie Rae. Pseudonym of Eleanor Rae Sherman (1929–   ), American writer.

Fleury, Delphine. Pseudonym of Sister Mary Amatora, contemporary American scholar.

Flexner, Stuart Berg (1928–   ). American writer, whose pseudonyms are *Adam Fletcher, Steve Mees,* and *Collier Santee.*

Flint, E. de P. See FIELDEN, THOMAS PERCEVAL.

Floren, Lee (1910–   ). American free-lance writer, whose pseudonyms are *Brett Austin, Claudia Hall, Wade Hamilton, Marguerite Nelson, Lew Smith, Lee Thomas, Len Turner, Will Watson,* and *Dave Wilson.*

Floris, Frans (1517?–1570). Flemish painter, etcher, and woodcut designer, whose real name was Frans de Vriendt.

Flynt, Josiah. Pseudonym of Josiah Flynt Willard (1869–1907), American sociologist and writer.

Fock, Gorch. Pseudonym of Johann Kinau (1880–1916), German novelist and playwright.

Foda, Aun. Pseudonym of Arthur N. Foxe (1902–   ), American scholar.

Foe, Daniel. See DEFOE, DANIEL.

Fogarty, Jonathan Titulescu, Esq. Pseudonym of James Thomas Farrell (1904–   ), American author.

Foley, Helen. Pseudonym of Helen Rosa Huxley Fowler (1917–   ), English writer.

Foley, John (1917–   ). English writer, whose pseudonyms are *John Sawyer* and *Ian Sinclair.*

Foley, Pearl. See DE MAR, PAUL.

Foley, Rae. See DENNISTON, ELINORE.

Folgore, Luciano. Pseudonym of Omero Vecchi (1888–   ), Italian poet and writer.

Folie, Franz. See ANSEL, FRANZ.

Folsom, Franklin Brewster (1907–   ). American writer, whose pseudonyms are *Benjamin Brewster, Samuel Cutler, Michael Gorham, Lyman Hopkins,* and *Troy Nesbit.*

Foot, Hugh Mackintosh. See CARADON, LORD.

Foote, Michael. See CATO.

Forbes, DeLoris Stanton (1923–   ). Mystery writer, whose pseudonyms are *De Forbes, Stanton Forbes,* and, with Helen B. Rydell, *Forbes Rydell.*

Forbes, Graham B. See STRATEMEYER, EDWARD L.

Forbes, Stanton. See FORBES, DELORIS STANTON.

Ford, Albert Lee. See STRATEMEYER, EDWARD L.

Ford, Corey. See RIDDELL, JOHN.

Ford, Elbur. See HIBBERT, ELEANOR BURFORD.

Ford, Ford Madox (1873–1939). English writer, whose original name was Ford Hueffer.

Ford, Fred. See DOERFFLER, ALFRED.

Ford, Hildegarde. Pseudonym of Velma Ford Morrison (1909–   ), American writer.

Ford, Leslie. See BROWN, ZENITH.

Ford, Marcia. See RADFORD, RUBY LORRAINE.

Forest, Felix C. See LINEBARGER, PAUL MYRON ANTHONY.

Forester, Frank. Pseudonym of Henry William Herbert (1807–1858), English writer.

Forio, Robert. Pseudonym of Irving J. Weiss (1921–   ), American scholar.

Forrest, Mark. See MORTON, GUY MAINWARING.

Forrest, Norman. See MORLAND, NIGEL.

Forrest, Sybil. See MARKUN, PATRICIA MALONEY.

Forrester, Alfred Henry. See CROWQUILL, ALFRED.

Forrester, Charles Robert. See CROWQUILL, ALFRED.

Forsman, Georg Zachris (1830–1903). Finnish historian, also known as *Yrjö Sakari Yrjö-Koskinen.*

Forsnas, V. A. See KOSKENNIEMI, V. A.

Forsythe, Robin. See DINGWALL, PETER.

Forteguerri, Niccolò. See CARTEROMACO.

Fortini, Franco. Pseudonym of Franco Lattes (1917–   ), Italian critic and writer.

Forward, Luke. See PATRIC, JOHNSTONE GILLESPIE.

Fosdick, Charles Austin. See CASTLEMON, HARRY.

Foss, John. Pseudonym of James Gordon (1912–   ), mystery writer.

Fossano, Ambrogio da. See BORGOGNONE, AMBROGIO.

Fosse, Giovanni Pietro delle. See VALERIANO, PIERIO.

Foster, George Cecil. See SEAFORTH.

Foster, Joanna. See DOUGHERTY, JOANNA FOSTER.

Foster, Margaret Rumer Godden (1907–   ). English novelist, whose principal pseudonym is *Rumer Godden.* She also uses the pseudonym *Rumer Godden Haynes-Dixon.*

Foster, Richard. See CROSSEN, KENDELL.

Fougasse. Pseudonym of Kenneth Bird (1887–   ), English writer.

Foulis, Hugh. Pseudonym of Neil Munro (1864–1930), mystery writer.

Fourest, Michel. See WYNNE-TYSON, JON.

Fournier, Henri Alban. See ALAIN-FOURNIER.

Fournier, Pierre. See GASCAR, PIERRE.

Fourth, Clifton. Pseudonym of H. Clifton Morse (1924–   ), American writer.

Fourth Brother, The. Pseudonym of Maung Htin Aung (1909–   ), British scholar.

Fouts, Edward Lee. See LEE, EDWARD.

Fowler, Helen Rosa Huxley. See FOLEY, HELEN.

Fowler, Sydney. Pseudonym of Sydney Fowler Wright (1874–), mystery writer.

Fox, David. See OSTRANDER, ISABEL EGENTON.

Fox, Gardner Francis (1911–). American free-lance writer, whose pseudonyms are *Jefferson Cooper, Jeffrey Gardner, James Kendricks,* and *Kevin Matthews.*

Fox, James M. See KNIPSCHEER, JAMES M. W.

Fox, Owen. Pseudonym of Bernard James Farmer (1902–), English writer.

Fox, Ruth. See IRVING, ALEXANDER.

Fox, Sebastian. Pseudonym of Gerald William Bullett (1894–1958), mystery writer.

Fox, V. Helen. Pseudonym of Helen Fox Couch (1907–), American writer.

Fox-Davies, Arthur Charles. See X.

Foxe, Arthur N. See FODA, AUN.

Fraddle, Farragut. Pseudonym of David Chambers Mearns (1899–), chief of the Manuscript Division at the Library of Congress.

Fraenkel, Heinrich (1897–). German-English writer, whose pseudonyms are *Assiac, Caissa,* and *Cinna.*

Fragner, Benjamin. See KLICHKA, BENJAMIN.

Frame, Janet. Pseudonym of Janet Paterson Frame Clutha (1924–), New Zealand writer.

France, Anatole. Pseudonym of Jacques Anatole François Thibault (1844–1924), French novelist, critic, poet, and playwright.

France, Claire. See DORE, CLAIRE MORIN.

Frances, Miss. Pseudonym of Frances R. Horwich (1908–), American writer.

Francesca, Piero della (1420–1492). Italian painter, whose real name was Piero de'i Franceschi.

Franceschi, Piero de'i. See FRANCESCA, PIERO DELLA.

Franceschini, Baldassare. See VOLTERRANO, IL.

Francesco, Domenico di. See MICHELINO, DOMENICO DI.

Francia, Francesco (c1450–1517). Italian painter and goldsmith, whose real name was Francesco di Marco di Giacomo Raibolini.

Franciabigio (1482?–1525). Florentine painter, whose real name was Francesco di Cristofano Bigi.

Francis, Basil Hoskins. See RHODE, AUSTEN.

Francis, C. D. E. Pseudonym of Patrick Howarth, contemporary mystery writer.

Francis, Dee. Pseudonym of Dorothy F. Haas, contemporary American writer.

Francis, Philip. Pseudonym of Roger Lockyer (1927–   ), English scholar.

Francis, Robert. Pseudonym of Robert Maxence (1909–   ), French novelist.

Francis, William. Pseudonym of William Francis Urell, contemporary mystery writer.

Franck, Frederick. See FREDERICKS, FRANK.

Francken, Fritz. Pseudonym of Frederik Edward (1893–   ), Dutch writer.

Franc-Nohain. Pseudonym of Maurice-Étienne Legrand (1873–1934), French poet and writer.

Frank, Theodore. Pseudonym of Dorothea Frances Gardiner, contemporary mystery writer.

Frank, Waldo David. See SEARCH-LIGHT.

Frankau, Julia Davis. See DANBY, FRANK.

Franklin, Benjamin (1706–1770). American statesman, scientist, and writer, whose pseudonyms are *Anthony Afterwit, The Busybody, Mrs. Silence Dogwood, Father Abraham, Philomath, Proteus Echo, Esq.,* and *Richard Saunders.*

Franklin, Charles. See USHER, FRANK.

Franklin, Cynthia. See NEVILLE, C. J.

Franklin, Elizabeth. Pseudonym of Hannah Campbell, contemporary free-lance writer and editor.

Franklin, Jay. See CARTER, JOHN FRANKLIN.

Franklin, Max. Pseudonym of Richard Deming (1915–   ), American free-lance writer.

Frapan-Akunian, Ilse. Pseudonym of Ilse Levien (1852–1908), German novelist.

Frare, Il. Cognomen of Francesco Bianchi-Ferrari (1460?–1510), Italian painter.

Fraser, Alex. Pseudonym of Henry Brinton (1901–   ), English writer.

Fraser, John A. See HAWKSHAW.

Fraser, Ronald. Pseudonym of Ronald Frank Tiltman (1901–   ), English free-lance journalist.

Frater Jocundus. Pseudonym of Wilhelm Müller (1845–1914), German-American writer.

Frazer, Andrew. See MARLOWE, STEPHEN.

Frederick, Dick. See DEMPEWOLFF, RICHARD FREDERIC.

Frederick, Oswald. Pseudonym of O. F. Snelling (1916–   ), English journalist and author.

Fredericks, Arnold. Pseudonym of Frederic Arnold Kummer (1873–1943), American mystery writer.

Fredericks, Frank. Pseudonym of Frederick Franck (1909–   ), Dutch-American writer, painter, and dental surgeon.

Fredricks, Frohm. See KERNER, FRED.

Free, John (d. 1465). English humanist, also known as *Phreas.*

Freedgood, Morton. See GODEY, JOHN.

Freeman, Artur. See LIEBERMANN, AHRON SAMUEL.

Freeman, Graydon La Verne (1904–   ). American scholar, whose pseudonyms are *Larry Freeman, James H. Thompson,* and *Sherry Wood.*

Freeman, James Dillet. See MANN, D. J.

Freeman, Kathleen. See FITT, MARY.

Freeman, Larry. See FREEMAN, GRAYDON LA VERNE.

Freidenstein, Nikolay Bernardovich. See FEL'ZEN, YURI.

Freihofer, Lois Diane. See BARTH, LOIS.

Fremlin, Celia. Pseudonym of Celia Fremlin Goller (1914–   ), English writer.

French, Alice. See THANET, OCTAVE.

French, Paul. Pseudonym of Isaac Asimov (1920–   ), Russian-American professor of biochemistry and science-fiction writer.

Frése, Dolores Warwick. See WARWICK, DOLORES.

Fresenus, Fritz. Occasional pseudonym of F. Lottmann (1880–1918), East Frisian novelist.

Frewin, Leslie Ronald. See DUPONT, PAUL.

Frey, Charles Weiser. See FINDLEY, FERGUSON.

Frey, Friedrich Herman. See GREIF, MARTIN.

Frey, Karl. Pseudonym of Konrad Falke (1880–1942), Swiss novelist, playwright, and poet.

Freyer, Frederic. See BALLINGER, WILLIAM SANBORN.

Frick, C. H. See IRWIN, CONSTANCE FRICK.

Frick, Constance. See IRWIN, CONSTANCE FRICK.

Frida, Emil. See VRCHLICKÝ, JAROSLAV.

Fridegard, Jan. See JOHANSSON, JOHAN FRIDOLF.

Friend, Oscar Jerome (1897–). American mystery writer, whose pseudonyms are *Owen Fox Jerome* and *Ford Smith.*

Friis, Babbis. See FRIIS-BAASTAD, BABBIS ELLINOR.

Friis-Baastad, Babbis Ellinor (1921–). Norwegian writer, whose pseudonyms are *Babbis Friis Baastad, Eleanor Babbis,* and *Babbis Friis.*

Friskey, Margaret Richards. See SHERMAN, ELIZABETH.

Fritschun. See FRIZZONI, GIAN BATTISTA.

Frizzoni, Gian Battista (c1725–after 1787). Raeto-Romansh poet, also known as *Fritschun.*

Frome, David. See BROWN, ZENITH.

Frost, Helen. See NICHOLS, DAVE.

Frosterus, Oskar. See PAKKALA, TEUVO.

Froy, Hearld. See DEGHY, GUY, and WATERHOUSE, KEITH.

Fry, Pete. Pseudonym of Clifford King (1914–), American mystery writer.

Fuchs, Summer. See LISKY, I. A.

Fucini, Renato. See TANFUCIO, NERI.

Fujiwara no Katako. See DAINI NO SAMMI.

Fujiwara no Sadaie (1162–1241). Japanese poet and scholar, also known as *Teika.*

Fujiwara no Toshinari (1114–1204). Japanese poet and scholar, also known as *Shunzei.*

Fujiwara Seika. Pseudonym of Fujiwara Shuku (1561–1619), Japanese writer.

Fujiwara Shuku. See FUJIWARA SEIKA.

Fukuzoya Chiyo (1703–1775). Japanese painter and haiku poet, whose pseudonyms are *Chiyojo, Chiyoni,* and *Kaga no Chiyo.*

Fuller, Henry Blake. See PAGE, STANTON.

Fuller, Iola. Pseudonym of Iola Fuller McCoy, contemporary American writer.

Funya no Yasuhide (c830–890). Japanese poet, also known as *Bunya no Yasuhide.*

Furai Sanjin. See HIRAGA KUNITOMO.

Furphy, Joseph. See COLLINS, TOM.

Furu, Paol. See BANG-HASEN, ODD.

Furukawa Mokuami. See MOKUAMI.

Fuseli, Henry. Anglicized name of Johann Heinrich Füssli (1741–1825), Swiss painter and writer.

Füssli, Johann Heinrich. See FUSELI, HENRY.

Futabatei Shimei. Pseudonym of Hasegawa Tatsunosuke (1864–1909), Japanese novelist.

Fuzuli. Pseudonym of Mehmed, Son of Suleyman (1494–1555), Turkish poet.

"*G*"

G.N. See KLOOS, WILLEM JOHAN THEODOOR.

Gabirol. See AVICEBRÓN.

Gabirol, Solomon ben Judah ibn-. See AVICEBRÓN.

Gabo, Naum (1890–   ). Russian sculptor and designer. His original surname was Pevsner.

Gabryella. Pseudonym of Narcyza Zmichowska (1819–1876), Polish novelist.

Gaddi, Dario. See GNOLI, DOMENICO.

Gaddis, Peggy. See DERN, PEGGY GADDIS.

Gaite, Francis. See COLES, CYRIL HENRY, and MANNING, ADELAIDE FRANCES OKE.

Gakyo-jin. See HOKUSAI.

Gakyo Rojin. See HOKUSAI.

Galaction, Gala. Pseudonym of Grigore Pişculescu (1879–1961), Rumanian writer.

Galbraith, Georgie Starbuck (1909–   ). American writer, whose pseudonyms are *G. S. Page, Ann Patrice, Penny Pennington,* and *Stuart Pennington.*

Galbraith, John Kenneth. See EPERNAY, MARK.

Gale, John. Pseudonym of Richard Gaze (1917–   ), American writer.

Gałecki, Tadeusz. See STRUG, ANDRZEJ.

Galen, Philipp. Pseudonym of Ernst Philipp Karl Lange (1813–1899), German novelist.

Galgario, Fra. See GHISLANDI, FRA VITTORE.

Galib, Seyh (1757–1798). Turkish poet, whose real name was Mehmed Esad.

Gallagher, Gale. Pseudonym of William Charles Oursler (1913–   ), American writer.

Gallerite, The. Pseudonym of Frederick Thomas Bason (1907–   ), English writer.

Gallinger, Osma Couch. Pseudonym of Osma Gallinger Tod (1898–   ), American writer.

Galsworthy, John. See SINJOHN, JOHN.

Galubok, Vladyslay. Pseudonym of Vladyslay Golub (1882–   ), White Russian writer and poet.

Galway, Norman. Pseudonym of Byron B. Gentry (1913–   ), American writer.

Gamar-Katiba. Occasional pseudonym of Rafael Patkanian (1830–1892), Armenian poet.

Gambarelli, Antonio. See ROSSELLINO, ANTONIO.

Gambarelli, Bernardo. See ROSSELLINO, BERNARDO.

Gambier, Kenyon. See LATHROP, LORIN ANDREWS.

Ganda, Theocritus à. See HEINSIUS, DANIEL.

Ganpat. Pseudonym of Martin Louis Alan Gompertz (1886–   ), mystery writer.

Gant, Jonathan. See ADAMS, CLIFTON.

García-Sarmiento, Félix Rubén. See DARÍO, RUBÉN.

Garcilaso de la Vega. See INCA, EL.

Garden, John. See FLETCHER, HARRY LUFT VERNE.

Gardiner, Dorothea Frances. See FRANK, THEODORE.

Gardner, Erle Stanley (1889–   ). American writer, whose pseudonyms are *A. A. Fair, Charles M. Green, Carleton Kendrake*, and *Charles J. Kenny.*

Gardner, Jeffrey. See FOX, GARDNER FRANCIS.

Gardner, Lawrence. See BRANNON, WILLIAM T.

Gardner, Nancy Bruff. See BRUFF, NANCY.

Garfield, Brian Wynne (1939–   ). American writer, whose pseudonyms are *Bennett Garland, Frank O'Brian, Brian Wynne*, and *Frank Wynne.*

Garland, Bennett. See GARFIELD, BRIAN WYNNE.

Garland, George. Pseudonym of Garland Roark (1904–   ), American writer.

Garland, Isabel. See LORD, GARLAND.

Garnett, Captain Mayn Clew. Pseudonym of Thornton Jenkins Hains (1866–   ), American mystery writer.

Garnett, Roger. See MORLAND, NIGEL.

Garofalo, Benvenuto da (1481?–1559). Italian painter, whose real name was Benvenuto Tisi.

Garrett, Randall. See JANIFER, LAURENCE MARK.

Garrett, Truman. Pseudonym of Margaret Haddican Judd (1906–   ), American author.

Garrison, Frederick. See SINCLAIR, UPTON BEALL.

Garrison, Joan. See NEUBAUER, WILLIAM ARTHUR.

Garrison, Webb Black. See WEBSTER, GARY.

Garrity. See GERRITY, DAVID JAMES.

Garst, Doris Shannon. See GARST, SHANNON.

Garst, Shannon. Pseudonym of Doris Shannon Garst (1894–   ), American writer.

Garth, Will. See KUTTNER, HENRY.

Garun, Ales'. Pseudonym of Alexander Vladimirovich Prushinski (1887–1921), White Russian poet.

Garve, Andrew. See WINTERTON, PAUL.

Garvin, Amelia Beers. See HALE, KATHERINE.

Gary, Romain. Pseudonym of Romain Kacev (1914–   ), French writer.

Gascar, Pierre. Pseudonym of Pierre Fournier (1916–   ), French novelist and journalist.

Gaspard-Poussin, Dughet. See DUGHET, GASPARD.

Gasparotti, Elizabeth Seifert. See SEIFERT, ELIZABETH.

Gaulden, Ray. See RAY, WESLEY.

Gaulli, Giovanni Battista. See BACICCIO, IL.

Gault, Mark. See COURNOS, JOHN.

Gauthier-Villars, Henry. See WILLY.

Gavarni. Pseudonym of Sulpice Guillaume Chevalier (1804–1866), French illustrator.

Gavrilescu, Alexandrina. See CAZIMIR, OTTILIA.

Gawsworth, John. Pseudonym of Terence Ian Fytton Armstrong (1912–   ), English poet and author.

Gay, Amelia. See HOGARTH, GRACE ALLEN.

Gay, Greer. Pseudonym of Hazel Belle Payne (1892–   ), mystery writer.

Gayle, Newton. Joint pseudonym of Muna Lee de Munoz Marin (1895–
) and Maurice C. Guinness, mystery writers.

Gaze, Richard. See GALE, JOHN.

Geber. See HAYYAN, JABIR IBN-.

Gehman, Betsy Holland. See KLAINIKITE, ANNE.

Gehman, Richard Boyd (1921–   ). American writer, whose pseudonyms are *Frederick Christian* and *Martin Scott.*

Geisel, Theodor Seuss (1904–   ). American author, illustrator, and
creator of nonsense creatures, whose pseudonyms are *Dr. Seuss* and,
unverified, *Theo LeSieg.*

Geldenhauer, Gerardus (1492–1512). Dutch theologian and historian,
also known as *Noviomagnus.*

Gellée (or Gelée), Claud(e). See LORRAIN, CLAUDE.

Gellis, Roberta L. Jacobs. See JACOBS, LEAH.

Genius, C. B. See BRONTË, CHARLOTTE.

Gennadius II (c1400–c1468). Byzantine scholar and patriarch of Con-
stantinople, whose monastic name was *Georgios Scholarius.*

Genoud, Antoine Eugène. See GENOUDE.

Genoude. Pseudonym of Antoine Eugène Genoud (1792–1849), French
journalist.

Gent, Joos van. 15th-century Flemish painter, also known as *Justus of
Ghent* and, to his Italian contemporaries, *Guisto da Guanto.*

Gentileschi, Orazio de' (1563–1647). Italian painter, whose real name
was Orazio Lomi.

Gentry, Byron B. See GALWAY, NORMAN.

Geoffrey, Charles. Pseudonym of Charles George Muller (1897–   ),
American writer.

George, Marion E. See BENJAMIN, CLAUDE.

George, Peter Bryan. See PETERS, BRYAN.

George, Prince of Prussia. See CONRAD GEORG.

George, Robert Esmonde Gordon. See SENCOURT, ROBERT.

George, Wilma. Pseudonym of Wilma Crowther (1918–   ), English
scholar.

George Monachus. Ninth-century Byzantine historian, also known as
Hamartolus the Sinner.

Gerahty, Digby George. See STANDISH, ROBERT.

Géraldy, Paul. Pseudonym of Paul Lefèvre (1885–   ), French poet.

Gérard, Jean Ignace Isidore. See GRANDVILLE.

Gerard, Morice. Pseudonym of John Jessop Teague (1856–1928), mystery writer.

Géraud, André. See PERTINAX.

Gérault, Charles. See PERTINAX.

Gerhardt, Dagobert von. See AMYNTOR, GERHARD VON.

Gerrare, Wirt. Pseudonym of William Oliver Greener (1862–   ), mystery writer.

Gerretson, Frederik Carel. See GOSSAERT, GEETEN.

Gerrity, David James (1923–   ). American mystery writer, whose pseudonyms are *Garrity, Calli Goran,* and *Mitch Hardin.*

Gersen, Alexander Ivanovich. See ISKANDER.

Gerson, Jean Charlier de (1363–1428). French ecclesiastic and writer, whose original name was Jean Charlier. The name was derived from his birthplace, Gerson.

Gersonides. See RALBAG.

Geweeten, Hendrik. Pseudonym of Hendrik Conscience (1812–1883), Dutch writer.

Gha'ani. See QA'ANI, HABIB ALLAH.

Ghazali, Muhammad. See QAZALI, ABU HAMID MUHAMMAD.

Ghelderode, Michel de. See MARTENS, ADEMAR.

Ghéon, Henri. Pseudonym of Henri Vangeon (1875–1944), French playwright.

Gherardi, Giovanni. See PRATO, GIOVANNI DA.

Gherardo della Notte (or delle Notti) ("Gerard of the Night Scene(s)"). Italian cognomen of Gerrit van Honthorst (1590–1656), Dutch painter.

Gherea, Ion. See DOBROGEANU-GHEREA, ION.

Gherus, Ranutius. See GRUTERUS, JANUS.

Ghica, Princess Helene. See DORA D'ISTRIA.

Ghil, René. Pseudonym of René Guilbert (1862–1925), French poet.

Ghine, Wunnakyawhtin U Ohn. Pseudonym of David Maurice (1899–   ), Australian writer.

Ghirlandajo (1449–1494). Florentine painter and goldsmith, whose real name was Domenico di Tommaso Bigordi.

Ghislandi, Fra Vittore (1655–1743). Italian painter, also known as *Fra Paolotto* and *Fra Galgario.*

Ghistele, Cornelis van (c1520?–1570). Dutch poet, also known as *Talpa* and *De Mol.*

Giamberti, Antonio. See SANGALLO.

Giamberti, Francesco. See SANGALLO.

Giamberti, Giovan Francesco. See SANGALLO.

Giamberti, Giuliano. See SANGALLO.

Giambologna (1529–1608). Flemish-Dutch painter. The name is a contraction of his real name, Giovanni Bologna.

Giannantonio. Nickname of Giovanni Antonio Volpi (1688–1766), Italian scholar and poet.

Gianuzzi, Giulio Pippi de'. See ROMANO, GIULIO.

Gibb, Lee. See DEGHY, GUY, and WATERHOUSE, KEITH.

Gibbon, Lewis Grassic. Pseudonym of James Leslie Mitchell (1901–1935), Scottish novelist.

Gibbs, Henry St. John Clair. See HARVESTER, SIMON.

Gibbs-Smith, Charles Harvard. See HARVARD, CHARLES.

Gibran, Kahlil (1883–1931). Syrian-American Arabic writer, also known as *Jubran Khalil Jubran.*

Gibson, Harry Clark. Pseudonym of Richard Gibson Hubler (1912–), American writer.

Gibson, Josephine. See HINE, SESYLE JOSLIN.

Gier-Ber, Ali. Pseudonym of Jean Baptiste du Val-de-Grâce, Baron de Cloots (1755–1794), German-French revolutionist, known as *Anacharsis Cloots.*

Gijsen, Marnix. Pseudonym of Jan-Albert Goris (1899–), Flemish author.

Gilbert, Anthony. See MALLESON, LUCY BEATRICE.

Gilbert, Marie Dolores Eliza Rosanna. See MONTEZ, LOLA.

Gilbert, Miriam. Pseudonym of Miriam Goldstein Presberg (1919–), American writer.

Gilbert, Nan. Pseudonym of Mildred Geiger Gilbertson (1908–), American writer.

Gilbert, Ruth Gallard Ainsworth. See AINSWORTH, RUTH.

Gilbert, Sir William Schwenck. See TOMLINE, F.

Gilbertson, Mildred Geiger. See GILBERT, NAN.

Gilden, Bert. See GILDEN, K. B.

Gilden, K. B. Joint pseudonym of Bert Gilden and his wife, Katya Gilden, contemporary American writers.

Gilden, Katya. See GILDEN, K. B.

Giles, Gordon A. See BINDER, OTTO OSCAR.

Giles, Kris. Pseudonym of Helen Berniece Nielsen (1918–   ), American writer.

Giles, Norman. Pseudonym of Norman Robert McKeown (1879–1947), South African novelist.

Gilford, C. B. (1920–   ). American writer, whose pseudonyms are *Donald Campbell, Douglas Farr*, and *Elizabeth Gregory*.

Gill, André. Professional name of Louis Alexandre Gosset de Guines (1840–1885), French painter, illustrator, and caricaturist.

Gill, Traviss. See ODELL, GILL.

Gille, Claud(e). See LORRAIN, CLAUDE.

Gillese, John Patrick (1920–   ). Irish-Canadian free-lance writer, whose pseudonyms are *Dale O'Hara* and *John A. Starr*.

Gilman, Dorothy. Pseudonym of Dorothy Gilman Butters (1723–   ), American writer.

Gilmer, Alice. See ROSS, DON.

Gilmer, Elizabeth. See DIX, DOROTHY.

Gilmore, James Roberts. See KIRKE, EDMUND.

Gilzean, Elizabeth Houghton Blanchet (1913–   ). Canadian-Welsh writer, whose pseudonyms are *Elizabeth Houghton* and *Mary Hunton*.

Ginzberg, Asher. See ACHAD, HAAM.

Ginzkey, Franz Karl. Pseudonym of Heinrich Hege (1871–   ), Austrian writer and poet.

Giordano, Luca. See FA PRESTO.

Giordano da Pisa (c1260–1311). Italian preacher, also called *Giordano da Rivalto*.

Giorgione, Il (c1478–1511). Venetian painter, whose original name was Giorgio Barbelli. He was also called *Giorgione da Castelfranco*.

Giovane, Il. See PALMA GIOVANE.

Giovanni, Domenico di. See BURCHIELLO, DOMENICO.

Giovanni, Piero di. See MONACO, LORENZO.

Giovanni, Stefano di. See SASSETTA.

Gippius, Z. N. (1869–1945). Russian author, also known as *Hippius*.

Giraldi, Giambattista Cinzio (1504–1573). Italian man of letters, also known simply as *Cinthio* or *Cynthius*.

Giraldi, Gregorio Giglio. See GYRALDUS, LILIUS GREGORIUS.

Girandole, Bernardo dalla. See BUONTALENTI, BERNARDO.

Girard, Antoine. See SAINT-AMANT, MARC-ANTOINE DE GÉRARD, SIEUR DE.

Giraud, Albert. Pseudonym of Marie Émile Albert Kayenbergh (1860–1929), Belgian poet.

Girkova, Lisabetta. See ELISHEVA.

Girling, Zoë. See HARE, MARTIN.

Girun, Gian. Pseudonym of Ursina Clauvot-Geer (1898–   ), Raeto-Romansh writer.

Gisander. Pseudonym of Johann Gottfried Schnabel (1690?–1750), German writer.

Gittings, Jo Grenville Manton. See MANTON, JO.

Giudeo, Manoello. See IMMANUEL BEN SOLOMON OF ROME.

Giurlani, Aldo. See PALAZZESCHI, ALDO.

Gjallandi, Porgils. Pseudonym of Jón Stefánsson (1851–1915), Icelandic writer.

Gjalski, Ksaver Sandor. Pseudonym of Ljuba Babic (1854–1935), Croatian writer.

Gladden, Washington (1836–1918). American congregational clergyman and writer, whose original name was Solomon Washington.

Glanndour, Maodez. Pseudonym of Loeiz Ar Flo'ch (1909–   ), Breton writer.

Glanville, Alec. Pseudonym of Alexander Haig Glanville Grieve (1902–   ), mystery writer.

Glanz, Aaron. See LEYELES, A.

Glaser, Eleanor Dorothy. Pseudonym of Eleanor Dorothy Zonik (1918–   ), English writer.

Glaser, Milton. See CATZ, MAX.

Glass, Justine. Pseudonym of Alice Enid Corrall (1916–   ), English writer.

Glassbrenner, Adolf. See BRENNGLAS, ADOLF.

Glassco, John (1909–   ). Canadian writer, whose pseudonyms are *Silas N. Gooch* and *Miles Underwood.*

Glasscock, Anne Bonner. See BONNER, MICHAEL.

Glazarovà, Jarmila. Pseudonym of Jarmila Podivínská (1901–   ), Czech writer.

Gleadow, Rupert Seeley. See CASE, JUSTIN.

Glen, Eugene. See FAWCETT, FRANK DUBREZ.

Glicenstein, Emanuel. See ROMANO, EMANUEL.

Glikberg, Alexander Mikhaylovich. See CHËRNY, SASHA.

Gloux, Olivier. See AIMARD, GUSTAVE.

Głowacki, Aleksander. See PRUS, BOLESŁAW.

Glück, Barbara Elisabeth. See PAOLI, BETTY.

Gluck, Sinclair. See DANNING, MELROD.

Gnapheus, Guilhelmus (1493–1568). Dutch Protestant writer, whose original name was Wiliem de Volder.

Gnoli, Domenico (1838–1915). Italian scholar and writer, whose pseudonyms were *Dario Gaddi* and *Giulio Orsini.*

Godden, Rumer. See FOSTER, MARGARET RUMER GODDEN.

Godey, John. Pseudonym of Morton Freedgood, contemporary mystery writer.

Godley, John. Pseudonym of John Raymond Godley Kilbracken (1920–), English free-lance journalist and author.

Godley, Robert. See JAMES, FRANKLIN.

Godwin, John. See STARK, JOHN.

Goedeke, Karl. See STAHL, KARL.

Goens, Rijklof Michaël van. See PHILOSOPHE SANS FARD, LE.

Goeverneur, Jan Jacob Antony. See RIJMER, JAN DE.

Gofman, Victor Victorovich (1884–1911). Russian modernist poet, also known as *Hufman.*

Gohman, Fred Joseph. See WEBB, SPIDER.

Gökalp, Ziya. See ZIYA, MEHMED.

Golaw, Salomon von. Pseudonym of Baron Friedrich von Logau (1604–1655), German poet and epigrammatist.

Goldenthal, Allan Benarria. See BENARRIA, ALLAN.

Goldfrank, Helen Colodny. See KAY, HELEN.

Goldsmith, Peter. Occasional pseudonym of John Boynton Priestley (1894–), British writer and scholar.

Goldstein, Isidore. See ISOU, ISIDORE.

Goldstein, William Isaac. See LODE, REX.

Goldston, Robert Conroy. See STARK, JAMES.

Goller, Celia Fremlin. See FREMLIN, CELIA.

Golodnyj, Michail. Pseudonym of Michail Semënovich Epstein (1903–1949), Russian poet.

Golssenau, Arnold Vieth von. See RENN, LUDWIG.

Golub, Vladyslay. See GALUBOK, VLADYSLAY.

Gomberg, V. See LIDIN, VLADIMIR GHERMANOVICH.

Gompertz, Martin Louis Alan. See GANPAT.

Gomulicki, Wiktor. See FANTAZY.

Gondola, Andrea di Pietro dalla. See PALLADIO, ANDREA.

Gondola, Giovanni. Italian name of Ivan Gundulić (1589–1638), Dalmatian poet.

Gonzaga, Tomaz Antônio. See DIRCEU.

González, José Vittoriano. See GRIS, JUAN.

Gooch, Silas N. See GLASSCO, JOHN.

Good, Edward. Pseudonym of M. Oved (1885–   ), Yiddish poet.

Good, Irving John. See DOOG, K. CAJ.

Goodchild, George (1888–   ). Mystery writer, whose pseudonyms are *Alan Dare, Wallace Q. Reid,* and *Jesse Templeton.*

Goodenough, Evelyn. Pseudonym of Evelyn G. Pitcher (1915–   ), American writer.

Goodrich, Samuel Griswold. See PARLEY, PETER.

Goodwin, Hal. See GOODWIN, HAROLD LELAND.

Goodwin, Harold Leland (1914–   ). American writer, whose pseudonyms are *John Blaine, Hal Goodwin,* and *Blake Savage.*

Goodwin, John. Pseudonym of Sidney Floyd Gowing (1878–   ), mystery writer.

Goossen, Agnes. Pseudonym of Margaret A. Epp, contemporary Canadian writer.

Góra. See GÓRNICKI, ŁUKASZ.

Góralczyk, Kozimierz. Pseudonym of Władysław Ludwik Anczyc (1823–1883), Polish playwright and poet.

Goran, Calli. See GERRITY, DAVID JAMES.

Gordon, Charles William. See CONNOR, RALPH.

Gordon, Donald. See PAYNE, DONALD GORDON.

Gordon, Frederick. Collective pseudonym. See STRATEMEYER, EDWARD L.

Gordon, Gordon. See GORDONS, THE.

Gordon, Ian. See FELLOWES-GORDON, IAN DOUGLAS.

Gordon, James. See FOSS, JOHN.

Gordon, Jan. See GORE, WILLIAM.

Gordon, Lew. See BALDWIN, GORDON C.

Gordon, Mildred. See GORDONS, THE.

Gordon, Neil. See MACDONELL, ARCHIBALD GORDON.

Gordon, Peter. See WILKES-HUNTER, RICHARD.

Gordon, Rex. See HOUGH, STANLEY BENNETT.

Gordon, Stewart. See SHIRREFFS, GORDON D.

Gordon, Yehuda Leib. See Y.L.G.

Gordons, The. Joint pseudonym of Gordon Gordon (1912–   ) and his
wife, Mildred Gordon (1912–   ), American writers.

Gore, William. Pseudonym of Jan Gordon (1882–1944), mystery
writer.

Gorenko, Anna Andreyevna. See AKHMATOVA, ANNA.

Gorey, Edward St. John. Contemporary American writer, whose
pseudonyms are *Eduard Blutig, Mrs. Regera Dowdy, Redway Grode,
O. Mude, Hyacinthe Phypps, Ogdred Weary,* and *Dreary Wodge.*

Gorham, Maurice Anthony Coneys. See RAULT, WALTER.

Gorham, Michael. See FOLSOM, FRANKLIN BREWSTER.

Goris, Jan-Albert. See GIJSEN, MARNIX.

Gorky (or Gorki), Maxim (or Maksim). Pseudonym of Alexey Maximovich Peshkov (1868–1936), Russian writer.

Górnicki, Łukasz (1527–1603). Polish political writer and historian,
whose original name was Góra.

Gorrio, Tobia. Anagrammatic pseudonym of Arrigo Boito (1842–1918),
Italian composer and librettist.

Górski, Artur. See QUASIMODO.

Goryan, Sirak. Pseudonym of William Saroyan (1908–   ), American
writer.

Goslicius, Wawrzyniec. See GÓSLICKI, WAWRZYNIEC GRZYMALA.

Góslicki, Wawrzyniec Grzymala (c1530–1607). Polish political writer
and bishop, also known as *Wawrzyniec Goslicius, Laurentius Grimaldus,* and *Laurentius Grimalius.*

Gossaert, Geeten. Pseudonym of Frederik Carel Gerretson (1884–1958),
Dutch poet and essayist.

Gosselin, Louis-Léon-Théodore. See LENÔTRE, GEORGES.

Gosset de Guines, Louis Alexandre. See GILL, ANDRÉ.

Gotthelf, Jeremias. Pseudonym of Albert Bitzius (1797–1854), Swiss
pastor and writer.

Gottlober, Abraham Baer (1811–1899). Hebrew poet and novelist,
whose pseudonyms were *Abag* and *Mahalel.*

Gottschalk, Laura Riding. See JACKSON, LAURA RIDING.

Gouge, Orson. Pseudonym of Jeremy Larner (1937–   ), American
writer.

Gould, Michael. Pseudonym of Michael Ayrton (1921–   ), English
writer.

Gould, Stephen. See FISHER, STEPHEN GOULD.

Govan, Christine Noble (1898–   ). American writer, whose pseudonyms are *Mary Allerton* and *J. N. Darby.*

Gowing, Sidney Floyd. See GOODWIN, JOHN.

Goyau, Georges. See GRÉGOIRE, LÉON.

Goyder, Margot. See NEVILLE, MARGOT.

Goyer (or Gooyer), Jacob de. See RUISDAEL, JACOB VAN.

Goyer (or Gooyer), Salomon de. See RUYSDAEL, SALOMON VAN.

Goyne, Richard. See COURAGE, JOHN.

Gozzoli, Benozzo (1420–1498). Florentine painter, whose real name was Benozzo di Lese di Sandro.

Graaf-Boukema, Bonny L. E. de. See CHEIXAOU, ELISABETH.

Graber, Alexander. See CORDELL, ALEXANDER.

Grabowski, Zbigniew Anthony. See HEYST, AXEL.

Grace, Joseph. See HORNBY, JOHN.

Gracián, Baltasar. See GRACIÁN, LORENZO.

Gracián, Lorenzo. Pseudonym of Baltasar Gracián (1601–1658), Spanish Jesuit and writer.

Gracq, Julien. Pseudonym of Louis Poirier (1910–   ), French novelist.

Grady, Tex. See WEBB, JACK.

Graeme, Bruce. See JEFFRIES, GRAHAM MONTAGUE.

Graeme, David. See JEFFRIES, GRAHAM MONTAGUE.

Graeme, Roderic. See JEFFRIES, GRAHAM MONTAGUE.

Graft, Guillaume van der. Pseudonym of Wilhelmus Barnard (1920–   ), Dutch poet and essayist.

Graham, Ennis. Pseudonym of Mary Louisa Molesworth (1839–1921), Scottish fiction writer.

Graham, Neill. See DUNCAN, W. MURDOCH.

Graham, Ramona. Pseudonym of Ramona Graham Cook, contemporary American poet.

Graham, Susan. See SUSAN.

Grainger, Francis Edward. See HILL, HEADON.

Grammaticus. Pseudonym of Edward Musgrave Blaiklock (1903–   ), English–New Zealand scholar.

Granadino, El. Cognomen of Alonso Cano (1601–1667), Spanish painter, sculptor, and architect.

Grand, Sarah. Pseudonym of Frances Elizabeth M'Fall (1862–1943), English fiction writer.

Grande Vitesse. See WALKERLEY, RODNEY LEWIS.

Grandi, Ercole di Giulio Cesare de'. See ROBERTI, ERCOLE DE.

Grandville. Professional name of Jean Ignace Isidore Gérard (1803–1847), French illustrator and caricaturist.

Grange, Cyril (1900–   ). English writer, whose pseudonyms are *Onlooker* and *Quill.*

Granite, Tony. See POLITELLA, DARIO.

Grant, Alan. Pseudonym of Gilbert Alan Kennington (1906–   ), mystery writer.

Grant, Ambrose. See RAYMOND, RENÉ.

Grant, Douglas. See OSTRANDER, ISABEL EGENTON.

Grant, Hilda Kay. See HILLIARD, JAN.

Grant, Joan. Pseudonym of Joan Marshall Kelsey (1907–   ), English free-lance writer.

Grant, Landon. See GRIBBLE, LEONARD REGINALD.

Grant, Richard. See CLARKE, J. CALVITT.

Grantham, Gerald. See WALLACE, JOHN.

Grantland, Keith. See BEAUMONT, CHARLES.

Grapho. See OAKLEY, ERIC GILBERT.

Graves, Charles Parlin. See PARLIN, JOHN.

Graves, Clotilde Inez Mary. See DEHAN, RICHARD.

Gray, Berkeley. See BROOKS, EDWY SEARLES.

Gray, Elizabeth Janet. Pseudonym of Elizabeth Gray Vining (1902–   ), American author, used for her books for children.

Gray, Ellington. Pseudonym of Naomi Ellington Jacob (1889–1964), English novelist.

Gray, George Hugh. See GRAY, TONY.

Gray, Jane. See EVANS, CONSTANCE MAY.

Gray, Jonathan. Pseudonym of Herbert Adams (1874–   ), mystery writer.

Gray, Tony. Pseudonym of George Hugh Gray (1922–   ), Irish-English author.

Gray, Walter. See MATTHAEI, CLARA.

Grayson, David. Pseudonym of Ray Stannard Baker (1870–   ), American journalist and essayist.

Grayson, Captain J. J. Pseudonym of Elsie N. Wright (1907–   ), American mystery writer.

Grayson, Richard. Pseudonym of Richard Grindal, contemporary mystery writer.

Grazzini, Antonio Francesco. See LASCA, IL.

Great Merlini. See RAWSON, CLAYTON.

Greco, El. Cognomen of Kyriakos Theotokopoulos (1541–1614), Greek-Spanish painter. He was also called *Domenico.*

Green, Alan Baer. See BURNE, GLEN, and DENBIE, ROGER.

Green, Charles M. See GARDNER, ERLE STANLEY.

Green, D. See CASEWIT, CURTIS.

Green, Edmund Fisk. See FISKE, JOHN.

Green, Gladys Elizabeth Blun. See BURNE, GLEN.

Green, Glint. Pseudonym of Margaret Peterson (1883–1933), mystery writer.

Green, Henry. Pseudonym of Henry Yorke (1905–   ), English writer.

Green, Julian. See DELAPORTE, THÉOPHILE.

Green, O. O. Pseudonym of Raymond Durgnat (1932–   ), English writer.

Green, Peter Morris. See DELANEY, DENIS.

Green, Robert. See DEINDORFER, ROBERT GREENE.

Green, Sheila Ellen. See GREENWALD, SHEILA.

Greene, Ward. See DUDLEY, FRANK.

Greener, William Oliver. See GERRARE, WIRT.

Greenhood, Clarence David. See SAWYER, MARK.

Greenwald, Sheila. Pseudonym of Sheila Ellen Green (1934–   ), American writer and illustrator.

Green-Wanstall, Kenneth. See WANSTALL, KEN.

Greenwood, Julia Eileen Courtney. See ASKHAM, FRANCIS.

Grégoire, Léon. Pseudonym of Georges Goyau (1869–1939), French historian.

Gregory, Elizabeth. See GILFORD, C. B.

Gregory, Hilton. Pseudonym of Charles W. Ferguson (1901–   ), American writer.

Gregory, Mason. See JONES, ADRIENNE, and MEEK, DORIS.

Gregory, Sean. See HOSSENT, HARRY.

Gregson, Paul. See OAKLEY, ERIC GILBERT.

Greif, Martin. Pseudonym of Friedrich Herman Frey (1839–1911), German poet and playwright.

Greig, Maysie (1902–   ). Mystery writer, whose pseudonyms are *Jennifer Ames, Ann Barclay, Madeline Thompson,* and *Mary Douglas Warren.*

Grendon, Edward. Pseudonym of Lawrence L. LeShan (1920–   ), American scholar.

Grenelle, Lisa. Occasional pseudonym of Elizabeth Lee Munroe (1910–   ), American writer and poet.

Grenvil, William. Pseudonym of Wyndham Martyn (1875–   ), mystery writer.

Gresham, Claude Hamilton, Jr. See GRESHAM, GRITS.

Gresham, Elizabeth F. See GREY, ROBIN.

Gresham, Grits. Pseudonym of Claude Hamilton Gresham, Jr. (1922–   ), American free-lance writer.

Grevelingen, H. van. Pseudonym of Johannes Willem Cornelis Verhage (1910–1947), Dutch writer.

Gréville, Henry. Pseudonym of Alice Durand (1842–1902), French novelist.

Grex, Leo. See GRIBBLE, LEONARD REGINALD.

Grey, A. F. Pseudonym of Adeline Phyllis Neal (1894–   ), mystery writer.

Grey, Donald. Pseudonym of Eugene Thomas (1894–   ), mystery writer.

Grey, Elizabeth. Pseudonym of Beth Tootill Hogg (1917–   ), English free-lance writer.

Grey, Louis. See GRIBBLE, LEONARD REGINALD.

Grey, Robin. Pseudonym of Elizabeth F. Gresham, contemporary mystery writer.

Grey Owl. Pseudonym of George Stanfeld Belaney (1888–1938), Canadian writer of nature stories. His Apache Indian name was Wa-Sha-Quon-Asin.

Gribble, Leonard Reginald (1908–   ). Mystery writer, whose pseudonyms are *Sterry Browning, Landon Grant, Leo Grex, Louis Grey,* and *Dexter Muir.*

Grien, Hans. See BALDUNG, HANS.

Grierson, Jane. Pseudonym of Edward Emberlin Woodward, contemporary mystery writer.

Grieve, Alexander Haig Glanville. See GLANVILLE, ALEC.

Grieve, Christopher Murray. See MACDIARMID, HUGH.

Griff. See FAWCETT, FRANK DUBREZ; MCKEAG, ERNEST L.

Griffin, C. F. Pseudonym of Eunice Cleland Fikso (1927–   ), American writer.

Griffith, Mr. & Mrs. E. G. See GRIFFITH, JASON.

Griffith, George Chetwynd. See LARA.

Griffith, Jason. Joint pseudonym of Mr. & Mrs. E. G. Griffith, contemporary mystery writers.

Griffith, Jeannette. Joint pseudonym of Jeannette Hyde Everly (1908–   ) and Valeria Winkler Griffith, American writers.

Griffith, John. See LONDON, JACK.

Griffith, Valeria Winkler. See GRIFFITH, JEANNETTE.

Griffith y Dexter, Maria Aline. See COUNTESS OF ROMANONES.

Grile, Dod. Pseudonym of Ambrose Bierce (1842–1914?), mystery writer.

Grimaldi, Giovanni Francesco. See BOLOGNESE, IL.

Grimaldus, Laurentius. See GÓSLICKI, WAWRZYNIEC GRZYMALA.

Grimalius, Laurentius. See GÓSLICKI, WAWRZYNIEC GRZYMALA.

Grimshaw, Mark. See MCKEAG, ERNEST L.

Grimsley, Gordon. See GROOM, ARTHUR WILLIAM.

Grin, Alexander. Pseudonym of Alexander Stepanovich Grinevetsky (1880–1932), Russian writer.

Grindal, Richard. See GRAYSON, RICHARD.

Grindel, Eugène. See ÉLUARD, PAUL.

Grinevetsky, Alexander Stepanovich. See GRIN, ALEXANDER.

Gringhuis, Dirk. Pseudonym of Richard H. Gringhuis (1918–   ), American writer and illustrator.

Gringhuis, Richard H. See GRINGHUIS, DIRK.

Gris, Juan (1887–1927). Spanish-French painter, whose real name was José Vittoriano González.

Griswold, George. Pseudonym of Robert George Dean, contemporary mystery writer.

Grode, Redway. See GOREY, EDWARD ST. JOHN.

Groeningen, August Pieter van. See OEVERE, WILLIAM VAN.

Gronon, Rose. Pseudonym of Martha Bellefroid (1901–   ), Dutch novelist.

Groom, Arthur William (1898–1964). English writer, whose pseudonyms are *Graham Adamson, George Anderson, Daphne du Blane, Gordon Grimsley, Bill Pembury, John Stanstead, Maurice Templar,* and *Martin Toonder.*

Groot, Huig de. See GROTIUS, HUGO.

Grosofsky, Leslie. Pseudonym of Leslie Gross (1927–   ), American writer.

Gross, Leslie. See GROSOFSKY, LESLIE.

Grossmann, Reuben. See AVINOAM.

Grotius, Hugo. Latinized name of Huig de Groot (1583–1645), Dutch theologian, poet, jurist, and playwright.

Grove, Will O. See BRISTER, RICHARD.

Gruber, Frank (1904–   ). American writer whose pseudonyms are *Stephen Acre, Charles K. Boston,* and *John K. Vedder.*

Grün, Hans. See BALDUNG, HANS.

Gruterus, Janus. Latinized name of Jan van Gruytère (1560–1627), Dutch humanist and Latin poet. He also used the pseudonym *Ranutius Gherus.*

Gruytère, Jan van. See GRUTERUS, JANUS.

Guanto, Guisto da. See GENT, JOOS VAN.

Guardati, Tommaso dei. See MASUCCIO DI SALERNO.

Guaspre, Le. See DUGHET, GASPARD.

Gubbins, Nathaniel. See MOTT, EDWARD SPENCER.

Gueran de Liost. Pseudonym of Jaume Bofill i Mates (1877–1933), Catalan poet, lawyer, and politician.

Guercino. Cognomen of Giovanni Francesco Barbieri (1591–1666), Italian painter, referring to his squint.

Guérin, Alexandre. See CHENEVIÈRE, JACQUES.

Guerrini, Olindo. See STECCHETTI, LORENZO.

Guest, Francis Narold. See SPENSER, JAMES.

Guichard, Karl Gottlieb. See ICILIUS, QUINTUS.

Guidi, Tommaso. See MASACCIO.

Guido. See KLOOS, WILLEM JOHAN THEODOOR.

Guigo, Ernest Philip. See HOLT, E. CARLETON.

Guilbert, René. See GHIL, RENÉ.

Guildford, John. Pseudonym of Bluebell Matilda Hunter (1887–   ), mystery writer.

Guimaraens, Alphonsus de. Pseudonym of Alfonso Henriques da Costa Guimarães (1870–1921), Brazilian poet.

Guinness, Maurice C. See GAYLE, NEWTON.

Guiot de Dijon (fl. c1220). French lyric poet, also known as *Jocelin.*

Gull, Cyril Arthur Edward Ranger. See THORNE, GUY.

Gundelfinger, Friedrich. See GUNDOLF, FRIEDRICH.

Gundolf, Friedrich. Pseudonym of Friedrich Gundelfinger (1880–1931), German writer and translator.

Gundulić, Ivan. See GONDOLA, GIOVANNI.

Gunn, James E. See JAMES, EDWIN.

Gunter, Archibald Clavering. See WARNEFORD, LIEUT.

Guthrie, John. Pseudonym of John Brodie (1905–   ), New Zealand–English novelist.

Guthrie, Thomas Anstey. See ANSTEY, F.

Gutmann, Simcha Alter. See BEN-ZION, SH.

Gwinn, William R. See RANDALL, WILLIAM.

Gyp. Pseudonym of Sibylle Gabrielle Marie-Antoinette de Riquetti de Mirabeau, Comtesse de Martel de Janville (1849–1932), French novelist and journalist.

Gyraldus, Lilius Gregorius. Latinized name of Gregorio Giglio Giraldi (1479–1552), Italian poet and humanist.

"H"

H.D. Pseudonym of Hilda Doolittle (1886–1961), American poet.

Haarer, Alex Ernest. See SHANWA.

Ha'ari ("The Lion"). Cognomen of Isaac Luria (1534–1572), Palestinian Jewish mystic.

Haas, Dorothy F. See FRANCIS, DEE.

Haasse, Willem Hendrik. See VAN EEMLANDT, W. H.

Haavio, Martti. See MUSTAPÄÄ, P.

Habbema, Koos. See HEIJERMANS, HERMAN.

Haddock, Albert. Pseudonym of Sir Alan Patrick Herbert (1890–   ), English journalist and writer.

Haddon, Christopher. See PALMER, JOHN LESLIE.

Hadfield, E. C. R. See HADFIELD, ELLIS CHARLES RAYMOND.

Hadfield, Ellis Charles Raymond (1909–   ). South African–English writer, whose pseudonyms are *Charles Alexander* and *E. C. R. Hadfield.*

Haedreyi, Abgad. Pseudonym of Alter Druyanov (1870–1938), Hebrew writer.

Haeften, Jacob van. See BENEDICTUS.

Haemstede, Jacob Eduard de Witte van (1763?–1853). Dutch poet and journalist, whose original name was Jacob Eduard de Witte. He changed his name after being released from prison.

Hage, J. van den. Pseudonym of Jan Frederik Oltmans (1806–1854), Dutch novelist and short-story writer.

Hagenau, Reinmar von. See REINMAR DER ALTE.

Haggard, Paul. See LONGSTREET, STEPHEN.

Haggard, William. Pseudonym of Richard Henry Michael Clayton (1907–   ), English author.

Hagymássy, Lajos. See TOLNAI, LAJOS.

Hailsham, Second Viscount. Pseudonym of Quintin McGarel Hogg (1907–   ), English scholar.

Haime, Agnes Irvine Constance. See PERSIS.

Hains, Thornton Jenkins. See GARNETT, CAPTAIN MAYN CLEW.

Hale, Arlene (1924–   ). American writer, whose pseudonyms are *Louise Christopher, Gail Everett,* and *Mary Anne Tate.*

Hale, Christopher. Pseudonym of Frances Moyer Ross Stevens (1895–   ), mystery writer.

Hale, Garth. Pseudonym of Albert Benjamin Cunningham (1888–   ), mystery writer.

Hale, Helen. Pseudonym of Lucille Burnett Mulcahy, contemporary American writer.

Hale, Katherine. Pseudonym of Amelia Beers Garvin (1878–   ), Canadian poet and essayist.

Hale, Michael. Pseudonym of Michael Bullock (1918–   ), English free-lance translator and writer.

Haliburton, Hugh. Pseudonym of James Logie Robertson (1846–1922), Scottish writer.

Haliburton, Thomas Chandler. See SLICK, SAM.

Halifax, Clifford. Pseudonym of Edgar Beaumont, contemporary mystery writer.

Hall, Adam. See TREVOR, ELLESTON.

Hall, Bennie Caroline. Contemporary American writer, whose pseudonyms are *Hall Bennett* and *Emily Marshall.*

Hall, Claudia. See FLOREN, LEE.

Hall, Elizabeth Wason. See WASON, BETTY.

Hall, Evan. See HALLERAN, EUGENE EDWARD.

Hall, Frédéric Sauser. See CENDRARS, BLAISE.
Hall, Holworthy. Pseudonym of Harold Everett Porter (1887–1936), American writer.
Hall, J. De P. Pseudonym of St. Clair McKelway (1905–   ), American author.
Hall, Josef Washington. See CLOSE, UPTON.
Hall, Maurits Cornelis van. See ARKEL, FRANK FLORISZOON VAN.
Hall, Oakley Maxwell. See MANOR, JASON.
Hall, Whyte. Pseudonym of Augustus Alfred Rayner (1894–   ), mystery writer.
Halleran, Eugene Edward (1905–   ), American Western writer, whose pseudonyms are *Donn Broward* and *Evan Hall.*
Hallgrimson, Jansson. See KAMBAN, GUDMUNDUR.
Halliday, Brett. See DRESSER, DAVIS.
Halliday, Michael. See CREASEY, JOHN.
Halm, Friedrich. Pseudonym of Baron Eligius Franz Joseph Freiherr von Münch-Bellinghausen (1806–1871), Austrian dramatist.
Halmar, Augusto d'. Pseudonym of Augusto Goemine Thompson (1880–1950), Chilean writer.
Hamadhani, al-. See BADI 'AL-ZAMAN.
Hamartolus the Sinner. See GEORGE MONACHUS.
Hambleton, Phyllis. See VANE, PHILLIPS.
Hamerling, Robert. Pseudonym of Rupert Johann Hammerling (1830–1889), Austrian poet.
Ha Mezayer ("The Painter"). Pseudonym of Mordecai Zui Manne (1859–1886), Hebrew poet and painter.
Hamill, Ethel. Pseudonym of Jean Francis Webb (1910–   ), American free-lance writer.
Hamilton, Alice. See CROMIE, ALICE HAMILTON.
Hamilton, Clive. See LEWIS, CLIVE STAPLES.
Hamilton, Ernest. See MERRIL, JUDITH.
Hamilton, Gail. Pseudonym of Mary Abigail Dodge (1833–1896), American writer.
Hamilton, Jack. See BRANNON, WILLIAM T.
Hamilton, Kay. See DE LEEUW, CATEAU.
Hamilton, Mary Agnes Adamson. See ICONOCLAST.
Hamilton, Michael. Pseudonym of Warren Chetham-Strode (1896–   ), English playwright.

Hamilton, Robert W. See STRATEMEYER, EDWARD L.

Hamilton, Wade. See FLOREN, LEE.

Hammam ben Ghalib ben Sacsaca. See FARAZDAQ, AL-.

Hammerling, Rupert John. See HAMERLING, ROBERT.

Hammett, Dashiell. See COLLINSON, PETER.

Hammond, Ralph. See HAMMOND INNES, RALPH.

Hammond Innes, Ralph (1913–   ). British writer, whose pseudonyms
are *Ralph Hammond* and *Hammond Innes.*

Hamp, Pierre. Pseudonym of Pierre Bourillon (1876–   ), French novelist.

Hampton, Kathleen. See STREET, LEE.

Hamsun, Knut. Pseudonym of Knut Pedersen (1859–1952), Norwegian
writer.

Han-fei-tzu ("Master Fei of Han"). Cognomen of Prince Fei of Han
(?–233 B.C.), Chinese philosophic writer.

Hankins, Arthur Preston (1880–   ). Mystery writer, whose pseudonyms are *H. Preston Arthur, Emart Kinsburn,* and *Arthur Preston.*

Hanley, Clifford. See CALVIN, HENRY.

Han Mac-Tu. Pseudonym of Nguya Trong-Tri (1913–1940), Vietnamese
poet.

Hanna, Frances Nichols. See NICHOLS, FRAN.

Hannay, James Owen. See BIRMINGHAM, GEORGE A.

Hansen, Anton. See TAMMSAARE, ANTON.

Hansen, Emil. See NOLDE, EMIL.

Hanshew, Hazel Phillips. See HANSHEW, MARY E., and HANSHEW,
THOMAS W.

Hanshew, Mary E. Mystery writer, whose pseudonyms, with Thomas
W. Hanshew (1857–1914), are *Hazel Phillips Hanshew* and *Anna
Kingsley.*

Hanshew, Thomas W. (1857–1914). Mystery writer, whose pseudonyms
are *Charlotte May Kingsley* and, with Mary E. Hanshew (1857–
1914), *Hazel Phillips Hanshew* and *Anna Kingsley.*

Hansson, Laura Mohr. See MARHOLM, LAURA.

Han Wen-kung (768–824). Chinese poet, essayist, and philosopher,
whose real name was Han Yu.

Han Yu. See HAN WEN-KUNG.

Hanzen, Klaas. See JACOBSE, MUUS.

Harbage, Alfred Bennett. See KYD, THOMAS.

Harbaugh, Thomas Chalmers. See CARTER, NICK, and OLD CAP COL-
LIER.

Harbinson, Robert. See BRYANS, ROBERT HARBINSON.

Harcourt, Melville. See CRITICUS.

Hardenberg, Baron Friedrich Leopold von. See NOVALIS.

Hardin, Clement. See NEWTON, DWIGHT BENNETT.

Hardin, Mitch. See GERRITY, DAVID JAMES.

Hardin, Peter. Pseudonym of Louis Vaczek (1913–   ), Hungarian-
American writer.

Hardin, Tom. See BAUER, ERWIN A.

Hardin, Wes. See KEEVIL, HENRY JOHN.

Hardinge, George. See MILNER, GEORGE.

Hardinge, Rex. See CAPSTAN.

Hardman, Richards Lynden. See HOWITZER, BRONSON.

Hard Pan. Pseudonym of Geraldine Bonner (1870–1930), mystery
writer.

Hardwick, Adam. See CONNOR, JOHN ANTHONY.

Hardy, Alice Dale. Collective pseudonym for the "Riddle Club" series.
See STRATEMEYER, EDWARD L.

Hardy, Douglas. See ANDREWS, CHARLES ROBERT DOUGLAS HARDY.

Hardy, Russ. See SNOW, CHARLES HORACE.

Hardy, Stuart. See SCHISGALL, OSCAR.

Hare, Cyril. Pseudonym of Alfred Alexander Gordon Clark (1900–
1958), British mystery writer.

Hare, Martin. Pseudonym of Zoë Girling, contemporary Irish writer.

Hare, Robert. Pseudonym of Robert Hare Hutchinson (1887–   ),
mystery writer.

Hargreaves, Reginald Charles. See AIGUILLETTE.

Häring, George Wilhelm. See ALEXIS, WILLIBALD.

Hark, Mildred. Pseudonym of Mildred Hark McQueen (1908–   ),
American writer.

Harkaway, Hal. See STRATEMEYER, EDWARD L.

Harland, Marion. Pseudonym of Mary Virginia Terhune (1830–1922),
American novelist. She was the mother of Albert Payson Terhune.

Harle, Elizabeth. See ROBERTS, IRENE.

Harlequin. Pseudonym of Alexander Wyclif Reed (1908–   ), New
Zealand writer.

Harley, John. See MARSH, JOHN.

Harper, Olive. Pseudonym of Helen D'Apery (1842–1915), mystery writer.

Harrington, K. See BEAN, KEITH F.

Harrington, Mark Raymond (1882–   ). American ethnologist, archaeologist, and writer, whose pseudonyms are *Ramon de las Cuevas, Jiskogo,* and *Tonashi.*

Harris, Colver. Pseudonym of Anne Colver (1908–   ), mystery writer.

Harris, John Beynon (1903–1969). Mystery writer, whose pseudonyms are *John Beynon* and *John Wyndham.*

Harris, Kathleen. See HUMPHRIES, ADELAIDE M.

Harris, Larry M. See JANIFER, LAURENCE MARK.

Harris, MacDonald. Pseudonym of Donald William Heiney (1921–   ), American writer.

Harris, Marion Rose. See YOUNG, ROSE.

Harris, Roger. Pseudonym of Roger Harris Lebus Wilson (1920–   ), American medical writer.

Harrison, Michael. See DOWNES, QUENTIN.

Harrison, Richard. See MOTTE, PETER.

Harsha (606–647). Sanskrit dramatist and poet, whose full name was Harshavardhana, Emperor of Kanauj.

Harshavardhana, Emperor of Kanauj. See HARSHA.

Harte, Marjorie. Pseudonym of Marjorie Harte McEvoy, contemporary English writer.

Hartman, Rachel Frieda. See WARD, JANICE.

Hartman, Roger. See MEHTA, RUSTAM JEHANGIR.

Hartmann, Helmut. See SEYMOUR, H.

Hartwell, Nancy. See CALLAHAN, CLAIRE WALLIS.

Harvard, Charles. Pseudonym of Charles Harvard Gibbs-Smith (1909–   ), English writer.

Harvester, Simon. Pseudonym of Henry St. John Clair Gibbs, contemporary English writer.

Harvey, Annie Jane Tennant. See HOPE, ANDRÉE.

Harvey, John Wilfred. See FARNDALE, JOHN.

Harwin, Brian. See HENDERSON, LEGRAND.

Harwood, Gina. Pseudonym of E. Georgina Harwood Battiscombe (1905–   ), English writer.

Hasebroek, Johannes Petrus. See JONATHAN.

Hasegawa Manjiro. See HASEGAWA NYOZEKAN.

Hasegawa Nyozekan. Pseudonym of Hasegawa Manjiro (1874–   ), Japanese writer.

Hasegawa Tatsunosuke. See FUTABATEI SHIMEI.

Haskin, Dorothy Clark. See CLARK, HOWARD.

Haslette, John. See VAHEY, JOHN GEORGE HASLETTE.

Haspels, George Frans. See COMPASSIONE.

Hastings, Alan. Pseudonym of Geoffrey Williamson (1897–   ), English writer.

Hastings, Brook. See EDGLEY, LESLIE.

Hastings, Harrington. See MARSH, JOHN.

Hastings, Phyllis Dora Hodge. Contemporary English writer, whose pseudonyms are *John Bedford, E. Chatterton Hodge, Rosina Land,* and *Julia Mayfield.*

Hatai. Pseudonym of Shah Ismail (1486–1524), Turkish poet and founder of the Safavid dynasty in Persia.

Hathaway, Jan. See NEUBAUER, WILLIAM ARTHUR.

Hattori Hikoemon. See RANSETSU.

Hauck, Louise Platt (1883–1943). Mystery writer, whose pseudonyms are *Lane Archer, Peter Ash,* and *Louise Landon.*

Hauenschild, Richard Georg Spiller von. See WALDAU, MAX.

Hauser, Kaspar. See TUCHOLSKY, KURT.

Hauser, Margaret L. See HEAD, GAY.

Hautzig, Esther Rudomin. See RUDOMIN, ESTHER.

Haverschmidt, François. See PAALTJENS, PIET.

Havlícek, Karel. See BOROVSKY, HAVEL.

Hawkins, Sir Anthony Hope. See HOPE, ANTHONY.

Hawkshaw. Pseudonym of John A. Fraser, contemporary mystery writer.

Hawley, Mabel C. Collective pseudonym for the "Four Little Blossoms" series. See STRATEMEYER, EDWARD L.

Hawton, Hector. See CURZON, VIRGINIA.

Hay, Frances. See ERIKSON, SIBYL ALEXANDRA.

Hay, Ian. Pseudonym of John Hay Beith (1876–1952), Scottish novelist and playwright.

Hayashi Gaho. See HAYASHI SHUNSAI.

Hayashi Jo. See HAYASHI SHUNSAI.

Hayashi Razan. Pseudonym of Hayashi Tadashi (1583–1657), Japanese scholar and writer. He was also called *Doshun.*

Hayashi Shunsai. Pseudonym of Hayashi Jo (1618–1680), Japanese writer, also called *Hayashi Gaho.* He was the son of Hayashi Razan.

Hayashi Suminori. See KAGAWA KAGESHIGE.

Hayashi Tadashi. See HAYASHI RAZAN.

Hayes, Evelyn. Pseudonym of Mary Ursula Bethell (1874–1945), New Zealand nature poet.

Hayes, Henry. Pseudonym of Ellen Warner Olney Kirk (1842–1928), American novelist.

Hayes, John F. See TERRENCE, FREDERICK J.

Hayes, Joseph. See ARNOLD, JOSEPH H.

Hayman. Pseudonym of Hazel Mary Peel (1930–   ), English writer.

Haynes, Alfred Henry. See CHRISTIE, KEITH.

Haynes, Anna. See MADLEE, DOROTHY.

Haynes, Linda. See SWINFORD, BETTY JUNE WELLS.

Haynes, Pat. See MCKEAG, ERNEST L.

Haynes-Dixon, Rumer Godden. See FOSTER, MARGARET RUMER GODDEN.

Hays, Elinor Rice. See RICE, ELINOR.

Hayward, Richard. Pseudonym of Baynard Hardwick Kendrick (1894–   ), American writer.

Hayyan, Jabir ibn- (fl. 721–776). Arabic scholar and scientific writer, also known as *Geber.*

Hazard, Jack. See BOOTH, EDWIN.

Hazelhoff, Hendrik. See DENDERMONDE, MAX.

Hazelton, Alexander. Pseudonym of William Alexander Armstrong (1912–   ), Scottish-English writer.

Head, Ann. Pseudonym of Anne Christensen Morse (1915–   ), American writer.

Head, Gay. Pseudonym of Margaret L. Hauser (1909–   ), American writer.

Head, Matthew. Pseudonym of John E. Canaday (1907–   ), American art critic and writer.

Headley, Elizabeth. See CAVANNA, ELIZABETH ALLEN.

Heal, Edith. See BERRIEN, EDITH HEAL.

Heard, Joseph Norman. See NORMAN, JOE.

Hearnden, Beryl. See BALFOUR, HEARNDEN.

Heartman, Harold. Pseudonym of John Mebane (1909–   ), American journalist and author.

Heath, Elizabeth Alden. Pseudonym of Edith Austin Holton (1881–   ), mystery writer.

Heathcott, Mary. See KEEGAN, MARY HEATHCOTT.

Heberden, Mary Violet. See LEONARD, CHARLES L.

Hébert, Jacques René (1755–1794). French journalist and revolutionary, called *Père Duchesne* after his best-known work.

Hector, Annie. See ALEXANDER, MRS.

Hedenstierna, Baron Alfred. See SIGURD.

Heelu, Jan van. 13th-century Dutch poet, whose real name was Jan van Leeuwe.

Heerberger, Helge. See BRENNER, ARVID.

Hege, Heinrich. See GINZKEY, FRANZ KARL.

Hegesippus. Pseudonym of Hugh J. Schonfield (1901–   ), English author, editor, and translator.

Heijermans, Herman (1864–1924). Dutch playwright, novelist, short-story writer, and editor, whose pseudonyms are *Samuel Falkland, Koos Habbema,* and *I. van Jelakowitch.*

Heiney, Donald William. See HARRIS, MACDONALD.

Heinlein, Robert Anson (1907–   ). American science-fiction writer, whose pseudonyms are *Anson MacDonald, Lyle Monroe, John Riverside,* and *Caleb Saunders.*

Heinsius, Daniel (1580–1655). Dutch humorist, also known as *Theocritus à Ganda* and *Janus Philodusus.*

Heiter, Amalie. Pseudonym of Amalie Marie Friedrike Auguste, Duchess of Saxony (1794–1870), dramatist and composer.

Heitner, Iris. See JAMES, ROBERT.

Helderenberg, Gery. Pseudonym of Hubert Buyle (1891–   ), Dutch poet and clergyman.

Helgesen, Poul. See HELIE, PAULUS.

Heliade-Radulescu, Ion. Pseudonym of Eliad Ion (1802–1872), Rumanian writer.

Helie, Paulus. Pseudonym of Poul Helgesen (c1485–1535), Danish theologian and writer.

Hellens, Franz. Pseudonym of Frédéric van Ermengem (1881–1920), Belgian writer.

Heller, Frank. Pseudonym of Martin Gunnar Serner (1886–1947), Swedish writer.

Helman, Albert. Pseudonym of Lou A. M. Lichtveld (1903–), Dutch writer.

Helmi, Jack. See SANDS, LEO G.

Heloise. Pseudonym of Heloise Cruse (1919–), American writer.

Hemerken, Thomas. See THOMAS À KEMPIS.

Hemingway, Taylor. See RYWELL, MARTIN.

Henderley, Brooks. Collective pseudonym for the "Y.M.C.A. Boys" series. See STRATEMEYER, EDWARD L.

Henderson, Donald Landels. See LANDELS, D. H.

Henderson, James Leal. See CURRIER, JAY L.

Henderson, LeGrand (1901–). American free-lance writer and illustrator, whose pseudonyms are *Brian Harwin* and *LeGrand.*

Henham, Ernest George. See TREVENA, JOHN.

Henjo. Pseudonym of Yoshimine no Munesada (816–890), Japanese poet.

Henriot, Émile. Pseudonym of Émile Maigrot (1889–1961), French poet and novelist.

Henry, O. Pseudonym of William Sydney Porter (1862–1910), American short-story writer.

Henschke, Alfred. See KLABUND.

Hensen, Herwig. Pseudonym of Florent Constant Albert Mielants, Jr. (1917–), Dutch poet and playwright.

Heraclius. See MAURICE.

Herbert, Sir Alan Patrick. See HADDOCK, ALBERT.

Herbert, Henry William. See FORESTER, FRANK.

Heredia, Marie-Louise-Antoinette de. See HOUVILLE, GÉRARD D'.

Hereford, John. See FLETCHER, HARRY LUFT VERNE.

Hériat, Philippe. Pseudonym of Raymond Gérard Payelle (1898–), French novelist and playwright.

Héricault, Charles d'. Pseudonym of Charles Joseph de Ricault (1823–1899), French historian and novelist.

Heritage, Martin. See HORLER, SIDNEY.

Hermanns, Peter. See BRANNON, WILLIAM T.

Hermon, Roparz. Pseudonym of L. P. Nemo (1900–), Breton writer.

Herne, Huxley. See BROOKER, BERTRAM.

Héroët, Antoine. See MAISONNEUVE, LA.

Heron, E. Pseudonym of Kate O'Brien Hesketh-Prichard, British mystery writer.

Heron, H. Pseudonym of Hesketh Vernon Hesketh-Prichard (1876–1922), British mystery writer.

Herpin, Clara Adèle Luce. See PEREY, LUCIEN.

Herring, Geilles. See SOMERVILLE, EDITH.

Herrnstein, Barbara. Pseudonym of Barbara Herrnstein Smith (1932–   ), American scholar.

Hertz, Henrik. Pseudonym of Henrik Heymann (1797–1870), Danish writer and poet.

Hervas y Cobo de la Torre, José Gerardo. See PITILLAS, JORGE.

Hervé, Aimé Marie Édouard. See VALNAY, RAOUL.

Hervey, Jane. Pseudonym of Naomi Blanche Thoburn McGaw, contemporary English writer.

Herzen, Alexander Ivanovich. See ISKANDER.

Herzog, Émile Salomon Wilhelm. See MAUROIS, ANDRÉ.

Heseltine, Philip Arnold. See WARLOCK, PETER.

Hesketh-Prichard, Hesketh Vernon. See HERON, H.

Hesketh-Prichard, Kate O'Brien. See HERON, E.

Hesse, Hermann (1877–1962). German-Swiss writer, whose pseudonyms were *Hermann Lauscher* and *Emil Sinclair*.

Hessels, Willem. Pseudonym of Hendrik Adriaan Mulder (1906–1949), Dutch poet and essayist.

Hetzel, Pierre Jules. See STAHL, P. J.

Hevesi, Ludwig. See ONKEL TOM.

Hewitt, Kathleen Douglas. See MARTIN, DOROTHEA.

Hexham, Lionel J. F. Pseudonym of Felix John De Hamel, contemporary mystery writer.

Hext, Harrington. Early pseudonym of Eden Phillpotts (1862–1960), English novelist and playwright.

Hextall, David. See PHILLIPS-BIRT, DOUGLAS.

Heyer, Georgette. See MARTIN, STELLA.

Heymann, Henrik. See HERTZ, HENRIK.

Heyst, Axel. Pseudonym of Zbigniew Anthony Grabowski (1903–   ), Polish writer.

Hiat, Elchik. Pseudonym of Menke Katz (1906–   ), Lithuanian-American poet.

Hibbert, Eleanor Burford (1906–   ). English writer, whose pseudonyms are *Eleanor Burford, Elbur Ford, Victoria Holt, Kathleen Kellow, Jean Plaidy,* and *Ellalice Tate.*

Hicks, Harvey. See STRATEMEYER, EDWARD L.

Hifni Nasif, Malak. See BAHITHAT AL-BADIYAH.

Higdon, Hal. See SMITH, LAFAYETTE.

Higgen, J. C. M. See BELLEW, JOHN CHIPPENDALL MONTESQUIEU.

Higgins, Rosalyn Cohen. See COHEN, ROSALYN.

Highsmith, Patricia. See MORGAN, CLAIRE.

Hildebrand. Pseudonym of Nikolaas Beets (1814–1903), Dutch parson, poet, and short-story writer.

Hildgard, Ferdinand Heinrich Gustav. See VILLARD, HENRY.

Hill, Brian. See MAGILL, MARCUS.

Hill, Dee. See ZUCKER, DOLORES MAE BOLTON.

Hill, Grace Brooks. Collective pseudonym for the "Corner House Girls" series. See STRATEMEYER, EDWARD L.

Hill, H. Haverstock. Pseudonym of James Morgan Walsh (1897–1952), mystery writer.

Hill, Headon. Pseudonym of Francis Edward Grainger (1857–   ), mystery writer.

Hill, Helen. Pseudonym of Helen Hill Miller (1899–   ), American writer.

Hill, King. See ROBERTSON, FRANK CHESTER.

Hill, Margaret (1915–   ). American writer, whose pseudonyms are *Rachel Bennett* and *Andrea Thomas.*

Hill, Monica. See WATSON, JANE WERNER.

Hill, Polly. Pseudonym of Mary Eglantyne Hill Humphreys (1914–   ), English scholar.

Hill, Roberta. See DAVIS, HARRY.

Hill, Ruth A. Pseudonym of Ruth Hill Viguers (1903–   ), American writer.

Hill, Ruth Livingston. Pseudonym of Ruth Hill Munce (1898–   ), American writer.

Hillas, Julian. Pseudonym of Robert Julian Dashwood (1899–   ), English writer.

Hilliard, Jan. Pseudonym of Hilda Kay Grant, contemporary Canadian writer.

Hilton, James. See TREVOR, GLEN.

Hilton, Richard. See DIL, ZAKHMI.

Hinckley, Helen. Pseudonym of Helen Hickley Jones (1903–   ), American writer.

Hinde, Thomas. Pseudonym of Sir Thomas Willes Chitty (1926–   ), mystery writer.

Hine, Sesyle Joslin (1929–   ). American writer, whose pseudonyms are *Josephine Gibson, Sesyle Joslin,* and *G. B. Kirtland.*

Hino, Ashihei. Pseudonym of Katsunori Tamai (1903–1960), Japanese soldier and writer.

Hinton, Richard W. Pseudonym of Charles Angoff (1902–   ), American writer, journalist, and editor.

Hipkins, Charles Hammond. See TALBOT, CARL.

Hippius. See GIPPIUS, Z. N.

Hippius. Pseudonym of Zinaida Nikolaevna Merezhkovskaya (1869–1945), Russian emigré novelist.

Hipsch Martin. See SCHONGAUER, MARTIN.

Hiraga Gennai. See HIRAGA KUNITOMO.

Hiraga Kunitomo (1729–1780). Japanese writer and dramatist, whose pseudonyms are *Furai Sanjin* and *Hiraga Kunitomo.*

Hirayama Togo. See IBARA SAIKAKU.

Hirazawa Tsunetomi. See KISANJI.

Hiroshige (1797–1858). Japanese painter and printmaker, whose real name was Ando Tokitaro. He was given the name *Utagawa Hiroshige* to indicate his affiliation with the Utagawa school of Ukiyo-e (the "painting of the Fleeting World").

Hirsch, William Randolph. See LINGEMAN, RICHARD R.

Hiscock, Leslie. See MARSH, PATRICK.

Hitchens, Dolores Birk Olsen (1907–   ). Mystery writer, whose pseudonyms are *Dolan Birkley* and *Noel Burke.*

Hitchin, Martin Mewburn. See MEWBURN, MARTIN.

Hlinka, Vojtěch. See PRAVDA, FRANTIŠEK.

Hoang Dao. Pseudonym of Nguyen Tuong-Long (1906–1948), Vietnamese writer.

Hobart, Black. Pseudonym of Ed Sanders (1939–   ), American poet, editor, and moviemaker.

Hobbes, John Oliver. Pseudonym of Pearl Mary Teresa Craigie (1867–1906), American-English novelist and playwright.

Hobsbawm, Eric John Ernest. See NEWTON, FRANCIS.

Hobson, Coralie von Werner. See SALT, SARAH.

Hobson, Hank. See HOBSON, HARRY.

Hobson, Harry (1908–   ). English writer, whose pseudonyms are *Hank Hobson* and *Hank Janson.*

Hobson, Laura Z. See QUIST, FELICIA.

Hobson, Polly. Pseudonym of Julia Evans (1913–   ), English writer.

Hockaby, Stephen. Pseudonym of Gladys Mitchell (1901–   ), English mystery writer.

Hodder, Alfred. See WALTON, FRANCIS.

Hodemart, Peter. Pseudonym of Pierre Audemars, contemporary mystery writer.

Hodge, E. Chatterton. See HASTINGS, PHYLLIS DORA HODGE.

Hodges, Turner. Pseudonym of Albert Hodges Morehead (1909–   ), American writer.

Hodgson, Norma. Pseudonym of Norma Hull Lewis Russell (1902–   ), English author.

Hoff, Gertrud. See MATTHAEI, CLARA.

Hoff, Harry Summerfield. See COOPER, WILLIAM.

Hoffmann, Elisabeth. See LANGGÄSSER, ELISABETH.

Hofman, V. V. See GOFMAN, VICTOR VICTOROVITCH.

Hogarth, Douglas. See PHILLIPS-BIRT, DOUGLAS.

Hogarth, Emmett. Joint pseudonym of Mitchell A. Wilson (1913–   ) and Abraham Polonsky, American mystery writers.

Hogarth, Grace Allen (1905–   ). Mystery writer, whose pseudonyms are *Amelia Gay* and, with Alice Mary Norton, *Allen Weston.*

Hogarth, Jr. Pseudonym of Rockwell Kent (1882–   ), American writer.

Hogg, Beth Tootill. See GREY, ELIZABETH.

Hogg, Quintin McGarel. See HAILSHAM, SECOND VISCOUNT.

Hogue, Dock. See HOGUE, WILBUR OWINGS.

Hogue, Wilbur Owings. Contemporary mystery writer, whose pseudonyms are *Dock Hogue* and *Carl Shannon.*

Hohenheim, Theophrast Bombast von. See PARACELSUS, PHILIPPOS AUREOLUS THEOPHRASTUS.

Hokusai (1760–1849). Japanese printmaker, whose father's name was Kawamura Ichiroemon. The name, first used in 1798, was one of more than fifty he used in his lifetime. His best-known pseudonyms are *Gakyo-jin, Hyakurin, I-itsu, Kako, Manji, Shinsai, Siunro, Sori,* and *Tokitaro.* Toward the end of his life he signed one document

Gakyo Rojin ("The Old Man Mad about Drawing").

Holbeche, Philippa Jack. See SHORE, PHILIPPA.

Holbrook, Sabra. Pseudonym of Sabra Rollins Erickson (1912–   ),
American writer.

Holdaway, Neville Aldridge. See TEMPLE-ELLIS, N. A.

Holden, Genevieve. Pseudonym of Genevieve Long Pou (1919–   ),
mystery writer.

Holden, Joanne. See CORBY, JANE.

Holden, Raymond Peckham. See PECKHAM, RICHARD.

Holland, Jan. See VITRINGA, ANNES JOHAN.

Holland, Katrin. See ALBRAND, MARTHA.

Holley, Marietta. See JOSIAH ALLEN'S WIFE.

Hollis, Jim. Pseudonym of Hollis Spurgeon Summers, Jr. (1916–   ),
American scholar.

Holloway, Brenda Wilmar. See VERNEY, SARAH.

Holloway, Teresa (1906–   ). American author of novels for young
adults, whose pseudonyms are *Elizabeth Beatty* and *Margaret Vail
McLeod.*

Holly, J. Hunter. Pseudonym of Joan Carol Holly (1932–   ), American science-fiction writer.

Holly, Joan Carol. See HOLLY, J. HUNTER.

Holm, Sven A. See FARMACEVTEN.

Holman, Clarence Hugh. See HUNT, CLARENCE.

Holmes, David Charles. See CHARLSON, DAVID.

Holmes, Gordon. Pseudonym of Louis Tracy (1863–1928) alone and
with Matthew Phipps Shiel (1865–1947), mystery writers.

Holmes, Grant. See KNIPSCHEER, JAMES M. W.

Holmes, H. H. See BOUCHER, ANTHONY.

Holmes, William Kersley. See SERRIFILE, F. O. O.

Holmvik, Oyvind (1914–   ). Norwegian author whose pseudonyms
are *Oy-vik, Paprika,* and *Sepia.*

Holt, E. Carleton. Pseudonym of Ernest Philip Guigo, contemporary
mystery writer.

Holt, Gavin. See RODDA, CHARLES.

Holt, Margaret. Pseudonym of Margaret Holt Parish (1937–   ),
American writer.

Holt, Stephen. Pseudonym of Harlan H. Thompson (1894–   ),
American writer.

Holt, Tex. See JOSCELYN, ARCHIE L.

Holt, Victoria. See HIBBERT, ELEANOR BURFORD.

Holton, Edith Austin. See HEATH, ELIZABETH ALDEN.

Holton, Leonard. See WIBBERLEY, LEONARD PATRICK O'CONNOR.

Home, Michael. Pseudonym of Christopher Bush (1885–   ), mystery writer.

Homersham, Basil Henry. See MANNINGHAM, BASIL.

Homes, Geoffrey. Pseudonym of Daniel Mainwaring (1902–   ), mystery writer.

Honeyman, William C. See M'GOVAN, JAMES.

Honeywell, E. L. See STANLEY, OLIN.

Hontheim, Johann Nikolaus von. See FEBRONIUS, JUSTINUS.

Honthorst, Gerrit van. See GHERARDO DELLA NOTTE.

Hook, Alfred Samuel. See COLTON, A. J.

Hook, Theodore Edward (1788–1841). English humorist and novelist, whose pseudonyms are *Vicesimus Blenkinsop, Richard Jones,* and *Mrs. Ramsbottom.*

Hooke, Charles Witherle. See FIELDING, HOWARD.

Hope, Andrée. Pseudonym of Annie Jane Tennant Harvey (d. 1898), mystery writer.

Hope, Anthony. Pseudonym of Sir Anthony Hope Hawkins (1863–1933), English novelist and playwright.

Hope, Frances Essex Theodora. See SMITH, ESSEX.

Hope, Felix. Pseudonym of Claude C. H. Williamson (1891–   ), English author.

Hope, Laura Lee. Collective pseudonym for the "Bobbsey Twins," "Blythe Girls," "Bunny Brown," "Make Believe Stories," "Outdoor Girls," and "Six Little Bunkers" series. See STRATEMEYER, EDWARD L.

Hopf, Alice L. See LIGHTNER, A. M.

Hopkins, A. T. Pseudonym of Annette Turngren, contemporary American free-lance writer, mainly for young people.

Hopkins, Kenneth (1914–   ). English poet and writer, whose pseudonyms are *Christopher Adams, Anton Burney, Warwick Mannon, Paul Marsh, Edmund Marshall,* and *Arnold Meredith.*

Hopkins, Lyman. See FOLSOM, FRANKLIN BREWSTER.

Hopley, George. See HOPLEY-WOOLRICH, CORNELL GEORGE.

Hopley-Woolrich, Cornell George (1903–1968). American writer, whose pseudonyms are *George Hopley, William Irish,* and *Cornell Woolrich.*

Horler, Sidney (1888–1954). Mystery writer, whose pseudonyms are *Peter Cavendish* and *Martin Heritage.*

Horn, Holloway. See WAGHORN, H. L.

Horn, W. O. von. Pseudonym of Philipp Friedrich Wilhelm Örtel (or Oertel) (1798–1867), German writer.

Hornby, John (1913–   ). English free-lance writer, whose pseudonyms are *Joseph Grace* and *Gordon Summers.*

Horne, Cynthia Miriam. See PILKINGTON, CYNTHIA.

Horne, Geoffrey. See NORTH, GIL.

Horne, Hugh Robert. See MADISON, JANE.

Horne, John. See TOOKE, JOHN.

Horwich, Frances R. See FRANCES, MISS.

Hosken, Clifford James Wheeler. See KEVERNE, RICHARD.

Hossent, Harry (1916–   ). English writer, whose pseudonyms are *Sean Gregory* and *Kevin O'Malley.*

Hough, Richard. See CARTER, BRUCE.

Hough, Stanley Bennett (1917–   ). English writer of fiction and travel books, whose pseudonyms are *Rex Gordon* and *Bennett Stanley.*

Houghton, Claude. Pseudonym of Claude Houghton Oldfield (1889–   ), mystery writer.

Houghton, Elizabeth. See GILZEAN, ELIZABETH HOUGHTON BLANCHET.

House, Anne W. Pseudonym of Elfrieda Babnick McCauley (1915–   ), American writer.

Houville, Gérard d'. Pseudonym of Marie-Louise-Antoinette de Heredia (1875–1963), French poet.

Houwink, Roel. See ELRO, H. VAN.

Howard, Coralie. Pseudonym of Coralie Cogswell (1930–   ), American writer.

Howard, Elizabeth. Pseudonym of Elizabeth Howard Mizner (1907–   ), American writer of historical novels for young people.

Howard, H. L. Pseudonym of Charles Jeremiah Wells (1799?–1879), English poet and playwright.

Howard, Hartley. See OGNALL, LEOPOLD HORACE.

Howard, Herbert Edmund. See PHILMORE, R.

Howard, James A. See FISHER, LAINE.

Howard, Keble. Pseudonym of John Keble Bell (1875–1928), English playwright and journalist.

Howard, Leigh. See KRISLOV, ALEXANDER.

Howard, Mark. See RIGSBY, HOWARD.

Howard, Peter D. See CATO.

Howard, Robert West. See CASE, MICHAEL.

Howard, Vechel. See RIGSBY, HOWARD.

Howarth, Patrick. See FRANCIS, C. D. E.

Howe, Muriel. See REDMAYNE, BARBARA.

Howitt, John Leslie Despard. Contemporary mystery writer, whose pseudonyms are *Leslie Despard* and *John Leslie.*

Howitzer, Bronson. Pseudonym of Richards Lynden Hardman (1924–), American professional writer.

Hozjusz. See DOBRACZYNSKI, JAN.

Hsiao Hsia. Pseudonym of Wu-chi Liu (1907–), Chinese-American scholar.

Hsieh Wan-ying. See PING-HSIN.

Hsü Pei-hung. See JUPÉON.

Hubler, Richard Gibson. See GIBSON, HARRY CLARK.

Hübsch Martin. See SCHONGAUER, MARTIN.

Huc, Philippe. See DERÈME, TRISTAN.

Hudson, Stephen. Pseudonym of Sydney Schiff (d. 1944), English novelist.

Hudson, William Cadwalader. See NORTH, BARCLAY.

Hueffer, Ford. See FORD, FORD MADOX.

Huel, Frits. Pseudonym of Godfried Eliza (1892–), Dutch economist and writer.

Huet, Conrad Busken (1826–1886). Dutch critic, historian, and writer, whose pseudonyms are *Een Geabonneerde, Fantasio,* and *Thrasybulus.*

Hugensz, Lucas. See LEYDEN, LUCAS VAN.

Huggard, John Needham. See WELCOME, JOHN.

Hughes, John Ceiriog. See CEIRIOG.

Hughes, M. Alison. Pseudonym of Mabel A. Steed (1894–), mystery writer.

Hulda. Pseudonym of Unnur Benediktsdóttir Bjarklind (1881–1946), Icelandic poet and novelist.

Hull, H. Braxton. Pseudonym of Helen Hull Jacobs (1908–   ), American writer.

Hull, Richard. Pseudonym of Richard Henry Sampson (1896–   ), mystery writer.

Hume, David. See TURNER, JOHN VICTOR.

Humfrey, C. Pseudonym of Charles Humfrey Caulfield Osborne, contemporary English scholar.

Humphreys, Eliza Margaret J. Gollan. See RITA.

Humphreys, Mary Eglantyne Hill. See HILL, POLLY.

Humphries, Adelaide M. (1898–   ). American author, whose pseudonyms are *Kathleen Harris, Wayne May,* and *Token West.*

Hungerford, Margaret Wolfe. See DUCHESS, THE.

Hunt, Clarence. Pseudonym of Clarence Hugh Holman (1914–   ), mystery writer.

Hunt, Edgar Hubert. See FIDELIO.

Hunt, Francis. Collective pseudonym for the "Mary and Jerry Mystery Stories" series. See STRATEMEYER, EDWARD L.

Hunt, Harrison. See BALLARD, TODHUNTER.

Hunt, Katharine Chandler. See NASH, CHANDLER.

Hunt, Kyle. See CREASEY, JOHN.

Hunt, Peter. Joint pseudonym of Charles Hunt Marshall and George Worthing Yates, contemporary mystery writers.

Hunter, Anson. Pseudonym of Arthur Orrmont (1922–   ), American writer.

Hunter, Bluebell Matilda. See GUILDFORD, JOHN.

Hunter, Christine. See HUNTER, MAUD LILY.

Hunter, Clementine. Pseudonym of Helen Mary Keynes, contemporary mystery writer.

Hunter, Evan (1926–   ). American writer, whose pseudonyms are *Hunt Collins, Ed McBain,* and *Richard Marsten.*

Hunter, Hall. Pseudonym of Edison Marshall (1894–1967), American free-lance writer.

Hunter, John (1891–   ). Mystery writer, whose pseudonyms are *John Addiscombe, L. H. Brenning, Anthony Dax, Anthony Drummond,* and *Peter Meriton.*

Hunter, John. See BALLARD, TODHUNTER.

Hunter, John. See HUNTER, MAUD LILY.

Hunter, Maud Lily (1910–   ). English writer, whose pseudonyms are

Christine Hunter, John Hunter, and *Charlotte Steer.*

Hunter, Paul. Pseudonym of Bertrand Weaver (1908–   ), American religious writer.

Hunter, Vickie MacLean. Pseudonym of Victoria Alberta Hunter (1929–   ), American author.

Hunter, Victoria Alberta. See HUNTER, VICKIE MACLEAN.

Huntingdon, John. Pseudonym of Gerald William Phillips (1884–   ), mystery writer.

Hunton, Mary. See GILZEAN, ELIZABETH HOUGHTON BLANCHET.

Hunzicker, Beatrice Plumb. See PLUMB, BEATRICE.

Hurban, Svetozar. See VAJANSKÝ, SVETOZAR HURBAN.

Hurd, Edith. See SAGE, JUNIPER.

Hurley, Doran. See MCGREGOR.

Hurley, Vic (1898–   ). American writer and naval officer, whose pseudonyms are *Jim Duane* and *Duane Richards.*

Husson, Jules François Felix (Fleury-). See CHAMPFLEURY.

Hutchinson, Robert Hare. See HARE, ROBERT.

Hutchison, Graham Seton. See SETON, GRAHAM.

Huxley, Herbert Henry. See STENUS.

Huxley, Julian Sorell. See BALBUS.

Huysman, Roelof. See AGRICOLA, RODOLPHUS.

Hviezdoslav. Pseudonym of Pavol Országh (1849–1921), Slovak poet and translator.

Hw'fa Môn. Bardic name of Rowland Williams (1823–1905), Welsh congregational minister and poet.

Hyakurin. See HOKUSAI.

Hyde, Douglas. See AOIBHINN, AN CRAOIBHÍN.

Hyde, Robin. Pseudonym of Iris Wilkinson (1906–1939), New Zealand journalist, novelist, and poet.

Hyndman, Jane Lee. Pseudonym of Lee Wyndham (1912–   ), Russian-American writer.

Hyne, Charles John Cutcliffe Wright. See CHESNEY, WEATHERBY.

"I"

Ibara Saikaku (1642–1693). Japanese poet and novelist, whose original name was probably Hirayama Togo.

Ibrahim, Taceddin. See AHMEDI.

Ibsen, Henrik. See BJARME, BRYNJOLF.

I-ching. Religious name of Chang Wen-ming (635–713), Buddhist monk and religious writer.

Icilius, Quintus. Pseudonym of Karl Gottlieb Guichard (or Guischard) (1724–1775), German soldier and writer.

Iconoclast. Pseudonym of Mary Agnes Adamson Hamilton (1883–), mystery writer.

Iependaal, Willem van. See KULK, WILLEM VAN DER.

Ieuan Glan Geirionydd. Pseudonym of Evan Evans (1795–1855), Welsh poet.

Ignotus. Pseudonym of Aleksyei Stepanovich Khomyakov (1804–1860), Russian mystery writer.

Ignotus. Pseudonym of Adam Müller-Guttenbrunn (1852–1923), Austrian writer.

Ignotus. Pseudonym of José de Elola y Guliérrez (1859–), Spanish writer.

Ignotus. Pseudonym of Hugo Veigelsberg (1869–1949), Hungarian poet and literary figure.

Iida. See SOGI.

I-itsu. See HOKUSAI.

Iker. Occasional pseudonym of Ivan Kerniskey (1913–), Ukrainian writer.

Iles, Bert. See ROSS, ZOLA HELEN.

Iles, Francis. See COX, ANTHONY BERKELEY.

Ilf, Illia. Pseudonym of Illia Arnoldovitsky Faizilber (1897–1937), Soviet Russian writer.

Ilyin, M. A. See OSORGIN, M. A.

Immanuel ben Solomon of Rome (1268/1272–1328). Italian-Hebrew humorist and poet, also called *Manoello Giudeo.*

Inca, El. Cognomen of Garcilaso de la Vega (c.1540–1616?), Spanish historian, who was the son of a Peruvian lady and a Spaniard.

Ind, Allison (1903–). American free-lance writer, whose pseudonyms are *Phil Stanley* and *Richard Wallace.*

Infield, Glen Berton (1920–). American writer, whose pseudonyms are *George Powers, Frank Rodgers,* and *Arthur Tolby.*

Ingelbrekt, Alf. Occasional pseudonym of Alf Larsen (1885–), Norwegian poet.

Ingenheim, Luciano von. See ZUCCOLI, LUCIANO.

Ingoldsby, Thomas. Pseudonym of Richard Harris Barham (1788–1845), English humorist.

Innes, Hammond. See HAMMOND INNES, RALPH.

Innes, Michael. Pseudonym of John Innes Mackintosh Stewart (1906–
), British writer.

Insight, James. Pseudonym of Robert William Alfred Coleman (1916–
), Egyptian-English writer.

Inspector F. See RUSSELL, WILLIAM.

Invrea, Gaspare. See ZENA, REMIGIO.

Inyart, Gene. Pseudonym of Gene Inyart Namovicz (1927–   ),
American writer.

Iolo Morganwg. Pseudonym of Edward Williams (1747–1826), Welsh
poet.

Ion, Eliad. See HELIADE-RADULESCU, ION.

Iqua. See BORCHARD, RUTH.

Irchan, Myroslav. Pseudonym of Andrey Babjuk (1897–1937), Ukrainian novelist and playwright.

Ireland, Michael. Pseudonym of Darrell Figgis (1882–1925), Irish poet
and novelist.

Irish, William. See HOPLEY-WOOLRICH, CORNELL GEORGE.

Iron, Ralph. Pseudonym of Olive Emilie Albertina Schreiner (1855–
1920), British writer.

Ironmaster, Maximus. Pseudonym of John Donald Wilkinson (1929–
), English religious writer.

Ironquill. Pseudonym of Eugene Fitch Ware (1841–1911), American
lawyer and poet.

Ironside, John. Pseudonym of Euphemia Margaret Tait, contemporary
mystery writer.

Irving, Alexander. Joint pseudonym of Anne Fahrenkopf and Ruth Fox,
contemporary American mystery writers.

Irving, Robert. Pseudonym of Irving Adler (1913–   ), American
scholar.

Irving, Washington (1783–1859). American writer, whose pseudonyms
are *Friar Antonio Agapida, Geoffrey Crayon, Jonathan Oldstyle,* and
Launcelot Wagstaffe.

Irwin, Constance Frick (1913–   ). American writer whose pseudonyms are *C. H. Frick* and *Constance Frick.*

Isa. See NECATI.

Isakov, M. V. See ISAKOVSKY, MICHAIL VASILIEVITCH.

Isakovsky, Michail Vasilievitch. Pseudonym of M. V. Isakov (1900–
), Russian poet.

Isaksen, Mathis. Pseudonym of Matti Aikio (1872–1929), Norwegian novelist.

Ischyrius. Latin pseudonym of Christiaen Vrijaldenhoven (fl. 1517–1536), Dutch neo-Latin poet. He was also known as *Sterck*.

Ishikawa Gabo. See ISHIKAWA MASAMOCHI.

Ishikawa Hajime. See ISHIKAWA TAKUBOKU.

Ishikawa Masamochi (1754–1830). Japanese writer, also known as *Ishikawa Gabo.*

Ishikawa Takuboku. Pseudonym of Ishikawa Hajime (1885–1912), Japanese poet.

Isis. See TORBETT, HARVEY DOUGLAS LOUIS.

Isis Copia. See ZIYADAH, MARIE.

Iskander. Pseudonym of Alexander Ivanovich Herzen (or Hertzen, Gertsen) (1812–1870), Russian writer and political agitator. His original surname was Yakovlev.

Islwyn. Pseudonym of William Thomas (1832–1878), Welsh poet.

Ismail, Shah. See HATAI.

Isou, Isidore. Pseudonym of Isidore Goldstein (1925–   ), French literary critic.

Israel ben Eliezer (c1700–1760). Jewish mystic, also known as *Baal Shem-Tov.*

Israeli, Isaac ben Solomon (845–c945). North African Hebrew writer, also known as *Isaac Iudaeus.*

Issachar. Pseudonym of John Keith Stanford (1892–   ), English writer.

Isserles, Moses (1525–1572). Polish-Hebrew religious writer, also known as *Ramaa.*

Ito Jinsai. Pseudonym of Ito Koresada (1627–1705), Japanese philosopher and writer.

Ito Koresada. See ITO JINSAI.

Ito Nagatane. See ITO TOGAI.

Ito Togai. Pseudonym of Ito Nagatane (1670–1736), Japanese writer and scholar.

Iudaeus, Isaac. See ISRAELI, ISAAC BEN SOLOMON.

Ivan, Gustave E. See IVAN, MARTHA MILLER PFAFF.

Ivan, Martha Miller Pfaff (1909–   ). American writer, whose pseudonyms are *Martha Miller* and, with her husband, Gustave E. Ivan, *Gus Tavo.*

Ivanov, Dimităr. See JOTOV, DIMITĂR IVANOV.

Ivanov, Razumnik Vasilyevich. See IVANOV-RAZUMNIK.

Ivanov-Razumnik. Pseudonym of Razumnik Vasilyevich Ivanov (1878–1946), Russian literary historian.

Ivnev, Ryurik. Pseudonym of Mikhail Alexandrovich Kovalev (1893–), Soviet Russian writer.

Ivry, Monsieur d'. See DELORME, PHILIBERT.

Iwase Nobuyoshi. See SANTO KYODEN.

Iwase Sei. See SANTO KYODEN.

Iwaszkiewicz, Jarosław. See ELEUTER.

Iwaya Sazanami. Pseudonym of Iwaya Sueo (1870–1933), Japanese writer.

Iwaya Sueo. See IWAYA SAZANAMI.

Izhaqi, Rabbi Shelomoh (1040–1105). French Jewish scholar and commentator, also known as *Rashi,* an acrostic of his name, and *Solomon ben Isaac.*

Izumi Kyoka. Pseudonym of Izumi Kyotaro (1873–1939), Japanese novelist.

Izumi Kyotaro. See IZUMI KYOKA.

Izumi Shikibu. Pseudonym of Oe Shikibu (974?–c1030), Japanese poet.

"J"

J.S. of Dale. Pseudonym of Frederic Jesup Stimson (1855–1943), American writer and lawyer.

Jackson, Caary Paul (1902–). American writer, whose pseudonyms are *Colin Lochlons* and *Jack Paulson.*

Jackson, Giles. See LEFFINGWELL, ALBERT.

Jackson, Laura Riding (1901–). American poet and author, whose pseudonyms are *Laura Riding Gottschalk, Barbara Rich,* and *Laura Riding.*

Jackson, Nora. Pseudonym of Nora Jackson Tennant (1915–), English writer.

Jackson, Sally. Pseudonym of Jean Kellogg (1916–), American writer.

Jackson, Wallace. See BUDD, WILLIAM JOHN.

Jacob, Naomi Ellington. See GRAY, ELLINGTON.

Jacob, P. L., Bibliophile. See LACROIX, PAUL.

Jacob ben Asher (c1269–1343). Spanish-Hebrew religious writer, also known as *Ba'al ha-Turim* and *Ribah.*

Jacob ben Meir (c1100–1171). Hebrew scholar, also known as *Rabenu Tam.*

Jacobs, Helen Hull. See HULL, H. BRAXTON.

Jacobs, Leah. Pseudonym of Roberta L. Jacobs Gellis (1927–), American writer.

Jacobs, T. C. H. See PENDOWER, JACQUES.

Jacobs, Thomas Curtis Hicks. See PENDOWER, JACQUES.

Jacobs, Walter Darnell. See OBOE, PETER.

Jacobse, Muus. Pseudonym of Klaas Hanzen (1909–), Dutch poet, essayist, and linguist.

Jacobsson, P. See OLDFELD, PETER.

Jacopo, Giovanni Battista di. See ROSSO, IL.

Jacot, B. L. Pseudonym of Bernard Louis Jacot de Boinod (1898–), English writer.

Jacot de Boinod, Bernard Louis. See JACOT, B. L.

Jacquot, Charles Jean Baptiste. See MIRECOURT, EUGÈNE DE.

Jadvigin, Anton. See LEVICKIJ, ANTON.

Jaffe, Gabriel. See POOLE, VIVIAN.

Jäger, Johann. See CROTUS RUBIANUS.

Jalal al-Din Muhammad Rumi. See MOWLAVI.

James, Andrew. See KIRKUP, JAMES.

James, Brian. See THOMAS, GORDON.

James, David Burnett Stephen. See VIZARD, STEPHEN.

James, Dynely. Joint pseudonym of William James Carter Mayne (1928–) and R. D. Caesar, English writers of children's books.

James, Edwin. Pseudonym of James E. Gunn (1923–), American author.

James, Florence Alice Price. See WARDEN, FLORENCE.

James, Franklin. Pseudonym of Robert Godley (1908–), mystery writer.

James, Godfrey Warden. See BROOME, ADAM.

James, Josephine. See STERNE, EMMA GELDERS.

James, Judith. See JENNINGS, LESLIE NELSON.

James, Robert. Pseudonym of Iris Heitner, contemporary mystery writer.

James, Ronald. Pseudonym of James Preston (1913–), Australian-English writer.

James, T. F. See FLEMING, THOMAS JAMES.

James, W. I. See BAXTER, YOUNG, and OLD CAP COLLIER.

Janifer, Laurence Mark (1933–   ). American writer, whose pseudonyms are *Andrew Blake, Larry M. Harris,* and, with Randall Garrett, *Mark Phillips.*

Janner, Greville Ewan. See MITCHELL, EWAN.

Jannsen, Lydia Emilie Florentine. See KOIDULA.

Jans, Emerson. See BIXBY, JEROME LEWIS.

Janson, Hank. See HOBSON, HARRY.

Jardin, Rex. See BURKHARDT, EVE, and BURKHARDT, ROBERT FERDI-NAND.

Järnefelt, Arvid. See KANILA, HILJA.

Jarrett, Cora Hardy. See KEENE, FARADAY.

Jarrett, Jeannette. Pseudonym of Lois Jeannette Fisher (1909–   ), American writer.

Jasienski, Bruno. Pseudonym of Bruno Zyskind (1901–1937), Polish poet and writer.

Jasmin, Jacques. Pseudonym of Jacques Boe (1798–1864), Gascon wigmaker and poet, last of the troubadours. He was also known as *The Barber Poet* and *Jasmin d'Agen.*

Jasmin d'Agen. See JASMIN, JACQUES.

Jasnorzewska, Maria. See PAWLIKOWSKA.

Jastrun, Mieczysław. Pseudonym of Mieczysław Agalstein (1903–   ), Polish poet.

Jaurand, Yvonne. See DUPLESSIS, YVES.

Javor, J. Pseudonym of Bartos Vlcek (1897–1926), Czech poet and novelist.

Javorov, Peju K. Pseudonym of Peju Kracholov (1877–1914), Bulgarian poet.

Jay, Charlotte. Pseudonym of Geraldine Jay (1919–   ), mystery writer.

Jay, Geraldine. See JAY, CHARLOTTE.

Jay, Simon. Pseudonym of Colin James Alexander (1920–   ), English writer.

Jaynes, Clare. Joint pseudonym of Jane Rothschild Mayer (1903–   ) and Clara Spiegel, American writers.

Jeake, Samuel, Jr. Pseudonym of Conrad Potter Aiken (1915–   ), Swedish scholar.

Jeames. See THACKERAY, WILLIAM MAKEPEACE.

Jean II, Lord of Nesle. See BLONDEL DE NESLE.

Jean Le Court. See BRISEBARRE, JEAN.
Jeanneret, Charles Édouard. See LE CORBUSIER.
Jean Paul. Pseudonym of Johann Paul Friedrich Richter (1763–1825), German writer.
Jebavý, Václav. See BŘEZINA, OTAKAR.
Jeffery, Grant. See TURNER, PETER PAUL.
Jeffries, Graham Montague (1900–   ). Mystery writer, whose pseudonyms are *Peter Bourne, Bruce Graeme, David Graeme,* and *Roderic Graeme.*
Jege. Pseudonym of Ladislav Nadasi (1866–1940), Slovak novelist.
Jelakowitch, I. van. See HEIJERMANS, HERMAN.
Jélanov. Pseudonym of Jus Kozak (1892–   ), Slovak writer.
Jenkins, William Fitzgerald. See LEINSTER, MURRAY.
Jenks, George Charles. See CARTER, NICK.
Jenneval. Pseudonym of Hippolyte Louis Alexandre Dechet (1801–1830), French comedian and poet.
Jennings, John E., Jr. (1906–   ). American writer, whose pseudonyms are *Bates Baldwin* and *Joel Williams.*
Jennings, Leslie Nelson (1890–   ). American writer, whose pseudonyms are *A. B. Brooke, Cyril Carfagne, James McGregor Cartwright, Baroness Julie Desplaines, Judith James,* and *Paul Rayson.*
Jennings, S. M. Pseudonym of Jerome Sydney Meyer (1895–   ), American writer.
Jennison, C. S. Pseudonym of Kaye Starbird (1916–   ), American writer.
Jensen, Pauline Marie. See LONG, ANN MARIE.
Jerome, Owen Fox. See FRIEND, OSCAR JEROME.
Jesse, Michael. Pseudonym of Michael Baldwin (1930–   ), English writer.
Jessey, Cornelia. Pseudonym of Cornelia Silver Sussman (1914–   ), American writer.
Jessup, Frances. Pseudonym of Margaret Frances Jessup Van Briggle (1917–   ), American writer.
Jesus, Mother Raymond de. Pseudonym of Sister Raymond de Jesus Dion (1918–   ), American author.
Jeż, Teodor Tomasz. Pseudonym of Zygmunt Fortunat Miłkowski (1824–1915), Polish novelist.

Jippensha Ikku. Pseudonym of Shigeta Sodakazu Ichijiro (1765–1831), Japanese humorist, also known as *Shigeta Ichijiro.*

Jiskogo. See HARRINGTON, MARK RAYMOND.

Jocelin. See GUIOT DE DIJON.

Jofriet, Jan Gerardus. See BRABANDER, GERARD DEN.

Johann, King of Saxony. See PHILALETHES.

Johansson, Johan Fridolf (1897–). Swedish writer, whose original name was Jan Fridegard.

John, Elizabeth Beaman. See ST. JOHN, BETH.

John, Eugenie. See MARLITT, EUGENIE.

Johns, Avery. See COUSINS, MARGARET.

Johns, Foster. See SELDES, GILBERT VIVIAN.

Johns, Kenneth. See BLUMER, HENRY KENNETH.

Johnson, A. See JOHNSON, ANNABEL JONES.

Johnson, A. E. See JOHNSON, ANNABEL JONES.

Johnson, Annabel Jones (1921–). American writer, whose pseudonyms are *A. Johnson* and, with her husband, Edgar Raymond Johnson (1912–), *A. E. Johnson.*

Johnson, Charles S. See EDWARDS, WILLIAM BENNETT.

Johnson, Christopher. See MCINTOSH, LOUIS.

Johnson, Crockett. Pseudonym of David Murray Leisk (1906–), American writer.

Johnson, Edgar Raymond. See JOHNSON, ANNABEL JONES.

Johnson, Marion Georgina Wikeley. See MASSON, GEORGINA.

Johnson, Pamela Hansford. See LOMBARD, NAP.

Johnson, Ronald. See CHAMBERLAIN, THEODORE.

Johnson, W. Bolingbroke. Pseudonym of Morris Bishop (1913–), American writer and professor of Romance languages.

Johnson, William. See CORY, WILLIAM.

Johnston, Anna. See CARBERY, EITHNE.

Johnston, Denis William. See TOCHER, E. W.

Johnstone, Charles. See ONCIROPOLOS.

Jolyot, Prosper. See CRÉBILLON.

Jonathan. Pseudonym of Johannes Petrus Hasebroek (1812–1896), Dutch essayist and poet.

Jones, Adrienne. Contemporary mystery writer, whose pseudonyms, with Doris Meek, are *Mason Gregory* and *Gregory Mason.*

Jones, Arthur Llewellyn. See MACHEN, ARTHUR.

Jones, Dorothy Holder. See JONES, DUANE.

Jones, Duane. Pseudonym of Dorothy Holder Jones (1925–   ), American writer.

Jones, Felix Edward Aylmer. See AYLMER, FELIX.

Jones, Helen Hickley. See HINCKLEY, HELEN.

Jones, Lucy M. See LUX.

Jones, Pat. Pseudonym of Virgil Carrington Jones (1906–   ), American writer and Civil War specialist.

Jones, Richard. See HOOK, THEODORE EDWARD.

Jones, Robert Ambrose. See EMRYS AP IWAN.

Jones, Susan Carleton. See CARLETON, S.

Jones, Virgil Carrington. See JONES, PAT.

Jones, Capt. Wilbur. See EDWARDS, WILLIAM BENNETT.

Jones, Zenith. See BROWN, ZENITH.

Jonkov, Nikola. See VAPCAROV, NIKOLA.

Jónsson, Hjálmar (1796–1875). Icelandic poet, also known as *Bólu-Hjálmar.*

Jordan, Gail. See DERN, PEGGY GADDIS.

Jorgensen, Mary Venn. See ADRIAN, MARY.

Joscelyn, Archie L. (1899–   ). American writer of popular Westerns whose pseudonyms are *A. A. Archer, Al Cody, Tex Holt, Evelyn McKenna,* and *Lynn Westland.*3

Joseph, James Herz. See ADAMS, LOWELL.

Joseph, Jonathan. Pseudonym of Irving Fineman (1893–   ), American writer.

Joséphin. Pseudonym of Joseph-Marie Soulary (1815–1891), French poet.

Josephs, Ray. See RAPHAEL, JAY.

Josiah Allen's Wife. Pseudonym of Marietta Holley (1836–1926), American humorist.

Joske, Neville Goyder. See NEVILLE, MARGOT.

Joslin, Sesyle. See HINE, SESYLE JOSLIN.

Jotov, Dimităr Ivanov (1878–1949). Bulgarian writer whose pseudonyms are *Elín-Pelín* and *Elin Pelin.* Also known as *Dimitâr Ivanov.*

Jouhandeau, Marcel. Pseudonym of Marcel Provence (1888–   ), French novelist.

Jovanović, Jovan. See ZMAJ.

Jubran Khalil Jubran. See GIBRAN, KAHLIL.

Judaeus, Leo. See ABARBANEL, JUDAH LEÓN.

Judd, Cyril. See MERRIL, JUDITH.

Judd, Frances K. Collective pseudonym for the "Kay Tracey Mystery Stories" series. See STRATEMEYER, EDWARD L.

Judd, Frederick Charles (1914–   ). English writer, whose pseudonyms are *John Courtney, A. Lester-Rands,* and *G. R. Miller.*

Judd, Margaret Haddican. See GARRETT, TRUMAN.

Judson, Edward Zane Carroll. See BUNTLINE, NED.

Judy, Will. See PORT, WYMAR.

June, Jennie. Pseudonym of Jane Croly (1829–1901), English-American writer and editor.

Jung, Heinrich. See JUNG-STILLING, JOHANN HEINRICH.

Jungle Doctor. Pseudonym of Paul Hamilton Hume White (1910–   ), Australian writer.

Jung-Stilling, Johann Heinrich (1740–1817). German writer, whose original name was Heinrich Jung. He was also known as *Heinrich Stilling.*

Jupéon (or **Ju Péon**). Gallicized name of Hsü Pei-hung (1895–1953), Chinese painter.

Jurij, Klen. Pseudonym of Oswald Burghardt (1891–1947), Ukrainian poet.

Justus of Ghent. See GENT, JOOS VAN.

"K"

K.R. Pseudonym of Grand Duke Constantine Romanov (1858–1915), Russian poet.

Kacev, Romain. See GARY, ROMAIN.

Kadłubec, Wincenty (c1160–1223). Polish-Latin chronicler, also known as *Cadlubco* and *Magister Vincentius.*

Kaga no Chiyo. See FUKUZOYA CHIYO.

Kagawa Kageshige (1768–1843). Japanese poet and scholar, whose original name was Hayashi Suminori. He was less correctly known as *Kagawa Kageki.*

Kagey, Rudolf H. S. See STEEL, KURT.

Kaibara Atsunobu. See KAIBARA EKIKEN.

Kaibara Ekiken. Pseudonym of Kaibara Atsunobu (1630–1754), Japanese essayist.

Kako. See HOKUSAI.

Kalin, Jeremìja. Pseudonym of Tine Debeljak (1903–   ), Slovak poet.

Kalmus, Ain. Pseudonym of Ewald Mand (1906–   ), Estonian-American writer.

Kamban, Gudmundur. Pseudonym of Jansson Hallgrimson (1888–1945), Icelandic playwright and writer.

Kambu, Joseph. Pseudonym of Joseph Godson Amamoo (1931–   ), African-English writer.

Kampf, Harold. See KAYE, HAROLD B.

Kanagaki Robin. Pseudonym of Nozaki Bunyo (1829–1894), Japanese novelist.

Kan'ami Kiyotsugo. Pseudonym of Yusaki Saburo Kiyotsugo (1333–1384), Japanese writer and actor of No plays.

Kane, Frank. See BOYD, FRANK.

Kangaku. See SOAMI.

Kanila, Hilja. Pseudonym of Arvid Järnefelt (1861–1932), Finnish novelist and playwright.

Kanze Motokiyo. See SE'AMI MOTOKIYO.

Kaplan, Anne Bernays. See BERNAYS, ANNE.

Kara, Giorg. Pseudonym of Gustav Brühl (1826–1903), German-American poet and physician.

Karai Hachiemon. See KARAI SENRYU.

Karai Senryu. Pseudonym of Karai Hachiemon (1718–1790), Japanese humorous poet.

Karasek, Josef Jiri Antonin. See KARASEK ZE LVOVIC, JIRI.

Karasek ze Lvovic, Jiri. Pseudonym of Josef Jiri Antonin Karasek (1871–1954), Czech writer.

Karig, Walter. See PATRICK, KEATS.

Kark, Nina Mary. See BAWDEN, NINA.

Karol, K. S. Pseudonym of Karol Kewes (1924–   ), Polish-French writer.

Karonin. Pseudonym of Nikolay E. Petropavlovsky (1857–1892), Russian writer.

Karpenko-Karyj, Ivan. Pseudonym of Ivan Karpovich Tobilevich (1845–1907), Ukrainian playwright.

Katerla, Jozef. See ZEROMSKI, STEFAN.

Kateyev, Evgeny. See PETROV, EVGENY PETROVICH.

Katib Celebi, Mustafa (1608–1657). Turkish writer and historian, also called *Hadji Khalifa.*

Katsunori Tamai. See HINO, ASHIHEI.

Katz, Menke. See HIAT, ELCHIK.

Katznelson, Yehuda Loeb. See BUKKI BEN YOGLI.

Kauffman, Ruth Hammitt. See WRIGHT, RUTH.

Kaufman, Louis. See KELLER, DAN.

Kaufman, Sue. Pseudonym of Sue Kaufman Barondess (1926–), American writer.

Kautilya. Hindu writer, usually identified with Chanakya, the minister of Magadha.

Kavan, Josef. See NOR, A. C.

Kavérin, Venyamin. Pseudonym of Venyamin Alexandrovich Zillberg (1902–), Soviet Russian writer.

Kawakami Akira. See KAWAKAMI BIZAN.

Kawakami Bizan. Pseudonym of Kawakami Akira (1869–1908), Japanese novelist.

Kawatake Mokuama. See MOKUAMI.

Kay, Ernest (1915–). English journalist and writer, whose pseudonyms are *George Ludlow* and *Alan Random.*

Kay, George. See LAMBERT, ERIC.

Kay, Helen. Pseudonym of Helen Colodny Goldfrank (1912–), American writer.

Kaye, Barbara. Pseudonym of Barbara K. Muir (1909–), English writer.

Kaye, Harold B. Pseudonym of Harold Kampf (1916–), mystery writer.

Kayenbergh, Marie Émile Albert. See GIRAUD, ALBERT.

Kayser, Ronal. See CLARK, DALE.

Keating, Lawrence A. (1903–). American free-lance writer, whose pseudonyms are *John Keith Bassett* and *H. C. Thomas.*

Keck, Maud. See ORBISON, KECK.

Keegan, Mary Heathcott (1914–). English free-lance writer and novelist, whose pseudonyms are *Mary Heathcott* and *Mary Raymond.*

Keel, Laura. Pseudonym of Carol Berge (1928–), American writer.

Keelivine, Christopher. Occasional pseudonym of Andrew Picken (1788–1833), Scottish novelist.

Keene, Carolyn. Pseudonym of Harriet Adams, contemporary American writer.

Keene, Carolyn. See STRATEMEYER, EDWARD L.

Keene, Faraday. Pseudonym of Cora Hardy Jarrett (1877–   ), mystery writer.

Keevil, Henry John (1914–   ). English writer, whose pseudonyms are *Clay Allison, Bill Bonney, Wes Hardin, Frank McLowery,* and *Johnny Ringo.*

Keichu. Pseudonym of Shimokawa Kushin (1640–1701), Japanese writer.

Keir, Christine. See POPESCU, CHRISTINE.

Keith, Carlton. Pseudonym of Keith Robertson (1914–   ), American free-lance writer.

Keith, David. See STEEGMÜLLER, FRANCIS.

Keith, Donald. See MONROE, KEITH.

Keith, J. Kilmeny. See MALLESON, LUCY BEATRICE.

Kell, Joseph. See BURGESS, ANTHONY.

Keller, Dan. Pseudonym of Louis Kaufman (1916–   ), mystery writer.

Kelley, Martha Mott. See WEBB, RICHARD WILSON.

Kelliher, Dan T. See SECRIST, KELLIHER.

Kellner, Esther. See COOPER, ESTHER.

Kellogg, Jean. See JACKSON, SALLY.

Kellow, Kathleen. See HIBBERT, ELEANOR BURFORD.

Kelsey, Joan Marshall. See GRANT, JOAN.

Kemp, Bernard. Pseudonym of Bernard Frans Van Vlierden (1926–   ), Dutch novelist, essayist, and critic.

Kendall, Lace. See STOUTENBURG, ADRIEN PEARL.

Kendall, Willmore. See MONK, ALAN.

Kendrake, Carleton. See GARDNER, ERLE STANLEY.

Kendrick, Baynard Hardwick. See HAYWARD, RICHARD.

Kendricks, James. See FOX, GARDNER FRANCIS.

Kennedy, Gerald Hamilton. See KISH, G. HOBAB.

Kennedy, Howard. See WOOLFOLK, JOSIAH PITTS.

Kennedy, John Pendleton. See LITTLETON, MARK.

Kennedy, Joseph. See KENNEDY, X. J.

Kennedy, Milward. See BURGE, MILWARD RODON KENNEDY.

Kenneth, Mr. See MARLOWE, KENNETH.

Kennedy, Robert Milward. See BURGE, MILWARD RODON KENNEDY.

Kennedy, X. J. Pseudonym of Joseph Kennedy (1929–   ), American poet and writer.

Kennington, Gilbert Alan. See GRANT, ALAN.

Kenny, Charles J. See GARDNER, ERLE STANLEY.
Kenny, Ellsworth Newcomb. See NEWCOMB, ELLSWORTH.
Kenny, Kathryn. See STACK, NICOLETE.
Kent, Alexander. Pseudonym of Kenneth Methold (1931–   ), English writer.
Kent, David. Pseudonym of Hoffman Birney (1891–   ), mystery writer.
Kent, Louise Andrews. See TEMPEST, THERESA.
Kent, Philip. See BLUMER, HENRY KENNETH.
Kent, Rockwell. See HOGARTH, JR.
Kent, Willis. Pseudonym of Wilson Collison (1893–1941), mystery writer.
Keogh, Lilian Gilmore. See PATRICK, LILIAN.
Kerekes, Tibor. See ROTARIUS.
Kerhouel, Gaétan. Pseudonym of Paul Vigné (1859–1943), French writer and politician, also known as *Vigné d'Octon.*
Kern, E. R. See KERNER, FRED.
Kerner, Fred (1921–   ). Canadian-American writer, whose pseudonyms are *Frohm Fredricks, E. R. Kern,* and *Frederick Kerr.*
Kerniskey, Ivan. See IKER.
Kerr, Ben. See ARD, WILLIAM THOMAS.
Kerr, Frederick. See KERNER, FRED.
Kerr, Norman D. Pseudonym of Sam Dixon Sieber (1931–   ), American writer.
Kerr, Orpheus C. Pseudonym of Robert Henry Newell (1836–1901), American journalist and humorist.
Kerry, Lois. See CARDOZO, LOIS STEINMETZ.
Kerverzhiou. Pseudonym of Gwilherm Bertou (1908–1951), Breton poet.
Kessel, Lipmann. See PAUL, DANIEL.
Kessler, Jascha. See ELY, FREDERICK.
Ketchum, Philip. See SAUNDERS, CARL McK.
Kettenfeier, Peter. See ROSEGGER, PETER.
Keverne, Richard. Pseudonym of Clifford James Wheeler Hosken (1882–   ), mystery writer.
Kewes, Karol. See KAROL, K. S.
Keynes, Helen Mary. See HUNTER, CLEMENTINE.

Keystone, Oliver. Pseudonym of James H. Mantinband, contemporary mystery writer.

Khai-Hung. Pseudonym of Tran Khanh-Giu (1896–1947), Vietnamese novelist.

Khalifa, Hadji. See KATIB CELEBI, MUSTAFA.

Khare, Narayan Bhaskar. See BAPU.

Khomyakov, Aleksyei Stepanovich. See IGNOTUS.

Kierkegaard, Søren Aabye (1813–1855). Danish philosopher and theologian, whose pseudonyms are *Anti-Climacus, Hilarius Bog-binder, Johannes Climacus, Victor Eremita,* and *Johannes de Si-lentio.*

Kieschner, Sidney. See KINGSLEY, SIDNEY.

Kikaku. Pseudonym of Takemoto (later Takarai or Enomoto) Yasoya (1661–1707), Japanese haiku poet.

Kikuchi Hiroshi. See KIKUCHI KAN.

Kikuchi Hisanori. See SHIKITEI SAMBA.

Kikuchi Kan (1888–1948). Japanese author, whose real name is Kikuchi Hiroshi.

Kikuchi Taisuke. See SHIKITEI SAMBA.

Kilbracken, John Raymond Godley. See GODLEY, JOHN.

Kim, Tomás. Pseudonym of Joaquim Fernandes Tomás Monteiro e Grilo (1915–   ), Portuguese poet and essayist.

Kinau, Johann. See FOCK, GORCH.

Kincaid, Alan. See RIKHOFF, JAMES C.

King, Charles Daly. See COURTNEY, ROBERT.

King, Clifford. See FRY, PETE.

King, Francis Henry. See CAULDWELL, FRANK.

King, Frank. See CONRAD, CLIVE.

King, John. See MCKEAG, ERNEST L.

King, Patricia. See WILDE, KATHEY.

King, Paul. Pseudonym of Philip Drackett (1922–   ), English writer.

King, Raymond Sherwood. See KING, SHERRY.

King, Sherry. Pseudonym of Raymond Sherwood King (1904–   ), mystery writer.

King-Hall, William Stephen Richard. See ETIENNE.

King of the Black Isles. Pseudonym of John Urban Nicolson (1885–   ), mystery writer.

Kingsley, Anna. See HANSHEW, MARY E., and HANSHEW, THOMAS W.

Kingsley, Charlotte May. See HANSHEW, THOMAS W.

Kingsley, Mary St. Leger. See MALET, LUCAS.

Kingsley, Robert. See CLARKE, JOHN.

Kingsley, Sidney. Pseudonym of Sidney Kieschner (1906–   ), British-American playwright.

Kinkaid, Matt. See ADAMS, CLIFTON.

Kinney, Thomas. Pseudonym of Curtis Thomas, contemporary mystery writer.

Ki no Kaion. Pseudonym of E'nami Kiemon (1663–1742), Japanese dramatist.

Kinross, Patrick Lord. See BALFOUR, PATRICK.

Kinsburn, Emart. See HANKINS, ARTHUR PRESTON.

Kirby, Jean. See ROBINSON, CHAILLE.

Kirk, Ellen Warner Olney. See HAYES, HENRY.

Kirk, Laurence. Pseudonym of Eric Andrew Simson (1895–   ), mystery writer.

Kirk, Richard. See CHURCH, JEFFREY.

Kirke, Edmund. Pseudonym of James Roberts Gilmore (1822–1903), American businessman, Civil War mediator, and writer.

Kirkup, James (1927–   ). English poet and writer, whose pseudonyms are *James Falconer, Andrew James,* and *Ivy B. Summerforest.*

Kirouac, Joseph Louis Conrad. See MARIE-VICTORIN, FRÈRE.

Kirtland, G. B. See HINE, SESYLE JOSLIN.

Kirwan, Molly Morrow. See MORROW, CHARLOTTE.

Kisanji. Pseudonym of Hirazawa Tsunetomi (1735–1813), Japanese writer and poet, also called *Meiseido Kisanji.*

Kish, G. Hobab. Pseudonym of Gerald Hamilton Kennedy (1907–   ), American scholar.

Kitamura Kigin. Pseudonym of Kitamura Kyunosuke (1625–1705), Japanese writer.

Kitamura Kyunosuke. See KITAMURA KIGIN.

Kitchin, Frederick Harcourt. See COPPLESTONE, BENNET.

Kite, Larry. See SCHNECK, STEPHEN.

Kivi, Alexis. Pseudonym of Alexis Stenvall (1834–1872), Finnish poet and writer.

Klabund. Pseudonym of Alfred Henschke (1890–1928), German poet.

Klainikite, Anne. Pseudonym of Betsy Holland Gehman (1932–), American free-lance writer.

Klaue, Lola Shelton. See SHELTON, LOLA.

Klein, Grace. See COOPER-KLEIN, NINA.

Kleinjan. Pseudonym of Jan R. L. Van Bruggen (1895–1948), South African writer.

Klichka, Benjamin. Pseudonym of Benjamin Fragner (1897–1943), Czech writer.

Klikspaan. Pseudonym of Johannes Kneppelhout (1814–1885), Dutch essayist.

Klingsor, Tristan. Pseudonym of Léon Leclère (1874–1966), French writer, painter, and musician.

Klonowic, Sebastian. See ACERNUS.

Kloos, Willem Johan Theodoor (1859–1938). Dutch poet, critic, and magazine editor, whose pseudonyms are *G.N.*, *Guido*, and *Sebastiaan*, *Sr.*

Klychkov, Sergey. Pseudonym of Sergey Antonovich Leshenkov (1889– 1930?), Soviet novelist.

Kneppelhout, Johannes. See KLIKSPAAN.

Knifesmith. Pseudonym of Ivor Cutler (1923–), English writer.

Knight, Adam. See LARIAR, LAWRENCE.

Knight, David. See PRATHER, RICHARD SCOTT.

Knight, James. See SCHNECK, STEPHEN.

Knight, Kathleen Moore. See AMOS, ALAN.

Knight-Patterson, W. M. See KULSKI, WLADYSLAW WSZEBOR.

Knipe, Emilie Benson. See BENSON, THÉRÈSE.

Knipscheer, James M. W. Contemporary mystery writer, whose pseudonyms are *James M. Fox* and *Grant Holmes.*

Knish, Anne. See BYNNER, WITTER.

Knott, William Cecil, Jr. See CAROL, BILL J.

Knotts, Raymond. See VOLK, GORDON.

Knox, Bill. See KNOX, WILLIAM.

Knox, Edmund George Valpy. See EVOE.

Knox, William (1928–). Scottish writer, whose pseudonyms are *Bill Knox* and *Robert MacLeod.*

Kobayashi Issa. Pseudonym of Kobayashi Nobuyuki (1763–1828), Japanese haiku poet.

Kobayashi Nobuyuki. See KOBAYASHI ISSA.

Kochkurov, Nikolay Ivanovich. See VESËLY, A.

Koidula. Pseudonym of Lydia Emilie Florentine Jannsen (1843–1886), Estonian poet.

Koikawa Harumachi. Pseudonym of Kurahashi Kiwame (1744–1789), Japanese novelist, also known as *Kurahashi Juhei.*

Kojuharov, Tudor (1894–1945). Bulgarian writer and journalist, whose pseudonyms are *Fedya Chorny* and *Captain Kopeykin.*

Kokhanovskaya. Pseudonym of Nadezhda Stephanovna Sockhanskaya (1825–1884), Russian writer.

Komenský, Jan Amos. See COMENIUS, JOHANNES AMOS.

Kondratowicz, Ludwik Władysław. See SYROKOMLA, WŁADYSŁAW.

Konishi Iemon. See KONISHI RAIZAN.

Konishi Raizan. Pseudonym of Konishi Iemon (1654–1716), Japanese haiku poet.

Koop, Katherine C. See LAMANCUSA, KATHERINE C.

Kopeykin, Captain. See KOJOHAROV, TUDOR.

Kornbluth, C. M. See MERRIL, JUDITH.

Korwin-Piotrowska, Gabriela (1860–1921). Polish author, whose pseudonyms are *Jozef Maskoff* and *Gabriela Zapolska.*

Korzeniowski, Theodor Józef Konrad. See CONRAD, JOSEPH.

Kosac, Ol'ha. See PCILKA, OLENA.

Kosinski, Jerzy. See NOVAK, JOSEPH.

Koskenniemi, V. A. Pseudonym of V. A. Forsnas (1885–1962), Finnish writer.

Kosma, Presbyter. 10th-century Belgian chronicler, also known as *St. Cosmas* (or *Kozma*).

Kossak, Zofia. See SZCZUCKA.

Köstlin, Christian Reinhold. See REINHOLD, C.

Kostrowitski, Wilhelm Apollinaris de. See APOLLINAIRE, GUILLAUME.

Kosugi Tamezo. See KOSUGI TENGAL.

Kosugi Tengal. Pseudonym of Kosugi Tamezo (1865–   ), Japanese novelist.

Kotta, Leo F. See FLAKE, OTTO.

Kouts, Hertha Pretorius. See PRETORIUS, HERTHA.

Kouyoumdjian, Dikron. See ARLEN, MICHAEL.

Kovalev, Mikhail Alexandrovich. See IVNEV, RYURIK.

Kozak, Jus. See JÉLANOV.

Kozma, Saint. See KOSMA, PRESBYTER.

Kracholov, Peju. See JAVOROV, PEJU K.

Kraenzel, Margaret. See BLUE, WALLACE.

Kramish, Arnold. See PAINE, J. LINCOLN.

Krapiva, Kandrat. Pseudonym of Kandrat Atrachovich (1896–), White Russian poet and playwright.

Krapp, R. M. Pseudonym of Robert Martin Adams (1915–), American scholar.

Krasko, Ivan. Pseudonym of Ján Botto (1876–), Slovak poet.

Krasney, Samuel A. See CURZON, SAM.

Krasnohorska, Eliska. Pseudonym of Eliska Pechova (1847–1926), Czech poet and publicist.

Kraszewski, Józef Ignacy. See BOLESLAWITA.

Krause, Ernst Ludwig. See CARUS, STERNE.

Krautter, Elisa Bialk. See BIALK, ELISA.

Kravchenko, Uliana. Pseudonym of Julia Shnaider (1860–1947), Ukrainian poet.

Kravchinsky, Sergey Mikhailovich. See STEPNYAK, SERGEY MIK-HAILOVICH.

Kremnitz, Mite (or Marie) (1852–1916). German writer, whose pseudonyms are *George Allan* and, with Queen Elizabeth of Rumania, *Dito und Idem.*

Krentel, Mildred White. See MIGGY, MRS.

Krislov, Alexander. Pseudonym of Leigh Howard, contemporary mystery writer.

Kristmundsson, Adalsteinn. See STEINARP, STEINN.

Krochmal, Nahman (1785–1840). Galician Jewish philosopher, also known as *Renaq.*

Krogzemju, Mikus. See AUSEKLIS.

Kropotkin, Piotr Alexeyevich. See BORODIN, LEVASIOV.

Krull, Felix. See WHITE, JAMES DILLON.

Krymov, Yuri. Pseudonym of Yuri Solomonovich Beklemishev (1908–1941), Russian writer.

K'uan-yu Lu. Pseudonym of Charles Luk (1898–), Chinese writer.

Kuehnelt-Leddihn, Erik Ritter von (1909–). Austrian scholar, whose pseudonyms are *Francis Stuart Campbell, Chester F. O'Leary,* and *Tomislav Vitezovic.*

Kuhar, Louro. See VORANC, PREZIHOV.

Kuhhorn, Martin. See ARETIUS FELINUS.

Kühn, Christoffel Hermanus. See MIKRO.

Kühne, August. See DEWALL, JOHANNES VAN.

Kuitenbrouwer, Louis Maria Albertus. See KUYLE, ALBERT.

Kukuchin, Martin. Pseudonym of Matej Bencur (1860–1928), Slovak novelist.

Kulk, Willem van der. Occasional pseudonym of Willem van Iependaal (1891–), Dutch poet and writer.

Kulmbach, Hans von (1476?–1522). German painter, whose real name was Hans Süss.

Kulski, Władysław Wszebor (1903–). Polish scholar, whose pseudonyms are *W. W. Coole, W. M. Knight-Patterson,* and *Politicus.*

Kumazawa Banzan. See KUMAZAWA HAKKEI.

Kumazawa Hakkei (1619–1691). Japanese philosopher whose pseudonyms are *Kumazawa Banzan* and *Kumazawa Ryokai.*

Kumazawa Ryokai. See KUMAZAWA HAKKEI.

Kummer, Frederic Arnold. See FREDERICKS, ARNOLD.

Kuncewicz, Maria S. See KUNCEWICZOWA, MARIA.

Kuncewiczowa, Maria. Pseudonym of Maria S. Kuncewicz (1899–), Polish-American author.

Kung. See FA-HSIEN.

Kunikida Doppo. Pseudonym of Kunikida Tetsuo (1871–1908), Japanese writer.

Kunikida Tetsuo. See KUNIKIDA DOPPO.

Kupala, Janka. Pseudonym of Ivan Daminikavich Lucevich (1882–1942), White Russian poet.

Kupper, C. E. M. See VAN DOESBURG, THEO.

Kurahashi Juhei. See KOIKAWA HARUMACHI.

Kurahashi Kiwame. See KOIKAWA HARUMACHI.

Kurata Hyakuzo (1891–1943). Japanese dramatist, essayist, and philosopher, more correctly called *Kurata Momozo.*

Kurata Momozo. See KURATA HYAKUZO.

Kurnitz, Harry. See PAGE, MARCO.

Kurowski, Eugeniusz. See DOBRACZYNSKI, JAN.

Kursh, Charlotte Olmsted. See OLMSTED, CHARLOTTE.

Kuttner, Henry (1914–1958). American mystery writer, whose pseudonyms are *Will Garth, Lewis Padgett,* and *Jack Vance.*

Kuyle, Albert. Pseudonym of Louis Maria Albertus Kuitenbrouwer (1904–1958), Dutch writer.

Kvitka, Grigori Petrovich. See OSNOVYANENKO.
Kvitka, Laryssa Petrovna. See UKRAINKA, LESYA.
Kyd, Thomas. Pseudonym of Alfred Bennett Harbage (1901–   ),
American scholar.
Kyle, Elisabeth. See DUNLOP, AGNES M. R.
Kyokutei Bakin. See BAKIN.
Kyorai. Pseudonym of Mukai Kanetoki (1651–1704), Japanese haiku
poet.

"L"

Laar, Pieter van. See BAMBOCCIO, IL.
Laer, Pieter van. See BAMBOCCIO, IL.
Labaigt, Laurent. See RAMEAU, JEAN.
Labberton, Johan Hendrik. See VAN AMEIDE, TH.
Labé, Louise. See BELLE CORDIÈRE, LA.
Labeo. See NOTKER.
Labronio, G. Pseudonym of Giovanni Marradi (1852–1922), Italian poet.
Labrunie, Gérard. See NERVAL, GÉRARD DE.
La Coste, Guy Robert. See BERTON, GUY.
Lacroix, Paul (1806–1884). French scholar and novelist, whose pseudo-
nyms are *Bibliophile Jacob, Pierre Dufour,* and *P. L. Jacob, Biblio-
phile.*
Lacroix, Ramon. See MCKEAG, ERNEST L.
Lady Geralda. See BRONTË, ANNE.
Lady of Quality, A. Pseudonym of Enid Bagnold (1889–   ), English
author.
Lady Packer. Pseudonym of Joy Packer (1905–   ), South African
writer.
La Fayette, Mme. de. See SEGRAIS.
Laing, Patrick. See LONG, AMELIA REYNOLDS.
Laird, Dorothy. Pseudonym of Dorothy Stevenson Laird Carr (1912–
    ), Scottish-English free-lance writer.
Lajolo, Davide. See ULISSE.
Lake, Joe Barry. See BARRY, JOE.
Laklan, Carli. See LAUGHLIN, VIRGINIA CARLI.
LaMancusa, Katherine C. Pseudonym of Katherine C. Koop (1923–
    ), American writer.
Lamb, Charles. See ELIA.
Lamber, Juliette. See ADAM, JULIETTE.

Lambert, Christine. See ALBRAND, MARTHA.

Lambert, Eric (1918–   ). English writer, whose pseudonyms are *Frank Brennand* and *George Kay.*

Lambert, Leslie Harrison. See ALAN, A. J.

Lambro. Pseudonym of Andrzej Niemojewski (1864–1921), Polish author.

Lamburn, John Battersby Crompton. See CROMPTON, JOHN.

Lamburn, Richmal Crompton. See CROMPTON, RICHMAL.

La Messine. See ADAM, JULIETTE.

Lampman, Evelyn Sibley. See BRONSON, LYNN.

Lancaster, G. B. Pseudonym of Edith J. Lyttleton (1873–1945), New Zealand writer.

Lancaster, William. See WARREN, JOHN BYRNE LEICESTER, 3RD BARON DE TABLEY.

Land, Rosina. See HASTINGS, PHYLLIS DORA HODGE.

Landau, Mark Alexandrovitch. See ALDANOV, MARK.

Landels, D. H. Pseudonym of Donald Landels Henderson (1905–   ), American mystery writer.

Landers, Ann. Pseudonym of Esther Pauline Friedman Lederer (1918–   ), American journalist and advice columnist.

Landesmann, Heinrich. See LORM, HIERONYMUS.

Landi, Lorenzo di Pietro di Giovanni di. See VECCHIETTA, IL.

Landi, Stefano. Pseudonym of Stefano Pirandello (1895–   ), Italian writer.

Landon, Louise. See HAUCK, LOUISE.

Lane, Grant. See FISHER, STEPHEN GOULD.

Lane, Kenneth Westmacott. See WEST, KEITH.

Lane, Yoti. See MAYO, MARK.

Lang, Anthony. See VAHEY, JOHN GEORGE HASLETTE.

Lang, Frances. See MANTLE, WINIFRED LANGFORD.

Lang, Gregor. See BIRREN, FABER.

Lang, Martin. See BIRREN, FABER.

Lang, Theo. See PIPER, PETER.

Lange, Antoni. See NAPIERSKI.

Lange, Ernst Philipp Karl. See GALEN, PHILIPP.

Langebehn, Theo. See PIPER, PETER.

Langenhoven, Cornelis Jacob. See ELSPET.

Langford, Jane. See MANTLE, WINIFRED LANGFORD.

Langgässer, Elisabeth. Pseudonym of Elisabeth Hoffmann (1899–1950), German novelist and poet.

Langhveldt, Joris van. See MACROPEDIUS, GEORGIUS.

Lanne, William F. See LEOPOLD, NATHAN F.

Lansel, Peider. Pseudonym of P. L. Derin (1863–1943), Italian poet.

Lanza del Vasto, Joseph Jean. Pseudonym of Giuseppe Giovanni Lanza di Trabia-Branciforte (1901–), Italian-French writer.

Lao-She. Pseudonym of Shu Ch'ing-ch'un (1897–), Chinese writer.

Lapauze, Jeanne. See LESUEUR, DANIEL.

Lara. Pseudonym of George Chetwynd Griffith, contemporary mystery writer.

Larbalestier, Philip George. See SCOTT, ARCHER G.

Lardner, Ring. Pseudonym of Ringgold Wilmer Lardner (1885–1933), American short-story writer and journalist.

Lardner, Ringgold Wilmer. See LARDNER, RING.

Laredo, Johnny. See CAESAR, EUGENE LEE.

Lariar, Lawrence (1908–). American writer, illustrator, and political cartoonist, whose pseudonyms are *Adam Knight, Michael Lawrence,* and *Michael Stark.*

Larner, Jeremy. See GOUGE, ORSON.

Laroche, Rene. See MCKEAG, ERNEST L.

Larra, Mariano José de. See FIGARO.

Larsen, Alf. See INGELBREKT, ALF.

Larsen, Erling. See BRAND, PETER.

Lasca, Il. Cognomen of Antonio Francesco Grazzini (1503–1584), Florentine apothecary and writer.

Laschever, Barnett D. See BARNETT, L. DAVID.

Lateur, Frank. See STREUVELS, STIJN.

Lathrop, Francis. Pseudonym of Fritz Leiber (1910–), mystery writer.

Lathrop, Lorin Andrews (1858–). Mystery writer, whose pseudonyms are *Kenyon Gambier* and *Andrew Loring.*

Latimer, Rupert. Pseudonym of Algernon Victor Mills (1905–), mystery writer.

Latouche, John. See CRAWFURD, OSWALD JOHN FREDERICK.

Lattes, Franco. See FORTINI, FRANCO.

Laughlin, Virginia Carli (1907–). American writer, whose pseudonyms are *John Clarke* and *Carli Laklan.*

Laugier, R. See CUMBERLAND, MARTEN.

Laurana, Luciano (fl. 1468–1489). Italian architect of the Palazzo Ducale Urbino. He was also known as *Luciano di Martino da Laurana* (or *Lauranna, Dellaurana*) and *Luciano da Urbino.*

Laurence, John. Pseudonym of John Laurence Pritchard (1885–   ), mystery writer.

Laurence, Will. Pseudonym of Willard Laurence Smith (1927–   ), American writer.

Lauscher, Hermann. See HESSE, HERMANN.

Lauter. Pseudonym of André Jules Louis Chamson (1900–   ), French author.

Lautréamont, Le Comte de. Pseudonym of Isidore-Lucien Ducasse (1847–1870), French writer.

Laver, James. See REVEL, JACQUES.

Lawless, Anthony. See MACDONALD, PHILIP.

Lawlor, Patrick Anthony (1893–   ). New Zealand writer, whose pseudonyms are *Shibli Bagarag* and *Christopher Penn.*

Lawrence, Jack. Pseudonym of Lawrence Pennybaker Fitzgerald (1906–   ), American writer.

Lawrence, Michael. See LARIAR, LAWRENCE.

Lawrence, Richard A. See LEOPOLD, NATHAN F.

Lawrence, Thomas Edward. See ROSS, J. H.

Lawson, Horace Lowe (1900–   ). American author whose pseudonyms are *M. C. Lawson* and *John A. Summers.*

Lawson, M. C. See LAWSON, HORACE LOWE.

Lawton, Sherman P. (1908–   ). American writer, whose pseudonyms are *Jack Paxton* and *Dr. John Paxton.*

Lazzari. See BRAMANTE, DONATO.

Leacroft, Eric. Pseudonym of Eric Brett Young, contemporary mystery writer.

Leaderman, George. Pseudonym of Richard Blundell Robinson (1905–   ), mystery writer.

Learmont, Thomas. See ERCELDOUNE, THOMAS OF.

Léataud, Paul. See BOISSARD, MAURICE.

Lebenson, Abraham Dov. See ADAM.

Lebenson, Micha Joseph. See MICHAL.

Le Bouvier, Gilles. See BERRY, LE HÉRAUT.

Lebrija, Elio Antonio de. See NEBRIJA, ELIO ANTONIO DE.

Le Caron, Henry. Pseudonym of Thomas Miller Beach (1841–1894), British secret-service agent and author.

Le Carré, John. Pseudonym of David John Moore Cornwell (1931–), British writer.

Lécavelé, Roland. See DORGELÈS, ROLAND.

Lechón, Jan. Pseudonym of Leszek Jozef Serafinowicz (1899–1956), Polish poet.

Leckie, Robert (1920–   ). American free-lance writer, whose pseudonyms are *Roger Barlow* and *Mark Porter.*

Leclère, Léon. See KLINGSOR, TRISTAN.

Le Corbusier. Pseudonym of Charles Édouard Jeanneret (1887–1965), Swiss-French architect. The name was derived from that of his maternal grandfather. He preferred to use his real name for his painting.

Lederer, Esther Pauline Friedman. See LANDERS, ANN.

Lee, Andrew. Pseudonym of Louis Stanton Auchincloss (1917–   ), American lawyer and novelist.

Lee, Austin (1904–   ). English author, whose pseudonyms are *John Austwick* and *Julian Callender.*

Lee, Babs. Pseudonym of Marion Van der Veer Lee (1914–   ), mystery writer.

Lee, Carol. See FLETCHER, HELEN JILL.

Lee, Carolina. See DERN, PEGGY GADDIS.

Lee, Edward. Pseudonym of Edward Lee Fouts (1902–   ), American mystery writer.

Lee, Lincoln. See COLLEN, NEIL.

Lee, Manfred B. (1905–   ). American mystery writer, whose pseudonyms, with Frederic Dannay, are *Daniel Nathan, Ellery Queen, Ellery Queen, Jr.,* and *Barnaby Ross.*

Lee, Marion Van der Veer. See LEE, BABS.

Lee, Mildred. Pseudonym of Mildred Lee Scudder (1908–   ), American free-lance writer.

Lee, Norman (1905–   ). Mystery writer, whose pseudonyms are *Raymond Armstrong* and *Mark Corrigan.*

Lee, Ranger. See SNOW, CHARLES HORACE.

Lee, Sir Sidney (1859–1926). Shakespearian scholar, whose original name was Solomon Lazarus Levy.

Lee, Vernon. Pseudonym of Violet Paget (1856–1935), English author.

Lee, William. See BURROUGHS, WILLIAM SEWARD.

Lee de Munoz Marin, Muna. See GAYLE, NEWTON.

Lees, Hannah. Pseudonym of Elizabeth Head Fetter (1904–), American writer.

Leeuwe, Jan van. See HEELU, JAN VAN.

Lefèvre, Paul. See GÉRALDY, PAUL.

Leffingwell, Albert (1895–1946). Mystery writer, whose pseudonyms are *Dana Chambers* and *Giles Jackson.*

Leffler, Anne Charlotte. See EDGREN, A. C.

Léger, Alexis (1887–). French scholar and poet, whose pseudonyms are *Saintléger Léger* and *Saint-John-Perse.*

Léger, Saintléger. See LÉGER, ALEXIS.

LeGrand. See HENDERSON, LE GRAND.

Legrand, Maurice-Étienne. See FRANC-NOHAIN.

Le Huu-Huan. See THUONG LA ONG HAI.

Le Huu Traco. See THUONG LA ONG HAI.

Leiber, Fritz. See LATHROP, FRANCIS.

Leigh, Johanna. Pseudonym of Dorothy Leigh Sayers (1893–1957), British writer.

Leighton, Florence. Pseudonym of Florence Leighton Pfalzgraf (1902–), mystery writer.

Leighton, Lee. See OVERHOLSER, WAYNE D.

Leino, Eino. Pseudonym of Armas Eino Leopold Lönnbohm (1878–1926), Finnish poet, playwright, and novelist.

Leinster, Murray. Pseudonym of William Fitzgerald Jenkins (1896–), American fiction writer.

Leisk, David Murray. See JOHNSON, CROCKETT.

Leisy, James Franklin. See LYNN, FRANK.

Leite, George Thurston. See SCOTT, THURSTON.

Lelio (1675?–1753). Italian actor and playwright, whose real name was Lodovico Riccoboni.

Lemmon, Laura Elizabeth. See WILSON, LEE.

Lemoine, Ernest. See ROY, EWELL PAUL.

Lenanton, C. Pseudonym of Carola Mary Anima Oman (1897–), English historical biographer.

Lenau, Nikolaus. Pseudonym of Nikolaus Franz Niembsch von Strehlenau (1802–1850), Austrian poet.

Lendon, Kenneth Harry. See VAUGHAN, LEO.

Lengyel, Cornel Adam. See ADAM, CORNEL.
Lenin, N. Pseudonym of Vladimir Ilich Ulyanov (1870–1924), Russian revolutionist leader and political theorist.
Lennon, Florence Becker. See BECKER, FLORENCE.
Lenôtre, Georges. Pseudonym of Louis-Léon-Théodore Gosselin (1857–1935), French writer.
Lent, Dora Geneva. See DORANT, GENE.
Lentini, Jacopo. See NOTO, IL.
Leo VI, the Wise. See MAURICE.
Leon, Henry Cecil. See CECIL, HENRY.
Leonard, A. B. Pseudonym of Earl Augustus Aldrich (1886–   ), mystery writer.
Leonard, Charles L. Pseudonym of Mary Violet Heberden (1906–   ), mystery writer.
Léon-Felipe. Pseudonym of Léon-Felipe Camino y Galicia (1884–   ), Spanish poet.
Leonid. See BOSWORTH, WILLAN GEORGE.
Leopold, Nathan F. (1904–   ). American–Puerto Rican author, whose pseudonyms are *William F. Lanne* and *Richard A. Lawrence.*
Lermoliev, Ivan. Pseudonym of Giovanni Morelli (1816–1891), Italian art critic.
Le Roi, David de Roche. See ROCHE, JOHN.
LeShan, Lawrence L. See GRENDON, EDWARD.
Leshenkov, Sergey Antonovich. See KLYCHKOV, SERGEY.
LeSieg, Theo. See GEISEL, THEODOR SEUSS.
Leslie, Cecilie. See MACADAM, EVE.
Leslie, Doris. Pseudonym of Lady Hannay Ferguson, contemporary English writer.
Leslie, John. See HOWITT, JOHN LESLIE DESPARD.
Leslie, O. H. Pseudonym of Henry Slesar (1927–   ), mystery writer.
Leslie, Ward S. Pseudonym of Elizabeth Honor Ward (1926–   ), English writer.
Lesman, B. See LESMIAN, BOLESŁAW.
Lesman, Jan Wiktor. See BRZECHWA, JAN.
Lesmian, Bolesław (1879–1937). Polish poet and translator, also known as *B. Lesman.*
Lesser, Milton. See MARLOWE, STEPHEN.
Lester, Frank. See USHER, FRANK.

Lester-Rands, A. See JUDD, FREDERICK CHARLES.

Lesueur, Daniel. Pseudonym of Jeanne Lapauze (1860–1921), French writer.

Levi ben Gerson. See RALBAG.

Levickij, Anton. Pseudonym of Anton Jadvigin (1869–1922), White Russian writer.

Levien, Ilse. See FRAPAN-AKUNIAN, ILSE.

Levin, Judah Leib. See YEHALEL.

Levin, Marcia Obrasky (1918–   ). American writer for children, whose pseudonyms are *Marcia Martin* and, with her husband, Martin P. Levin, *Jeremy Martin.*

Levin, Martin P. See LEVIN, MARCIA OBRASKY.

Levine, Philip. See POE, EDGAR.

Levine, William. See LEVINREW, WILL.

Levinrew, Will. Pseudonym of William Levine (1881–   ), mystery writer.

Levinsky, Elchanan Leib. See RABBI KAROV.

Levita, Elijah (or **Elias**) (1469–1549). Jewish scholar, whose real name was Elijah ben Asher ha-Levi. He was also known as *Elijah Ashkenazi, Elijah Bachur* (or *Bahur*) and *Elijah Tishbi.*

Levy, Solomon Lazarus. See LEE, SIR SIDNEY.

Lewin, C. L. See BRISTER, RICHARD.

Lewin, Leonard C. See CASE, L. L.

Lewis, Alfred Henry. See QUIN, DAN.

Lewis, Cecil Day. See BLAKE, NICHOLAS.

Lewis, Charles Bertrand. See QUAD, M.

Lewis, Clive Staples (1898–1963). English writer, whose pseudonyms are *N. W. Clerk* (used to publish *A Grief Observed,* reflections on the death of his wife) and *Clive Hamilton.*

Lewis, D. B. See BIXBY, JEROME LEWIS.

Lewis, Ethelreda. See BAPTIST, R. HERNEKIN.

Lewis, Howel Elvet. See ELFED.

Lewis, Janet. Pseudonym of Janet Lewis Winters (1899–   ), American novelist and poet.

Lewis, Lange. Pseudonym of Jane Beynon (1915–   ), mystery writer.

Lewis, Mary Christianna Milne (1907–   ). British mystery writer, whose pseudonyms are *Christianna Brand* and *Mary Roland.*

Lewis, Matthew Gregory. See LEWIS, MONK.

Lewis, Mildred D. See DE WITT, JAMES.

Lewis, Monk. Pseudonym of Matthew Gregory Lewis (1775–1818), English novelist and playwright.

Lexau, Joan M. See NODSET, JOAN L.

Ley, Willy. See WILLEY, ROBERT.

Leyden, Lucas van (1494–1533). Dutch painter, whose real name was Lucas Hugensz. The name was derived from his birthplace, Leyden.

Leyeles, A. Pseudonym of Aaron Glanz (1889–   ), Yiddish poet.

L'Hermite, François. See TRISTAN L'HERMITE.

Liang Feng-tzu. See LIANG K'AI.

Liang K'ai (1175?–1246?). Chinese painter, also called *Po Liang* and *Liang Feng-tzu.*

Lichtenberg, Elisabeth Jacoba. See SOMEREN, LIESJE VAN.

Lichtveld, Lou A. M. See HELMAN, ALBERT.

Liddy, James (1934–   ). Irish writer, whose pseudonyms are *Brian Lynch* and *Liam O'Connor.*

Lidin, Vladimir Ghermanovich. Pseudonym of V. Gomberg (1894–   ), Soviet Russian writer.

Liebeler, Jean Mayer. See MATHER, VIRGINIA.

Liebermann, Ahron Samuel (1840–1880). Hebrew essayist, whose pseudonyms are *Bar Drora, Danial Yish Chamudot,* and *Artur Freeman.*

Lieknis, Edvarts. See VIRZA, EDVARTS.

Li Fei-kan. See PA-CHIN.

Lightner, A. M. Pseudonym of Alice L. Hopf (1904–   ), American free-lance writer.

Li Kung-lin (c1040–1106). Chinese painter, also known as *Li Po-shih* and *Li Lung-mien,* the latter a nickname he received from spending his last years in the Lung-mien Mountains.

Lilia, Georg. See STIERNHIELM, GEORG.

Lilley, Peter. See BUCKINGHAM, BRUCE.

Li Lung-mien. See LI KUNG-LIN.

Limbourg, Pol, Hermann, and **Jehanequin de.** Fifteenth-century Belgian painters, also known as *Malouel* (or *Maelwael, Maelweel*) after their uncle Jean Malouel, the titular painter of Philip the Bold.

Limburg Brouwer, Petrus Abraham Samuel van. See LUIK, ABRAHAM VAN.

Limnelius, George. See ROBINSON, LEWIS GEORGE.

Lin, Adet Jusu. See TAN YUN.
Linde Jansz, Gerrit van de. See SCHOOLMEESTER, DE.
Lindegard, Mai. See CHRISTIANSEN, SYNNØVE.
Linden, Oliver. See ABRAHAMS, DORIS CAROLINE.
Lindholm, Anna Chandler. See FAY, DOROTHY.
Lindo, Mark Prager. See OUDE HEER SMITS, DE.
Lindsay, Barbara. See STERNE, EMMA GELDERS.
Lindsay, Jack (1900–   ). Australian-English writer, whose pseudonyms are *Peter Meadows* and *Richard Preston.*
Lindsay, John. See MURIEL, JOHN SAINT CLAIR.
Lindsay, John Maurice. See BROCK, GAVIN.
Lindsay, Kathleen (1903–   ). Mystery writer, whose pseudonyms are *Margaret Cameron* and *Mary Richmond.*
Lindsay, Perry. See DERN, PEGGY GADDIS.
Lindström, Sigfrid. See TRISTAN.
Linebarger, Paul Myron Anthony (1913–   ). American scholar, whose pseudonyms are *Felix C. Forest* and *Carmichael Smith.*
Lingeman, Richard R. (1931–   ). American writer, whose pseudonyms are *Niles Chignon* and *William Randolph Hirsch.*
Linington, Elizabeth (1921–   ). American writer of historical novels and mysteries, whose pseudonyms are *Anne Blaisdell, Lesley Egan, Egan O'Neill,* and *Dell Shannon.*
Linklater, J. Lane. Pseudonym of Alex Watkins, contemporary mystery writer.
Linnankoski, Johannes. Pseudonym of Juho Vihtori Peltonen (1869–1913), Finnish writer.
Linschoten, Paulus Hubert Adriann Jan Strick van. See ELEUTHEROPHILOS.
Li Po-shih. See LI KUNG-LIN.
Lippi, Lorenzo. See ZIPOLI, PERLONE.
Lirio. See BRUNCLAIR, VICTOR J.
Lisky, I. A. Pseudonym of Summer Fuchs (1903–   ), Yiddish novelist.
Lissandrino (1667?–1749). Italian painter whose real name was Alessandro Magnasco.
Liston, Jack. Pseudonym of Ralph Liston Maloney (1927–   ), American writer.
Lite, James. See SCHNECK, STEPHEN.
Little, Frances. Pseudonym of Fannie Macaulay (1863–1941), American writer.

Little, Paul H. (1915–   ). American writer, whose pseudonyms are *Paula Little, Paula Minton,* and *Hugo Paul.*

Little, Paula. See LITTLE, PAUL H.

Little, Thomas. See MOORE, THOMAS.

Littleboy, Sheila M. Pseudonym of Sheila Mary Littleboy Ary (1929–   ), English-American author.

Littleton, Mark. Pseudonym of John Pendleton Kennedy (1795–1870), American Congressman and novelist.

Litwos. Pseudonym of Henryk Sienkiewicz (1846–1916), Polish author.

Liverton, Joan. See MEDHURST, JOAN.

Livingston, Kenneth. Pseudonym of Kenneth Livingston Stewart (1894–   ), mystery writer.

Lloyd J. Ivester (1905–   ). English writer, whose pseudonyms are *Babbler, Peter Farmer,* and *The Lodger.*

Lobaugh, Elma K. See LOWE, KENNETH.

Lobowski, Edward. See SPIRIDION.

Lochener, Stefan. See LOCHNER, STEFAN.

Locher, Jakob. See PHILOMUSUS.

Lochlons, Colin. See JACKSON, CAARY PAUL.

Lochner, Stefan (c1410/15–1451/52). German painter, also known as *Stefan Loechener* (or *Lochener*). At one time the name was misread as *Loethener.*

Lock, Arnold Charles Cooper. See COOPER, CHARLES.

Locke, Clinton W. Collective pseudonym for the "Perry Pierce Mystery" series. See STRATEMEYER, EDWARD L.

Locke, David Ross. See NASBY, PETROLEUM V.

Locke, Martin. See DUNCAN, W. MURDOCH.

Locke, Peter. Pseudonym of John Wilson McCutchan (1909–   ), American-Canadian scholar.

Lockridge, Frances Louise Davis. See RICHARDS, FRANCIS.

Lockridge, Richard Orson. See RICHARDS, FRANCIS.

Lockyer, Roger. See FRANCIS, PHILIP.

Lode, Rex. Joint pseudonym of William Isaac Goldstein (1932–   ) and Boyd Boyland, American writers.

Loder, Vernon. See VAHEY, JOHN GEORGE HASLETTE.

Lodewyk. Pseudonym of Lodewijk Mulder (1822–1907), Dutch novelist, playwright, and poet.

Lodger, The. See LLOYD, J. IVESTER.

Lodowich. See BARRY, LORD.

Loechener, Stefan. See LOCHNER, STEFAN.

Loeiz Ar Flo'ch. See GLANNDOUR, MAODEZ.

Loethener, Stefan. See LOCHNER, STEFAN.

Lofts, Norah Robinson. See CURTIS, PETER.

Logan, Ford. See NEWTON, DWIGHT BENNETT.

Logau, Baron Friedrich von. See GOLAW, SALOMON VON.

Loges, François des. See VILLON, FRANÇOIS.

Loghem, Martinus Gesinus Lambert van. See FIORE DELLA NEVE.

Lo Kuan-chung. Courtesy name of Lo Pen (c1330–c1400), Chinese novelist.

Lomas, Steve. Pseudonym of Joseph Lomas Brennan, contemporary American writer.

Lombard, Nap. Joint pseudonym of Pamela Hansford Johnson (Lady C. P. Snow) (1912–   ) and Neil Stewart, British writers.

Lombardi, Cynthia. Pseudonym of Georgina M. Lombardi, contemporary mystery writer.

Lombardi, Georgina M. See LOMBARDI, CYNTHIA.

Lomi, Orazio. See GENTILESCHI, ORAZIO DE'.

London, Jack. Pseudonym of John Griffith (1875–1916), American novelist and short-story writer.

Long, Amelia Reynolds (1904–   ). Mystery writer, whose pseudonyms are *Patrick Laing, Adrian Reynolds, Peter Reynolds*, and, with Edna McHugh, *Kathleen Buddington Coxe*.

Long, Ann Marie. Pseudonym of Pauline Marie Jensen (1900–   ), American free-lance writer.

Long, Gabrielle Margaret Vere (1888–1952). English novelist and playwright, whose pseudonyms are *Marjorie Bowen, Robert Paye, George Runnell Preedy, Joseph Shearing*, and *John Winch*.

Long, Helen Beecher. Collective pseudonym for the "Do Something" series. See STRATEMEYER, EDWARD L.

Long, John Frederick Lawrence. See LONGSWORD, JOHN.

Long, Lily Augusta. See DOUBLEDAY, ROMAN.

Longchamps, Nigel de. See WIREKER.

Longhi, Pietro (1702–1785). Venetian painter, whose original name was Pietro Falca. The origin of the name Longhi is uncertain.

Longinus, Johannes. Latinized name of Jan Długosz (1415?–1480), Polish chronicler.

Longrigg, Jane Chichester. See CHICHESTER, JANE.

Longrigg, Roger Erskine. See ERSKINE, ROSALIND.

Longstreet, Stephen (1907–   ). American writer, whose pseudonyms are *Thomas Burton, Paul Haggard, David Ormsbee,* and *Henri Weiner.*

Longsword, John. Pseudonym of John Frederick Lawrence Long (1917–   ), English-German writer.

Lönnbohm, Armas Eino Leopold. See LEINO, EINO.

Loomis, Noel Miller (1905–1969). American writer, whose pseudonyms are *Sam Allison, Benjamin Miller, Frank Miller,* and *Silas Water.*

Looy, Jacobus van. See BROUWER, A.

Lo Pen. See LO KUAN-CHUNG.

Lopresti, Lucia Longhi. See BANTI, ANNA.

Lorac, E. C. R. See RIVETT, EDITH CAROLINE.

Lord, Garland. Joint pseudonym of Isabel Garland (1903–   ) and Mindret Lord, mystery writers.

Lord, Jeremy. Occasional pseudonym of Ben Ray Redman (1896–1961), American journalist and writer.

Lord, Mindret. See LORD, GARLAND.

Lording. See BARRY, LORD.

Lorena, Claudio di. See LORRAIN, CLAUDE.

Lorenese, Il. See LORRAIN, CLAUDE.

Lorenzini, Carlo. See COLLODI, CARLO.

Loring, Andrew. See LATHROP, LORIN ANDREWS.

Loring, Emilie Baker. See STORY, JOSEPHINE.

Loring, Peter. See SHELLABARGER, SAMUEL.

Lorm, Hieronymus. Pseudonym of Heinrich Landesmann (1821–1902), German writer.

L'Orme (or **Lorme**), **de.** See DELORME, PHILIBERT.

Lorne, Charles. Pseudonym of Charles Neville Brand (1895–   ), mystery writer.

Lorning, Ray. Pseudonym of Malcolm Braly (1925–   ), American writer.

Lorrain, Claude (1600–1682). French landscape painter, whose real name was Claude Gellée (or Gelée, Gille). The name was derived from Lorraine, the region from which he came. At an early age he moved to Rome, where his contemporaries referred to him as *Claudio di Lorena* and *Il Lorenese.* He signed himself simply as *Claud(e)* or *Claudio,* with or without his original surname.

Lorrain, Jean. Pseudonym of Paul Duval (1850?–1906), French poet and playwright.

Lotarёv, Igor Vasilyevich. See SEVERYANIN, IGOR.

Loti, Pierre. Pseudonym of Louis Marie Julien Viaud (1850–1923), French novelist.

Lottich, Kenneth V. See CONRAD, KENNETH.

Lottmann, F. See FRESENUS, FRITZ.

Louis, Father M. Pseudonym of Thomas James Merton (1915–1969), American scholar.

Louis, Pierre. See LOUÿS, PIERRE.

Lourie, Helen. See STORR, CATHERINE.

Louÿs, Pierre. Pseudonym of Pierre Louis (1870–1925), French poet.

Lovehill, C. B. See BEAUMONT, CHARLES.

Loveling, Virginie. See WALTER, W. E. C.

Lovell, Ingraham. Pseudonym of Josephine Dodge Daskam Bacon (1876–1961), mystery writer.

Low, Gardner. See RODDA, CHARLES.

Lowe, Kenneth. Pseudonym of Elma K. Lobaugh (1907–   ), mystery writer.

Lowell, James Russell. See BIGLOW, HOSEA.

Lowndes, Belloc. Pseudonym of Marie Adelaide Belloc (1868–1947), English mystery writer and novelist.

Lowry, Joan Catlow. See CATLOW, JOANNA.

Łozinski, Władysław. See LUBON, W.

Lubicz-Milosz, Oscar Wenceslas de. See MILOSZ.

Lubliner, Hugo. See BÜRGER, HUGO.

Lubon, W. Pseudonym of Władysław Łozinski (1843–1913), Polish novelist and historian.

Lucanius. See CALVIN, JOHN.

Lucas, Victoria. Pseudonym of Sylvia Plath (1932–1963), American-English poet and writer.

Lucevich, Ivan Daminikavich. See KUPALA, JANKA.

Lu-ch'iao. Pseudonym of Nelson I. Wu (1919–   ), Chinese-American scholar.

Luciani, Sebastiano. See SEBASTIANO DEL PIOMBO.

Lucianus. See CALVIN, JOHN.

Lucy, Sir Henry. See TOBY, M.P.

Ludlow, Geoffrey. See MEYNELL, LAURENCE WALTER.

Ludlow, George. See KAY, ERNEST.

Ludlum, Mabel Cleland. See WIDDEMER, MABEL CLELAND.

Lu Domine (d. c1447). Venetian painter, whose real name was Domenico da Udine.

Ludovici, Anthony M. (1882–   ). English writer, whose pseudonyms are *Cobbett, Huntley Paterson,* and *David Valentine.*

Ludwell, Bernice. Pseudonym of Manning Lee Stokes, contemporary mystery writer.

Ludwig, Emil (1881–1948). German writer, whose original surname was Cohn.

Luff, Stanley George Anthony. See FARNASH, HUGH.

Lugansky, Kazak. Pseudonym of Vladimir Ivanovich Dahl (1801–1872), Russian linguist.

Luik, Abraham van. Pseudonym of Petrus Abraham Samuel van Limburg Brouwer (1829–1873), Dutch writer.

Luk, Charles. See K'UAN-YU LU.

Lum, Peter. Pseudonym of Bettina Lum Crowe (1911–   ), American-English writer.

Lund, A. Morten. See BORCH, TED.

Lund, Lars. See BANG-HASEN, ODD.

Luria, Isaac. See HA'ARI.

Luria, Solomon (c1510–1573). Polish Jewish religious writer and Hebrew poet, known as *Rashal* and *Maharshal.*

Lusin. Pseudonym of Chou Shu-jen (1881–1936), Chinese short-story writer and essayist.

Lu Te-ming. Courtesy name of Lu Yuan-lang (c550–c620), Chinese scholar.

Lutero, Battista di (d. 1548). Italian painter, also known as *Battista Dossi.* He was the brother of Dosso Dossi, with whom he collaborated.

Lutero, Giovanni di. See DOSSI, DOSSO.

Lux. Pseudonym of Lucy M. Jones, contemporary mystery writer.

Lu Yuan-lang. See LU TE-MING.

Lyall, David. Pseudonym of Helen Buckingham Reeves (1853–1920), English novelist.

Lyall, Edna. Pseudonym of Ada Ellen Bayly (1857–1903), English novelist and supporter of women's rights.

Lyall, Katharine Elizabeth. See WHITEHORN, KATHARINE.

Lyashchenko, Nikolay Nikolayevich. See LYASHKO, NIKOLAY.

Lyashko, Nikolay. Pseudonym of Nikolay Nikolayevich Lyashchenko (1884–   ), Soviet Russian novelist and short-story writer.

Lyman, Albert Robinson. See OLD SETTLER, THE.

Lynch, Brian. See LIDDY, JAMES.

Lynch, Lawrence L. Pseudonym of Emma Murdoch Van Deventer, contemporary mystery writer.

Lynd, Robert. See Y.Y.

Lynn, Frank. Pseudonym of James Franklin Leisy (1927–   ), American writer.

Lyon, Jessica. See DE LEEUW, CATEAU.

Lyon, Lyman R. See DECAMP, LYON SPRAGUE.

Lys, Christian. Pseudonym of Percy James Brebner (1864–1922), mystery writer.

Lyte, Richard. See WHELPTON, GEORGE ERIC.

Lyttleton, Edith J. See LANCASTER, G. B.

Lytton, Edward Robert Bulwer. See MEREDITH, OWEN.

"M"

M. E. R. Pseudonym of Maria Elizabeth Rothmann (1875–   ), Afrikaans writer.

Maartens, Maarten. Pseudonym of Joost Marius Willem van der Poorten-Schwartz (1858–1915), Dutch novelist.

MacAdam, Eve. Pseudonym of Cecilie Leslie (1914–   ), Indian-English writer.

McAllister, Alister (1877-1943). Irish writer, whose pseudonyms are *Lynn Brock* and *Anthony Wharton.*

MacAlpine, Margaret H. See CARMICHAEL, ANN.

MacArthur, David Wilson. See WILSON, DAVID.

McArthur, John. Pseudonym of Arthur Wise (1923–   ), English writer.

Macaulay, Fannie. See LITTLE, FRANCES.

McBain, Ed. See HUNTER, EVAN.

McCabe, Cameron. Pseudonym of Ernest Borneman (1915–   ), German writer.

McCann, Coolidge. See FAWCETT, FRANK DUBREZ.

McCarthy, Shaun (1928–). English writer, whose pseudonyms are *Theo Callas* and *Desmond Cory.*

MácCathmhaoil, Seosamh. See CAMPBELL, JOSEPH.

McCauley, Elfrieda Babnick. See HOUSE, ANNE W.

McCaull, M. E. Pseudonym of Edna McCaull Bohlman (1897–), American writer.

McChesney, Mary F. See RAYTER, JOE.

McClary, Jane Stevenson. See MCILVAINE, JANE.

McClintock, Marshall (1906–). American free-lance writer, whose pseudonyms are *Gregory Duncan, Mike McClintock, Douglas Marshall,* and *William Starret.*

McClintock, Mike. See MCCLINTOCK, MARSHALL.

McCloskey, Robert. See DANGERFIELD, BALFOUR.

MacClure, Victor. See CRAIG, PETER.

McConnell, James Douglas Rutherford (1915–). American mystery writer, whose pseudonyms are *Douglas Rutherford* and, with Francis Durbridge (1912–), *Paul Temple.*

McCormick, Wilfred (1903–). American writer, whose pseudonyms are *Rand Allison* and *Lon Dunlap.*

McCorquodale, Barbara. Pseudonym of Barbara Cartland (1904–), English author.

McCoy, Iola Fuller. See FULLER, IOLA.

McCready, Jack. Pseudonym of Talmage Powell (1920–), American free-lance writer.

McCutchan, John Wilson. See LOCKE, PETER.

MacDiarmid, Hugh. Pseudonym of Christopher Murray Grieve (1892–), Scottish poet and essayist.

MacDonald, Aeneas. Pseudonym of George Malcolm Thomson (1899–), Scottish-English writer.

MacDonald, Anson. See HEINLEIN, ROBERT ANSON.

Macdonald, John. See MILLAR, KENNETH.

Macdonald, John Ross. See MILLAR, KENNETH.

MacDonald, Philip. Contemporary mystery writer, whose pseudonyms are *Oliver Fleming, Anthony Lawless,* and *Martin Porlock.*

Macdonald, Ross. See MILLAR, KENNETH.

Macdonell, Archibald Gordon (1895–1941). Mystery writer, whose pseudonyms are *John Cameron* and *Neil Gordon.*

Macdonnell, James Edmond. See MACNELL, JAMES.

MacDouall, Robertson. Pseudonym of George Brown Mair (1914–
    ), Scottish writer.

MacDowell, Katherine Sherwood. See BONNER, SHERWOOD.

McElfresh, Elizabeth Adeline (1918–   ). American writer, whose
    pseudonyms are *John Cleveland, Jane Scott,* and *Elizabeth Wesley.*

McEvoy, Harry K. See MACK, KIRBY.

McEvoy, Marjorie Harte. See HARTE, MARJORIE.

M'Fall, Frances Elizabeth. See GRAND, SARAH.

MacFarlane, Kenneth. Pseudonym of Kenneth MacFarlane Walker
    (1882–1966), British medical writer.

MacFarlane, Stephen. Pseudonym of John Keir Cross (1914–   ),
    mystery writer.

MacFee, Maxwell. See RENNIE, JAMES ALAN.

McGaw, Naomi Blanche Thoburn. See HERVEY, JANE.

McGinnis, K. K. Pseudonym of Grover Page, Jr. (1918–   ), American
    writer.

McGivern, Maureen Daly. See DALY, MAUREEN.

McGlinn, Dwight. See BRANNON, WILLIAM T.

McGloin, Joseph Thaddeus. See O'FINN, THADDEUS.

M'Govan, James. Pseudonym of William C. Honeyman, contemporary
    mystery writer.

McGregor. Pseudonym of Doran Hurley (1900–   ), American writer.

MacGregor, Alasdair Alpin. See FEATHERSTONEHAUGH, FRANCIS.

MacGregor, James. See MCINTOSH, J. T.

McGrew, Fenn. Joint pseudonym of Caroline K. Fenn and Julia
    McGrew, contemporary mystery writers.

McGrew, Julia. See MCGREW, FENN.

MacHaye, Eric. Pseudonym of Arthur Somers Roche (1883–1935),
    mystery writer.

Machen, Arthur. Pseudonym of Arthur Llewellyn Jones (1863–1947),
    Anglo-Welsh translator and short-story writer.

Machshoves Baal. Pseudonym of Isidore Eliashiv (1873–1924), Yiddish
    writer.

McHugh, Edna. See LONG, AMELIA REYNOLDS.

McHugh, Jay. See MACQUEEN, JAMES WILLIAM.

Maciejowski, Ignacy. See SEWER.

McIlvaine, Jane. Pseudonym of Jane Stevenson McClary (1919–), American writer.

Macintosh, Edith Joan Burbridge. See COCKIN, JOAN.

McIntosh, J. T. Pseudonym of James MacGregor (1925–), Scottish free-lance writer.

McIntosh, Louis. Pseudonym of Christopher Johnson (1931–), English writer.

McIntyre, John Thomas. See O'NEIL, KERRY.

MacIre, Esor B. See AMBROSE, ERIC.

Mačiulis-Mačiulevicius, Jonas. See MAIRONIS.

Mack, Evalina. Pseudonym of Lena Brooke McNamara (1891–), American mystery writer.

Mack, Kirby. Pseudonym of Harry K. McEvoy (1910–), American writer.

McKay, Claude. See EDWARDS, ELI.

Mackay, Mary. See CORELLI, MARIE.

McKeag, Ernest L. (1896–). English free-lance writer, whose pseudonyms are *Jacque Braza, Griff, Mark Grimshaw, Pat Haynes, John King, Ramon Lacroix, Rene Laroche, Eileen McKeay, Jack Maxwell,* and *Roland Vane.*

McKeay, Eileen. See MCKEAG, ERNEST L.

McKelway, St. Clair. See HALL, J. DE P.

McKenna, Evelyn. See JOSCELYN, ARCHIE L.

MacKenna, Stephen. See DALY, MARTIN.

Mackenzie, Dr. Willard. See STRATEMEYER, EDWARD L.

McKeown, Norman Robert. See GILES, NORMAN.

Mackie, Albert David. See MACNIB.

McKillop, Norman. See BEG, TORAN.

Mackinnon, Charles Roy (1924–). British–West African writer, whose pseudonyms are *Vivian Donald, Hilary Rose, Charles Stuart,* and *Iain Torr.*

Mackintosh, Elizabeth (1896–1952). English writer, whose pseudonyms are *Gordon Daviot* and *Josephine Tey.*

Maclagan, Bridget. Pseudonym of Mary Borden (1886–), American-English author.

Maclaren, Ian. Pseudonym of John Watson (1850–1907), Scottish-American novelist and Free Church minister.

Macleod, Fiona. Occasional pseudonym of William Sharp (1856?–1905), Scottish poet and man of letters.

Macleod, Jean Sutherland. See AIRLIE, CATHERINE.

MacLeod, Joseph. See DRINAN, ADAM.

McLeod, Margaret Vail. See HOLLOWAY, TERESA.

MacLeod, Robert. See KNOX, WILLIAM.

McLowery, Frank. See KEEVIL, HENRY JOHN.

McMeekin, Clark. Joint pseudonym of Dorothy Park Clark (1899–) and Isabel McLennan McMeekin (1895–), American authors.

McMeekin, Isabel McLennan. See MCMEEKIN, CLARK.

MacMullan, Charles Walden Kirkpatrick. See MUNRO, CHARLES KIRKPATRICK.

MacNamara, Brinsley. Pseudonym of John Weldon (1890–), Irish novelist and playwright.

McNamara, Lena Brooke. See MACK, EVALINA.

MacNeil, Neil. See BALLARD, TODHUNTER.

McNeile, Cyril. See SAPPER.

MacNell, James. Pseudonym of James Edmond Macdonnell (1917–), Australian writer.

MacNib. Pseudonym of Albert David Mackie (1904–), Scottish writer.

Mac Orlan, Pierre (1882–). French novelist, whose original name was Pierre Dumarchais.

MacPhail, James A. See CROCKETT, JAMES.

MacPherson, Thomas George. See PARSONS, TOM.

McQuade, Ann Aikman. See AIKMAN, ANN.

MacQueen, James William (1900–). American mystery writer, whose pseudonyms are *James G. Edwards* and *Jay McHugh*.

McQueen, Mildred Hark. See HARK, MILDRED.

MacRae, Donald G. See CAMPBELL, CLIVE.

McRae, Lindsay. Pseudonym of Arthur Lindsay McRae Sowerby (1899–), English writer.

MacRae, Travis. Pseudonym of Anita MacRae Feagles (1926–), American writer.

Macrin. Pseudonym of Jean Salmon (1490–1557), French neo-Latin poet.

Macropedius, Georgius. Latinized name of Joris van Langhveldt (1475–1558), Dutch playwright.

Madden, Warren. Pseudonym of Kenneth Neill Cameron (1908–   ), English-American scholar.

Madison, Jane. Pseudonym of Hugh Robert Horne (1915–   ), American writer.

Madlee, Dorothy (1917–   ). American free-lance writer, whose pseudonyms are *Anna Haynes* and *Wade Rogers.*

Madrigal, Alonso de. Pseudonym of Alonso Tostado (d. 1455?), Spanish writer and scholar, derived from his birthplace, Madrigal de la Sierra.

Maelwael (or Maelweel). See LIMBOURG, POL, HERMANN, and JEHANE-QUIN DE.

Maestro Gaio (1388–c1460). Italian-Hebrew poet and historian, whose real name was Moses di Rieti.

Magee, William Kirkpatrick. See EGLINTON, JOHN.

Magill, Marcus. Pseudonym of Brian Hill (1896–   ), English writer.

Magister Islebius. See AGRICOLA, JOHANNES.

Magnasco, Alessandro. See LISSANDRINO.

Magnus, Philip. Pseudonym of Sir Philip Magnus-Allcroft (1906–   ), English author.

Magnus-Allcroft, Sir Philip. See MAGNUS, PHILIP.

Magnusson, Jón Gudmundur. See TRAUSTI, JÓN.

Magny, Renaut de. See CHASTELAIN DE COUCI, LE.

Magoon, Carey. Joint pseudonym of Elisabeth Carey (no dates available) and Marian Austin Magoon (1885–   ), mystery writers.

Magoon, Marian Austin. See MAGOON, CAREY.

Magoun, F. Alexander. See WRIGHT, AMOS.

Maguire, Robert Augustine Joseph. See TAAFFE, MICHAEL.

Mahalel. See GOTTLOBER, ABRAHAM BAER.

Maharan. See NAHMAN OF BRATZLAV.

Maharshal. See LURIA, SOLOMON.

Mahen, Jiri. Pseudonym of Antonin Vancura (1882–1939), Czech writer.

Mahony, Francis Sylvester. See FATHER PROUT.

Maigrot, Émile. See HENRIOT, ÉMILE.

Maimonides, Moses (1135–1204). Spanish-Jewish religious writer and philosopher, whose formal name was Rabbi Moses ben Maimon. He was also known as *Rambam*, an acronym of Ra(bbi) M(oses) b(en) M(aimon).

Mainprize, Don. See ROCK, RICHARD.

Mainwaring, Daniel. See HOMES, GEOFFREY.

Mainzer. See ELLOPOSCLEROS, HULDRICH.

Mair, George Brown. See MACDOUALL, ROBERTSON.

Mair, Margaret. Pseudonym of Margaret Norah Mair Crompton (1901–), English author.

Maironis. Pseudonym of Jonas Mačiulis-Mačiulevicius (1862–1932), Lithuanian poet.

Maison, Margaret M. See CLARE, MARGARET.

Maisonneuve, La (d. 1568). French clergyman and poet, whose real name was Antoine Héroët.

Maizel, C. L. See MAIZEL, CLARICE MATTHEWS.

Maizel, Clarice Matthews (1919–). English author, whose pseudonyms are *C. L. Maizel* and *Leah Maizel.*

Maizel, Leah. See MAIZEL, CLARICE MATTHEWS.

Majerova, Marie. Pseudonym of Marie Tusarova (1882–), Czech novelist.

Majnun ("Madman"). Cognomen of Qays, 7th-century Arabic poet, derived after an unhappy love affair caused him to lose his reason.

Major, Charles. See CASKODEN, SIR EDWIN.

Malet, Lucas. Pseudonym of Mary St. Leger Kingsley (1852–1931), English novelist.

Malin, Peter. Pseudonym of Patrick Reardon Conner (1907–), British writer.

Malinovsky, Alexander Alexandrovich. See BOGDANOV, ALEXANDER ALEXANDROVICH.

Malleson, Lucy Beatrice (1899–). Mystery writer, whose pseudonyms are *Anthony Gilbert, J. Kilmeny Keith,* and *Anne Meredith.*

Mallet, David (c1705–1765). Scottish poet, whose original surname was Malloch.

Malloch, David. See MALLET, DAVID.

Malloch, Peter. See DUNCAN, W. MURDOCH.

Maloney, Pat. See MARKUN, PATRICIA MALONEY.

Maloney, Ralph Liston. See LISTON, JACK.

Malouel. See LIMBOURG, POL, HERMANN, and JEHANEQUIN DE.

Mand, Ewald. See KALMUS, AIN.

Mandelkorn, Eugenia Miller. See MILLER, EUGENIA.

Manfred, Frederick Feikema. See FEIKEMA, FEIKE.

Manfred, Robert. Pseudonym of Erica Elizabeth Marx (1909–   ), English writer.

Maniu, Miculu. See CLAIN, SAMUIL.

Manji. See HOKUSAI.

Mankowska, Joyce Kells Batten. See BATTEN, JOYCE MORTIMER.

Mann, Avery. Pseudonym of Jim Patrick Breetveld (1925–   ), American writer.

Mann, D. J. Pseudonym of James Dillet Freeman (1912–   ), American writer.

Manne, Mordecai Zui. See HA MEZAYER.

Mannering, Julia. Pseudonym of Madeleine Bingham (1912–   ), English author.

Mannes, Marya. See SEC.

Manngian, Peter. See MONGER, IFOR DAVID.

Manning, Adelaide Frances Oke. Contemporary English writer, whose pseudonyms, with Cyril Henry Coles, are *Manning Coles* and *Francis Gaite.*

Manning, Hilda. See REACH, JAMES.

Manning, Rosemary. See COLE, MARGARET ALICE; VOYLE, MARY.

Manningham, Basil. Pseudonym of Basil Henry Homersham (1902–   ), mystery writer.

Mannon, M. M. Joint pseudonym of Martha Mannon (1909–   ) and Mary Ellen Mannon (1913–   ), mystery writers.

Mannon, Martha. See MANNON, M. M.

Mannon, Mary Ellen. See MANNON, M. M.

Mannon, Warwick. See HOPKINS, KENNETH.

Mannyng, Robert (c1264–1340). English poet, also known as *Robert of Brunne.*

Manor, Jason. Pseudonym of Oakley Maxwell Hall (1920–   ), American free-lance writer.

Mansfield, Katherine. Pseudonym of Kathleen Mansfield Beauchamp (1888–1923), English short-story writer.

Mantegna, Andrea (1431?–1506). Italian painter and engraver, also known as *Andrea di Vicentia.*

Mantinband, James H. See KEYSTONE, OLIVER.

Mantle, Winifred Langford. Contemporary English writer of novels and short stories, whose pseudonyms are *Anne Fellowes, Frances Lang,* and *Jane Langford.*

Manton, Jo. Pseudonym of Jo Grenville Manton Gittings (1919–), English writer.

Manton, Peter. See CREASEY, JOHN.

Mantovano, Battista. Pseudonym of Giovan Battista Spagnoli (1448–1516), Italian humanist and poet.

Mantu, Lucia. Pseudonym of Cornelia Nadejde (1906–), Rumanian writer.

Manuchihri. Pseudonym of Ahmad Abu'l-Najm (d. c1041), Persian poet.

Manuel, Nikolaus (1484–1530). Swiss painter and satirist, also known as *Nikolaus Deutsch.*

Manzoli, Pier Angelo de la Stellata (1500?–1543?). Italian poet, now identified with Palingenio.

Mao-tun. Pseudonym of Shen Yen-ping (1896–), Chinese novelist and short-story writer.

Mar, Esmeralda de. See MELLEN, IDA MAY.

Maras, Karl. See BLUMER, HENRY KENNETH.

Marcelino. Pseudonym of Edith J. Agnew (1897–), American author.

March, Jermyn. Pseudonym of Dorothy Anna Maria Webb, contemporary mystery writer.

March, William. Pseudonym of William Edward March Campbell (1894–1954), American novelist and short-story writer.

Marchant, Catherine. Pseudonym of Catherine Cookson (1906–), American author.

Marchant, Romano Isabel. Pseudonym of Grace Isabel Colbron (1869–1948), mystery writer.

Marcoussis, Louis Casimir Ladislas (1882?–1941). Polish painter, whose original surname was Markus.

Marek, Kurt W. See CERAM, C. W.

Margerson, David. Pseudonym of David Margerison Davies (1923–), British author.

Marholm, Laura. Pseudonym of Laura Mohr Hansson (1854–1928), Swedish writer.

Mariano, Agnolo di Cosimo di. See BRONZINO, IL.

Marie-Victorin, Frère. Religious name of Joseph Louis Conrad Kirouac (1895–1944), French-Canadian botanist and author.

Marisa. Pseudonym of Marisa Lonette Nucera (1959–   ), American poet.

Mark, Matthew. Pseudonym of Frederic Babcock (1896–   ), American writer and editor.

Markham, Robert. Pseudonym of Kingsley Amis (1922–   ), English writer.

Markovich, Maria Alexandrovna. See MARKO, VOVCHOK.

Markun, Patricia Maloney (1924–   ). American writer, whose pseudonyms are *Sybil Forrest, Pat Maloney,* and *Patricio Marroquin.*

Markus, Louis Casimir Ladislas. See MARCOUSSIS, LOUIS CASIMIR LADISLAS.

Marlinski, Cossack. Pseudonym of Alexander Alexandrovich Bestuzhev (1797–1837), Russian novelist and poet.

Marlitt, Eugenie. Pseudonym of Eugenie John (1825–1887), German novelist.

Marlowe, Amy Bell. Collective pseudonym. See STRATEMEYER, EDWARD L.

Marlowe, Hugh. See PATTERSON, HENRY.

Marlowe, Kenneth (1926–   ). American writer, whose pseudonyms are *Mr. Kenneth* and *Leslie Stuart.*

Marlowe, Stephen (1928–   ). American writer, whose pseudonyms are *Andrew Frazer, Milton Lesser, Jason Ridway,* and *C. H. Thames.*

Marquand, John Phillips. See PHILLIPS, JOHN.

Marquard, Leopold. See BURGER, JOHN.

Marquess of Anglesey, The. Pseudonym of George Charles Henry Victor Paget (1922–   ), English–North Welsh writer.

Marquis of Douro, The. See BRONTË, CHARLOTTE.

Marradi, Giovanni. See LABRONIO, G.

Marric, J. J. See CREASEY, JOHN.

Marr-Johnson, Diana Maugham. See MAUGHAM, DIANA.

Marroquin, Patricio. See MARKIN, PATRICIA MALONEY.

Marsh, J. E. See MARSHALL, EVELYN.

Marsh, Jean. See MARSHALL, EVELYN.

Marsh, John (1907–   ). English author, whose pseudonyms are *John Elton, John Harley, Harrington Hastings, Grace Richmond,* and *Lilian Woodward.*

Marsh, Patrick. Pseudonym of Leslie Hiscock (1902–   ), mystery writer.

Marsh, Paul. See HOPKINS, KENNETH.

Marsh, Rebecca. See NEUBAUER, WILLIAM ARTHUR.

Marshall, Charles Hunt. See HUNT, PETER.

Marshall, Douglas. See MCCLINTOCK, MARSHALL.

Marshall, Edison. See HUNTER, HALL.

Marshall, Edmund. See HOPKINS, KENNETH.

Marshall, Emily. See HALL, BENNIE CAROLINE.

Marshall, Evelyn (1897–   ). English writer, whose pseudonyms are *Lesley Bourne, J. E. Marsh,* and *Jean Marsh.*

Marshall, Gary. See SNOW, CHARLES HORACE.

Marshall, James Vance. See DOONE, JICE; PAYNE, DONALD GORDON.

Marshall, Lovat. See DUNCAN, W. MURDOCH.

Marshall, Margaret Wiley. See WILEY, MARGARET L.

Marshall, Percy. Pseudonym of Percy M. Young (1912–   ), English writer on music and sports.

Marshall, Raymond. See RAYMOND, RENÉ.

Marshall, Stephen. See SMECTYMNUUS.

Marsten, Richard. See HUNTER, EVAN.

Martel, Charles. Pseudonym of Thomas Delf (1810–1865), mystery writer.

Martens, Ademar. Occasional pseudonym of Michel de Ghelderode (1898–1962), Belgian playwright.

Martens, Paul. See SOUTHWOLD, STEPHEN.

Marti, Bernart. See PINTOR, LE.

Martin, Basil Kingsley. See CRITIC.

Martin, Dorothea. Pseudonym of Kathleen Douglas Hewitt (1893–   ), mystery writer.

Martin, Eugene. Collective pseudonym for the "Sky Flyers" series. See STRATEMEYER, EDWARD L.

Martin, Jeremy. See LEVIN, MARCIA OBRASKY.

Martin, John. See TATHAM, LAURA.

Martin, Marcia. See LEVIN, MARCIA OBRASKY.

Martin, Mr. See BURROUGHS, WILLIAM SEWARD.

Martin, Nell Columbia Boyer. See BOYER, COLUMBIA.

Martin, Oliver. Pseudonym of Ernest Davies (1873–   ), mystery writer.

Martin, Patricia Miles. See MILES, MISKA.

Martin, Paul. Pseudonym of Kenneth Edwin Lee Deale (1907–   ), Irish writer.

Martin, Paul. Pseudonym of Paul Martin Rade (1857–1940), German Lutheran theologian.

Martin, R. Johnson. See MEHTA, RUSTAM JEHANGIR.

Martin, Richard. See CREASEY, JOHN.

Martin, Robert. See ROBERTS, LEE.

Martin, Robert Bernard. See BERNARD, ROBERT.

Martin, Sam. Pseudonym of Sam Moskowitz (1920–   ), American free-lance writer.

Martin, Stella. Pseudonym of Georgette Heyer (1902–   ), mystery writer.

Martin, Violet (1862–1915). Irish novelist, whose pseudonyms are *Martin Ross* and, with her cousin, Edith Somerville, *Somerville & Ross.*

Martínez Ruíz, José. See AZORÍN.

Martínez Zuviría, Gustavo. See WAST, HUGO.

Marting, Ruth Lenore. See BAILEY, HILEA.

Martinson, Moa. Pseudonym of Maria Helga Swartz (1890–   ), Swedish writer.

Martoncsik, László. See MÉCS, LÁSZLÓ.

Martyn, Edward. See SIRIUS.

Martyn, Oliver. Pseudonym of Herbert Martyn Oliver White (1885–   ), mystery writer.

Martyn, Wyndham. See GRENVIL, WILLIAM.

Martyr, Peter (1459–1526). Italian humanist, resident of Spain after 1487, whose real name was Pietro Martire d'Anghiera. He was also known as *Anglerius.*

Marvel, Ik. Pseudonym of Donald Grant Mitchell (1822–1908), American author.

Marvell, Holt. Pseudonym of Eric Maschwitz (1901–   ), mystery writer.

Marvin, John T. See RICHARDS, CHARLES.

Marvin, W. R. See CAMERON, LOU.

Marx, Erica Elizabeth. See MANFRED, ROBERT.

Marx, Olga. See VALHOPE, CAROL NORTH.

Mary, André. Pseudonym of Jean-Vorle Monniot (1879–   ), French poet.

Mary Estelle, Sister. See CASALANDRA, ESTELLE.

Mary Francis, Mother. See CLARE, FRANCIS D.

Mary Gilbert, Sister. See DEFREES, MADELINE.

Masaccio ("a coarse, rough fellow"). Cognomen of Tommaso Guidi (1401–1428), Florentine painter.

Masako Matsuno. Pseudonym of Masako Matsuno Kobayashi (1935–   ), Japanese author.

Masako Matsuno Kobayashi. See MASAKO MATSUNO.

Masamune Hakucho. Pseudonym of Masamune Tadao (1879–   ), Japanese writer.

Masamune Tadao. See MASAMUNE HAKUCHO.

Masaoka Shiki. Pseudonym of Masaoka Tsunenori (1867–1902), Japanese writer.

Masaoka Tsunenori. See MASAOKA SHIKI.

Maschwitz, Eric. See MARVELL, HOLT.

Masetti, Pirro. See MASTRI, PIETRO.

Maskoff, Jozef. See KORWIN-PIOTROWSKA, GABRIELA.

Masolino da Panicale (1383?–1447). Florentine painter, identified with Tommaso di Cristoforo Fini.

Mason, Charles. See MASON, S. C.

Mason, Eudo Colecestra. See MAURER, OTTO.

Mason, Francis van Wyck (1901–   ). American author, whose pseudonyms are *Geoffrey Coffin, Frank W. Mason,* and *Ward Weaver.*

Mason, Frank W. See MASON, FRANCIS VAN WYCK.

Mason, Gregory. See JONES, ADRIENNE, and MEEK, DORIS.

Mason, Harry. See STRATEMEYER, EDWARD L.

Mason, Howard. Pseudonym of Jennifer Ramage, contemporary mystery writer.

Mason, Madeline (1913–   ). American scholar, whose pseudonyms are *David Bartlett* and *Tyler Mason.*

Mason, Philip. See WOODRUFF, PHILIP.

Mason, S. C. Pseudonym of Charles Mason, contemporary mystery writer.

Mason, Tally. Pseudonym of August William Derleth (1909–   ), mystery writer.
Mason, Tyler. See MASON, MADELINE.
Massio, Gentile di Nicolò di. See FABRIANO, GENTILE DA.
Masson, Georgina. Pseudonym of Marion Georgina Wikeley Johnson (1912–   ), British-Italian writer.
Massys, Quentin (1465/66–1530). Flemish painter, also known as *Matsys* and *Metsys.*
Masters, Kelly R. See BALL, ZACHARY.
Masters, William. See COUSINS, MARGARET.
Masterson, Whit. See MILLER, BILL, and WADE, BOB.
Mastri, Pietro. Pseudonym of Pirro Masetti (1868–1932), Italian poet.
Masuccio di Salerno. Pseudonym of Tommaso dei Guardati (c1430–1500?), Italian writer.
Matcha, Jack (1919–   ). American writer, whose pseudonyms are *Jackson Mitchell* and *John Tanner.*
Matheolus. See MATTHIEU LE BIGAME.
Mather, Virginia. Pseudonym of Jean Mayer Liebeler, contemporary mystery writer.
Mathews, Evelyn Craw. See CLEAVER, NANCY.
Mathieu, Noël. See EMMANUEL, PIERRE.
Matsunaga Katsuguma. See MATSUNAGA TEITOKU.
Matsunaga Teitoku. Pseudonym of Matsunaga Katsuguma (1571–1654), Japanese poet.
Matsys, Quentin. See MASSYS, QUENTIN.
Matthaei, Clara (1884–1934). German-American novelist, whose pseudonyms are *Walter Gray* and *Gertrud Hoff.*
Matthew, Thomas. Pseudonym of John Rogers (1500?–1555), English Protestant martyr.
Matthews, Kevin. See FOX, GARDNER FRANCIS.
Matthieu le Bigame. Cognomen of Matheolus (fl. 1270–1300), French Latin poet, derived from an alleged bigamous marriage.
Maugham, Diana. Pseudonym of Diana Maugham Marr-Johnson (1908–   ), English writer.
Maugham, Robert Cecil Romer. See MAUGHAM, ROBIN.
Maugham, Robin. Pseudonym of Robert Cecil Romer Maugham (1916–   ), English writer.

Maule, Hamilton Bee. See MAULE, TEX.

Maule, Tex. Pseudonym of Hamilton Bee Maule (1915–   ), American writer.

Maurer, Otto. Pseudonym of Eudo Colecestra Mason (1901–   ), English scholar.

Maurice. Pseudonym of various authors who worked on the *Tactica*, a Byzantine military handbook. Among the contributors were Urbicius (fl. 491–510) and the Eastern Roman emperors Maurice (539?–602), Heraclius (575?–641), and Leo VI, the Wise (866–912).

Maurice, David. See GHINE, WUNNAKYAWHTIN U OHN.

Maurice, Furnley. Pseudonym of Frank Leslie Thomson Wilmot (1881–1942), Australian poet.

Maurice, Michael. Pseudonym of Conrad Arthur Skinner (1889–   ), mystery writer.

Maurois, André. Pseudonym of Émile Salomon Wilhelm Herzog (1885–1967), French writer.

Mauropous, John. Eleventh-century Byzantine scholar, also known simply as *John of Euchaita.*

Mavor, Osborne Henry. See BRIDIE, JAMES.

Maxence, Robert. See FRANCIS, ROBERT.

Maxtone Graham, Joyce. See STRUTHER, JAN.

Maxwell, Jack. See MCKEAG, ERNEST L.

Maxwell, Ronald. See SMITH, RONALD GREGOR.

May, Henry John. See SCHLOSBERG, H. J.

May, Sophie. Pseudonym of Rebecca Sophia Clarke (1833–1906), American writer.

May, Wayne. See HUMPHRIES, ADELAIDE M.

Mayer, Charles Leopold. See REYAM.

Mayer, Jane Rothschild. See JAYNES, CLARE.

Mayfield, Julia. See HASTINGS, PHYLLIS DORA HODGE.

Mayne, Rutherford. Pseudonym of Sam Waddell (1878–   ), Irish playwright.

Mayne, William James Carter. See JAMES, DYNELY.

Mayo, Mark. Pseudonym of Yoti Lane, Irish writer, journalist, and drama critic.

Mayrant, Drayton. See SIMONS, KATHERINE DRAYTON MAYRANT.

Maysi, Kadra. See SIMONS, KATHERINE DRAYTON MAYRANT.

Mayy. See ZIYADAH, MARIE.

Mazzola (or Mazzuoli), Girolamo Francesco Maria. See PAR-
MIGIANINO, IL.

Meade, Lillie Thomas. Pseudonym of Elizabeth Thomasina Meade
Smith (1854–1914), mystery writer.

Meadowcroft, Enid LaMonte. Pseudonym of Enid Meadowcroft Wright
(1898–   ), American writer for young people.

Meadows, Peter. See LINDSAY, JACK.

Means, Mary. See SCOTT, DENIS.

Mearns, David Chambers. See FRADDLE, FARRAGUT.

Measday, George. See SODERBERG, PERCY MEASDAY.

Mebane, John. See HEARTMAN, HAROLD.

Meccherino, Il. See BECCAFUMI, DOMENICO.

Mécs, László. Pseudonym of László Martoncsik (1895–   ), Hungarian poet.

Medhurst, Joan. Pseudonym of Joan Liverton (1913–   ), English
free-lance writer.

Medley, Anne. See BORCHARD, RUTH.

Medolla, Andrea. See SCHIAVONE, ANDREA.

Meek, Doris. Contemporary mystery writer, whose pseudonyms, with
Adrienne Jones, are *Mason Gregory* and *Gregory Mason.*

Meel, Jan. See VITE, GIOVANNI DELLA.

Mees, Steve. See FLEXNER, STUART BERG.

Megerle, Johann Ulrich. See ABRAHAM A SANCTA CLARA.

Mehmed, Son of Suleyman. See FUZULI.

Mehta, Rustam Jehangir (1912–   ). Indian writer, whose pseudonyms are *Roger Hartman, R. Johnson Martin,* and *Plutonius.*

Mei Fei (1051–1107). Chinese painter, whose name until 1091 was Mi
Fu. He was also known as *Yüan-chang.*

Meigs, Cornelia Lynde. See ALDON, ADAIR.

Meikle, Clive. Pseudonym of Jeremy Brooks (1926–   ), English author.

Meiring, Desmond. Pseudonym of Desmond Charles Rice (1924–
    ), South African–Venezuelan writer.

Meiseido Kisanji. See KISANJI.

Meisetsu. See NAITO MEISETSU.

Melanchthon. Grecized surname of Philipp Schwarzert (1497–1560),
German humanist.

Melaro, Constance L. See BRUCE, MONICA.

Meldolla, Andrea. See SCHIAVONE, ANDREA.

Mélesville. Pseudonym of Anne Honoré Joseph Duveyrier (1787–1865), French playwright.

Melik-Iakobian, Jacob. See RAFFI.

Melissus, Paulus. Latinized name of Paul Schede (1539–1602), German humanist.

Mellen, Ida May (1877–   ). American writer, whose pseudonyms are *Esmeralda de Mar* and *George Otis.*

Melshin, L. Pseudonym of Peter Filippovich Yakubovich (1860–1911), Russian poet and revolutionary writer.

Melville, Alan. Pseudonym of William Melville Caverhill (1910–   ), mystery writer.

Melys, Atis. See SPINNIKER, ADRIAEN.

Mendel, David. See NEANDER, JOHANN AUGUST WILHELM.

Mendel, Jo. Pseudonym of Gladys Baker Bond (1912–   ), American author.

Mendele Mocher Sforim ("Mendele the Bookseller"). Pseudonym of Sholem Jacob Abramovich (1835–1917), Polish-Yiddish writer.

Mendelsohn, Oscar. See MILSEN, OSCAR.

Menen, Aubrey (1912–   ). English writer, whose original name was Salvator Aubrey Clarence Menon.

Menon, Salvator Aubrey Clarence. See MENEN, AUBREY.

Mentzer. See FISCHART, JOHANN.

Menzel, Johanna. Pseudonym of Johanna Menzel Meskill (1930–   ), German-American scholar.

Meo, Desiderio. See SETTIGNANO, DESIDERIO DA.

Mercader, Enrique. Pseudonym of Pere Corominas (1870–1939), Catalan writer and economist.

Mercer, Cecil William. See YATES, DORNFORD.

Mercer, Jessie. See SHANNON, TERRY.

Meredith, Anne. See MALLESON, LUCY BEATRICE.

Meredith, Arnold. See HOPKINS, KENNETH.

Meredith, David William. Pseudonym of Earl Schenck Miers (1910–   ), American writer.

Meredith, Nicolete. See STACK, NICOLETE.

Meredith, Owen. Pseudonym of Edward Robert Bulwer Lytton, 1st Earl of Lytton (1831–1891), English poet and writer.

Meredith, Peter. See WORTHINGTON-STUART, BRIAN ARTHUR.

Merezhkovskaya, Zinaida Nikolaevna. See HIPPIUS.

Merher, Alojzij. See SARDENKO, SILVIN.

Merisi, Michelangelo. See CARAVAGGIO, MICHELANGELO DA.

Meriton, Peter. See HUNTER, JOHN.

Merrick, Leonard (1864–1939). English novelist and playwright, whose original surname was Miller.

Merril, Judith (1923–   ). American writer, whose pseudonyms are *Ernest Hamilton, Rose Sharon, Eric Thorstein,* and, with C. M. Kornbluth, *Cyril Judd.*

Merrill, P. J. See ROTH, HOLLY.

Merriman, Henry Seton. Pseudonym of Hugh Stowell Scott (1862–1903), English novelist.

Merton, Giles. See CURRAN, MONA ELISA.

Merton, Thomas James. See LOUIS, FATHER M.

Meskill, Johanna Menzel. See MENZEL, JOHANNA.

Messager, Charles. See VILDRAC, CHARLES.

Methold, Kenneth. See KENT, ALEXANDER.

Metsys, Quentin. See MASSYS, QUENTIN.

Mewburn, Martin. Pseudonym of Martin Mewburn Hitchin (1917–   ), English writer.

Meyer, Heinrich. See MEYER, K. H. HOUSTON.

Meyer, Jerome Sydney. See JENNINGS, S. M.

Meyer, K. H. Houston. Pseudonym of Heinrich Meyer (1904–   ), German-American novelist.

Meynell, Laurence Walter (1899–   ). Mystery writer, whose pseudonyms are *Valerie Baxter, Robert Eton, Geoffrey Ludlow,* and *A. Stephen Tring.*

Michaels, Dale. Pseudonym of Shepard Rifkin (1918–   ), American editor and writer.

Michaels, Steve. See AVALLONE, MICHAEL ANGELO, JR.

Michaildis, Kleanthis. See EFTALIOTIS, ARJYRIS.

Michal. Pseudonym of Micha Joseph Lebenson (1828–1852), Hebrew poet.

Miche, Josef. Pseudonym of Joseph M. Bochenski (1902–   ), Polish author.

Michel, Claude. See CLODION.

Michele Cione, Andrea di. See VERROCCHIO, ANDREA DEL.

Michelino, Domenico di (1417–1491). Florentine painter, also known as *Domenico di Francesco.*

Michelozzi, Michelozzo. See MICHELOZZO.

Michelozzo (1396–1472). Florentine bronze caster, sculptor, and architect, whose full name was Michelozzo di Bartolommeo. He was also known as *Michelozzo Michelozzi.*

Middleton-Murry, John. See MURRY, COLIN.

Miel, Jan. See VITE, GIOVANNI DELLA.

Mielants, Florent Constant Albert, Jr. See HENSEN, HERWIG.

Miers, Earl Schenck. See MEREDITH, DAVID WILLIAM.

Mi Fu. See MEI, FEI.

Miggy, Mrs. Pseudonym of Mildred White Krentel (1921–   ), American writer.

Mihkelson, Friedebert. See TUGLAS, FRIEDEBERT.

Mikan, Baron. See BARBA, HARRY.

Mikhaylovsky, Nikolay Grigoryevich. See GARIN, N. G.

Mikkola, Maria Winter. See TALVIO, MAILA.

Mikro. Pseudonym of Christoffel Hermanus Kühn (1903–   ), Afrikaans novelist.

Miles. See SOUTHWOLD, STEPHEN.

Miles, John. See BICKHAM, JACK MILES.

Miles, Miska. Pseudonym of Patricia Miles Martin, contemporary American writer.

Militant. See SANDBURG, CARL AUGUST.

Miłkowski, Zygmunt Fortunat. See JEŻ, TEODOR TOMASZ.

Mill, C. R. Pseudonym of Milos Crnjanski (1893–   ), Hungarian-English writer.

Millar, Kenneth (1915–   ). American writer, whose pseudonyms are *John Macdonald, John Ross Macdonald,* and *Ross Macdonald.*

Millay, Edna St. Vincent. See BOYD, NANCY.

Millburn, Cynthia. See BROOKS, ANNE TEDLOCK.

Miller, Benjamin. See LOOMIS, NOEL MILLER.

Miller, Bill (1920–   ). American mystery writer, whose pseudonyms, with Bob Wade, are *Whit Masterson* and *Wade Miller.*

Miller, Cincinnatus Hiner. See MILLER, JOAQUIN.

Miller, Eugenia. Pseudonym of Eugenia Miller Mandelkorn (1916–   ), American writer.

Miller, Frank. See LOOMIS, NOEL MILLER.

Miller, G. R. See JUDD, FREDERICK CHARLES.

Miller, Harriet. See MILLER, OLIVE THORNE.

Miller, Helen Hill. See HILL, HELEN.

Miller, Joaquin. Pseudonym of Cincinnatus Hiner Miller (1750–1814), American poet and playwright.

Miller, John. See SAMACHSON, JOSEPH.

Miller, Leonard. See MERRICK, LEONARD.

Miller, Margaret J. Pseudonym of Margaret Jessy Miller Dale (1911–), English author.

Miller, Marc. Pseudonym of Marceil Genée Kolstad Baker (1911–), mystery writer.

Miller, Martha. See IVAN, MARTHA MILLER PFAFF.

Miller, Mary. Pseudonym of William Cecil Northcott (1902–   ), English writer.

Miller, Olive Thorne. Pseudonym of Harriet Miller (1831–1918), American ornithologist and writer.

Miller, Thomas. See BASKET-MAKER, THE.

Miller, Wade. See MILLER, BILL, and WADE, BOB.

Milligan, Spike. Pseudonym of Terence Alan Milligan (1918–   ), English free-lance writer.

Milligan, Terence Alan. See MILLIGAN, SPIKE.

Mills, Algernon Victor. See LATIMER, RUPERT.

Mills, Osmington. Pseudonym of Vivian Collin Brooks, contemporary mystery writer.

Milner, George. Pseudonym of George Hardinge, contemporary mystery writer.

Milner, Marion. See FIELD, JOANNA.

Milosz (1877–1939). French poet whose full name was *Oscar Wenceslas de Lubicz-Milosz.*

Milsen, Oscar. Pseudonym of Oscar Mendelsohn (1896–   ), Australian writer.

Milton, Gladys Alexandra. See CARLYLE, ANTHONY.

Miner, Opal Irene Frazine Sevrey. See SEVREY, OPAL IRENE.

Minervius. See SCHAIDENREISSER, SIMON.

Minier, Nelson. See STOUTENBURG, ADRIEN PEARL.

Minsky, Betty Jane Toebe. See TOBY, LIZ.

Minsky, N. Pseudonym of Nikolay Maximovich Vilenkin (1855–1937), Russian poet.

Minton, Paula. See LITTLE, PAUL H.

Mirabeau, Sybille Gabrielle Marie-Antoinette de Riquetti de, Comtesse de Martel de Janville. See GYP.

Miracola, Giovanni. See BRAGAGLIA, ANTON GIULIO.

Mirecourt, Eugène de. Pseudonym of Charles Jean Baptiste Jacquot (1812–1880), French journalist.

Miriam. Pseudonym of Zenon Przesmycki (1861–1944), Polish author.

Mistral, Gabriela. Pseudonym of Lucila Godoy de Alcayaga (1889–), Chilean poet.

Mistrik, Ludo. See ONDREJOV, LUDO.

Mitchell, Donald Grant. See MARVEL, IK.

Mitchell, Ewan. Pseudonym of Greville Ewan Janner (1928–), English writer on legal subjects.

Mitchell, Gladys. See HOCKABY, STEPHEN.

Mitchell, Jackson. See MATCHA, JACK.

Mitchell, James. See MONRO, JAMES.

Mitchell, James Leslie. See GIBBON, LEWIS GRASSIC.

Mitchell, Kerry. See WILKES-HUNTER, RICHARD.

Mitchell, Langdon Elwyn. See VARLEY, JOHN PHILIP.

Mizner, Elizabeth Howard. See HOWARD, ELIZABETH.

Mobachus, Vesalius. Pseudonym of Hendrik de Veer (1829–1890), Dutch writer and journalist.

Mo-ch'i. See WANG WEI.

Mo-ching-tao-jen. See WU LI.

Modell, Merriam. See PIPER, EVELYN.

Modena, Tommaso da (1325/26–1379). Italian painter, whose father's name was Barisino da Barisini. The name was derived from his birthplace, Modena.

Mo-han chai ("Ink-mad Studio"). Pseudonym of Feng Meng-lung (1574?–1645), Chinese writer.

Moineaux, Georges. See COURTELINE, GEORGES.

Moir, David Macbeth. See DELTA.

Mokuami. Pseudonym of Yoshimura Shinshichi (1816–1893), Japanese playwright, also called *Kawatake* (or *Furukawa*) *Mokuami.*

Mole, William. Pseudonym of William Antony Younger (1917–), mystery writer.

Molesworth, Mary Louisa. See GRAHAM, ENNIS.

Molière. Pseudonym of Jean Baptiste Poquelin (1622–1673), French dramatist.

Molina, Tirso de. Pseudonym of Gabriel Téllez (1571?–1648), Spanish monk, dramatist, and novelist.

Monaco, Lorenzo (1370/71–1425/26). Italian painter, apparently known in Siena as *Piero di Giovanni.*

Monger, Ifor David (1908–   ). British author, whose pseudonyms are *Peter Manngian* and *Peter Richards.*

Monig, Christopher. See CROSSEN, KENDELL.

Monk, Alan. Pseudonym of Willmore Kendall (1909–   ), American scholar.

Monkshood, G. F. Pseudonym of William James Clarke (1872–   ), mystery writer.

Monniot, Jean-Vorle. See MARY, ANDRÉ.

Monro, James. Pseudonym of James Mitchell (1926–   ), English writer.

Monroe, Keith (1917–   ). American author, whose pseudonyms are *Dale Colombo* and *Donald Keith.*

Monroe, Lyle. See HEINLEIN, ROBERT ANSON.

Mont, Pol de. Pseudonym of Karel Maria Polydoor (1857–1931), Flemish poet and art critic.

Montagu of Beaulieu, third baron. Pseudonym of Edward John Barrington Douglas-Scott-Montagu (1926–   ), English writer.

Montclair, Dennis. See SLADEN, NORMAN ST. BARBE.

Montcorbier, François de. See VILLON, FRANÇOIS.

Monteiro e Grilo, Joaquim Fernandes Tomás. See KIM, TOMÁS.

Montez, Lola. Stage name of Marie Dolores Eliza Rosanna Gilbert (1818?–1861), British dancer, writer, and adventuress.

Montgomery, Leslie Alexander. See DOYLE, LYNN.

Montgomery, Robert Bruce. See CRISPIN, EDMUNDS.

Montgomery, Rutherford George (1894–   ). American free-lance writer, whose pseudonyms are *Al Avery* and *Everitt Proctor.*

Montoro, Antón de. See ROPERO, EL.

Mooney, Canice Albert James. See O MAONAIGH, CAINNEACH.

Moore, Austin. Pseudonym of Augustus Muir, contemporary English writer.

Moore, Fenworth. Collective pseudonym for the "Jerry Ford Wonder Stories" series. See STRATEMEYER, EDWARD L.

Moore, Rosalie. Pseudonym of Rosalie Gertrude Moore Brown (1910–   ), American writer.

Moore, Thomas (1779–1852). Irish poet, whose pseudonyms are *Thomas Little* and *Thomas Brown the younger.*

Moorhouse, Herbert Joseph. See MOORHOUSE, HOPKINS.

Moorhouse, Hilda Vansittart. See VANSITTART, JANE.

Moorhouse, Hopkins. Pseudonym of Herbert Joseph Moorhouse (1882–), mystery writer.

Moorshead, Henry. Pseudonym of Leslie Gilbert Pine (1907–), English writer.

Moraes, Frank Robert. See ARIEL.

Moran, Mike. See ARD, WILLIAM THOMAS.

Moravia, Alberto. Pseudonym of Alberto Pincherle (1907–), Italian journalist and novelist.

Mordaunt, Eleanor. See MORDAUNT, EVELYN MAY.

Mordaunt, Elinor. See MORDAUNT, EVELYN MAY.

Mordaunt, Evelyn May (1877–1942). Mystery writer, whose pseudonyms are *Eleanor Mordaunt, Elinor Mordaunt,* and *A. Riposte.*

More, Caroline. Pseudonym of Margaret Pitcairn Strachan (1908–), American writer.

Moréas, Jean. Pseudonym of Ioannis Papadiamantopoulos (1856–1910), Greco-French poet.

Moreau, Hégésippe. Pseudonym of Pierre Jacques Roulliot (1810–1838), French poet.

Morehead, Albert Hodges. See HODGES, TURNER.

Morel, Dighton. Pseudonym of Kenneth Lewis Warner (1915–), English-German novelist.

Morelli, Giovanni. See LERMOLIEV, IVAN.

Moreno, Bento. Pseudonym of Francisco Teixeira de Queirós (1848–1919), Portuguese novelist and short-story writer.

Moresby, Louis. See BECK, LILY ADAMS.

Moreton, John. Pseudonym of Morton Norton Cohen (1921–), American writer.

Moretto, Il. Cognomen of Alessandro Bonvicino (or Buonvicino) (1498–1554), Italian painter. He was also known as *Moretto da Brescia.*

Morey, Charles. See FLETCHER, HELEN JILL.

Morgan, Claire. Pseudonym of Patricia Highsmith (1921–), mystery writer.

Morgan, Emanuel. See BYNNER, WITTER.

Morgan, Michael. Joint pseudonym of C. E. Carle and Dean M. Dorn, contemporary mystery writers.

Morgan, Murray Cromwell. See MURRAY, CROMWELL.

Morgan, Nicholas. See MORGAN, THOMAS BRUCE.

Morgan, Stephen. Pseudonym of Thomas C. Murray, one of "the Cork realists," used in writing *The Serf* (1920).

Morgan, Thomas Bruce (1926–   ). American writer, whose pseudonyms are *Nicholas David* and *Nicholas Morgan*.

Morgan, Thomas Christopher. See MUIR, JOHN.

Mori Ogai. Pseudonym of Mori Rintaro (1862–1922), Japanese writer.

Mori Rintaro. See MORI OGAI.

Morin, Claire. See DORE, CLAIRE MORIN.

Morita Sohei. Pseudonym of Morita Yonematsu (1881–   ), Japanese writer and translator of Spanish novels.

Morita Yonematsu. See MORITA SOHEI.

Morland, Nigel (1905–   ). Mystery writer, whose pseudonyms are *Mary Dane, John Donavan, Norman Forrest, Roger Garnett,* and *Neal Shephard.*

Morris, Ruth. Pseudonym of Ruth Enid Borlase Morris Webb (1926–   ), Australian writer.

Morris, Sara. See BURKE, JOHN FREDERICK.

Morrison, Gert W. See STRATEMEYER, EDWARD L.

Morrison, Velma Ford. See FORD, HILDEGARDE.

Morrison, William. See SAMACHSON, JOSEPH.

Morrow, Charlotte. Pseudonym of Molly Morrow Kirwan (1906–   ), English writer.

Morse, Anne Christensen. See HEAD, ANN.

Morse, H. Clifton. See FOURTH, CLIFTON.

Mort, Vivian. See CROMIE, ALICE HAMILTON.

Mortimer, Chapman. Pseudonym of William Charles Chapman-Mortimer (1907–   ), Scottish-Swedish author.

Mortimer, Peter. Pseudonym of Dorothy James Roberts (1903–   ), American author.

Morton, Anthony. See CREASEY, JOHN.

Morton, Guy Mainwaring (1896–   ). English novelist and playwright, whose pseudonyms are *Mark Forrest* and *Peter Traill.* His original surname was Dunstan.

Morton, Sarah Wentworth. See PHILENIA.

Morton, William. Pseudonym of William Blair Morton Ferguson (1882–   ), American mystery writer.

Moscherosch, Johann Michael. See SITTEWALD, PHILANDER VON.

Moselly, Émile. Pseudonym of Émile Chénin (1870–1918), French novelist.

Mosenrosh, Johann Michael. See SITTEWALD, PHILANDER VON.

Moses ben Maimon. See MAIMONIDES, MOSES.

Moskowitz, Sam. See MARTIN, SAM.

Moss, Nancy. See MOSS, ROBERT.

Moss, Robert (1903–   ). English writer, whose pseudonyms are *Nancy Moss* and *Roberta Moss.*

Moss, Roberta. See MOSS, ROBERT.

Moth. See FLEMING, PETER.

Motley, Mary. Pseudonym of Mary Margaret Motley Sheridan De Reneville (1912–   ), English writer.

Mott, Edward Spencer (1844–1910). Mystery writer, whose pseudonyms are *Nathaniel Gubbins* and *Edward Spencer.*

Motte, Peter. Pseudonym of Richard Harrison (1901–   ), mystery writer.

Moulié, Charles. See SANDRE, THIERRY.

Mowbray, John. See VAHEY, JOHN GEORGE HASLETTE.

Mowlavi ("Whirling Dervish"). Pseudonym of Jalal al-Din Muhammad Rumi (1207–1273), Persian poet and mystic.

Mu-ch'i. 13th-century Chinese painter, also known as *Fa-ch'ang.*

Muddock, Joyce Emmerson Preston. See DONOVAN, DICK.

Mude, O. See GOREY, EDWARD ST. JOHN.

Mudgett, Herman W. See BOUCHER, ANTHONY.

Muensterberg, Hugo. See TERBERG, HUGO.

Muhammad-i Mas'ud. See DIHATI, MUHAMMAD-I MAS'UD.

Mühlbach, Luise. Pseudonym of Klara Mundt (1814–1873), German novelist.

Muir, Augustus. See MOORE, AUSTIN.

Muir, Barbara K. See KAYE, BARBARA.

Muir, Dexter. See GRIBBLE, LEONARD REGINALD.

Muir, Jane. Pseudonym of Jane Muir Petrone (1929–   ), American writer.

Muir, John. Pseudonym of Thomas Christopher Morgan, contemporary mystery writer.

Muir, Kenneth Arthur. See FINNEY, MARK.

Muir, Marie (1904–   ). English writer, whose pseudonyms are *Monica Blake, Monica Clynder,* and *Jean Scott.*

Mukai Kanetoki. See KYORAI.

Mulcahy, Lucille Burnett. See HALE, HELEN.

Mulder, Hendrik Adriaan. See HESSELS, WILLEM.

Mulder, Lodewijk. See LODEWYK.

Muller, Charles George. See GEOFFREY, Charles.

Müller, Johann. See REGIOMONTANUS.

Müller, Wilhelm. See FRATER JOCUNDUS.

Müller-Guttenbrunn, Adam. See IGNOTUS.

Mullins, Ann. Pseudonym of Ann Mullins Dally (1926–   ), English writer.

Multatuli. Pseudonym of Eduard Douwes Dekker (1820–1887), Dutch novelist, playwright, and essayist.

Munce, Ruth Hill. See HILL, RUTH LIVINGSTON.

Münch-Bellinghausen, Baron Eligius Franz Joseph Freiherr von. See HALM, FRIEDRICH.

Mundt, Klara. See MÜHLBACH, LUISE.

Munefusa, Matsuo. See BASHO.

Munger, Al. Pseudonym of Maurice Albert Unger (1917–   ), American writer.

Munk, Kaj. Pseudonym of Kaj Harald Leininger Peterson (1878–1944), Danish poet and playwright.

Muñoz, Eugenio. See NOEL, EUGENIO.

Munro, Charles Kirkpatrick. Pseudonym of Charles Walden Kirkpatrick MacMullan (1889–   ), British playwright.

Munro, Hector Hugh. See SAKI.

Munro, Neil. See FOULIS, HUGH.

Munroe, Elizabeth Lee. See GRENELLE, LISA.

Munroe, James. Pseudonym of Roderick George James Munroe Cave (1935–   ), English writer.

Munthe, Frances. See COWEN, FRANCES.

Murad Efendi. Pseudonym of Franz von Werner (1834–1881), Austrian-Turkish poet and playwright.

Murai Gensai. Pseudonym of Murai Hiroshi (1863–1927), Japanese novelist.

Murai Hiroshi. See MURAI GENSAI.

Murano, Antonio da (c1420–1476/1484). Venetian painter, whose real name was Antonio Vivarini. His brother and son are also well-known under the family name Vivarini. The name was derived from the island Murano, in the Venetian lagoon, where his family lived.

Murasaki Shikibu (c978–1031?). Japanese novelist and poet, whose real name is unknown except for the fact that she belonged to the Fujiwara clan.

Murfree, Mary Noailles. See CRADDOCK, CHARLES EGBERT.

Muriel, John Saint Clair (1909–   ). British mystery writer, whose pseudonyms are *Simon Dewes* and *John Lindsay.*

Muro Kyuso. Pseudonym of Muro Naokiyo (1658–1734), Japanese writer.

Muro Naokiyo. See MURO KYUSO.

Murray, Adrian. See CURRAN, MONA ELISA.

Murray, Cromwell. Pseudonym of Murray Cromwell Morgan (1916–   ), mystery writer.

Murray, John. See COMBS, ROBERT.

Murray, Thomas C. See MORGAN, STEPHEN.

Murry, Colin. Pseudonym of John Middleton-Murry (1926–   ), English writer.

Musketeer. Pseudonym of Arthur James Barker (1918–   ), English writer.

Mustapää, P. Pseudonym of Martti Haavio (1899–   ), Finnish poet.

Mutanabbi al- (915–965). Arabic poet, whose name is a cognomen meaning "one who pretends to be a prophet." His real name is unknown.

Mutt, R. See DUCHAMP, MARCEL.

Muzakova, Johanna. See SVETLA, KAROLINA.

Muziano, Girolamo (1528?–1592). Italian painter, also known as *Girolamo Bressano* and *Brescianino.*

Mykolaitis, Vincas. See PUTINAS.

Myles, Devera. See ZUCKER, DOLORES MAE BOLTON.

Myrnyj, Panas Jakovich. Pseudonym of Rudcenko Panas (1849–1920), Ukrainian writer.

"N"

Nabokov, Vladimir Vladimirovich. See SIRIN, VLADIMIR.

Nabuco, Joaquim. Pseudonym of Joachim Aurelio Barreto Nabuco de Araujo (1849–1910), Brazilian writer.

Nachmanides, Rabbi Moses ben Nahman Gerondi (1194–c1270). Spanish-Hebrew religious writer and poet, known as *Ramban* and, in Spain, *Bonastruc da Porta.*

Nadar. Pseudonym of Félix Tournachon (1820–1910), French writer.

Nadasi, Ladislav. See JEGE.

Nadejde, Cornelia. See MANTU, LUCIA.

Nadir, Moishe. Pseudonym of Yitzchok Reiz (1885–1943), Yiddish satirist.

Nagai Kafu. Pseudonym of Nagai Sokichi (1879–   ), Japanese writer.

Nagai Sokichi. See NAGAI, KAFU.

Nagdela, Samuel ben Joseph ibn-. See SAMUEL HA-NAGID.

Nagel, Willen Hendrik. See CHARLES, J. B.

Na Gopaleen, Myles. See Ó NUALLAIN, BRIAIN.

Nagrela, Samuel ben Joseph ibn-. See SAMUEL HA-NAGID.

Nahman of Bratzlav (1770–1811). Russian Jewish writer. Also known as *Maharan.*

Naili. Pseudonym of Mustafa Celebi (d. 1668), Turkish poet.

Naimy, Mikha'il (1889–   ). Syrian-American Arabic literary critic and essayist, also known as *Mikha'il Nu'aimah.*

Naito Meisetsu. Pseudonym of Naito Soko (1847–1926), Japanese haiku poet, also known simply as *Meisetsu.*

Naito Soko. See NAITO MEISETSU.

Nakamura Kichizo. Pseudonym of Nakamura Tsuneharu (1877–1941), Japanese dramatist and novelist.

Nakamura Tsuneharu. See NAKAMURA KICHIZO.

Nakazato Kaizan. Pseudonym of Nakazato Yanosuke (1885–1944), Japanese novelist.

Nakazato Yanosuke. See NAKAZATO KAIZAN.

Nakiko. See SEI SHONAGON.

Namiki Senryu. Pseudonym of Namiki Sosuke (c1695–1751), Japanese writer of puppet plays.

Namiki Sosuke. See NAMIKI SENRYU.

Namovicz, Gene Inyart. See INYART, GENE.

Nandakumar, Prema. See ASWIN.

Napierski. Pseudonym of Antoni Lange (1861–1929), Polish poet.

Narayana. See RAMDAS, MARATHI.

Nasby, Petroleum V. Pseudonym of David Ross Locke (1833–1888), American journalist.

Nascimento, Francisco Manoel do. See ELYSIO, FILINTO.

Nash, Chandler. Pseudonym of Katharine Chandler Hunt, contemporary mystery writer.

Nash, Simon. Pseudonym of Raymond Chapman (1924–   ), British author.

Nash, Thomas. See PASQUIL.

Nasier, Alcofribas. Anagrammatic pseudonym of François Rabelais (1494?–1553), monk and novelist.

Nason, Leonard Hastings. See STEAMER.

Nast, Elsa Ruth. See WATSON, JANE WERNER.

Nathan, Daniel. See DANNAY, FREDERIC, and LEE, MANFRED B.

Natsume Kinnosuke. See NATSUME SOSEKI.

Natsume Soseki. Pseudonym of Natsume Kinnosuke (1867–1916), Japanese novelist, essayist, critic, and poet. He was also known simply as *Soseki.*

Nauticus. Pseudonym of Sir William Laird Clowes (1856–1905), English naval writer.

Naydenov, S. Pseudonym of Sergey Alexandrovich Alexeyev (1869–1922), Russian playwright.

Neal, Adeline Phyllis. See GREY, A. F.

Neal, Harry. See BIXBY, JEROME LEWIS.

Neal, Hilary. See NORTON, OLIVE.

Neander, Hippophilus. Grecized name of Philip Numan (c1550–1617), Dutch poet.

Neander, Johann August Wilhelm (1789–1850). German Protestant church historian and theologian, whose original name was David Mendel.

Nebrija (or Lebrija), Elio Antonio de. Pseudonym of Antonio Martínez de Cala (1444?–1532), Spanish humanist.

Necati. Pseudonym of Isa (d. 1509), Turkish poet.

Neckham, Alexander (1157–1217). English grammarian, poet, and cleric. His name is a fourteenth-century corruption of his cognomen, *Nequam* ("Worthless," "Good-for-nothing"). The earliest authorities call him simply *Alexander of St. Albans.*

Neera. Pseudonym of Anna Radius Zuccari (1846–1918), Italian writer of romantic stories.

Nef'i. Pseudonym of Omer (d. 1634), Turkish poet and satirist.

Nehajev, Milutin. pseudonym of Milutin Cihlar (1880–1931), Croatian writer.

Nelli, Pietro. See BERGAMO, ANDREA DA.

Nelms, Henning. See TALBOT, HAKE.

Nelson, Lawrence. See TRENT, PETER.

Nelson, Marguerite. See FLOREN, LEE.

Nelson, Michael Harrington. See STRATTON, HENRY.

Nemi, Orsola. Pseudonym of Flora Vezzani (1905–   ), Italian writer.

Nemo, L. P. See HERMON, ROPARZ.

Nepveu, André. See DURTAIN, LUC.

Nerval, Gérard de. Pseudonym of Gérard Labrunie (1808–1855), French poet.

Nesbit, Troy. See FOLSOM, FRANKLIN BREWSTER.

Nesimi. Pseudonym of Seyid Imadeddin (d. 1417), Turkish poet and mystic.

Nesmith, Robert I. See CLARKE, CAPTAIN JAFER.

Neubauer, William Arthur (1916–   ). American writer, whose pseudonyms are *William Arthur, Christine Bennett, Norman Bligh, Ralph Carter, Joan Garrison, Jan Hathaway, Rebecca Marsh, Norma Newcomb,* and *Gordon Semple.*

Neuwert. See NOWACZYNSKI, ADOLF.

Neverov, Alexander (1886–1923). Soviet author, also known as *Alexander Sergeyevich Skobelev.*

Neville, Barbara Alison Boodson. See CANDY, EDWARD.

Neville, C. J. Pseudonym of Cynthia Franklin, contemporary American mystery writer.

Neville, Margot. Joint pseudonym of Margot Goyder (1903–   ) and Neville Goyder Joske (1893–   ), mystery writers.

Newby, Eric. See PARKER, JAMES.

Newcomb, Ellsworth. Occasional pseudonym of Ellsworth Newcomb Kenny (1909–   ), American free-lance writer.

Newcomb, Norma. See NEUBAUER, WILLIAM ARTHUR.

Newcomen, Matthew. See SMECTYMNUUS.

Newell, Robert Henry. See KERR, ORPHEUS C.

Newman, Bernard. See BETTERIDGE, DON.

Newman, John. See BLUMER, HENRY KENNETH.

Newton, Dwight Bennett (1916–   ). American writer, whose pseudonyms are *Dwight Bennett, Clement Hardin, Ford Logan,* and *Dan Temple.*

Newton, Francis. Pseudonym of Eric John Ernest Hobsbawm (1917–   ), British scholar.

Nguya Trong-Tri. See HAN MAC-TU.

Nguyen Tuong-Long. See HOANG DAO.

Nichols, Dale. See POLMAN, WILLEM DE.

Nichols, Dave. Pseudonym of Helen Frost (1898–   ), American writer.

Nichols, Fran. Pseudonym of Frances Nicholas Hanna, contemporary mystery writer.

Nicholson, David. See ROC, JOHN.

Nicholson, Margaret Beda Larminie. See YORKE, MARGARET.

Nicolai, Joannes. See SECUNDUS, JANUS.

Nicolaie, Louis François. See CLAIRVILLE, LOUIS FRANÇOIS.

Nicoll, Sir William Robertson. See CLEAR, CLAUDIUS.

Nicolson, John Urban. See KING OF THE BLACK ISLES.

Nielsen, Helen Berniece. See GILES, KRIS.

Nielsen, Jean Sarver. See SARVER, HANNAH.

Niemojewski, Andrzej. See LAMBRO.

Nienkarken, Boysen van. See BOYSEN, JOHANN WILHELM.

Nies, Konrad. See ALZEY, KONRAD VON.

Niese, Charlotte. See BÜRGER, LUCIAN.

Nieuwenhuys, Robert. See BRETON DE NIJS, E.

Niger, Shmuel. Pseudonym of Shmuel Charni (1884–   ), Yiddish literary critic and essayist.

Nikolaeva, Galina Evgenevna. Pseudonym of Galina Evgenevna Volyanskaya (1914–   ), Russian writer.

Nimrod. Pseudonym of Charles James Apperley (1777?–1843), Welsh sporting writer.

Nishiyama Toyokazu. See SOIN.

Nisot, Mavis Elizabeth Hocking. See PENMARE, WILLIAM.

Nodset, Joan L. Pseudonym of Joan M. Lexau, contemporary American writer.

Noel, Eugenio. Pseudonym of Eugenio Muñoz (1885–1936), Spanish intellectual and polemicist.

Noel, L. Pseudonym of Leonard Noel Barker (1882–   ), mystery writer.

Nöel, Marie. Pseudonym of Marie-Mélanie Rouget (1883–   ), French poet.

Nolan, Jeannette Covert. See TUCKER, CAROLINE.

Nolan, William Francis (1928–   ). American science-fiction writer, whose pseudonyms are *Frank Anmar*, *F. E. Edwards*, and *Michael Phillips*.

Nolde, Emil (1867–1956). German painter and graphic artist, whose original surname was Hansen. The name was derived from his birthplace, Nolde, in northern Germany.

Noll, Bink. Pseudonym of Lou Barker Noll (1927–   ), American writer.

Noll, Lou Barker. See NOLL, BINK.

Noll, Martin. Pseudonym of Martin Buxbaum (1913–   ), American writer.

Nor, A. C. Pseudonym of Josef Kavan (1903–   ), Czech novelist.

Norcross, John. See CONROY, JOHN WESLEY.

Nordau, Max Simon. Pseudonym of Max Simon Südfeld (1849–1923), German writer.

Norden, Charles. See DURRELL, LAWRENCE GEORGE.

Nordhausen, Richard. See CALIBAN.

Norman, James. Pseudonym of James Norman Schmidt (1912–   ), mystery writer.

Norman, Joe. Pseudonym of Joseph Norman Heard (1922–   ), American writer.

Norris, Benjamin Franklin. See NORRIS, FRANK.

Norris, Frank. Pseudonym of Benjamin Franklin Norris (1870–1902), American novelist.

Norse, Alan Edward. See EDWARDS, AL.

North, Andrew. See NORTON, ALICE MARY.

North, Barclay. Pseudonym of William Cadwalader Hudson (1843–1915), mystery writer.

North, Charles W. See BAUER, ERWIN A.

North, Christopher. Pseudonym of John Wilson (1785–1854), Scottish journalist.

North, Eric. See CRONIN, BERNARD.

North, Gil. Pseudonym of Geoffrey Horne (1916–   ), English writer.

North, William (b. 1869). Mystery writer, whose pseudonyms are *Ralph Rodd* and *John Vanner*.

Northcote. See COTES, PETER.

Northcott, William Cecil. See MILLER, MARY.

Northumbrian Gentleman, The. See TEGNER, HENRY.

Norton, Alice Mary. Contemporary American writer, whose pseudonyms are *Andrew North, Andre Norton*, and, with Grace Allen Hogarth, *Allen Weston*.

Norton, Andre. See NORTON, ALICE MARY.

Norton, Bess. See NORTON, OLIVE.

Norton, Olive (1913–). English writer, whose pseudonyms are *Hilary Neal, Bess Norton,* and *Kate Norway.*

Norway, Kate. See NORTON, OLIVE.

Norway, Nevil Shute. See SHUTE, NEVIL.

Norwood, John. Pseudonym of Raymond Stark, contemporary mystery writer.

Notker (950–1022). Germanic writer and monk of the Abbey of St. Gaul, called *Labeo* and *Teutonicus.*

Notker. See BALBULUS THE STAMMERER.

Noto, Il. Cognomen of Jacopo (or Giacomo) da Lentini (1180/90–c1240), Italian poet.

Novachovitch, Lippe Benzion. See Winchevsky, Morris.

Novak, Joseph. Pseudonym of Jerzy Kosinski (1933–), Polish-American writer.

Novak, Karel. See NOVY, KAREL.

Novalis. Pseudonym of Baron Friedrich Leopold von Hardenberg (1772–1801), German poet.

Novelli, Enrico. See YAMBO.

Noventa, Giacomo. Pseudonym of Giacomo Zorzi (1878–1960), Italian poet.

Noviomagnus. See GELDENHAUER, GERARDUS.

Novodvorsky, Andrey Osipovich. See OSIPOVICH, A.

Novomiski, Moishe. See OLGIN, M. J.

Novy, Karel. Pseudonym of Karel Novak (1890–), Czech writer.

Nowaczynski, Adolf (1876–1944). Polish writer, whose pseudonyms are *Neuwert* and *Przyjaciel.*

Nowakowski, Zygmunt. See TEMPKA, ZYGMUNT.

Nozaki Bunyo. See KANAGAKI ROBIN.

Nu'aimah, Mikha'il. See NAIMY, MIKHA'IL.

Nucera, Marisa Lonette. See MARISA.

Nugent, John Peter. See EXALL, BARRY.

Nuitter. Anagrammatic pseudonym of Charles Louis Étienne Truinet (1828–1899), French playwright.

Numan, Philip. See NEANDER, HIPPOPHILUS.

Núñez de Guzmán, Hermán. See COMENDADOR GRIEGO, EL.

Nunn, William Curtis (1908–). American professor of history, whose pseudonyms are *Will Curtis* and *Ananias Twist.*

Nuraini. Pseudonym of Katharine Sim (1913–   ), English writer.
Nye, Nelson Coral (1907–   ). American writer, whose pseudonyms
are *Clem Colt, Drake C. Denver,* and *Montague Rockingham.*

"O"

Oakley, Eric Gilbert (1916–   ). English writer, whose pseudonyms
are *Peter Capon, Grapho,* and *Paul Gregson.*
Oberholtzer, Peter. See BRANNON, WILLIAM T.
Oboe, Peter. Pseudonym of Walter Darnell Jacobs (1922–   ), Ameri-
can scholar.
O'Brian, Frank. See GARFIELD, BRIAN WYNNE.
O'Brien, Dean D. See BINDER, OTTO OSCAR.
O'Brien, Flann. See Ó NUALLAIN, BRIAIN.
O'Brien, Howard Vincent. See PERRIN, CLYDE.
Occidente, María del. Pseudonym of Maria Brooks (1794?–1845),
American poet.
O'Connell, Peg. Pseudonym of Margaret McCrohan Ahern (1921–
    ), American free-lance cartoonist, illustrator, and writer.
O'Connor, Frank. Pseudonym of Michael O'Donovan (1903–1966),
Irish writer.
O'Connor, Liam. See LIDDY, JAMES.
O'Connor, Sister Mary Catharine. See FARRELL, CATHARINE.
O'Connor, Patrick. See WIBBERLEY, LEONARD PATRICK O'CONNOR.
O'Connor, Thomas Power. See TAY PAY.
Odell, Carol. See ODELL, GILL.
Odell, Gill. Joint pseudonym of Traviss Gill (1891–   ) and Carol
Odell, English writers.
Odem, J. Pseudonym of Jacob A. Rubin (1910–   ), Austrian-Ameri-
can journalist and author.
O'Donovan, Michael. See O'CONNOR, FRANK.
Oe Shikibu. See IZUMI SHIKIBU.
Oevere, William van. Pseudonym of August Pieter van Groeningen
(1865–1894), Dutch writer.
O'Farachain, Roibeard. Gaelic name of Robert Farren (1909–   ),
Irish poet.
O'Finn, Thaddeus. Pseudonym of Joseph Thaddeus McGloin (1917–
    ), American writer.

Ogawa Kensaku. See OGAWA MIMEI.

Ogawa Mimei. Pseudonym of Ogawa Kensaku (1882–   ), Japanese novelist.

Ognall, Leopold Horace (1908–   ). British writer, whose pseudonyms are *Harry Carmichael* and *Hartley Howard.*

Ognëv, Nikolay. Pseudonym of Michail Grigorevich Rozanov (1888–1938), Russian writer.

O'Grady, Rohan. Pseudonym of June O'Grady Skinner (1922–   ), Canadian author.

Ogyu Soemon. See OGYU SORAI.

Ogyu Sorai. Pseudonym of Ogyu Soemon (1666–1728), Japanese writer.

O'Hara, Dale. See GILLESE, JOHN PATRICK.

O'Hara, Kevin. See CUMBERLAND, MARTEN.

O'Hara, Mary. Pseudonym of Mary O'Hara Alsop (1885–   ), American writer.

Ohon. See BARBA, HARRY.

O Judeu (1705–1739). Portuguese playwright, whose real name was Antônio José da Silva.

Okoński, Władysław. Pseudonym of Aleksander Swietochowski (1849–1938), Polish playwright and short-story writer.

Oksanen. Pseudonym of Carl August Engelbrekt Ahlqvist (1826–1889), Finnish philosopher and poet.

Ó Laoghaire, An Tathair Peadar. Gaelic name of Peter O'Leary (1839–1920), Irish writer and playwright.

Olbracht, Ivan. Pseudonym of Kamil Zeman (1882–1952), Czech novelist.

Old Cap Collier. Pseudonym used by various authors of the series: W. I. James (no dates available), Thomas C. Harbaugh (1849–1924), and Bernard Wayde (no dates available).

Oldfeld, Peter. Joint pseudonym of Vernon Bartlett (1894–   ) and P. Jacobsson, mystery writers.

Oldfield, Claude Houghton. See HOUGHTON, CLAUDE.

Old Settler, The. Pseudonym of Albert Robinson Lyman (1880–   ), American writer.

Oldstyle, Jonathan. See IRVING, WASHINGTON.

O'Leary, Chester F. See KUEHNELT-LEDDIHN, ERIK RITTER VON.

O'Leary, Peter. See Ó LAOGHAIRE, AN TATHAIR PEADAR.

Olgin, M. J. Pseudonym of Moishe Novomiski (1878–1939), Yiddish writer.

Oliver, Gail. See SCOTT, MARIAN GALLAGHER.

Oliver, George. See ONIONS, OLIVER.

Oliver, Jane. Pseudonym of Helen Christina Easson Rees (1903–   ), English writer.

Olmsted, Charlotte. Pseudonym of Charlotte Olmsted Kursh (1912–   ), American writer.

Olofsson, Georg. See STIERNHIELM, GEORG.

Olsen, John Edward. See RHOADES, JONATHAN.

Olsen, Theodore Victor (1932–   ). American writer, whose pseudonyms are *Joshua Stark* and *Christopher Storm.*

Oltmans, Jan Frederik. See HAGE, J. VAN DEN.

O'Malley, Frank. Pseudonym of Frank O'Rourke (1916–   ), mystery writer.

O'Malley, Kevin. See HOSSENT, HARRY.

Oman, Carola Mary Anima. See LENANTON, C.

O Maonaigh, Cainneach. Gaelic name of Canice Albert James Mooney (1911–   ), Irish writer.

Omer. See NEF'I.

Ompteda, Baron Georg von. See EGESTORFF, GEORG.

O'Nair, Mairi. See EVANS, CONSTANCE MAY.

Onciropolos ("Son of the Dreamer"). Pseudonym of Charles Johnstone (1719–1800), Irish author.

Ondere, Jochem van. See VITRINGA, ANNES JOHAN.

Ondrejov, Ludo. Pseudonym of Ludo Mistrik (1901–   ), Slovak writer.

O'Neil, Kerry. Pseudonym of John Thomas McIntyre (1871–1951), mystery writer.

O'Neill, Egan. See LININGTON, ELIZABETH.

O'Neill, Moira. Pseudonym of Agnes Skrine, contemporary Irish poet.

O'Niell, C. M. See WILKES-HUNTER, RICHARD.

Onions, Oliver. Pseudonym of George Oliver, contemporary mystery writer.

Onkel Adam. Pseudonym of Carl Anton Wetterbergh (1804–1889), Swedish writer.

Onkel Tom. Pseudonym of Ludwig Hevesi (1843–1910), Austro-Hungarian journalist.

Onlooker. See GRANGE, CYRIL.

Ó Nuallain, Briain (1890–1966). Irish author. As *Myles na Gopaleen* he is a satirical columnist and dramatist. His name in English is Flann O'Brien.

Oom Warden. Pseudonym of Edward Vermeulen (1861–1943), Flemish novelist.

Oppenheim, Edward Phillips. See PARTRIDGE, ANTHONY.

Oppenheimer, Joel Lester. See AQUARIAN.

Oppmann, Artur. See OR-OT.

Optic, Oliver. Pseudonym of William Taylor Adams (1822–1887), American writer of boys' books.

Orbison, Keck. Joint pseudonym of Maud Keck and Olive Orbison, contemporary mystery writers.

Orbison, Olive. See ORBISON, KECK.

Orcagna, Andrea (fl. 1343–1368). Florentine painter, sculptor, and architect, whose real name was Andrea di Cione. The name was derived from his cognomen, *Arcagnuolo* ("Archangel").

Orchella, R. L. Pseudonym of Herman George Scheffauer (1878–1927), German-American writer and translator.

O'Reilly, Montagu. Pseudonym of Wayne Andrews (1913–   ), American author.

O'Rell, Max. Pseudonym of Paul Blouet (1848–1903), French writer.

Organ, John (1925–   ). English writer, whose pseudonyms are *Graham Ashley* and *Desmond Farrell.*

O'Riordan, Conal O'Connell. See CONNELL, NORREYS.

Orkan, Władysław. Pseudonym of Franciszek Smreczyński (1876–1930), Polish writer.

Orland, Claude. See ROY, CLAUDE.

Ormiston, Roberta. Pseudonym of Adele Fletcher (1898–   ), American free-lance writer.

Ormsbee, David. See LONGSTREET, STEPHEN.

Or-ot. Pseudonym of Artur Oppmann (1867–1931), Polish poet.

O'Rourke, Frank. See O'MALLEY, FRANK.

Orr, Mary. See DENHAM, MARY ORR.

Orrmont, Arthur. See HUNTER, ANSON.

Orsini, Giulio. See GNOLI, DOMENICO.

Ors y Rovira, Eugenio D'. See XENIUS.

Országh, Pavol. See HVIEZDOSLAV.

Örtel, Philipp Friedrich Wilhelm. See HORN, W. O. VON.

Orvar Odd. Pseudonym of Oscar Patrik Sturzen-Becker (1811–1869), Swedish poet and writer, whose original name was Sturtzen-Becher.

Orwell, George. Pseudonym of Eric Arthur Blair (1903–1950), English essayist and novelist.

Orwid, Władysław. See DANILOWSKI, GUSTAW.

Osborne, Charles Humfrey Caulfield. See HUMFREY, C.

Osceola. See BLIXEN-FINECKE, BARONESS KAREN CHRISTENTZE.

O Siochain, P. A. See SHEEHAN, PATRIC AUGUSTINE.

Osipovich, A. Pseudonym of Andrey Osipovich Novodvorsky (1853–1882), Russian writer.

Osman. See RUHI.

Osnovyanenko. Pseudonym of Grigori Petrovich Kvitka (1778–1843), Ukrainian writer.

Osorgin, M. A. Pseudonym of M. A. Ilyin (1878–1942), Russian émigré writer.

Osorio, Miguel Ángel. See BARBA-JACOB, PORFIRIO.

Ostrander, Isabel Egenton (1883–1924). Mystery writer, whose pseudonyms are *Robert Orr Chipperfield, David Fox,* and *Douglas Grant.*

O'Sullivan, Seumas. Pseudonym of James Sullivan Starkey (1879–1958), Irish poet and essayist.

Ota Nampo. See OTA TAN.

Ota Tan (1749–1823). Japanese comic writer, whose pseudonyms are *Ota Nampo* and *Shokusanjin.*

Otis, George. See MELLEN, IDA MAY.

Ott, Peter. Pseudonym of Dietrich Von Hildebrand (1889–   ), Italian-American scholar.

Ottesen, Thea Tauber. See BANK-JENSEN.

Oude Heer Smits, De ("Old Mr. Smits"). Pseudonym of Mark Prager Lindo (1819–1879), Dutch humorous writer.

Oudshoorn, J. van. Pseudonym of J. K. Feylbrief (1877–1951), Dutch novelist.

Ouida. Pseudonym of Marie Louise de la Ramée (1839–1908), English novelist.

Oursler, Charles Fulton. See ABBOT, ANTHONY.

Oursler, William Charles. See GALLAGHER, GALE.

Oved, M. See GOOD, EDWARD.

Overholser, Wayne D. (1906–). American writer, whose pseudonyms are *John S. Daniels, Lee Leighton, Wayne Roberts, Dan J. Stevens,* and *Joseph Wayne.*

Owen, Frank. See CATO.

Owen, Harry Collinson. See ADDISON, HUGH.

Owl, Sebastian. Pseudonym of Hunter S. Thompson (1939–), American free-lance writer.

Oxenham, John (1861?–1941). English businessman and writer, whose original name was William Arthur Dunkerley.

Oy-vik. See HOLMVIK, OYVIND.

Ozaki, Milton K. See SABER, ROBERT O.

Ozaki Koyo. Pseudonym of Ozaki Tokutaro (1868–1903), Japanese novelist.

Ozaki Tokutaro. See OZAKI KOYO.

Ozawa Genchu. See OZAWA ROAN.

Ozawa Roan. Pseudonym of Ozawa Genchu (1723–1801), Japanese poet.

Ozy. Pseudonym of Benjamin Charles Rosset (1910–), Russian-Irish writer.

"P"

Paaltjens, Piet. Pseudonym of François Haverschmidt (1835–1894), Dutch Reformed Church preacher and poet.

Paasche, Johan Fredrik (1886–1943). Norwegian literary historian, whose original surname was Amundsen.

Pab. Pseudonym of Percy A. Blooman (1906–), English–South African writer.

Pace, Domenico di. See BECCAFUMI, DOMENICO.

Pace, Peter. See BURNETT, DAVID.

Pa-chin. Pseudonym of Li Fei-kan (1905–), Chinese writer.

Pachter, Henry M. See RABASSEIRE, HENRY.

Packer, Joy. See LADY PACKER.

Padecopeo, Gabriel. See VEGA, LOPE DE.

Padgett, Lewis. See KUTTNER, HENRY.

Padovanino, Il. Cognomen of Alessandro Varotari (1590–1650), Italian painter.

Page, Eileen. See BERRIEN, EDITH HEAL.

Page, Evelyn. See SCARLETT, ROGER.

Page, G. S. See GALBRAITH, GEORGIE STARBUCK.

Page, Grover, Jr. See MCGINNIS, K. K.

Page, Marco. Pseudonym of Harry Kurnitz (1908–1968), American mystery writer.

Page, Stanton. Occasional pseudonym of Henry Blake Fuller (1857–1929), American novelist.

Page, Walter Hines. See WORTH, NICHOLAS.

Paget, George Charles Henry Victor. See MARQUESS OF ANGLESEY, THE.

Paget, Violet. See LEE, VERNON.

Pagnini, Antonio Luca. See ELEUTERO.

Pailleterie, Alexandre Davy de la. See DUMAS, ALEXANDRE.

Paine, J. Lincoln. Pseudonym of Arnold Kramish (1923–   ), American writer.

Pakkala, Teuvo. Pseudonym of Oskar Frosterus (1862–1925), Finnish writer.

Palacios, Pedro Bonifacio. See ALMAFUERTE.

Palazzeschi, Aldo. Pseudonym of Aldo Giurlani (1885–   ), Italian poet and writer.

Palestrant, Simon S. (1907–   ). American scholar whose pseudonyms are *Stephen Edwards, S. P. Stevens,* and *Paul E. Strand.*

Palingenio. See MANZOLI, PIER ANGELO DE LA STELLATA.

Palinurus. Pseudonym of Cyril Vernon Connolly (1903–   ), English writer and critic.

Palladio, Andrea (1508–1580). Italian architect, whose real name was Andrea di Pietro dalla Gondola.

Palma, Jacopo. See PALMA GIOVANE; PALMA VECCHIO.

Palma Giovane. Cognomen of Jacopo Palma (1544–1628), Venetian painter, grandnephew of Palma Vecchio. He was also called *Il Giovane* ("The Younger").

Palma Vecchio. Cognomen of Jacopo Palma (1480?–1528), Venetian painter, great-uncle of Palma Giovane. He was also called *Il Vecchio* ("The Elder").

Palmer, Elsie Pavitt. See PALMER, PETER.

Palmer, John Leslie (1885–1944). English writer, whose pseudonyms are *Christopher Haddon* and, with Hilary Aidan St. George Saunders, *Francis Beeding* and *David Pilgrim.*

Palmer, Peter. Pseudonym of Elsie Pavitt Palmer (1922–   ), American writer.

Palmer, Stuart. See STEWART, JAY.

Paltenghi, Madeleine. Pseudonym of Madeleine Paltenghi Anderson (1899–   ), American poet and writer of children's books.

Pan. Pseudonym of Leslie Beresford, contemporary mystery writer.

Panaitescu, D. See PERPESSICIUS.

Panas, Rudcenko. See MYRNYJ, PANAS JAKOVICH.

Panbourne, Oliver. See ROCKEY, HOWARD.

Panc, Petro Josypovich. Pseudonym of Petro Josypovich Pancenko (1891–   ), Ukrainian writer.

Pancenko, Petro Josypovich. See PANC, PETRO JOSYPOVICH.

Panneton, Philippe. See RINGUET.

Pannonius, Janus. Latinized name of János Csezmiczey (1434–1472), Hungarian poet.

Panormita. See BECCADELLI, ANTONIO.

Panowski, Eileen Thompson. See THOMPSON, EILEEN.

Panter, Peter. See TUCHOLSKY, KURT.

Pantycelyn, Williams. See WILLIAMS, WILLIAM.

Paoli, Betty. Pseudonym of Barbara Elisabeth Glück (1814–1894), Austrian poet.

Paolotto, Fra. See GHISLANDI, FRA VITTORE.

Papadiamantopoulos, Ioannis. See MORÉAS, JEAN.

Paprika. See HOLMVIK, OYVIND.

Paracelsus, Philippus Aureolus Theophrastus (1493–1541). Physician, alchemist, and mystic writer, whose original name was Theophrast Bombast von Hohenheim.

Paradijs, Cornelis. Occasional pseudonym of Frederik van Eeden (1860–1932), Dutch author, critic, and social reformer.

Pareja, Juan de. See ESCLAVO, EL.

Pares, Marion. See CAMPBELL, JUDITH.

Pargeter, Edith Mary. See PETERS, ELLIS.

Paris, Alexandre de. See BERNAI, ALEXANDRE DE.

Parish, Margaret Holt. See HOLT, MARGARET.

Parker, James. Pseudonym of Eric Newby (1919–   ), English writer.

Parley, Peter. Pseudonym of Samuel Griswold Goodrich (1793–1860), American writer.

Parlin, John. Pseudonym of Charles Parlin Graves (1911–   ), American free-lance writer.

Parmigianino, Il. Cognomen of Girolamo Francesco Maria Mazzola (or Mazzuoli) (1503–1540), Italian painter.

Parra, Teresa de la. Pseudonym of Ana Teresa Parra Sanojo, contemporary Venezuelan novelist.

Parrish, Mary. See COUSINS, MARGARET.

Parry, Hugh J. See CROSS, JAMES.

Parry, John. See WHELPTON, GEORGE ERIC.

Parsons, Tom. Pseudonym of Thomas George MacPherson (1915–), English writer.

Partington, F. H. Pseudonym of Harry W. Yoxall (1896–), English writer.

Partridge, Anthony. Pseudonym of Edward Phillips Oppenheim (1866–1946), mystery writer.

Pascoais, Teixeira de. Pseudonym of Joaquim Pereira Teixeira de Vasconcelos (1878–), Portuguese poet.

Pasquil. Pseudonym of Thomas Nash (or Nashe) (1567–1601), English satirical pamphleteer and playwright.

Pasquin, Anthony. Pseudonym of John Williams (1761–1818), English satirist.

Pa-ta-shan-jen (1625/26–1705). Chinese painter, whose real name was Chu Ta.

Paterson, Andrew Barton. See BANJO, THE.

Paterson, Huntley. See LUDOVICI, ANTHONY M.

Patkanian, Rafael. See GAMAR-KATIBA.

Patric, Johnstone Gillespie (1918–). Scottish-American writer, whose pseudonyms are *Luke Forward* and *Star-Man's Padre.*

Patrice, Ann. See GALBRAITH, GEORGIE STARBUCK.

Patrick, Keats. Pseudonym of Walter Karig (1898–1956), mystery writer.

Patrick, Leal. Pseudonym of Patti Stone (1926–), American author.

Patrick, Lilian. Pseudonym of Lilian Gilmore Keogh (1927–), Irish writer.

Patrick, Q. See WEBB, RICHARD WILSON, and WHEELER, HUGH CALLINGHAM.

Patterson, Harry. See PATTERSON, HENRY.

Patterson, Henry (1929–). English author, whose pseudonyms are *Martin Fallon, Hugh Marlowe,* and *Harry Patterson.*

Patterson, Jane. Pseudonym of Mattie Lula Cooper Britton (1914–), American writer.

Paul, Auren. Pseudonym of Auren Uris (1913–), American writer.
Paul, Daniel. Pseudonym of Lipmann Kessel (1914–), English writer.
Paul, Elliot Harold. See RUTLEDGE, BRETT.
Paul, Emily. See EICHER, ELIZABETH.
Paul, Hugo. See LITTLE, PAUL H.
Paul, John. Pseudonym of Charles Henry Webb (1834–1905), American journalist.
Paul, William. See EICHER, ELIZABETH.
Paulson, Jack. See JACKSON, CAARY PAUL.
Pavshich, Vladimir. See BOR, MATEJ.
Pawlikowska. Pseudonym of Maria Jasnorzewska (1899–1945), Polish poet and playwright.
Paxton, Jack. See LAWTON, SHERMAN P.
Paxton, Dr. John. See LAWTON, SHERMAN P.
Paye, Robert. See LONG, GABRIELLE MARGARET VERE.
Payelle, Raymond Gérard. See HÉRIAT, PHILIPPE.
Payne, Donald Gordon (1924–). English writer, whose pseudonyms are *Ian Cameron, Donald Gordon,* and *James Vance Marshall.*
Payne, Hazel Belle. See GAY, GREER.
Pcilka, Olena. Occasional pseudonym of Ol'ha Kosac (1849–1930), Ukrainian poet.
Pearl, Eric. Pseudonym of Richard M. Elman (1934–), American professional writer.
Pechey, Archibald Thomas (1876–1961). Mystery writer, whose pseudonyms are *Mark Cross* and *Valentine.*
Pechova, Eliska. See KRASNOHORSKA, ELISKA.
Peckham, Richard. Pseudonym of Raymond Peckham Holden (1894–), American writer.
Pecsok, Mary Bodell. See BODELL, MARY.
Pedersen, Knut. See HAMSUN, KNUT.
Peel, Frederick. See SLINGSBY, RUFUS.
Peel, Hazel Mary. See HAYMAN.
Peeslake, Gaffer. See DURRELL, LAWRENCE GEORGE.
Péladan, Joseph. See PÉLADAN, MÉRODACK SAR.
Péladan, Mérodack Sar. Pseudonym of Joseph (or Joséphin) Péladan (1859–1918), French playwright.
Pelin, Elin. See JOTOV, DIMITĂR IVANOV.

Pell, Franklyn. Pseudonym of Frank E. Pelligrin, contemporary mystery writer.

Pelligrin, Frank E. See PELL, FRANKLYN.

Pellisson, Paul (1624–1693). French historian and poet, also known as *Pellisson-Fontanier.*

Pellisson-Fontanier, Paul. See PELLISSON, PAUL.

Peltonen, Juho Vihtori. See LINNANKOSKI, JOHANNES.

Pembury, Bill. See GROOM, ARTHUR WILLIAM.

Pender, Lex. See PENDOWER, JACQUES.

Pender, Marilyn. See PENDOWER, JACQUES.

Pendower, Jacques (1899–   ). English author, whose pseudonyms are *Tom Curtis, Penn Dowers, T. C. H. Jacobs, Thomas Curtis Hicks Jacobs, Lex Pender, Marilyn Pender,* and *Anne Penn.*

Penmare, William. Pseudonym of Mavis Elizabeth Hocking Nisot (1893–   ), mystery writer.

Penn, Anne. See PENDOWER, JACQUES.

Penn, Christopher. See LAWLOR, PATRICK ANTHONY.

Penni, Gianfrancesco. See FATTORE, IL.

Pennington, Penny. See GALBRAITH, GEORGIE STARBUCK.

Pennington, Stuart. See GALBRAITH, GEORGIE STARBUCK.

Penrose, Margaret. Collective pseudonym for the "Campfire Girls," "Dorothy Dale," and "Motor Girls" series. See STRATEMEYER, EDWARD L.

Pensador Mexicano, El ("The Thinking Mexican"). Pseudonym of José Joaquín Fernández de Lizardi (1776–1827), Mexican novelist. The name was derived from the title of a journal he founded in 1812.

Pentecost, Hugh. Pseudonym of Judson Pentecost Philips (1903–   ), mystery writer.

People, Granville Church. See CHURCH, GRANVILLE.

Pepper, Joan. Pseudonym of Joan Alexander Wetherell-Pepper (1920–   ), English writer.

Pepperpod, Pip. Pseudonym of Charles Warren Stoddard (1843–1909), American traveler and writer.

Percy, Florence. Pseudonym of Elizabeth Allen (1832–1911), American poet.

Père, Duchesne. See HÉBERT, JACQUES RENÉ.

Peregrina, La ("The Strange One"). Pseudonym of Gertrudis Gómez de Avellaneda y Arteaga (1814–1873), Spanish writer.

Peregrine. Pseudonym of Isaac Deutscher (1907–1967), Polish author.

Pereira, Harold Bertram (1890–   ). Indian-English free-lance writer on travel, civil aviation, and heraldry, whose pseudonyms are *Hussaini Muhammad Askari* and *Mabel Yeates*.

Pereira, José Maria dos Reis. See RÉGIO, JOSÉ.

Perelman, Joseph. See DYMOV, OSIP ISIDOROVICH.

Perelmann, Eliezer. See BEN YEHUDA.

Perey, Lucien. Pseudonym of Clara Adèle Luce Herpin (1845–1914), French historian and biographer.

Pericoli, Niccolò. See TRIBOLO, IL.

Perkins, Faith. Pseudonym of Jennie Perkins Bramer (1900–   ), American writer.

Perovsky, Alexey. See POGORELSKY, ANTON.

Perpessicius. Pseudonym of D. Panaitescu (1891–   ), Rumanian poet and literary critic.

Perrin, Clyde. Pseudonym of Howard Vincent O'Brien (1888–1947), mystery writer.

Persis. Pseudonym of Agnes Irvine Constance Haime (1884–   ), English writer.

Pertcheval, Jan (c1455–1523). Dutch poet, also known as *Jan Steemaer.*

Pertinax. Joint pseudonym of Charles Gérault (1878–   ) and André Géraud (1882–   ), French journalists.

Perugino, Il. Cognomen of Pietro di Cristoforo di Vannucci (1446–1523), Florentine painter, probably derived after he painted frescoes (lost) in the council chamber of the Palazzo dei Priori in Perugia. He was also called *Pier della Pieve.*

Pesarese, Il. Cognomen of Simone Cantarini (1612–1648), Italian painter, derived from his birthplace, Pesaro.

Peshkov, Alexey Maximovich. See GORKY, MAXIM.

Pesis, Nicolaus de. See PISANO, NICOLA.

Pessoa, Fernando (1888–1935). Portuguese poet, whose pseudonyms, which he claimed represented distinct personalities, are *Alberto Caeiro, Ricardo Reis,* and *Alvaro de Campos.*

Petachya ben Jacob ha-Lavan. See PETHAHIAH OF REGENSBURG.

Peters, Bryan. Pseudonym of Peter Bryan George (1924–1966), mystery writer.

Peters, Caroline. Pseudonym of Eva Kelly Betz, contemporary American free-lance writer.

Peters, Ellis. Pseudonym of Edith Mary Pargeter (1913–   ), English novelist and translator.

Peters, S. T. See BRANNON, WILLIAM T.

Petersen, H. A. See BERGSTEDT, HARALD ALFRED.

Peterson, James. Pseudonym of Henry A. Zeiger (1930–   ), American free-lance writer.

Peterson, Kaj Harald Leininger. See MUNK, KAJ.

Peterson, Margaret. See GREEN, GLINT.

Peterson, Robert E. See SAYA, PETER.

Pethahiah ben Jacob ha-Lavan. See PETHAHIAH OF REGENSBURG.

Pethahiah of Regensburg (fl. 1175–1190). German Jewish travel writer, also called *Pethahiah* (or *Petachya*) *ben Jacob ha-Lavan*.

Petiot, Henri. See DANIEL-ROPS, HENRI.

Peto. See WHITE, JAMES DILLON.

Peto, James. See WHITE, JAMES DILLON.

Petrone, Jane Muir. See MUIR, JANE.

Petropavlovsky, Nikolay E. See KARONIN.

Petrov, Evgeny Petrovich. Pseudonym of Evgeny Kateyev (1903–1942), Soviet writer, who collaborated with Ilya Arnoldovich (1897–1939) in producing satirical novels.

Petrov, Stepan Gavrilovich. See SKITALETS.

Petrovsky-Sitianovich, Simeon Emelyanovich. See POLOTSKY, SIMEON.

Pevsner, Naum. See GABO, NAUM.

Pfalzgraf, Florence Leighton. See LEIGHTON, FLORENCE.

Philalethes ("Lover of Truth"). Pseudonym of Johann (Nepomuk Maria Joseph) (1801–1873), King of Saxony.

Philenia. Pseudonym of Sarah Wentworth Morton (1759–1846), American poet.

Philipp, Elliot Elias (1915–   ). English writer, whose pseudonyms are *Philip Embey* and *Victor Tempest*.

Philips, Judson Pentecost. See PENTECOST, HUGH.

Phillips, Alan Meyrick Kerr. See PHILLIPS, MICKEY.

Phillips, D. J. (1924–   ). English writer, whose pseudonyms are *Peter Chambers* and *Peter Chester*.

Phillips, Gerald William. See HUNTINGDON, JOHN.

Phillips, Jack. See SANDBURG, CARL AUGUST.

Phillips, John. Occasional pseudonym of John Phillips Marquand (1893–1960), American writer, used for his mysteries.

Phillips, Mac. Pseudonym of Maurice Jack Phillips (1914–   ), American editor and writer.

Phillips, Mark. See JANIFER, LAURENCE MARK.

Phillips, Maurice Jack. See PHILLIPS, MAC.

Phillips, Michael. See NOLAN, WILLIAM FRANCIS.

Phillips, Mickey. Pseudonym of Alan Meyrick Kerr Phillips (1916–), English writer.

Phillips, Pauline Esther. See VAN BUREN, ABIGAIL.

Phillips-Birt, Douglas (1920–). English writer, whose pseudonyms are *Argus, David Hextall,* and *Douglas Hogarth.*

Phillpotts, Eden. See HEXT, HARRINGTON.

Philmore, R. Pseudonym of Herbert Edmund Howard (1900–), mystery writer.

Philodusus, Janus. See HEINSIUS, DANIEL.

Philomath. See FRANKLIN, BENJAMIN.

Philomusus. Pseudonym of Jakob Locher (1471–1528), Swabian humorist.

Philosophe sans Fard, Le ("The Philosopher without Pretense"). Pseudonym of Rijklof Michaël van Goens (1748–1810), Dutch essayist.

Phipps, Margaret. See TATHAM, LAURA.

Phipson, Joan. Pseudonym of Joan Margaret Fitzhardinge (1912–), Australian author of children's books.

Phoenix, John. See DERBY, GEORGE HORATIO.

Phreas. See FREE, JOHN.

Phypps, Hyacinthe. See GOREY, EDWARD ST. JOHN.

Picasso, Pablo (1881–). Spanish painter, whose real name is José Ruiz Blasco.

Pichumerio, Giovanni. See AURISPA, GIOVANNI.

Pickel, Konrad. See CELTIS, CONRADUS.

Picken, Andrew. See KEELIVINE, CHRISTOPHER.

Pickering, Percival. Pseudonym of Anna Maria Diana Wilhelmina Stirling (b. 1865), English writer.

Pickle, Peregrine. Pseudonym of George Putnam Upton (1834–1919), American journalist and music critic.

Pickles, M. Elizabeth. See BURGOYNE, ELIZABETH.

Pienaar, Andries Albertus. See SANGIRO.

Pierce, John Robinson. See COUPLING, J. J.

Piestre, Fernand Anne. See CORMON.

Piestre, Pierre Étienne. See CORMON, EUGÈNE.

Pietro, Guido di. See ANGELICO, FRA.

Pieve, Pier della. See PERUGINO, IL.

Pike, Robert L. Pseudonym of Robert L. Fish (1912–   ), American writer.

Pilgrim, Anne. See ALLAN, MABEL ESTHER.

Pilgrim, David. See PALMER, JOHN LESLIE, and SAUNDERS, HILARY AIDAN ST. GEORGE.

Pilio, Gerone. Pseudonym of John Humphreys Whitefield (1906–   ), English scholar.

Pilkington, Cynthia. Pseudonym of Cynthia Miriam Horne (1939–   ), English writer.

Pilnyak, Boris Andreyevich. Pseudonym of Boris Andreyevich Vogau (1894–1938), Russian fiction writer.

Pincherle, Alberto. See MORAVIA, ALBERTO.

Pindar, Peter. Pseudonym of John Wolcot (1738–1819), English satirist.

Pine, Leslie Gilbert. See MOORSHEAD, HENRY.

Ping-hsin. Pseudonym of Hsieh Wan-ying (1902–   ), Chinese writer.

Pino, E. Pseudonym of Elizabeth Wittermans, contemporary Indonesian-American writer.

Pintor, Le. Cognomen of Bernart Marti (fl. c1260), Provençal troubador.

Pinturicchio (or **Pintoricchio**) ("Worthless Painter"). Cognomen of Bernardino Betti (or di Betto) di Biagio (1454–1513), Italian painter.

Piombo, Sebastiano del. See SEBASTIANO DEL PIOMBO.

Piper, Evelyn. Pseudonym of Merriam Modell (1908–   ), mystery writer.

Piper, Peter. Pseudonym of Theo Lang, contemporary mystery writer, whose original name was Theo Langebehn.

Pirandello, Stefano. See LANDI, STEFANO.

Pisa, Giordano da (c1260–1311). Italian preacher and religious writer, also known as *Giordano da Rivalto.*

Pisançon. see BISINZO, ALBERIC VON.

Pisanello, Il. See PISANO, ANTONIO.

Pisano, Andrea (1270?–1348). Italian sculptor, also called *Andrea da Pontedera.*

Pisano, Antonio (1397?–1455). Italian painter and medalist, whose father's name was Puccio di Giovanni da Cereto. He was called *Il Pisanello,* and he signed his name *Pisanus.* Vasari mistakenly calls him *Vittore.*

Pisano, Nicola (1220–1284). Italian sculptor, active in Pisa, Siena, Pistoria, Perugia, and Bologna. He was also known as *Nicholas de Apulia, Nicholas Pietri de Apulia,* and *Nicolaus de Pesis.*

Pisanus. See PISANO, ANTONIO.

Pişculescu, Grigore. See GALACTION, GALA.

Pisistratus, Sextus Amarcius Gallus. see AMARCIUS.

Pitati, Bonifazio di. See BONIFAZIO VERONESE.

Pitcher, Evelyn G. See GOODENOUGH, EVELYN.

Pitcher, Gladys (1890–). American free-lance composer, arranger, editor, and consultant, whose pseudonyms are *Betsy Adams, Barbara Wentworth,* and *Ann Weston.*

Pitigrilli. Pseudonym of Dino Segre (1893–), Italian writer.

Pitillas, Jorge. Pseudonym of José Gerardo de Hervás y Cobo de la Torre (d. 1742), Spanish satirist and cleric.

Pitt, Jeremy. See WYNNE-TYSON, JON.

Pizzicolli, Ciriaco de. See ANCONA, CIRIACO DE.

Place, Marian Templeton (1910–). American juvenile writer, whose pseudonyms are *Dale White* and *R. D. Whitinger.*

Plácido ("calm, placid"). Pseudonym of Gabriel de la Concepción Valdés (1809–1844), Cuban poet.

Plaidy, Jean. See HIBBERT, ELEANOR BURFORD.

Plath, Sylvia. See LUCAS, VICTORIA.

Platina, Il (1421–1481). Italian humanist, whose real name was Bartolommeo de' Sacchi.

Pleydell, Susan. Pseudonym of Isabel Janet Couper Syme Senior, contemporary English writer.

Pliekšans, Jan. See RAINIS, JAN.

Pliny the Youngest. Pseudonym of Stanley Kidder Wilson (1879–), mystery writer.

Plomer, William Charles Franklin (1903–). South African writer, also known as *William D'Arfey.*

Ploug, Parmo Carl. See RYTTER, Poul.

Pluff, Barbara Littlefield. See CLAYTON, BARBARA.

Plumb, Beatrice. Pseudonym of Beatrice Plumb Hunzicker (1886–), British-American writer.

Plummer, Thomas Arthur. See SARNE, MICHAEL.

Plummy. Pseudonym of John Dellbridge (1887–), mystery writer.

Plutonius. see MEHTA, RUSTAM JEHANGIR.

Poccetti, Bernardino (1548?–1612). Italian painter, whose real name was Bernardino (or Bernardo) Barbatelli.

Podivínská, Jarmila. See GLAZAROVÀ, JARMILA.

Poe, Edgar. Pseudonym of Philip Levine (1928–   ), American scholar.

Pogodin, Nikolay Fëdorovich. Pseudonym of Nikolay Fëdorovich Stukalov (1900–   ), Soviet Russian playwright.

Pogorelsky, Anton. Occasional pseudonym of Alexey Perovsky (1787–1836), Russian novelist.

Poirier, Louis. See GRACQ, JULIEN.

Po Liang. See LIANG K'AI.

Politella, Dario (1921–   ). American author, whose pseudonyms are *Tony Granite* and *David Stewart.*

Politian. See POLIZIANO, ANGELO.

Politicus. See KULSKI, WLADYSLAW WSZEBOR.

Politis, Kosmas. Pseudonym of P. Taveludi (1888–   ), Greek fiction writer.

Poliziano, Angelo (1454–1494). Italian poet and humanist, whose original name was Angiolo Ambrogini. He was called *Politian* after his birthplace, Mons Politianus.

Pollaiuolo, Antonio (1431/32?–1498), and **Piero** (1443/47?–1496?). Italian painters, goldsmiths, and sculptors, whose original surname was Benci. Their name was derived from the poultry trade of their father.

Polman, Willem de. Pseudonym of Dale Nichols (1904–   ), American writer.

Polonsky, Abraham. See HOGARTH, EMMETT.

Polotsky, Simeon. Pseudonym of Simeon Emelyanovich Petrovsky-Sitianovich (1629–1680), Russian monk, poet, and dramatist.

Polydoor, Karel Maria. See MONT, POL DE.

Pomeranus. See BUGENHAGEN, JOHANN.

Pomeroy, Florence Mary. Pseudonym of Florence Mary Pomeroy Powley (1892–   ), English poet and playwright.

Pomeroy, Hub. Pseudonym of Harold Claassen (1905–   ), American sportswriter.

Pomfret, Baron. Pseudonym of Lawrence Dame (1898–   ), American writer.

Pommer, Dr. See BUGENHAGEN, JOHANN.

Ponsonby, Doris Almon. See RYBOT, DORIS.

Ponsonby, Frederick Edward Neuflize. See TENTH EARL OF BESS-BOROUGH, THE.

Ponte, Lorenzo da (1749–1838). Italian poet and writer, whose real name was Emanuele Conegliano.

Pontedera, Andrea da. See PISANO, ANDREA.

Pontormo, Jacopo da (1494–1556/57). Italian painter, whose real name was Jacopo Carrucci. His name was derived from his birthplace, Pontormo.

Poole, Michael. Pseudonym of Reginald Heber Poole (1885–   ), mystery writer.

Poole, Reginald Heber. See POOLE, MICHAEL.

Poole, Vivian. Pseudonym of Gabriel Jaffe (1923–   ), English writer.

Poor Robin. Pseudonym of William Winstanley (1628?–1698), English writer.

Poorten-Schwartz, Joost Marius Willem van der. See MAARTENS, MAARTEN.

Poot, Linke. Pseudonym of Alfred Döblin (1878–1957), German writer.

Pope, Alexander. See SCRIBLERUS, MARTINUS.

Popescu, Christine (1930–   ). English writer, whose pseudonyms are *Christine Kier* and *Christine Pullein-Thompson*.

Popov, Alexander Serafimovich. See SERAFIMOVICH, ALEXANDER.

Poppi, Mino da. See FIESOLE, MINO DA.

Poquelin, Jean Baptiste. See MOLIÈRE.

Porcupine, Peter. Pseudonym of William Cobbett (1762–1835), English journalist and essayist.

Porlock, Martin. See MACDONALD, PHILIP.

Port, Wymar. Pseudonym of Will Judy (1891–   ), American writer.

Porta, Bartolommeo (or Baccio) della. See BARTOLOMMEO, FRA.

Porta, Bonastruc da. See NACHMANIDES, RABBI MOSES BEN NAHMAN GERONDI.

Portaas, Herman. See WILDENVEY, HERMAN.

Porter, Gene. See STRATTON-PORTER, GENE.

Porter, Harold Everett. See HALL, HOLWORTHY.

Porter, Kathryn. See SWINFORD, BETTY JUNE WELLS.

Porter, Mark. See LECKIE, ROBERT.

Porter, William Sydney. See HENRY, O.

Posner, Jacob D. See DEAN, GREGORY.

Postl, Karl Anton. See SEALSFIELD, CHARLES.
Posznanski, Alfred. See SAVOIR, ALFRED.
Potter, George William, Jr. See WITHERS, E. L.
Potter, Margaret. See BETTERIDGE, ANNE.
Pou, Genevieve Long. See HOLDEN, GENEVIEVE.
Pound, Ezra Loomis (1885–   ). American author, whose pseudonyms are *William Atheling* and *Alfred Venison.*
Powell, Richard Stillman. Pseudonym of Ralph Henry Barbour (1870–1944), mystery writer.
Powell, Talmage. See MCCREADY, JACK.
Power, Cecil. See ALLEN, GRANT.
Powers, George. See INFIELD, GLEN BERTON.
Powers, Margaret. See BERRIEN, EDITH HEAL.
Powley, Florence Mary Pomeroy. See POMEROY, FLORENCE MARY.
Powley, Jean. See CARDWELL, ANN.
Prather, Richard Scott (1921–   ). American mystery writer, whose pseudonyms are *David Knight* and *Douglas Ring.*
Prato, Giovanni da. Pseudonym of Giovanni Gherardi (c1367–1442), Italian poet.
Pratt, Eleanor Blake Atkinson (1899–   ). Mystery writer, whose pseudonyms are *E. A. Blake* and *Eleanor Blake.*
Pratt, John. See WINTON, JOHN.
Pratt, Theodore. See BRACE, TIMOTHY.
Pravda, František. Pseudonym of Vojtěch Hlinka (1817–1904), Czech writer.
Prebble, John Edwards Curtis. See CURTIS, JOHN.
Prebble, Marjorie Mary Curtis (1912–   ). English writer, whose pseudonyms are *Ann Compton, Denise Conway*, and *Marjorie Curtis.*
Preedy, George Runnell. See LONG, GABRIELLE MARGARET VERE.
Premont, Brother Jeremy. See WILLETT, BROTHER FRANCISCUS.
Presberg, Miriam Goldstein. See GILBERT, MIRIAM.
Presland, John. Pseudonym of Gladys Williams Bendit (1885–   ), Australian-English author.
Preston, Arthur. See HANKINS, ARTHUR PRESTON.
Preston, George F. See WARREN, JOHN BYRNE LEICESTER, 3RD BARON DE TABLEY.
Preston, James. See JAMES, RONALD.

Preston, James. Pseudonym of John Unett, contemporary English writer.

Preston, Richard. See LINDSAY, JACK.

Prete Genovese, Il. See STROZZI, BERNARDO.

Pretorius, Hertha. Pseudonym of Hertha Pretorius Kouts (1922–   ), American writer.

Price, Evadne. Pseudonym of Helen Zenna Smith, contemporary mystery writer.

Price, George. See PRICE, RHYS.

Price, Rhys. Pseudonym of George Price (1910–   ), Welsh author.

Pridvorov, Efim Alexeyevich. See BEDNY, DEMYAN.

Priestley, Clive Ryland. See RYLAND, CLIVE.

Priestley, John Boynton. See GOLDSMITH, PETER.

Primm, Brother Orrin. See WILLETT, BROTHER FRANCISCUS.

Pring-Mill, Robert D. F. See DUGUID, ROBERT.

Prins, Ary. See COOPLANDT, A.

Prins, Jan. Pseudonym of Christiaan Louis Schepp (1876–1948), Dutch poet and translator.

Pritchard, John Laurence. See LAURENCE, JOHN.

Probazki, Boris. Pseudonym of Maurits Rudolf Jöell Dekker (1896–1962), Dutch novelist and playwright.

Procter, Adelaide Anne. See BERWICK, Mary.

Procter, Bryan Waller. See CORNWALL, BARRY.

Proctor, Everitt. See MONTGOMERY, RUTHERFORD GEORGE.

Pro-Rok. Pseudonym of Antoni Słonimski (1895–   ), Polish painter and writer.

Proudfoot, Walter. See VAHEY, JOHN GEORGE HASLETTE.

Provence, Marcel. See JOUHANDEAU, MARCEL.

Prudhomme, René François. See SULLY PRUDHOMME.

Prud'hon, Pierre-Paul. Pseudonym of Pierre Prudon (1758–1823), French historical painter.

Prudon, Pierre. See PRUD'HON, PIERRE-PAUL.

Pruitt, Alan. Pseudonym of Alvin Emanuel Rose, contemporary mystery writer.

Prus, Bolesław. Pseudonym of Aleksander Głowacki (1847–1912), Polish novelist.

Prushinski, Alexander Vladimirovich. See GARUN, ALES.

Pryde, Anthony. Pseudonym of Agnes Russell Weekes, contemporary mystery writer.

Przesmycki, Zenon. See MIRIAM.

Przyjaciel. See NOWACZYNSKI, ADOLF.

Ptochoprodromus ("Poor Prodromus"). Cognomen of Theodore Prodromus (d. 1166), Byzantine writer and poet, who was always be-
moaning his poverty.

Pullè, Leopoldo. See CASTELNUOVO, LEO DI.

Pullein-Thompson, Christine. See POPESCU, CHRISTINE.

Pullein-Thompson, Diana. Pseudonym of Diana Pullein-Thompson
Farr, contemporary English-American author.

Pulling, Christopher Robert Druce. See DRUCE, CHRISTOPHER.

Pulsford, Norman George. See TREVOR, A. C.

Pumpernickel. Pseudonym of Sol Weinstein (1928–   ), American
writer.

Punnett, Ivar. See SIMONS, ROGER.

Punnett, Margaret. See SIMONS, ROGER.

Puthoste, Roger. See THÉRIVE, ANDRÉ.

Putinas. Pseudonym of Vincas Mykolaitis (1894–   ), Lithuanian poet
and scholar.

"Q"

Q. Pseudonym of Sir Arthur Thomas Quiller-Couch (1863–1944), British mystery writer.

Qa'ani, Habib Allah (d. 1854). Persian poet, also known as *Gha'ani*.

Qays. See MAJNUN.

Qazali, Abu Hamid Muhammad (1058–1111). Persian theologian and
mystic, also known as *Muhammad Ghazali*.

Quad, M. Pseudonym of Charles Bertrand Lewis (1842–1924), American humorist.

Quasimodo. Pseudonym of Arthur Gorski (1870–   ), Polish poet,
writer, and translator.

Queen, Ellery. See DANNAY, FREDERIC, and LEE, MANFRED B.

Queen, Ellery, Jr. See DANNAY, FREDERIC, and LEE, MANFRED B.

Queirós, Francisco Teixeira de. See MORENO, BENTO.

Quentin, Patrick. See WEBB, RICHARD WILSON, and WHEELER, HUGH
CALLINGHAM.

Quill. See GRANGE, CYRIL.

Quiller-Couch, Sir Arthur Thomas. See Q.

Quin, Dan. Pseudonym of Alfred Henry Lewis (1857–1914), mystery writer.

Quin, Mike. See RYAN, PAUL WILLIAM.

Quince, Peter. Pseudonym of George Harold Day (1900–   ), English writer.

Quinlan, Red. Pseudonym of Sterling C. Quinlan (1916–   ), American writer.

Quinlan, Sterling C. See QUINLAN, RED.

Quintanilla, Maria Aline Griffith y Dexter, Condesa de. See COUNTESS OF ROMANONES.

Quist, Felicia. Pseudonym of Laura Z. Hobson (1900–   ), American writer.

"R"

Raabe, Wilhelm. See CORVINUS, JAKOB.

Rabasseire, Henry. Pseudonym of Henry M. Pachter (1907–   ), German-American writer.

Rabbi Karov. Pseudonym of Elchanan Leib Levinsky (1857–1910), Hebrew novelist.

Rabelais, François. See NASIER, ALCOFRIBAS.

Rabenu Tam. See JACOB BEN MEIR.

Rabinovitch, M. See BEN AMI.

Rabinowitz (or **Rabinovitz**), **Solomon.** See ALEICHEM, SHALOM.

Rachilde. Pseudonym of Marguerite Vallette (1860?–1953), French novelist and critic.

Racin, Kosta. Pseudonym of Koco Apostolov Solev (1909–1943), Macedonian poet.

Radcliffe, Henry Garnett. See TRAVERS, STEPHEN.

Rade, Paul Martin. See MARTIN, PAUL.

Radek, Karl Bernardovich. Pseudonym of Karl Sobelsohn (1885–   ), Russian political writer and international lawyer.

Radford, Ruby Lorraine (1891–   ). American writer, whose pseudonyms are *Matilda Bailey* and *Marcia Ford*.

Radványi, Netty. See SEGHERS, ANNA.

Raffi. Pseudonym of Jacob Melik-Iakobian (1837–1888), Armenian novelist.

Ragg, Thomas Murray. See THOMAS, MURRAY.

Raibolini, Francesco di Marco di Giacomo. See FRANCIA, FRANCESCO.

Raimann, Ferdinand. See RAIMUND, FERDINAND.

Raimar, Freimund. Pseudonym of Friedrich Rückert (1788–1866), German poet, used to publish an anti-Napoleonic sonnet.

Raimond, C. E. Pseudonym of Elizabeth Robins (1862?–1952), American actress and writer.

Raimund, Ferdinand. Professional name of Ferdinand Raimann (1790–1836), Austrian dramatist.

Raine, Allen. Pseudonym of Anne Adalisa (1836–1908), Welsh novelist.

Rainham, Thomas. Pseudonym of Charles Barren (1913–   ), English writer.

Rainis, Jan. Pseudonym of Jan Pliekšans (1865–1929), Latvian poet and playwright.

Rai Noboru. See RAI SANYO.

Rai Sanyo. Pseudonym of Rai Noboru (1781–1832), Japanese writer and poet.

Ralbag (1288–1344). Provençal Hebrew philosopher and scientific writer, whose real name was Levi ben Gerson. He was also called *Gersonides.*

Ralston, Jan. See DUNLOP, AGNES M. R.

Ramaa. See ISSERLES, MOSES.

Ramage, Jennifer. See MASON, HOWARD.

Rambam. See MAIMONIDES, MOSES.

Ramban. See NACHMANIDES, RABBI MOSES BEN NAHMAN GERONDI.

Ramboldoni, Vittorino de'. See FELTRE, VITTORINO DA.

Ramdas ("Slave of Rama"), **Marathi** (1608–1681). Indian poet and guru, whose original name was Narayana.

Rame, David. Occasional pseudonym of Arthur Durham Divine (1904–   ), South African novelist, journalist, and war correspondent.

Rameau, Jean. Pseudonym of Laurent Labaigt (1859–1942), French poet and novelist.

Ramée, Marie Louise de la. See OUIDA.

Ramel, Walter. Occasional pseudonym of Walter De La Mare (1873–1956), English poet.

Ramenghi, Bartolommeo. See BAGNACAVALLO, IL.

Ramos, João de Deus (1830–1896). Portuguese poet, also known simply as *João de Deus.*

Ramsbottom, Mrs. See HOOK, THEODORE EDWARD.

Ramskill, Valerie Patricia Roskams. See BROOKE, CAROLE.

Rand, John. See REACH, JAMES.

Randall, Clay. See ADAMS, CLIFTON.

Randall, Janet. Pseudonym of Janet Randall Young (1919–), American free-lance writer.

Randall, William. Pseudonym of William R. Gwinn, contemporary mystery writer.

Randolf, Ellen. See ROSS, DON.

Randolph, Marion. Pseudonym of Marie Freid Rodell (1912–), mystery writer.

Random, Alan. See KAY, ERNEST.

Ranger, Ken. See CREASEY, JOHN.

Ransetsu. Pseudonym of Hattori Hikoemon (1654–1707), Japanese haiku poet.

Ransom, Jay Ellis. See ADAMS, HENRY T.

Ransome, Stephen. See DAVIS, FREDERICK CLYDE.

Raphael (1483–1520). Italian painter and architect, whose real name was Raffaello Sanzio (or Santi).

Raphael, Chaim. See DAVEY, JOCELYN.

Raphael, Jay. Pseudonym of Ray Josephs (1912–), American writer on Latin-American subjects.

Rapisarda, Antonio. See ANIANTE, ANTONIO.

Rappaport, Solomon Samuel. See AN-SKI, SH. A.

Rappoport, Solomon Judah Leib. See SHIR.

Raq. Pseudonym of Glyn Kinnaird Evens, contemporary mystery writer.

Raschgolski, Hillel. See BABLI, HILLEL.

Rash, Dora Eileen Agnew Wallace. See WALLACE, DOREEN.

Rashal. See LURIA, SOLOMON.

Rashba. See ADRET, SOLOMON.

Rashbam. Acronym of Rabbi Samuel ben Me'ir (c1085–c1174), French Hebrew religious writer.

Rashi. See IZHAQI, RABBI SHELOHMOH.

Rath, E. J. Joint pseudonym of Chauncey Corey Brainerd and Edith Rathbone Jacobs Brainerd, contemporary mystery writers.

Ratigan, Eleanor Eldridge. See WHARTON, VIRGINIA.

Ratisbonne, Louis Fortuné Gustave. See TRIM.

Rattray, Simon. See TREVOR, ELLESTON.

Rau, Santha Rama. Pseudonym of Santha Rama Rau Bowers, Indian-American writer (1923–   ).

Rault, Walter. Pseudonym of Maurice Anthony Coneys Gorham (1902–   ), English-Irish writer.

Rawicz, Wacław. Pseudonym of Wacław Berent (1873–1940), Polish novelist.

Rawlins, Eustace (b. 1854). Mystery writer, whose pseudonyms are *Eustace Barton* and *Robert Eustace.*

Rawson, Clayton (1906–   ). Mystery writer, whose pseudonyms are *Great Merlini* and *Stuart Towne.*

Ray, Oscar. Pseudonym of Aladar A. Farkas (1895–1969), Hungarian-American novelist.

Ray, Wesley. Pseudonym of Ray Gaulden (1914–   ), American free-lance writer.

Raymond, Mary. See KEEGAN, MARY HEATHCOTT.

Raymond, René (1906–   ). Mystery writer, whose pseudonyms are *James Hadley Chase, James Docherty, Ambrose Grant,* and *Raymond Marshall.*

Raymond, Robert. See ALTER, ROBERT EDMOND.

Rayner, Augustus Alfred. See HALL, WHYTE.

Rayner, Olive Pratt. See ALLEN, GRANT.

Rayson, Paul. See JENNINGS, LESLIE NELSON.

Rayter, Joe. Pseudonym of Mary F. McChesney, contemporary mystery writer.

Reach, James. Contemporary American writer, whose pseudonyms are *Bruce Abbott, Ward Bremer, Hilda Manning, John Rand, George Ressieb, Thomas Sutton, Tom West, Pete Williams,* and *Richard Williams.*

Read, Miss. Pseudonym of Dora Jessie Saint (1913–   ), English writer.

Rebhu, Jan. See BEER, JOHANN.

Reddaway, W. Brian. See ACADEMIC INVESTOR.

Redfield, Martin. Pseudonym of Alice Brown (1857–1948), American writer.

Redman, Ben Ray. See LORD, JEREMY.

Redmayne, Barbara. Pseudonym of Muriel Howe, contemporary English author.

Reed, Alexander Wyclif. See HARLEQUIN.

Reed, Blair. See RING, ADAM.

Reed, Elizabeth Stewart. See STEWART, ELIZABETH GREY.

Reed, Kit. Pseudonym of Lillian Craig Reed (1932–   ), American journalist and writer.

Reed, Lillian Craig. See REED, KIT.

Reehany, Amin (1876–1940). Syrian-American Arabic author, also known as *Ar-Raihant.*

Rees, Dilwyn. Pseudonym of Glyn Edmund Daniel (1914–   ), mystery writer.

Rees, Helen Christina Easson. See OLIVER, JANE.

Reeve, Joel. Pseudonym of William R. Cox, contemporary American writer.

Reeves, Helen Buckingham. See LYALL, DAVID.

Régio, José. Pseudonym of José Maria dos Reis Pereira (1901–   ), Portuguese poet and playwright.

Regiomontanus (1436–1476). German mathematician, writer, and astrologer, whose real name was Johann Müller. The name was derived from the Latin for his birthplace, Konigsburg.

Reid, Eleanor. Pseudonym of Constance Isabel Smith (1894–   ), mystery writer.

Reid, Frances Pugh. See ALLISON, MARIAN.

Reid, James Macarthur. See WALKINSHAW, COLIN.

Reid, Wallace Q. See GOODCHILD, GEORGE.

Reilly, Helen Kieran. See ABBY, KIERAN.

Reilly, William K. See CREASEY, JOHN.

Reims, Chardon de. See CROISILLES, CHARDON DE.

Reims, Robert de. See CHIEVRE, LA.

Reiner, Max. See CALDWELL, JANET MIRIAM TAYLOR HOLLAND.

Reinfeld, Fred. See YOUNG, EDWARD.

Reinhold, C. Pseudonym of Christian Reinhold Köstlin (1813–1856), German jurist and poet.

Reinmar der Alte ("Reinmar the Old") (fl. 1190–1210). Viennese minnesinger and poet, also known as *Reinmar von Hagenau.*

Reis, Ricardo. See PESSOA, FERNANDO.

Reiz, Yitzchok. See NADIR, MOISHE.

Reizenstein, Elmer. See RICE, ELMER.

Remark, Erich Paul. See REMARQUE, ERICH MARIA.

Remarque, Erich Maria. Pseudonym of Erich Paul Remark (1898–   ), German novelist.

Remenham, John. See VLASTO, JOHN ALEXANDER.

Rémy, Caroline. See SÉVERINE.

Renaq. See KROCHMAL, NAHMAN.

Renier, Elizabeth. Pseudonym of Betty D. Baker (1916–   ), English writer.

Renn, Ludwig. Pseudonym of Arnold Vieth von Golssenau (1889–   ), German writer.

Renner, Karl (1870–1950). Austrian statesman and writer, whose pseudonyms are *Rudolf Springer* and *Synopticus*.

Rennie, Christopher. See AMBROSE, ERIC.

Rennie, James Alan (1899–   ). Scottish writer, whose pseudonyms are *Morton Cleland, Boone Denver,* and *Maxwell MacFee*.

Renton, Julia. See COLE, MARGARET ALICE.

Ressich, John. See BAXTER, GREGORY.

Ressieb, George. See REACH, JAMES.

Retla, Robert. See ALTER, ROBERT EDMOND.

Reubeni, Aaron. Pseudonym of Aaron Shimshelevitz (1886–   ), Hebrew writer.

Revel, Jacques. Occasional pseudonym of James Laver (1899–   ), English writer.

Revere, M. P. See WILLIAMSON, ALICE MURIEL LIVINGSTON.

Rey, Hans Agusto. See UNCLE GUS.

Reyam. Pseudonym of Charles Leopold Mayer (1881–   ), French scientist and writer.

Reynolds, Adrian. See LONG, AMELIA REYNOLDS.

Reynolds, Dickson. See REYNOLDS, HELEN MARY CAMPBELL.

Reynolds, Helen Mary Campbell (1884–   ). Canadian writer and illustrator, whose pseudonyms are *Helen Dickson* and *Dickson Reynolds*.

Reynolds, Liggett. Pseudonym of Robert Alfred Simon (1897–   ), mystery writer.

Reynolds, Peter. See LONG, AMELIA REYNOLDS.

Rheinau, Bild aus. See BEATUS RHENANUS.

Rhoades, Jonathan. Pseudonym of John Edward (Jack) Olsen (1925–   ), American writer.

Rhode, Arvid. Pseudonym of Paal Emanuel Brekke (1923–   ), Norwegian critic.

Rhode, Austen. Pseudonym of Basil Hoskins Francis (1906–   ), English free-lance journalist and author.

Rhode, John. See STREET, CECIL JOHN CHARLES.

Rhode, Winslow. See ROE, F. GORDON.

Ribah. See JACOB BEN ASHER.

Ricault, Charles Joseph de. See HÉRICAULT, CHARLES D'.

Ricciarelli, Daniele. See VOLTERRA, DANIELE DA.

Riccio, Andrea (1470?–1532). Italian sculptor and architect, whose real name was Andrea Briosco.

Riccio, Domenico. See BRUSASORCI, IL.

Riccoboni, Lodovico. See LELIO.

Rice, Craig (1908–1957). Mystery writer, whose pseudonyms are *Daphne Sanders* and *Michael Venning*.

Rice, Desmond Charles. See MEIRING, DESMOND.

Rice, Dorothy Mary (1913–   ). Irish-English author of children's books, whose pseudonyms are *Dorothy Borne* and *Dorothy Vicary.*

Rice, Elinor. Pseudonym of Elinor Rice Hays, contemporary American writer.

Rice, Elmer. Pseudonym of Elmer Reizenstein (1892–1967), American writer.

Rich, Barbara. See JACKSON, LAURA RIDING.

Richards, Allen. Pseudonym of Richard A. Rosenthal (1925–   ), American writer.

Richards, Charles. Pseudonym of John T. Marvin (1906–   ), American writer on dogs.

Richards, Clay. See CROSSEN, KENDELL.

Richards, Duane. see HURLEY, VIC.

Richards, Francis. Joint pseudonym of Frances Louise Davis Lockridge and Richard Orson Lockridge (1898–   ), mystery writers.

Richards, Peter. See MONGER, IFOR DAVID.

Richards, Phyllis. Pseudonym of Phyllis Auty (1910–   ), English scholar.

Richardson, Henrietta. See RICHARDSON, HENRY HANDEL.

Richardson, Henry Handel. Pseudonym of Henrietta Richardson (1870–1946), Australian novelist.

Richmond, George. See BRISTER, RICHARD.

Richmond, Grace. See MARSH, JOHN.

Richmond, Mary. See LINDSAY, KATHLEEN.

Richter, Fernande. See FERN, EDNA.

Richter, Johann Paul Friedrich. See JEAN PAUL.

Rickert, Corinne Holt. Pseudonym of Corinne Holt Sawyer, contemporary American writer.

Rictus, Jehan. Pseudonym of Gabriel Randon de Saint Amand.(1867–1933), French poet.

Riddell, Charlotte Eliza Lawson. See TRAFFORD, F. G.

Riddell, John. Pseudonym of Corey Ford (1902–   ), American mystery writer.

Ridder, Alfons Joseph de. See ELSSCHOT, WILLEM.

Rideaux, Charles de Balzac. See CHANCELLOR, JOHN.

Riding, Laura. See JACKSON, LAURA RIDING.

Ridley, Nat, Jr. Collective pseudonym for the "Nat Ridley Detective Stories" series. See STRATEMEYER, EDWARD L.

Ridway, Jason. See MARLOWE, STEPHEN.

Rieti, Moses di. See MAESTRO GAIO.

Rifkin, Shepard. See MICHAELS, DALE.

Righetti, Carlo. See ARRIGHI, CLETTO.

Rigsby, Howard (1909–   ). American writer, whose pseudonyms are *Mark Howard* and *Vechel Howard.*

Rijmer, Jan de. Pseudonym of Jan Jacob Antony Goeverneur (1809–1889), Dutch poet.

Rikhoff, James C. (1931–   ). American free-lance writer on outdoor life, whose pseudonyms are *Jim Cornwall, Joe Fargo,* and *Alan Kincaid.*

Riley, Tex. See CREASEY, JOHN.

Ring, Adam. Pseudonym of Blair Reed, contemporary mystery writer.

Ring, Douglas. See PRATHER, RICHARD SCOTT.

Ringo, Johnny. See KEEVIL, HENRY JOHN.

Ringuet. Pseudonym of Philippe Panneton (1895–1960), French-Canadian novelist.

Rios, Tere. Pseudonym of Marie Teresa Rios Versace (1917–   ), American writer.

Riposte, A. See MORDAUNT, EVELYN MAY.

Rita. Pseudonym of Eliza Margaret J. Gollan Humphreys, contemporary mystery writer.

Ritchie, Lewis. See BARTIMEUS.

Rittner, Tadeusz. See CZASKA, TOMASZ.

Rivalto, Giordano da. See PISA, GIORDANO DA.

Riverside, John. See HEINLEIN, ROBERT ANSON.

Riverton, Stein. Pseudonym of Sven Elvestad (1884–1934), Norwegian novelist.

Rives, Leigh. Pseudonym of William W. Seward, Jr. (1913–   ), American scholar.

Rivett, Edith Caroline (1894–1958). Mystery writer, whose pseudonyms are *Carol Carnac* and *E. C. R. Lorac.*

Roark, Garland. See GARLAND, GEORGE.

Robbins, Clarence Aaron. See ROBBINS, TOD.

Robbins, Tod. Pseudonym of Clarence Aaron Robbins (1888–1949), mystery writer.

Robert de Reims. See CHIEVRE, LA.

Roberti, Ercole de (1451/52–1496). Italian painter, also known as *Ercole di Giulio Cesare de' Grandi.*

Roberts, Anthony. Pseudonym of John B. Watney (1915–   ), English writer.

Roberts, Carl Eric Bechhofer. See EPHESIAN.

Roberts, Don. See ROSS, DON.

Roberts, Dorothy James. See MORTIMER, PETER.

Roberts, Eric. See ROBIN.

Roberts, Irene (1926–   ). English romantic novelist whose pseudonyms are *Roberta Carr, Elizabeth Harle, Ivor Roberts,* and *Iris Rowland.*

Roberts, Ivor. See ROBERTS, IRENE.

Roberts, Jim. See BATES, BARBARA S.

Roberts, Julian. See BARDENS, DENNIS CONRAD.

Roberts, Lee. Occasional pseudonym of Robert Martin (1908–   ), American writer.

Roberts, Tom. Pseudonym of R. Murray Thomas (1921–   ), American scholar.

Roberts, Wayne. See OVERHOLSER, WAYNE D.

Robertson, Constance Noyes. See SCOTT, DANA.

Robertson, Frank Chester (1890–   ). American writer of Westerns, whose pseudonyms are *Robert Crane, Frank Chester Field,* and *King Hill.*

Robertson, Helen. Pseudonym of Helen Jean Mary Edmiston (1913–   ), mystery writer.

Robertson, James Logie. See HALIBURTON, HUGH.

Robertson, Keith. See KEITH, CARLTON.

Robertson, Thomas Anthony. See TOMASITO, DON.

Robin. Pseudonym of Eric Roberts (1914–   ), English free-lance writer.

Robins, Elizabeth. See RAIMOND, C. E.

Robinson, Chaille. Contemporary American writer, whose pseudonyms are *Jean Kirby* and *Kathleen Robinson.*

Robinson, Elizabeth Cameron. Contemporary American writer, whose pseudonyms are *Elizabeth Cameron* and *Elizabeth Clemons.*

Robinson, Joan Mary Gale Thomas. See THOMAS, JOAN GALE.

Robinson, Kathleen. See ROBINSON, CHAILLE.

Robinson, Lewis George (1886–   ). Mystery writer, whose pseudonyms are *George Braha* and *George Limnelius.*

Robinson, Richard Blundell. See LEADERMAN, GEORGE.

Robinson, Therese Albertine Louise. See TALVJ.

Robusti, Jacopo. See TINTORETTO.

Roc, John. Pseudonym of David Nicholson, contemporary English playwright and travel writer.

Rocha, Adolfo Correia de. See TORGA, MIGUEL.

Roche, Arthur Somers. See MACHAYE, ERIC.

Roche, John. Pseudonym of David de Roche Le Roi (1905–   ), American-English writer.

Rock, Richard. Pseudonym of Don Mainprize (1930–   ), American writer.

Rockey, Howard (1886–1934). Mystery writer, whose pseudonyms are *Ronald Bryce* and *Oliver Panbourne.*

Rockingham, Montague. See NYE, NELSON CORAL.

Rockwood, Harry. Pseudonym of Ernest A. Young, contemporary mystery writer.

Rockwood, Roy. Collective pseudonym for the "Dave Fearless," "Great Marvel," "Bomba Books," and "Speedwell Boys" series. See STRATEMEYER, EDWARD L.

Roda Roda, Alexander Friedrich Ladislaus (1872–1945), Slavonic writer, whose original name was Rosenfeld.

Rodd, Kylie Tennant. See TENNANT, KYLIE.

Rodd, Ralph. See NORTH, WILLIAM.

Rodda, Charles (1891–   ). Australian-English writer, whose pseudonyms are *Gavin Holt, Gardner Low,* and, with Eric Ambler (1909–   ), *Eliot Reed.*

Rodell, Marie Freid. See RANDOLPH, MARION.

Rodgers, Frank. See INFIELD, GLEN BERTON.

Rodman, Maia. Pseudonym of Maia Wojciechowska (1927–), Polish-American writer.

Rodney, Bob. Pseudonym of Robert Rodrigo (1928–), English writer, usually on sports.

Rodrigo, Robert. See RODNEY, BOB.

Rodríquez del Padrón, Juan (c1405–1440). Spanish poet and novelist, also known as *Juan de la Cámara.*

Rodt, Rudolf. Pseudonym of Ludwig Eichrodt (1827–1892), German humorous poet and jurist.

Rodziewiczówna, Maria. See ŻMOGAS.

Roe, F. Gordon (1894–). English writer, whose pseudonyms are *Criticus, Winslow Rhode,* and *Uncle Gordon.*

Roe, Harry Mason. See STRATEMEYER, EDWARD L.

Rogers, John. See MATTHEW, THOMAS.

Rogers, Ruth. See ALEXANDER, RUTH.

Rogers, Wade. See MADLEE, DOROTHY.

Rohmer, Sax. Pseudonym of Arthur Sarsfield Ward (1883–1959), English mystery writer.

Roland, Mary. See LEWIS, MARY CHRISTIANNA MILNE.

Rolfe, Frederick William. See CORVO, FREDERICK BARON.

Rollins, Kathleen. See DRESSER, DAVIS.

Rollins, William. See STACY, O'CONNOR.

Rolls, Anthony. Pseudonym of Colwyn Edward Vulliamy (1886–), mystery writer.

Romaine, Lawrence B. See WEATHERCOCK, THE.

Romains, Jules. Pseudonym of Louis Farigoule (1885–), French poet.

Romani, Girolamo. See ROMANINO, IL.

Romanino, Il. Cognomen of Girolamo Romani (1485–1566), Italian painter.

Romano, Emanuel (1904–). Italian-American painter, whose original surname was Glicenstein.

Romano, Enotrio. Occasional pseudonym of Giosuè Carducci (1835–1907), Italian poet and critic.

Romano, Giulio (1499–1546). Italian painter and architect, whose real name was Giulio Pippi de' Gianuzzi.

Romanones, Countess of. See COUNTESS OF ROMANONES.

Romanousky, N. K. See CHORNY, KUZMA.

Romanov, Grand Duke Constantine. See K.R.

Rome, Anthony. Pseudonym of Marvin H. Albert, contemporary mystery writer.

Ronald, E. B. Pseudonym of Ronald Ernest Barker (1920–   ), mystery writer.

Ronns, Edward. See AARONS, EDWARD SIDNEY.

Roos, Audrey Kelley. See ROOS, KELLEY.

Roos, Kelley. Joint pseudonym of Audrey Kelley Roos (1912–   ) and William Roos (1911–   ), mystery writers.

Roos, William. See ROOS, KELLEY.

Roosdorp, Frits. Pseudonym of Frederik Cornelis Marie Schröder (1874–1898), Dutch writer.

Ropero, El. Cognomen of Antón de Montoro (1404–c1480), Spanish poet.

Ropes, Arthur Reed. See ROSS, ADRIAN.

Ropshin. Pseudonym of Boris Viktorovich Savinkov (1879–1926), Russian revolutionary writer.

Rosa, Salvator. See SALVATORIELLO.

Roscoe, John. See ROSCOE, MIKE.

Roscoe, Mike. Joint pseudonym of John Roscoe (1921–   ) and Michael Ruso, mystery writers.

Rose, Alvin Emanuel. See PRUITT, ALAN.

Rose, George. See SKETCHLEY, ARTHUR.

Rose, Hilary. See MACKINNON, CHARLES ROY.

Rosegger, Peter (1843–1918). Austrian writer, whose original name was Peter Kettenfeier.

Rosenberg, Elsa. See ASPAZIA.

Rosenberg, Léon Nikolayevich. See BAKST, LÉON NIKOLAYEVICH.

Rosenfeld, Morris. Pseudonym of Moshe Jacob Alter (1862–1923), Yiddish poet.

Rosenplüt, Hans (fl. c1430–1460). German poet, also called *Hans Schnepperer.*

Rosenstok, J. See TZARA, TRISTAN.

Rosenthal, Richard A. See RICHARDS, ALLEN.

Rosh. See ASHER BEN YEHIEL.

Roskolenko, Harry. See ROSS, COLIN.

Rosny, J. H. Joint pseudonym of Joseph-Henri Boëx (1856–1940) and his brother, Justin Boëx (1859–1948), French novelists. After 1908 they published separately as *Rosny aîné* and *Rosny jeune.*

Rosny aîné. See ROSNY, J. H.

Rosny jeune. See ROSNY, J. H.

Ross, Adrian. Pseudonym of Arthur Reed Ropes (1859–1933), English writer and librettist, used for his stage works.

Ross, Barnaby. See DANNAY, FREDERIC, and LEE, MANFRED B.

Ross, Colin. Pseudonym of Harry Roskolenko (1907–   ), American author.

Ross, Don. Contemporary American writer, whose pseudonyms are *Rose Dana, Alice Gilmer, Ellen Randolf, Don Roberts, Marilyn Ross,* and *Jane Rossiter.*

Ross, Eulalie Steinmetz. See STEINMETZ, EULALIE.

Ross, J. H. Pseudonym of Thomas Edward Lawrence (1888–1935), popularly known as Lawrence of Arabia, English soldier, adventurer, and writer. In 1927 he changed his name to *Thomas Edward Shaw.*

Ross, Katherine. See WALTER, DOROTHY BLAKE.

Ross, Leonard Q. Pseudonym of Leo Rosten (1908–   ), Polish-American scholar.

Ross, Marilyn. See ROSS, DON.

Ross, Martin. See MARTIN, VIOLET.

Ross, Sutherland. Pseudonym of Thomas Henry Callard (1912–   ), English writer.

Ross, Zola Helen (1912–   ). Mystery writer, whose pseudonyms are *Helen Arre* and *Bert Iles.*

Rossellino, Antonio (1427–1479). Florentine sculptor, brother of Bernardo Rossellino. His family name is Gambarelli, his father being Matteo di Domenico Gambarelli. The name was derived from *rosellino,* an agricultural term for a certain kind of olive, fern, and grape.

Rossellino, Bernardo (1409–1464). Florentine sculptor and architect, brother of Antonio Rossellino. His father was named Matteo di Domenico Gambarelli. The name was derived from *rosellino,* an agricultural term for a certain kind of olive, fern, and grape.

Rosset, Benjamin Charles. See OZY.

Rossi, Francesco de'. See SALVIATI, CECCO DI.

Rossi, Gian Vittorio. See ERYTHRAEUS, IANUS NICIUS.

Rossiter, Ian. Pseudonym of Hugh Ross Williamson (1901–   ), English writer.

Rossiter, Jane. See Ross, Don.

Rosso, Il. Cognomen of Giovanni Battista di Jacopo (1495–1540), Florentine painter.

Ross Williamson, Hugh. See Rossiter, Ian.

Rosten, Leo. See Ross, Leonard Q.

Ro Tae-yong. Pseudonym of Richard Rutt (1925–   ), English writer.

Rotarius. Pseudonym of Tibor Kerekes (1893–   ), Hungarian-American scholar.

Roth, Holly (d. 1964). American mystery writer, whose pseudonyms are *K. G. Ballard* and *P. J. Merrill.*

Rothmann, Maria Elizabeth. See M.E.R.

Rotwil, Konrat von. See Witz, Konrad.

Rouget, Marie-Mélanie. See Noël, Marie.

Roulliot, Pierre Jacques. See Moreau, Hégésippe.

Roux, Paul. See Saint-Pol-Roux.

Rowans, Virginia. See Tanner, Edward Everett, III.

Rowland, Iris. See Roberts, Irene.

Rowlands, Richard. Pseudonym of Richard Verstegan (or Verstegen) (c1550–1640), English-Dutch novelist, used while in England.

Roy, Claude. Pseudonym of Claude Orland (1915–   ), French critic and writer.

Roy, Ewell Paul (1929–   ). American writer, whose pseudonyms are *Victor Bonnette* and *Ernest Lemoine.*

Roy, Liam. Pseudonym of Patricia Scarry (1924–   ), Canadian-American writer of children's books and for radio and television.

Rozanov, Michail Grigorevich. See Ognëv, Nikolay.

Rozanski, A. See Wogler, Elchanan.

Rozenberg, Elza. See Aspazia.

Rubianus, Crotus. Pseudonym of Johann Jäger (c1480–1539). German humanist.

Rubin, Jacob A. See Odem, J.

Rückert, Friedrich. See Raimar, Freimund.

Rudd, Steele. Pseudonym of Arthur Hoey Davis (1868–1935), Australian writer.

Rudomin, Esther. Pseudonym of Esther Rudomin Hautzig (1930–   ), Polish-American writer.

Ruedi, Norma Paul. Pseudonym of Norma Ainsworth, contemporary American author.

Ruffle, The. See TEGNER, HENRY.

Ruhi. Pseudonym of Osman (d. 1605), Turkish satirical poet.

Ruisdael, Jacob van (1628–1682). Dutch painter, whose original surname was de Goyer (or de Gooyer). The name was probably derived from Castle Ruysendael, where the family originally lived. He was the nephew of Salomon van Ruysdael, who used another spelling.

Ruíz, José Martínez. See AZORÍN.

Runyon, Charles W. See WEST, MARK.

Rupert, Raphael Rudolph. See TATRAY, ISTVAN.

Rushd, ibn-. See AVERROËS.

Rushton, Charles. Pseudonym of Charles Rushton Shortt (1904–   ), mystery writer.

Ruso, Michael. See ROSCOE, MIKE.

Russell, Albert. See BIXBY, JEROME LEWIS.

Russell, George William. See Æ.

Russell, J. See BIXBY, JEROME LEWIS.

Russell, John. See THRICE, LUKE.

Russell, Norma Hull Lewis. See HODGSON, NORMA.

Russell, William. Contemporary mystery writer, whose pseudonyms are *Inspector F* and *Waters*.

Rutherford, Douglas. Pseudonym of James Douglas Rutherford McConnell (1915–   ), Irish-English writer.

Rutherford, Mark. Pseudonym of William Hale White (1831–1913), English novelist, critic, and philosopher.

Rutledge, Brett. Pseudonym of Elliot Harold Paul (1891–1958), mystery writer.

Rutledge, Dom Denys. Pseudonym of Edward William Rutledge (1906–   ), English writer.

Rutledge, Edward William. See RUTLEDGE, DOM DENYS.

Rutledge, Nancy. See BRYSON, LEIGH.

Rutt, Richard. See RO TAE-YONG.

Ruysdael, Salomon van (1600/02–1670). Dutch painter, whose original surname was de Goyer (or de Gooyer). The name was probably derived from Castle Ruysendael, where the family originally lived. He was the uncle of Jacob van Ruisdael, who used another spelling.

Ruzzante, Il. Cognomen of Angelo Beolco (1502–1542), Italian playwright and comic actor. The name was derived from his best-known character, the peasant Ruzzante (from *ruzzare*, "to romp"), a role he acted.

Ryall, William Bolitho. See BOLITHO, WILLIAM.

Ryan, Paul William (1906–1947). American mystery writer, whose pseudonyms are *Robert Finnegan* and *Mike Quin.*

Rybot, Doris. Pseudonym of Doris Almon Ponsonby, contemporary English author.

Rydell, Forbes. see FORBES, DELORIS STANTON.

Rydell, Helen B. See FORBES, DELORIS STANTON.

Ryerson, Lowell. Pseudonym of Winfred Van Atta (1910–   ), mystery writer.

Rygier-Nałkowska, Zofia. See NAŁKOWSKA, ZOFJA.

Ryland, Clive. Pseudonym of Clive Ryland Priestley (1892–   ), mystery writer.

Rysselberghe, Maria van. See SAINT-CLAIR, M.

Rytter, Poul. Pseudonym of Parmo Carl Plough (1813–1894), Danish poet.

Ryutei Tanehiko. Pseudonym of Takaya Tomohisa (1783-1842), Japanese novelist and essayist, also called *Takaya Hikoshiro.*

Rywell, Martin (1905–   ). American author and specialist in American firearms, whose pseudonyms are *Taylor Hemingway* and *Deane Sears.*

Rzewuski, Count Henryk. See BEJLA, J.

"S"

SEC. Occasional pseudonym of Marya Mannes (1904–   ), American editor and writer.

Sabellico, Marcantonio. Latinized name of Marcantonio Coccio (1436?–1505), Italian humanist.

Saber, Robert O. Pseudonym of Milton K. Ozaki, contemporary mystery writer.

Sabini, John Anthony. See ANTHONY, JOHN.

Sacchi, Bartolommeo de'. See PLATINA, IL.

Sachs, Maurice. Pseudonym of Maurice Ettinghausen (1906–1945), French writer.

Sadino, Elmano. Academic name of Manuel Maria Barbosa du Bocage (or Boccage) (1765–1805), Portuguese poet.

Saeki Mana. See KOBO DAISHI.

Sage, Juniper. Joint pseudonym of Edith Hurd (1910–   ) and Margaret Wise Brown, American authors of children's books.

Sa'igh, ibn-al-. See AVEMPACE.

Saigyo. Pseudonym of Sato Norikiyo (1118–1190), Japanese poet.

Saint, Dora Jessie. See READ, MISS.

St. Albans, Alexander of. See NECKHAM, ALEXANDER.

Saint Amand, Gabriel Randon de. See RICTUS, JEHAN.

Saint-Amant, Marc-Antoine de Gérard, Sieur de (1594–1661). French poet, whose original name was Antoine Girard.

Saint-Aubain, Andreas Nicolai de. See BERNHARD, KARL.

Saint Briavels, James. See WOOD, JAMES PLAYSTED.

Saint-Clair, M. Pseudonym of Maria Van Rysselberghe (1866–   ), Belgian novelist and essayist.

St. Cosmas. See KOSMA, PRESBYTER.

Saint-Denis, Michel Jacques. See DUCHESNE, JACQUES.

Saintine, Xavier. Pseudonym of Joseph Xavier Boniface (1798–1865), French novelist and playwright.

St. James, Andrew. Pseudonym of James Stern (1904–   ), mystery writer.

St. John, Beth. Pseudonym of Elizabeth Beaman John (1907–   ), American writer.

St. John, J. Hector. Pseudonym of Michel Guillaume Jean de Crèvecoeur (1735–1813), French writer.

St. John, John. Pseudonym of Richard Sale (1911–   ), American writer.

Saint-John-Perse. See LÉGER, ALEXIS.

St. Myer, Ned. See STRATEMEYER, EDWARD L.

Saint-Pol-Roux. Pseudonym of Paul Roux (1861–1940), French poet.

Saint-Serge, Monsieur de. See DELORME, PHILIBERT.

Saki. Pseudonym of Hector Hugh Munro (1870–1916), English writer.

Saks, Elmer Eliot. See FAWCETT, FRANK DUBREZ.

Salamatullah. Pseudonym of Salamat Ullah (1913–   ), Indian scholar.

Sale, Richard. See SAINT JOHN, JOHN.

Salmon, Geraldine Gordon. See SARASIN, J. G.

Salmon, Jean. See MACRIN.

Salt, Sarah. Pseudonym of Coralie von Werner Hobson (1891–   ), mystery writer.

Salten, Felix. Pseudonym of Felix Salzmann (1869–1945), Hungarian writer.

Saltykov, Mikhail Evgrafovich. See SHCHEDRIN, N.

Salustri, Carlo Alberto. See TRILUSSA.

Salvatoriello. Nickname of Salvator Rosa (1615–1673), Italian painter and poet.

Salviati, Cecco di (1510–1563). Italian painter, whose real name was Francesco de' Rossi.

Salzmann, Felix. See SALTEN, FELIX.

Samachson, Dorothy. See SAMACHSON, JOSEPH.

Samachson, Joseph (1906–   ). American science writer who also writes jointly with his wife, Dorothy Samachson, under the pseudonyms *John Miller* and *William Morrison.*

Sampson, Richard Henry. See HULL, RICHARD.

Samuel ben Me'ir. See RASHBAM.

Samuel ha-Nagid (993–1055). Spanish-Hebrew poet, also known as *Samuel ben Joseph ibn-Nagdela* (or *Nagrela*).

Samuilu. See CLAIN, SAMUIL.

Sanborn, B. X. See BALLINGER, WILLIAM SANBORN.

Sánchez de las Bronzas, Francisco. See BRONCENSE, EL.

San Cristóbal, Diego de. See ESTELLA, FRATE DIEGO DE.

Sand, George. Pseudonym of Amandine Aurore Lucie Dupin (1804–1876), French novelist. The name was derived from that of Jules Sandeau, French novelist and playwright, with whom she had a prolonged affair. She was also known as *Aurore Dudevant,* from the name of her divorced husband, Baron Casimir Dudevant.

Sandburg, Carl August (1878–1967). American scholar, whose pseudonyms are *Militant, Jack Phillips,* and *Charles A. Sandburg.*

Sandburg, Charles A. See SANDBURG, CARL AUGUST.

Sandel, Cora. Pseudonym of Sara Fabricius (1880–   ), Norwegian novelist.

Sanders, Daphne. See RICE, CRAIG.

Sanders, Ed. See HOBART, BLACK.

Sanders, Kent. See WILKES-HUNTER, RICHARD.

Sanders, Winston P. Pseudonym of Paul William Anderson (1926–   ), American mystery and science-fiction writer.

Sanderson, Douglas (1922–   ). Mystery writer, whose pseudonyms are *Martin Brett* and *Malcolm Douglas*.

Sandre, Thierry. Pseudonym of Charles Moulié (1890–   ), French novelist.

Sandro, Benozzo di Lese di. See GOZZOLI, BENOZZO.

Sands, Leo G. (1912–   ). American free-lance writer, whose pseudonyms are *Lee Craig* and *Jack Helmi*.

Sandys, Oliver. See EVANS, MARGUERITE FLORENCE HÉLÈNE.

Sangallo. Name given to a group of Florentine artists who were members of the Giamberti and Cordiani families. It was derived from the gate of San Gallo in Florence, near which they lived.

> **Antonio the Elder** (1453–1534). Architect, whose real name was Antonio Giamberti.

> **Antonio the Younger** (1483–1546). Architect, whose real name was Antonio Cordiani.

> **Aristotile** (1481–1551). Architect, painter, and decorator, whose real given name was Bastiano. He was a son of a sister of Giuliano Giamberti.

> **Francesco** (1405–1480). Woodworker and musician, whose real name was Francesco Giamberti.

> **Giovan Francesco** (1482–1530). Architect, whose real name was Giovan Francesco Giamberti.

> **Giuliano** (1443–1516). Architect, whose real name was Giuliano Giamberti.

> **Gobbo, Il** ("The Hunchback") (1496–1552). Architect, whose real name was Battista Cordiani.

> **Margotta, Il** ("The Layerer," obs. for "mason") (1494–1576). Sculptor, whose real name was Francesco Giamberti.

Sangiro ("Rabbit"). Swahili cognomen of Andries Albertus Pienaar (1894–   ), Afrikaans writer, derived from his swiftness as a runner.

Sannazzaro, Jacopo. See ACTIUS SYNCERUS.

Sanojo, Ana Teresa Parra. See PARRA, TERESA DE LA.

Sansovino, Andrea (c1460–1529). Italian sculptor and architect, whose real name was Andrea Contucci.

Sansovino, Jacopo (1486–1570). Italian sculptor and architect, whose original surname was Tatti. The name was derived from that of his teacher, Andrea Sansovino.

Santa María, Pablo de (1350–1435). Spanish theologian and historian, whose original name was Solomon ha-Levi. He was a Jew who converted to Christianity, took orders, and became Bishop of Burgos.

Santee, Collier. See FLEXNER, STUART BERG.

Santi, Raffaello. See RAPHAEL.

Santob de Carrión de los Condes. Early fourteenth-century Spanish-Hebrew poet, also called *Sem Tob ibn-Ardutiel ben Isaac.*

Santo Kyoden. Pseudonym of Iwase Sei (1761–1816), Japanese novelist and writer, also called *Iwase Nobuyoshi.*

Sanzio, Raffaello. See RAPHAEL.

Sapientis, Conradus. See WITZ, KONRAD.

Sapper. Pseudonym of Cyril McNeile (1888–1937), British army officer and writer.

Sara. Pseudonym of Sally Mirliss Blake (1925–   ), American writer.

Sarasin, J. G. Pseudonym of Geraldine Gordon Salmon (1897–   ), mystery writer.

Sarcey, Francisque. See BINET, SATANÉ.

Sardenko, Silvin. Pseudonym of Alojzij Merher (1875–1942), Slovak poet.

Sarfatti, Margherita (1886–1961). Italian writer and literary critic, whose pseudonyms are *Cidiè* and *El Sereno.*

Sargidzhan, Amir. See BORODIN, SERGEY PETROVICH.

Sarne, Michael. Pseudonym of Thomas Arthur Plummer, contemporary mystery writer.

Saroyan, William. See GORYAN, SIRAK.

Sarpi, Paolo. Religious name of Pietro Sarpi (1552–1623), Italian ecclesiastical historian.

Sarpi, Pietro. See SARPI, PAOLO.

Sarto, Ben. See Fawcett, Frank Dubrez.

Sartorius, E. Pseudonym of Heinrich Emil Schneider (1839–1928), German-American poet.

Sarver, Hannah. Pseudonym of Jean Sarver Nielsen (1922–   ), American author.

Sasaki Sadataka. See TAMENAGA SHUNSUI.

Sassetta (1392?–1450). Sienese painter, whose real name was Stefano di Giovanni, with which he signed his works. The name was apparently established in the 18th century.

Satomi. Pseudonym of Yamanouchi Hideo (1888–   ), Japanese novelist.

Sato Norikiyo. See SAIGYO.

Satterly, Weston. Pseudonym of William Sunners (1903–   ), American writer.

Sauer, Muriel Strafford. See HEINLEIN, ROBERT ANSON.

Saunders, Carl McK. Pseudonym of Philip Ketchum (1902–   ), mystery writer.

Saunders, Hilary Aidan St. George (1898–   ). English writer, whose pseudonyms, with John Leslie Palmer, are *Francis Beeding* and *David Pilgrim.*

Saunders, Ione. See COLE, MARGARET ALICE.

Saunders, Lawrence. Joint pseudonym of Burton Davis (1893–   ) and Claire Ogden Davis (1892–   ), mystery writers.

Saunders, Richard. See FRANKLIN, BENJAMIN.

Saunders, Theodore. See SCOTT, DENIS.

Sava, George. See BANKOFF, GEORGE ALEXIS.

Savage, Blake. See GOODWIN, HAROLD LELAND.

Savallo, Teresa de, Marquesa d'Alpens. See WILLIAMSON, ALICE MURIEL LIVINGSTON.

Savinio, Alberto. Occasional pseudonym of Andrea De Chirico (1891–1952), Italian painter, musician, novelist, essayist, and playwright.

Savinkov, Boris Viktorovich. See ROPSHIN, V.

Savior, Alfred. Pseudonym of Alfred Posznanski (1883–1934), French playwright.

Saviozzo, Il. Cognomen of Simone Serdini (c1360–c1420), Italian poet.

Sawyer, Corinne Holt. See RICKERT, CORINNE HOLT.

Sawyer, Eugene T. See CARTER, NICK.

Sawyer, John. See FOLEY, JOHN.

Sawyer, Mark. Pseudonym of Clarence David Greenhood (1895–   ), American poet and prose writer.

Saxon, Gladys Relyea. Contemporary American writer, whose pseudonyms are *M. Borden* and *Marion Seyton.*

Saya, Peter. Pseudonym of Robert E. Peterson (1928–   ), American author.

Sayers, Dorothy Leigh. See LEIGH, JOHANNA.

Sayre, Gordon. See WOOLFOLK, JOSIAH PITTS.

Scannabue, Aristarco. Pseudonym of Giuseppe Marc' Antonio Baretti (1719–1789), Italian critic.

Scantrel, Félix-André-Yves. See SAURÈS, ANDRÉ.

Scarlett, Roger. Joint pseudonym of Evelyn Page (1902–) and Dorothy Blair, American free-lance writers.

Scarry, Patricia. See ROY, LIAM,

Schabacher, Simon. See DUVERNOIS, HENRI.

Schaffy, Mirza. See BODENSTEDT, FRIEDRICH VON.

Schaidenreisser, Simon (d. 1573). German writer and translator, also called *Minervius.*

Schakovskoy, Princess Zinaida. See CROISE, JACQUES.

Schaumburg, Paul. See BURG, PAUL.

Schede, Paul. See MELISSUS, PAULUS.

Scheffauer, Herman George. See ORCHELLA, R. L.

Scheffler, Johannes. See SILESIUS, ANGELUS.

Schepp, Christiaan Louis. See PRINS, JAN.

Schiavone, Andrea (1522?–1582). Italian painter, whose real name was Andrea Medolla (or Meldolla).

Schiff, Sydney. See HUDSON, STEPHEN.

Schisgall, Oscar (1901–). Mystery writer, whose pseudonyms are *Jackson Cole* and *Stuart Hardy.*

Schlemihl, Peter. Occasional pseudonym of Ludwig Thoma (1867–1921), German playwright and writer.

Schlosberg, H. J. Pseudonym of Henry John May (1903–), Rhodesian–English–South African writer.

Schmidt, Anton Franz. See DIETZENSCHMIDT.

Schmidt, Eduard. See BASS, EDUARD; EDSCHMID, KASIMIR.

Schmidt, James Norman. See NORMAN, JAMES.

Schmidt, Kasper. Pseudonym of Max Stirner (1806–1856), German philosopher.

Schmidt, Otto Ernst. See ERNST, OTTO.

Schmidt, Wilhelm. See SCHMIDTBONN, WILHELM.

Schmidt, Wilhelmina Angela. See CORSARI, WILLY.

Schmidtbonn, Wilhelm. Pseudonym of Wilhelm Schmidt (1876–1952), German playwright, novelist, and poet.

Schmillauer, Alois. See SMILOVSKÝ, ALOIS VOJTECH.

Schmitz, Ettore. See SVEVO, ITALO.

Schnabel, Johann Gottfried. See GISANDER.

Schneck, Stephen (1933–). American satirist, whose pseudonyms are *Ben Bite, Mack Fite, Larry Kite, James Knight, James Lite,* and *Sam Spit.*

Schneider, Heinrich Emil. See SARTORIUS, E.

Schneider, Louis. See BOTH, L. W.

Schnepperer, Hans. See ROSENPLÜT, HANS.

Schnitter, Johannes. see AGRICOLA, JOHANNES.

Scholarius, Georgios. See GENNADIUS II.

Scholasticus. 6th-century Greek ascetic and religious writer, whose original name was John Climacus.

Scholefield, Edmund O. See BUTTERWORTH, WILLIAM EDMUND, III.

Schön, Martin. See SCHONGAUER, MARTIN.

Schonfield, Hugh J. See HEGESIPPUS.

Schongauer, Martin (1445?–1491). German engraver and printer, also known as *Hipsch* (or *Hübsch*) ("Handsome") *Martin* and *Martin Schön.*

Schoolmeester, De. Pseudonym of Gerrit van de Linde Jansz (1808–1858). Dutch humorous poet.

Schopfer, Jean. See ANET, CLAUDE.

Schosberg, Paul Allyn. See ALLYN, PAUL.

Schreiner, Olive Emilie Albertina. See IRON, RALPH.

Schröder, Frederik Cornelis Marie. See ROOSDORP, FRITS.

Schwarzefeld, Gertrude von. Pseudonym of Gertrude E. L. Cochrane de Alencar (1906–   ), Austrian writer.

Schwarzert, Philipp. See MELANCHTHON.

Schwarzmann, Lev Isaakovich. See SHESTOV, LEV.

Scipione. Pseudonym of Gino Bonichi (1904–1933), Italian poet and painter.

Scott, Anthony. See DRESSER, DAVIS.

Scott, Archer G. Pseudonym of Philip George Larbalestier, contemporary mystery writer.

Scott, Cora Annett. See ANNETT, CORA.

Scott, Dan. See BARKER, S. OMAR.

Scott, Dan. See STRATEMEYER, EDWARD L.

Scott, Dana. Pseudonym of Constance Noyes Robertson (1897–   ), mystery writer.

Scott, Denis. Joint pseudonym of Mary Means and Theodore Saunders, contemporary mystery writers.

Scott, Evelyn. See SOUZA, ERNEST.

Scott, Frances V. Pseudonym of Frances Wing (1907–   ), American writer.

Scott, Hugh Stowell. See MERRIMAN, HENRY SETON.

Scott, Jane. See MCELFRESH, ELIZABETH ADELINE.

Scott, Jean. See MUIR, MARIE.

Scott, Jody. See SCOTT, THURSTON.

Scott, Marian Gallagher. Contemporary mystery writer, whose pseudonyms are *Gail Oliver* and *Katherine Wolffe.*

Scott, Martin. See GEHMAN, RICHARD BOYD.

Scott, Thurston. Joint pseudonym of George Thurston Leite (1920–
) and Jody Scott (1923–   ), mystery writers.

Scott, Warwick. See TREVOR, ELLESTON.

Scriblerus, Martinus. Joint pseudonym of John Arbuthnot (1667–1735),
         Alexander Pope (1688–1744), and Jonathan Swift (1667–1745),
         used for *Memoirs of Martinus Scriblerus.*

Scudder, Mildred Lee. See LEE, MILDRED.

Seaforth. Pseudonym of George Cecil Foster (1893–   ), mystery
         writer.

Sea-Lion. Pseudonym of Geoffrey Bennett (1909–   ), English writer.

Sealsfield, Charles. Pseudonym of Karl Anton Postl (1793–1864), German novelist and travel writer. He took the name when he gave up
         the priesthood and came to America in 1864. He returned to
         Europe, however, and died in Switzerland.

Seaman, Elizabeth. See BLY, NELLIE.

Seamark. Pseudonym of Austin J. Small (d. 1929), mystery writer.

Se'ami Motokiyo. Pseudonym of Yusaki Saemondayu Motokiyo (1363–
         1443), Japanese writer of No plays, also known as *Kanze Motokiyo.*
         His father was Kan'ami Kiyotsugo, co-founder, with his son, of the
         No drama.

Search-light. Pseudonym of Waldo David Frank (1889–1967), American mystery writer.

Sears, Deane. See RYWELL, MARTIN.

Sebastiaan, Sr. See KLOOS, WILLEM JOHAN THEODOOR.

Sebastiano del Piombo (1485?–1547). Italian painter, whose real name
         was Sebastiano Luciani. The name was derived from the papal seals
         (piombatore papale), of which he was appointed keeper. Vasari refers to him as *Sebastiano Veneziano,* after his birthplace, Venice.

Secrist, Kelliher. Joint pseudonym of Dan T. Kelliher and W. G. Secrist,
         contemporary mystery writers.

Secrist, W. G. See SECRIST, KELLIHER.

Secundus, Janus (1511–1536). Neo-Latin poet, also called *Joannes Everardi* or *Joannes Nicolai.*

Sedges, John. Occasional pseudonym of Pearl Buck (1892–   ), American novelist.

Sedmak, Pavle. See BEVK, FRANCE.

Seebord, G. R. See SODERBERG, PERCY MEASDAY.

Seferiadis, Jorgos. See SEFERIS, GEORGE.

Seferis, George. Pseudonym of Jorgos Seferiadis (1900–   ), neo-Hellenic poet.

Seger, Herkeles. See SEGHERS, HERCULES PIETERZ.

Seghers, Anna. Pseudonym of Netty Radványi (1900–   ), German writer.

Seghers, Hercules Pieterz (1589/90–1633?). Dutch painter and etcher, also known as *Herkeles Seger.*

Segrais. Pseudonym of Mme. de La Fayette (1634–1693), French writer.

Segre, Dino. See PITIGRILLI.

Seid, Ruth. See SINCLAIR, JO.

Seifert, Elizabeth. Pseudonym of Elizabeth Seifert Gasparotti (1897–   ), American writer.

Sélavy, Rose. See DUCHAMP, MARCEL.

Seldes, Gilbert Vivian (1893–   ). American writer, whose pseudonyms are *Lucien Bluphocks, Sebastian Cauliflower, Foster Johns,* and *Vivian Shaw.*

Seldon, George. Pseudonym of George Seldon Thompson (1929–   ), American free-lance writer.

Seldon-Truss, Leslie. See SELMARK, GEORGE.

Sellari, Girolamo de'. See CARPI, GIROLAMO DA.

Sellers, Isaiah. See TWAIN, MARK.

Selmark, George. Pseudonym of Leslie Seldon-Truss (1892–   ), English writer.

Semple, Gordon. See NEUBAUER, WILLIAM ARTHUR.

Sencourt, Robert. Pseudonym of Robert Esmonde Gordon George (1890–   ), New Zealand–English scholar.

Senior, Isabel Janet Couper Syme. See PLEYDELL, SUSAN.

Senkovsky, Osip Ivanovich. See BRAMBEUS, BARON.

Sepia. See HOLMVIK, OYVIND.

Serafimovich, Alexander. Pseudonym of Alexander Serafimovich Popov

(1863–1949), Russian author of Cossack origin and one-time member of Gorky's Znanie group of writers.

Serafinowicz, Leszek Jozef. See LECHOŃ, JAN.

Serdini, Simone. See SAVIOZZO, IL.

Sereno, El. See SARFATTI, MARGHERITA.

Serner, Martin Gunnar. See HELLER, FRANK.

Serrifile, F. O. O. Pseudonym of William Kersley Holmes (1882–), English writer.

Sesshu (1420–1506). Japanese painter, also known as Unkoku Toyo. Many of his works before 1464 are signed simply *Toyo.*

Seton, Ernest Thompson (1860–1946). English-Canadian writer and illustrator, whose original surname was Thompson.

Seton, Graham. Pseudonym of Graham Seton Hutchison (1890–), mystery writer.

Settignano, Desiderio da (1428?–1464). Florentine sculptor, also known as *Desiderio Meo.*

Settle, Edith. Pseudonym of William Linton Andrews (1886–), British writer.

Seuss, Dr. See GEISEL, THEODOR SEUSS.

Séverine. Pseudonym of Carline Rémy (1855–1929), French journalist and writer.

Severn, David. Pseudonym of David Storr Unwin (1918–), English writer.

Severyanin, Igor. Pseudonym of Igor Vasilyevich Lotarëv (1887–1942), Russian writer.

Sevrey, Opal Irene. Pseudonym of Opal Irene Frazine Sevrey Miner, contemporary American writer.

Seward, William W., Jr. See RIVES, LEIGH.

Sewer. Pseudonym of Ignacy Maciejowski (1839–1901), Polish novelist.

Seyhi. Pseudonym of Yusuf Sinan (d. 1426), Turkish poet and physician.

Seyid Imadeddin. See NESIMI.

Seymour, H. Pseudonym of Helmut Hartmann, contemporary mystery writer.

Seyton, Marion. See SAXON, GLADYS RELYEA.

Sforim, Mendele Mocher. See MENDELE MOCHER SFORIM.

Shackleton, C. C. Pseudonym of Brian Wilson Aldiss (1925–), English author.

Shaffer, Anthony. See ANTHONY, PETER.

Shaffer, Peter. See ANTHONY, PETER.

Shalkovitz, Arieh Leib. See BEN-AVIGDOR.

Shalom Aleichem. See ALEICHEM, SHALOM.

Shane, Susannah. Pseudonym of Harriette Ashbrook (1898–1946), mystery writer.

Shannon, Carl. See HOGUE, WILBUR OWINGS.

Shannon, Dell. See LININGTON, ELIZABETH.

Shannon, Terry. Pseudonym of Jessie Mercer, contemporary American juvenile writer.

Shanwa. Pseudonym of Alex Ernest Haarer (1894–   ), English writer.

Shapiro, Konstantin (1839–1900). Hebrew poet, also called *Asher* and *Ab'a.*

Sharman, Maisie. See BOLTON, MAISIE SHARMAN.

Sharon, Rose. See MERRIL, JUDITH.

Sharp, Luke. Pseudonym of Robert Barr (1850–1912), mystery writer.

Sharp, William. See MACLEOD, FIONA.

Shauki, Ahmad Bey. See SHAUQI, AHMAD.

Shauki, Ahmed. See SHAUQI, AHMAD.

Shauqi, Ahmad (1868–1932). Egyptian-Arab poet, dramatist, and novelist, also known as *Ahmad Bey Shauki* and *Ahmed Shauki.*

Shaw, Charles. See SINGER, BANT.

Shaw, Henry Wheeler (1818–1885). American humorist, whose pseudonyms are *Josh Billings* and *Uncle Esek.*

Shaw, Thomas Edward. See ROSS, J. H.

Shaw, Vivian. See SELDES, GILBERT VIVIAN.

Shayne, Gordon. See WINTER, BEVIS.

Shchedrin, N. Pseudonym of Mikhail Evgrafovich Saltykov (1826–1889), Russian writer.

Shea, John Gerald. See FITZGERALD, JACK.

Shearing, Joseph. See LONG, GABRIELLE MARGARET VERE.

Sheehan, Patric Augustine. Pseudonym of P. A. O Siochain (1905–   ), Irish writer.

Sheldon, Ann. Collective pseudonym for the "Linda Craig" series. See STRATEMEYER, EDWARD L.

Sheldon, George E. See STAHL, LE ROY.

Shellabarger, Samuel (1888–1954). American mystery writer, whose pseudonyms are *John Esteven* and *Peter Loring.*

Shelley, Peter. See DRESSER, DAVIS.
Shelton, Lola. Pseudonym of Lola Shelton Klaue (1903–   ), American writer.
Shen Yen-ping. See MAO-TUN.
Shepherd, Joan. Pseudonym of B. J. Buchanan, contemporary mystery writer.
Shepherd, John. See BALLARD, TODHUNTER.
Shepherd, Neal. See MORLAND, NIGEL.
Shepherd, Robert Henry Wishart. See WISHART, HENRY.
Sheppard, Lancelot Capel. See CAPEL, ROGER.
Sherashevski, Boris. Pseudonym of John J. Brown (1916–   ), Canadian financial writer.
Sherman, Eleanor Rae. See FLEURIDAS, ELLIE RAE.
Sherman, Elizabeth. Pseudonym of Margaret Richards Friskey (1901–   ), American editor and free-lance writer.
Sherman, Joan. See DERN, PEGGY GADDIS.
Shestov, Lev. Pseudonym of Lev Isaakovich Schwarzmann (1866–1938), Russian philosopher and author.
Shiba Shiro. See TOKAI SANSHI.
Shiel, Matthew Phipps. See HOLMES, GORDON.
Shigeta Ichijiro. See JIPPENSHA IKKU.
Shigeta Sadakazu. See JIPPENSHA Ikku.
Shikitei Samba. Pseudonym of Kikuchi Hisanori (1776–1822), Japanese novelist, also called *Kikuchi Taisuke.*
Shimazaki Haruki. See SHIMAZAKI TOSON.
Shimazaki Toson. Pseudonym of Shimazaki Haruki (1872–1943), Japanese poet, novelist, and playwright.
Shimokawa Kushin. See KEICHU.
Shimshelevitz, Aaron. See REUBENI, AARON.
Shina Norishige. See SOKAN.
Shinsai. See HOKUSAI.
Shir. Pseudonym of Solomon Judah Leib Rappoport (1790–1867), Galician-Hebrew poet.
Shirreffs, Gordon D. (1914–   ). American writer, whose pseudonyms are *Gordon Donalds* and *Stewart Gordon.*
Shnaider, Julia. See KRAVCHENKO, ULIANA.
Shokusanjin. See OTA TAN.
Sholl, Anna McClure. See CORSON, GEOFFREY.

Shore, Philippa. Pseudonym of Philippa Jack Holbeche (1919–   ), English writer.

Shortt, Charles Rushton. See RUSHTON, CHARLES.

Shoyo. See TSUBOUCHI SHOYO.

Shu Ch'ing-ch'un. See LAO-SHE.

Shulberg, Alan. See WILKES-HUNTER, RICHARD.

Shunzei. See FUJIWARA NO TOSHINARI.

Shura, Mary Francis. Pseudonym of Mary Francis Craig (1923–   ), American writer.

Shute, Nevil. Professional name of Nevil Shute Norway (1899–1960), English aeronautical engineer and writer.

Siddle, Charles. See SLINGSBY, RUFUS.

Sieber, Sam Dixon. See KERR, NORMAN D.

Siegel, Doris. See WELLS, SUSAN.

Sienkiewicz, Henryk. See LITWOS.

Sieroszewski, Wacław (1858–1945). Polish author, whose pseudonyms are *K. Bagrynowski* and *Sirko.*

Sifadda, Siful. Pseudonym of Henrik Arnold Wergeland (1808–1845), Norwegian poet, playwright, and essayist.

Sigimori Nobumori. See CHICKAMATSU MONZAEMON.

Sigurd. Pseudonym of Baron Alfred Hedenstierna (1852–1906), Swedish writer.

Silentio, Johannes de. See KIERKEGAARD, SØREN AABYE.

Silesius, Angelus. Latinized name of Johannes Scheffler (1624–1677), German religious poet and mystic.

Siller, Van. Pseudonym of Hilda Van Siller, contemporary mystery writer.

Silone, Ignazio. Pseudonym of Secondo Tranquilli (1900–   ), Italian novelist.

Silva, Antônio José da. See O JUDEU.

Silviana. Pseudonym of Elisabeth Wolff-Bekker (1738–1804), Dutch novelist, poet, and essayist.

Sim, Georges. See SIMENON, GEORGES.

Sim, Katharine. See NURAINI.

Simenon, Georges. Pseudonym of Georges Sim (1903–   ), French novelist.

Simmons, Edward (1852–1931). American painter, whose original name was Edward Emerson.

Simon. See BURFORD, ROGER D'ESTE.

Simon, Charlie May. Pseudonym of Charlie May Hogue Fletcher (1897–), American writer.

Simon, Robert Alfred. See REYNOLDS, LIGGETT.

Simon, S. J. Pseudonym of Simon Jasha Skidelsky, contemporary mystery writer.

Simonides. See SZYMONOWICZ, SZYMON.

Simons, Katherine Drayton Mayrant (1892–   ). American writer, whose pseudonyms are *Drayton Mayrant* and *Kadra Maysi*.

Simons, Roger. Joint pseudonym of Ivar Punnett and Margaret Punnett, contemporary mystery writers.

Simpson, Bertram Lenox. See WEALE, PUTNAM.

Sims, George Robert. See DAGONET.

Simson, Eric Andrew. See KIRK, LAURENCE.

Sina, ibn-. See AVICENNA.

Sinan (1489–1578/88). Turkish architect, commonly known as *Koca Mimar Sinan* ("The Great Architect Sinan") to avoid confusion with Atik Sinan and Sinan of Balikesir, also architects.

Sinclair, Emil. See HESSE, HERMANN.

Sinclair, Ian. See FOLEY, JOHN.

Sinclair, Jo. Pseudonym of Ruth Seid (1913–   ), American author.

Sinclair, Upton Beall (1878–1968). American author, whose pseudonyms are *Clarke Fitch* and *Frederick Garrison*.

Singer, Bant. Pseudonym of Charles Shaw (1900–   ), mystery writer.

Sinjohn, John. Early pseudonym of John Galsworthy (1867–1933), English novelist and playwright.

Sirin, Vladimir. Occasional pseudonym of Vladimir Vladimirovich Nabokov (1899–   ), Russian emigré author.

Sirius. Pseudonym of Edward Martyn (1859–1923), Irish dramatist and founder of the Irish Literary Theatre (1899).

Sirko. See SIEROSZEWSKI, WACLAW.

Sittenfeld, Konrad. See ALBERTI, KONRAD.

Sittewald, Philander von. Pseudonym of Johann Michael Moscherosch (properly Mosenrosh) (1601–1669), German satirist.

Siunro. See HOKUSAI.

Sjöberg, Erik. See VITALIS.

Sketchley, Arthur. Pseudonym of George Rose (1817–1882), English clergyman and humorous writer.

Skidelsky, Simon Jasha. See SIMON, S. J.

Skinner, Conrad Arthur. See MAURICE, MICHAEL.

Skinner, June O'Grady. See O'GRADY, ROHAN.

Skitalets. Pseudonym of Stepan Gavrilovich Petrov (1868–1941), Russian writer.

Skobelev, Alexander Sergeyevich. See NEVEROV, ALEXANDER.

Skrine, Agnes. See O'NEILL, MOIRA.

Skrine, Mary Nesta. See FARRELL, M. J.

Sladen, Norman St. Barbe. Contemporary English author, whose pseudonyms are *Rodney Bullingham* and *Dennis Montclair.*

Sladkovich, Andrey. Pseudonym of Ondrey Braxatoris (1820–1872), Slovak poet.

Slančiková, Božena. See TIMRAVA.

Slaney, George Wilson. See WODEN, GEORGE.

Slater, Frances Charlotte. See BANCROFT, F.

Slaughter, Frank Gill. See TERRY, C. V.

Slavitt, David. See SUTTON, HENRY.

Slesar, Henry. See LESLIE, O. H.

Slick, Sam. Pseudonym of Thomas Chandler Haliburton (1796–1865), Canadian jurist and humorist.

Slingsby, Jonathan Freke. Pseudonym of John Francis Waller (1810–1894). Irish journalist, editor, poet, and songwriter.

Slingsby, Rufus. Joint pseudonym of Frederick Peel (1888–   ) and Charles Siddle (1892–   ), mystery writers.

Słonimski, Antoni. See PRO-ROK.

Slustre. See SLUTER, CLAUS.

Sluter, Claus (d. 1405/6). Dutch-Burgundian sculptor, also known, according to the region in which he was residing, as *(Claes, Claux,* and *Klaas) de Sluter, Seluster, Slustre, Sluyter, Slutre, Celoistre, Celustre,* and *Celuister.*

Slutre. See SLUTER, CLAUS.

Sluyter. See SLUTER, CLAUS.

Small, Austin J. See SEAMARK.

Small, William. Pseudonym of David Edward Charles Eversley (1921–   ), German-English demographic scholar.

Smectymnuus. Pseudonym derived from the initials of Stephen Marshall, Edmund Calamy, Thomas Young, Matthew Newcomen, and

William Spurstow. They used this pseudonym in publishing a tract attacking episcopacy (1641).

Smeken, Jan (c1450–1517). Dutch poet in the Rederijker tradition, also known as *Jan de Baertmaker.* From 1485 he was town poet of Brussels.

Smidovich, Vikenti Vikentievich. See VERESAYEV, VIKENTI.

Smilovský, Alois Vojtech. Pseudonym of Alois Schmillauer (1837–1883), Czech novelist.

Smith, Barbara Herrnstein. See HERRNSTEIN, BARBARA.

Smith, Caesar. See TREVOR, ELLESTON.

Smith, Carmichael. See LINEBARGER, PAUL MYRON ANTHONY.

Smith, Charles Henry. See ARP, BILL.

Smith, Constance Isabel. See REID, ELEANOR.

Smith, Dodie. See ANTHONY, C. L.

Smith, Elizabeth Thomasina Meade. See MEADE, LILLIE THOMAS.

Smith, Ernest Bramah. See BRAMAH, ERNEST.

Smith, Essex. Pseudonym of Frances Essex Theodora Hope, contemporary mystery writer.

Smith, Florence Margaret. See SMITH, STEVIE.

Smith, Ford. See FRIEND, OSCAR JEROME.

Smith, Frederick Escreet. See FARRELL, DAVID.

Smith, Helen Zenna. See PRICE, EVADNE.

Smith, Howard Van. See SOMMERS, DAVID.

Smith, Lafayette. Pseudonym of Hal Higdon (1931–   ), American free-lance magazine writer.

Smith, Lew. See FLOREN, LEE.

Smith, Linell Nash. See CHENAULT, NELL.

Smith, Ronald Gregor (1913–   ). Scottish writer, whose pseudonyms are *Sam Browne* and *Ronald Maxwell.*

Smith, Sarah. Pseudonym of Hesba Stretton (1832–1911), novelist and juvenile writer.

Smith, Seba. See DOWNING, MAJOR JACK.

Smith, Shelley. Pseudonym of Nancy Bodington (1912–   ), mystery writer.

Smith, Stevie. Pseudonym of Margaret Smith Florence (1902–   ), English writer and poet.

Smith, Wade. See SNOW, CHARLES HORACE.

Smith, Willard Laurence. See LAURENCE, WILL.
Smithells, Roger. See CASH, SEBASTIAN.
Smolski, Mihail. See SORBUL, MIHAIL.
Smreczyński, Franciszek. See ORKAN, WŁADYSŁAW.
Smrek, Jan. See CHIETEK, JAN.
Snakenburg, Theodor van. See A.L.F.
Sneider, Johannes. See AGRICOLA, JOHANNES.
Snelling, O. F. See FREDERICK, OSWALD.
Snow, Charles Horace (1877–   ). Mystery writer, whose pseudonyms
    are *H. C. Averill, Charles Ballew, Russ Hardy, Ranger Lee, Gary
    Marshall, Wade Smith, Dan Wardle,* and *Chester Wills.*
Soami (1472?–1525/30). Japanese painter, of the family Ami, surname
    Shinso. He is also known by the pseudonym *Kangaku.*
Soares, António da Fonseca. See CHAGAS, ANTÓNIO DAS.
Sobelsohn, Karl. See RADEK, KARL BERNARDOVICH.
Sockhanskaya, Nadezhda Stephanovna. See KOKHANOVSKAYA.
Soderberg, Percy Measday (1901–   ). English writer of works mainly
    concerning animals, whose pseudonyms are *George Measday, G. R.
    Seebord,* and *Peter Underhill.*
Sodoma, Il. Cognomen of Giovanni Antonio Bazzi (1477–1549), Italian
    painter. According to Vasari, the painter was subject to the views his
    name implies.
Sogi. Pseudonym of Iida (1421–1502), Japanese poet, whose personal
    name is unknown. He was the most famous of the "chain-poetry"
    poets.
Sohomonjàn, Egiše. See ČARENC, EGIŠE.
Sohr, Martin. See AGRICOLA, MARTIN.
Soin. Pseudonym of Nishiyama Toyokazu (1605–1682), Japanese poet.
Sokan. Pseudonym of Shina Norishige (1465–1553), Japanese haiku
    poet, also known as *Yamazaki Sokan.*
Solev, Koco Apostolov. See RACIN, KOSTA.
Sologub, Fëdor. Pseudonym of Fëdor Kuzmich Teternikov (1863–1927),
    Russian poet and writer.
Solomon ben Isaac. See IZHAQI, RABBI SHELOHMOH.
Solomon ha-Levi. See SANTA MARÍA, PABLO DE.
Solovyëv, Evgeny Andreyevich. See ANDREYEVICH.
Soluster. See SLUTER, CLAUS.

Soman, Shirley. See CAMPER, SHIRLEY.

Someren, Liesje van. Pseudonym of Elisabeth Jacoba Lichtenberg (1913–   ), English author.

Somers, Paul. See WINTERTON, PAUL.

Somerville, Edith (1858–1949). Irish novelist, whose pseudonyms are *Geilles Herring* and, with her cousin, Violet Martin, *Somerville & Ross.*

Somerville & Ross. See MARTIN, VIOLET, and SOMERVILLE, EDITH.

Sommers, David. Pseudonym of Howard Van Smith (1910–   ), American writer.

Sorbul, Mihail. Pseudonym of Mihail Smolski (1886–   ), Rumanian playwright.

Sori. See HOKUSAI.

Sorokin, Pitirim Alexandrovich. See TCHAADAIEFF.

Soseki. See NATSUME SOSEKI.

Soudley, Henry. See WOOD, JAMES PLAYSTED.

Soulary, Joseph-Marie. See JOSÉPHIN.

Soulès, Jean Georges. See ABELLIO, RAYMOND.

Sousa, José Oswald de. See ANDRADE, OSWALD DE.

South, Clark. Pseudonym of Dwight V. Swain (1915–   ), American free-lance writer.

Southard, Helen Fairbairn. See FAIRBAIRN, HELEN.

Southwold, Stephen (1887–1964). Mystery writer, whose pseudonyms are *Neil Bell, Paul Martens,* and *Miles.*

Souza, Ernest. Pseudonym of Evelyn Scott (1893–   ), mystery writer.

Sowerby, Arthur Lindsay McRae. See MCRAE, LINDSAY.

Spagnoli, Giovan Battista. See MANTOVANO, BATTISTA.

Spain, John. See ADAMS, CLEVE FRANKLIN.

Sparks, Timothy. See DICKENS, CHARLES JOHN HUFFAM.

Spaulding, Leonard. Pseudonym of Ray Douglas Bradbury (1920–   ), American science-fiction writer.

Spencer, Edward. See MOTT, EDWARD SPENCER.

Spencer, Geoffrey. Pseudonym of Alexander Wilson (1893–   ), mystery writer.

Spencer, John. Pseudonym of Roy Vickers (1899–   ), mystery writer.

Spenser, James. Pseudonym of Francis Narold Guest (1901–   ), mystery writer.

Speranza. Pseudonym of Lady Jane Francesca Wilde (c1820–1896), Irish poet and collector of Irish legends. She was the mother of Oscar Wilde.

Sperry, Jane. Pseudonym of Jane Sperry Eisenstat (1920–), American writer.

Sperry, Raymond, Jr. Collective pseudonym for the "Larry Dexter" and "White Ribbon Boys" series. See STRATEMEYER, EDWARD L.

Spewack, Samuel. See ABBOTT, A. A.

Spicer, Bart. See BARBETTE, JAY.

Spiegel, Clara. See JAYNES, CLARE.

Spigna, N. U. Occasional pseudonym of Eduard Bezzola (or Betschla) (1875–1948), Raeto-Romansh poet.

Spillane, Frank Morrison. See SPILLANE, MICKEY.

Spillane, Mickey. Pseudonym of Frank Morrison Spillane (1918–), American mystery writer.

Spinello Aretino (1330?–1410). Florentine painter, whose real name was Luca Spinello.

Spinello, Luca. See SPINELLO ARETINO.

Spinniker, Adriaen (1678–1754). Dutch poet, whose real name was Atis Melys.

Spiridion. Pseudonym of Edward Lobowski (1837–1923), Polish playwright and novelist.

Spit, Sam. See SCHNECK, STEPHEN.

Spitteler, Carl. See TANDEM, CARL FELIX.

Spoelstra, Cornelis. See DOOLAARD, A. DEN.

Sprigg, Christopher St. John. See CAUDWELL, CHRISTOPHER.

Spring, Philip. Pseudonym of E. Philip Dobson (1910–), English free-lance writer.

Springer, Rudolf. See RENNER, KARL.

Spurstowe, William. See SMECTYMNUUS.

Squibob. See DERBY, GEORGE HORATIO.

Squire, Sir John Collings. See EAGLE, SOLOMON.

Squires, Phil. See BARKER, S. OMAR.

Stabili, Francesco degli. See ASCOLI, CECCO D'.

Stack, Nicolete (1896–). American writer, whose pseudonyms are *Kathryn Kenny* and *Nicolete Meredith*.

Stacy, O'Connor. Pseudonym of William Rollins (1897–), mystery writer.

267 Stark, Raymond

Stagge, Jonathan. See WEBB, RICHARD WILSON, and WHEELER, HUGH CALLINGHAM.
Stahl, Heinrich. Pseudonym of Jodocus Donatus Hubertus Temme (1798–1881), German jurist, criminologist, and novelist.
Stahl, Karl. Pseudonym of Karl Goedeke (1814–1887), German scholar.
Stahl, Le Roy (1908–   ). American free-lance writer, whose pseudonyms are *George E. Sheldon* and *Kirk Wood.*
Stahl, P. J. Pseudonym of Pierre Jules Hetzel (1814–1886), French publisher and writer.
Stalwart, John. See TRAUSTI, JÓN.
Stancioff, Panait. See CERNA, PANAIT.
Standish, Robert. Pseudonym of Digby George Gerahty, contemporary mystery writer.
Stanford, John Keith. See ISSACHAR.
Stang, Judit. See VARGA, JUDY.
Stanhope, Philip Dormer, 4th Earl of Chesterfield. See BROADBOTTOM, GEFFERY.
Stanislavski. Professional name of Konstantin Sergeyevich Alekseyev (1863–1938), Russian producer and theatrical writer.
Stanley, Bennett. See HOUGH, STANLEY BENNETT.
Stanley, Olin. Pseudonym of E. L. Honeywell, contemporary mystery writer.
Stanley, Phil. See IND, ALLISON.
Stansfeld, Anthony. See BUCKINGHAM, BRUCE.
Stanstead, John. See GROOM, ARTHUR WILLIAM.
Stanton, Schuyler. See BAUM, LYMAN FRANK.
Stapleton, D. Joint pseudonym Dorothy Stapleton and Douglas Stapleton, contemporary mystery writers.
Stapleton, Dorothy. See STAPLETON, D.
Stapleton, Douglas. See STAPLETON, D.
Starbird, Kaye. See JENNISON, C. S.
Stark, James. Pseudonym of Robert Conroy Goldston (1927–   ), professional American writer.
Stark, John. Pseudonym of John Godwin (1928–   ), Australian writer.
Stark, Joshua. See OLSEN, THEODORE VICTOR.
Stark, Michael. See LARIAR, LAWRENCE.
Stark, Raymond. See NORWOOD, JOHN.

Stark, Richard. Pseudonym of Donald E. Westlake (1933–), American writer.

Starkey, James Sullivan. See O'SULLIVAN, SEUMAS.

Star-Man's Padre. See PATRIC, JOHNSTONE GILLESPIE.

Starr, John A. See GILLESE, JOHN PATRICK.

Starr, Richard Harry. See ESSEX, RICHARD.

Starret, William. See MCCLINTOCK, MARSHALL.

Stasek, Anatal. Pseudonym of Antonín Zeman (1843–1931), Czech writer.

Stauffer, Don. See BERKEBILE, FRED DONOVAN.

Steamer. Pseudonym of Leonard Hastings Nason (1895–), mystery writer.

Stecchetti, Lorenzo. Pseudonym of Olindo Guerrini (1845–1916), Italian poet.

Steed, Mabel A. See HUGHES, M. ALISON.

Steegmuller, Francis (1906–). American mystery writer, whose pseudonyms are *David Keith* and *Byron Steel.*

Steel, Byron. See STEEGMÜLLER, FRANCIS.

Steel, Kurt. Pseudonym of Rudolf H. S. Kagey (1904–), mystery writer.

Steele, Chester K. See STRATEMEYER, EDWARD L.

Steele, Richard. See BICKERSTAFF, ISAAC.

Steemaer, Jan. See PERTCHEVAL, JAN.

Steer, Charlotte. See HUNTER, MAUD LILY.

Stefanescu, Barbu. See DELAVRANCEA, BARBU.

Stefani, Ambrogio. See BORGOGNONE, AMBROGIO.

Stefano, Ambrogio di. See BORGOGNONE, AMBROGIO.

Stefánsson, Jón. See GJALLANDI, PORGILS.

Stefánsson, Magnús. See ARNARSON, ØRN.

Steffan, Alice Kennedy. See STEFFAN, JACK.

Steffan, Jack. Pseudonym of Alice Kennedy Steffan (1907–), American writer.

Stein, Aaron Marc (1906–). American free-lance writer, whose pseudonyms are *George Bagby* and *Hampton Stone.*

Steinarp, Steinn. Pseudonym of Adalsteinn Kristmundsson (1908–1958), Icelandic poet.

Steindler, R. A. See TREMAINE, BOB.

Steinmetz, Eulalie. Pseudonym of Eulalie Steinmetz Ross (1910–), American writer.

Stendhal. Pseudonym of Marie Henri Beyle (1783–1842), French novelist.

Stenus. Pseudonym of Herbert Henry Huxley (1916–   ), English scholar.

Stenvall, Alexis. See KIVI, ALEXIS.

Stepnyak, Sergey Mikhailovich. Pseudonym of Sergey Mikhailovich Kravchinsky (1852–1895), Russian terrorist and writer.

Steptoe, Lydia. Pseudonym of Djuna Barnes (1892–   ), American writer.

Sterck. See ISCHYRIUS.

Sterling, Anthony. See CAESAR, EUGENE LEE.

Sterling, Stewart. See WINCHELL, PRENTICE.

Stern, Daniel. Pseudonym of Marie Catherine Sophie de Flavigny, Comtesse d'Agoult (1805–1876), French writer, noted for her liaison with Franz Liszt, Hungarian composer.

Stern, David. See STIRLING, PETER.

Stern, James. See ST. JAMES, ANDREW.

Stern, Philip Van Doren. See STORME, PETER.

Sternberg, Alexander von. Pseudonym of Baron Alexander von Ungern-Sternberg (1806–1868), German novelist.

Sterne, Emma Gelders (1894–   ). American writer, whose pseudonyms are *Emily Brown* and, with Barbara Lindsay, *Josephine James.*

Stevens, Dan J. See OVERHOLSER, WAYNE D.

Stevens, E. S. Pseudonym of Ethel Stefana May Drower (1879–   ), English author, who has lived and traveled in the Middle East.

Stevens, Fae Hewston. Pseudonym of Frances Isted Stevens (1907–   ), Australian writer.

Stevens, Frances Isted. See STEVENS, FAE HEWSTON.

Stevens, Frances Moyer Ross. See HALE, CHRISTOPHER.

Stevens, S. P. See PALESTRANT, SIMON S.

Stevenson, William. See CHEN HWEI.

Stewart, Alfred Walter (1880–1947). Mystery writer, whose pseudonyms are *J. J. Connington* and *John Jervis Connington.*

Stewart, David. See POLITELLA, DARIO.

Stewart, Elizabeth Grey. Pseudonym of Elizabeth Stewart Reed (1914–   ), American writer.

Stewart, Frances. See WILMOT, JAMES REGINALD.

Stewart, Jay. Pseudonym of Stuart Palmer (1905–   ), American mystery writer.

Stewart, John Innes Mackintosh. See INNES, MICHAEL.
Stewart, Kenneth Livingston. See LIVINGSTON, KENNETH.
Stewart, Neil. See LOMBARD, NAP.
Stewart, Will. Pseudonym of John Stewart Williamson (1908–   ), American author.
Stiernhielm, Georg (1598–1672). Swedish poet and philosopher, whose original surname was Olofsson. In 1614 he took the name *Lilia,* and in 1631 he received the name Stiernhielm by ennoblement.
Stille, Karl. Pseudonym of Hermann Christoph Gottfried Demme (1760–1822), German novelist and poet.
Stillfried, Felix. Pseudonym of Adolf Brandt (1851–1910), Low German writer.
Stilling, Heinrich. See JUNG-STILLING, JOHANN HEINRICH.
Stimson, Frederic Jesup. See J.S. OF DALE.
Stirling, Anna Maria Diana Wilhelmina. See PICKERING, PERCIVAL.
Stirling, Peter. Pseudonym of David Stern (1909–   ), mystery writer.
Stirner, Max. See SCHMIDT, KASPER.
Stitny, Tomas. See TOMAS ZE STITNEHO.
Stockley, Cynthia. See WEBB, LILIAN JULIAN.
Stoddard, Charles Warren. See PEPPERPOD, PIP.
Stokes, Francis William. See EVERTON, FRANCIS.
Stokes, Manning Lee. See LUDWELL, BERNICE.
Stokes, Simpson. See FAWCETT, FRANK DUBREZ.
Stoll, Dennis G. See CRAIG, DENYS.
Stone, Alan. Collective pseudonym for the "Tolliver" series. See STRATEMEYER, EDWARD L.
Stone, Hampton. See STEIN, AARON MARC.
Stone, Patti. See PATRICK, LEAL.
Stone, Raymond. Collective pseudonym for the "Tommy Tiptop" series. See STRATEMEYER, EDWARD L.
Stone, Richard A. See STRATEMEYER, EDWARD L.
Stone, Simon. Pseudonym of Howard Barrington (1906–   ), mystery writer.
Stoneham, Charles Thurley. See THURLEY, NORGOVE.
Stonor, Oliver (1903–   ). English author, journalist, and critic, whose pseudonyms are *E. Morchard Bishop, Evelyn Morchard Bishop,* and *Morchard Bishop.*
Stookey, Aaron W. Pseudonym of Jerome Beatty, Jr. (1918–   ), American free-lance writer.

Storasta, Vilius. See VYDUNAS.

Storm, Christopher. See OLSEN, THEODORE VICTOR.

Storm, Virginia. See TEMPEST, JAN.

Storme, Peter. Pseudonym of Philip Van Doren Stern (1900–   ), American author.

Storr, Catherine (1913–   ). English writer, whose pseudonyms are *Irene Adler* and *Helen Lourie.*

Story, Josephine. Pseudonym of Emilie Baker Loring (d. 1951), mystery writer.

Stoss, Veit. See STWOSZ, WIT.

Stoutenburg, Adrien Pearl (1916–   ). American author, whose pseudonyms are *Barbie Arden, Lace Kendall,* and *Nelson Minier.*

Stowe, Harriet Elizabeth Beecher. See CROWFIELD, CHRISTOPHER.

Strachan, Margaret Pitcairn. See MORE, CAROLINE.

Straeten, Emiel van der (1887–1918). Flemish novelist, short-story writer, poet, and playwright, whose real name was Emiel Delrue.

Strafford, Muriel. Pseudonym of Muriel Strafford Sauer, contemporary American free-lance newspaper and magazine writer.

Strand, Paul E. See PALESTRANT, SIMON S.

Strandberg, Carl Vilhelm August. See TALIS QUALIS.

Strange, John Stephen. Pseudonym of Dorothy Stockbridge Tillett (1896–   ), mystery writer.

Stranger, Joyce. Pseudonym of Joyce M. Wilson, contemporary English writer on wildlife.

Stratemeyer, Edward L. (1862–1930). American writer of boys' stories and founder of the Stratemeyer Syndicate. He both wrote and hired writers to contribute to numerous popular young people's series under the collective pseudonyms *Manager Henry Abbott, Harrison Adams, Captain Ralph Bonehill, Jim Bowie, Franklin Calkins, Allen Chapman, Louis Charles, James R. Cooper, Jim Daly, Spencer Davenport, Julie Edwards, Albert Lee Ford, Robert W. Hamilton, Hal Harkaway, Harvey Hicks, Dr. Willard Mackenzie, Ned St. Myer, Chester K. Steele, E. Ward Strayer, Arthur M. Winfield, Edna Winfield,* and *Nat Woods.* The Stratemeyer Syndicate pseudonyms were: *Victor Appleton, Victor Appleton II, Richard Barnum, Philip A. Bartlett, May Hollis Barton, Charles Amory Beach, Captain James Carson, Lester Chadwick, John R. Cooper, Elmer A. Dawson, Franklin W. Dixon, Julia K. Duncan, Alice B. Emerson, James Cody Ferris, Graham B. Forbes, Frederick Gordon, Alice Dale Hardy, Ma-*

bel C. Hawley, Brooks Henderley, Grace Brooks Hill, Laura Lee Hope, Francis Hunt, Frances K. Judd, Carolyn Keene, Clinton W. Locke, Helen Beecher Long, Amy Bell Marlowe, Eugene Martin, Harry Mason, Fenworth Moore, Gert W. Morrison, Margaret Penrose, Nat Ridley, Jr., Roy Rockwood, Harry Mason Roe, Dan Scott, Ann Sheldon, Raymond Sperry, Jr., Alan Stone, Raymond Stone, Richard A. Stone, Helen Louise Thorndyke, Frank A. Warner, Frank V. Webster, Jerry West, Janet D. Wheeler, Ramy Allison White, and *Clarence Young.*

Stratton, Henry. Pseudonym of Michael Harrington Nelson (1921–), English writer.

Stratton-Porter, Gene (1868–1924). American novelist and nature writer, also known as *Gene Porter.*

Strayer, E. Ward. See STRATEMEYER, EDWARD L.

Street, Cecil John Charles (1884–). Mystery writer, whose pseudonyms are *Miles Burton, F.O.O.,* and *John Rhode.*

Street, Lee. Pseudonym of Kathleen Hampton (1923–), American writer.

Street, Robert. See THOMAS, GORDON.

Strehlenau, Nikolaus Franz Niembsch von. See LENAU, NIKOLAUS.

Stretton, Hesba. See SMITH, SARAH.

Streuvels, Stijn. Pseudonym of Frank Lateur (1871–), Flemish novelist and short-story writer.

Strix. See FLEMING, PETER.

Strong, Charles. See EPSTEIN, SAMUEL.

Stroosnyder, Jan. Sixteenth-century Dutch poet, also known as *Jan de Costere.*

Strover, Dorothea. Contemporary English writer, whose pseudonyms are *Dorothea Tinne* and *E. D. Tinne.*

Strozzi (or **Strozza**), **Bernardo** (1581–1644). Italian painter and engraver, whose cognomens were *Il Capuccino* and *Il Prete Genovese.* The names were derived from his membership in a Capuchin monastery.

Strubberg, Friedrich Armand (1806–1889). German novelist whose pseudonyms are *Armand* and *Farnwald.*

Strübe, Hermann. See BURTE, HERMANN.

Strug, Andrzej. Pseudonym of Tadeusz Gałecki (1873–1937), Polish novelist.

Struther, Jan. Pseudonym of Joyce Maxtone Graham (1901–1953), English writer.

Stuart, Alex. See STUART, VIVIAN.

Stuart, Brian. See WORTHINGTON-STUART, BRIAN ARTHUR.

Stuart, Charles. See MACKINNON, CHARLES ROY.

Stuart, Leslie. See MARLOWE, KENNETH.

Stuart, Sheila. Pseudonym of Mary Gladys Baker (1892–   ), Scottish author and journalist.

Stuart, Vivian (1914–   ). English romantic novelist, whose pseudonyms are *Barbara Allen, Finona Finlay,* and *Alex Stuart.*

Stubbs, Harry C. See CLEMENT, HAL.

Stuber, Stanley I. See ERASMUS, M. NOTT.

Stukalov, Nikolay Fëdorovich. See POGODIN, NIKOLAY FËDOROVICH.

Stúñiga. See ESTÚÑIGA, LOPE DE.

Sturzen-Becker, Oscar Patrik. See ORVAR ODD.

Stuyvesant, Alice. See WILLIAMSON, ALICE MURIEL LIVINGSTON, and WILLIAMSON, CHARLES NORRIS.

Stwosz, Wit. Polish name of Veit Stoss (1447?–1533), German sculptor, painter, and engraver, who was active in Cracow.

Styles, Showell. See CARR, GLYN.

Suardi, Bartolommeo. See BRAMANTINO, IL.

Suarès, André. Pseudonym of Félix-André-Yves Scantrel (1866–1948), French writer.

Subík, Frantisek. See ZARNOV, ANDREJ.

Su Chien. See SU MAN-SHU.

Südfeld, Max Simon. See NORDAU, MAX SIMON.

Sudo Mitsutheru. See SUDO NANSUI.

Sudo Nansui. Pseudonym of Sudo Mitsutheru (1858–1920), Japanese novelist.

Suk, Ratibor. See VASEK, VLADIMIR.

Sully Prudhomme. Pseudonym of René François Prudhomme (1839–1907), French poet and essayist.

Su Man-shu. Religious name of Su Chien (1884–1918), Chinese poet, essayist, and novelist.

Summerforest, Ivy B. See KIRKUP, JAMES.

Summers, Gordon. See HORNBY, JOHN.

Summers, Hollis Spurgeon, Jr. See HOLLIS, JIM.

Summers, John A. See LAWSON, HORACE LOWE.

Sunners, William. See SATTERLY, WESTON.

Surfaceman. Pseudonym of Alexander Anderson (1845–1909), Scottish poet, derived from his occupation as a railroad-track layer, or surfaceman.

Surrey, Richard. See BROOKER, BERTRAM.

Susan. Pseudonym of Susan Graham (1912–   ), New Zealand writer.

Süss, Hans. See KULMBACH, HANS VON.

Sussex, Gordon. See VOLK, GORDON.

Sussman, Cornelia Silver. See JESSEY, CORNELIA.

Sutherland, William. Pseudonym of John Murray Cooper (1908–   ), mystery writer.

Suttles, Shirley. See CONGER, LESLEY.

Sutton, Henry. Pseudonym of David Slavitt (1935–   ), American writer.

Sutton, Maurice Lewis. See SUTTON, STACK.

Sutton, Stack. Pseudonym of Maurice Lewis Sutton (1927–   ), American author.

Sutton, Thomas. See REACH, JAMES.

Svetla, Karolina. Pseudonym of Johanna Muzakova (1830–1899), Czech novelist.

Svevo, Italo. Pseudonym of Ettore Schmitz (1861–1928), Italian writer.

Swain, Dwight V. See SOUTH, CLARK.

Swartz, Maria Helga. See MARTINSON, MOA.

Swatridge, Charles. See CHARLES, THERESA.

Swatridge, Irene. See CHARLES, THERESA.

Swayne, Geoffrey. Pseudonym of Sidney Ronald Campion (1891–   ), English free-lance writer.

Swedberg, Emanuel. See SWEDENBORG, EMANUEL.

Swedenborg, Emanuel (1688–1772). Swedish philosopher and mystic, whose original surname was Swedberg. In 1719 he received the name Swedenborg by ennoblement.

Swietochowski, Aleksander. See OKOŃSKI, WŁADYSŁAW.

Swift, Anthony. Pseudonym of Joseph Jefferson Farjeon (1883–1955), mystery writer.

Swift, Jonathan. See BICKERSTAFF, ISAAC, and SCRIBLERUS, MARTINUS.

Swift, Julian. Pseudonym of Arthur Applin (1883–   ), mystery writer.

Swinford, Betty June Wells (1927–   ). American free-lance writer, whose pseudonyms are *Linda Haynes, Kathryn Porter, Bob Swinford*, and *June Wells*.

Swinford, Bob. See SWINFORD, BETTY JUNE WELLS.

Sylva, Carmen. See ELIZABETH, QUEEN OF RUMANIA.

Synopticus. See RENNER, KARL.

Syntax, John. See DENNETT, HERBERT VICTOR.

Syrokomla, Władysław. Pseudonym of Ludwik Władysław Kondratowicz (1823–1862), Polish poet and playwright.

Szczucka. Pseudonym of Zofia Kossak (1890–1968), Polish author.

Sztyrmer, Eleonora. See SZTYRMER, LUDWIK.

Sztyrmer, Ludwik (1809–1886). Polish novelist, whose pseudonyms were *Gerwazy Bomba* and *Eleonora Sztyrmer*.

Szymonowicz, Szymon (1558–1629). Polish Latin poet, playwright, and translator, also known as *Simonides*. In 1590 he was knighted and took the name *Szymon Bendonski*.

"T"

T.N.T. See THOMAS, CORNELIUS DICKINSON.

Taaffe, Michael. Pseudonym of Robert Augustine Joseph Maguire (1898–   ), British scholar.

Tabor, Paul. Pseudonym of Paul Tabori (1908–   ), Hungarian author.

Tabori, Paul. See TABOR, PAUL.

Taceddin Ibrahim. See AHMEDI.

Tad. Pseudonym of Thomas Aloysius Dorgan (1877–1929), American journalist.

Tagger, Theodor. See BRUCKNER, FERDINAND.

Tait, Euphemia Margaret. See IRONSIDE, JOHN.

Takaya Hikoshiro. See RYUTEI TANEHIKO.

Takayama Chogyu. Pseudonym of Takayama Rinjiro (1871–1902), Japanese writer and critic.

Takayama Rinjiro. See TAKAYAMA CHOGYU.

Takaya Tomohisa. See RYUTEI TANEHIKO.

Takeda Izumo. Pseudonym of Takeda Kiyosada (1691–1756), Japanese dramatist and producer.

Takeda Kiyosada. See TAKEDA IZUMO.

Takemoto (or **Takarai, Enomoto**) **Yasoya.** See KIKAKU.

Takizawa Okikuni (or **Tokuru**). See BAKIN.

Talbot, Carl. Pseudonym of Charles Hammond Hipkins (1893–), mystery writer.

Talbot, Hake. Pseudonym of Henning Nelms, contemporary mystery writer.

Talis Qualis. Pseudonym of Carl Vilhelm August Strindberg (1818–1877), Swedish poet and journalist.

Talpa. See GHISTELE, CORNELIS VAN.

Talvio, Maila. Pseudonym of Maria Winter Mikkola (1871–1952), Finnish playwright and novelist.

Talvj. Pseudonym of Therese Albertine Louise Robinson, née von Jakob (1797–1870), German-American novelist and historian, taken from her initials.

Tamai, Katsunori. See HINO, ASHIHEI.

Tamenaga Shunsui. Pseudonym of Sasaki Sadataka (1789–1844), Japanese novelist.

Tammsaare, Anton. Pseudonym of Anton Hansen (1878–1940), Estonian author.

Tan. Pseudonym of Vladimir Germanovich Bogoraz (1865–1936), Russian ethnographer and novelist.

Tandem, Carl Felix. Pseudonym of Carl Spitteler (1845–1924), Swiss poet and essayist.

Tanfucio, Neri. Anagrammatic pseudonym of Renato Fucini (1843–1921), Italian dialect poet and writer.

Taniguchi Tora. See BUSON.

Tanner, Edward Everett, III (1921–). American novelist, whose pseudonyms are *Patrick Dennis* and *Virginia Rowans.*

Tanner, John. See MATCHA, JACK.

Tan Yun. Pseudonym of Adet Jusulin (1923–), Chinese writer.

T'ao-chi-chu-shin. See WU LI.

Tardivaux, René. See BOYLESVE, RENÉ.

Tarassov, Lev. See TROYAT, HENRI.

Tarn, Pauline M. See VIVIEN, RENÉE.

Tashrak. Pseudonym of Israel Joseph Zevin (1872–1926), Russian-American journalist and short-story writer.

Tate, Ellalice. See HIBBERT, ELEANOR BURFORD.

Tate, Mary Anne. See HALE, ARLENE.

Tatham, Campbell. See ELTING, MARY.

Tatham, Laura (1919–   ). English author, whose pseudonyms are *John Martin* and *Margaret Phipps.*

Tatray, Istvan. Pseudonym of Raphael Rudolph Rupert (1910–   ), Hungarian-Irish writer.

Tattersall, Muriel Joyce. See WAUD, ELIZABETH.

Tatti, Jacopo. See SANSOVINO, JACOPO.

Taveludi, P. See POLITIS, KOSMAS.

Tavo, Gus. See IVAN, MARTHA MILLER PFAFF.

Tayama Katai. Pseudonym of Tayama Rokuya (1872–1930), Japanese novelist.

Tayama Rokuya. See TAYAMA KATAI.

Taylor, Constance Lindsay. See CULLINGFORD, GUY.

Taylor, Phoebe Atwood. See TILTON, ALICE.

Taylor, Richard. See CRONUS, DIODORUS.

Tay Pay. Pseudonym of Thomas Power O'Connor (1848–1929), Irish journalist and nationalist leader.

Tchaadaieff. Pseudonym of Pitirim Alexandrovich Sorokin (1889–1968), Russian-American scholar.

Tchalsky, Shmuel Yoseph. See AGNON, SHEMUEL JOSEPH.

Tchatsky, Shmuel Yoseph. See AGNON, SHEMUEL JOSEPH.

Teague, John Jessop. See GERARD, MORICE.

Tedesco, Il ("The German"). Cognomen of Adam Elsheimer (1578–1610), German painter and etcher.

Teffy. Pseudonym of Nadezhda Alexeyevna Buchinskaya (1876–1952), Russian writer.

Tegner, Henry (1901–   ). English writer, whose pseudonyms are *The Northumbrian Gentleman* and *The Ruffle.*

Teika. See FUJIWARA NO SADAIE.

Teishitsu. Pseudonym of Yasuhara Masaakira (1610–1673), Japanese haiku poet.

Tekan. Occasional pseudonym of Yosano Hiroshi (1873–1935), Japanese poet.

Telfair, Nancy. Pseudonym of Louise Jones DuBose (1901–   ), American writer.

Téllez, Gabriel. See MOLINA, TIRSO DE.

Telmann, Konrad. Pseudonym of Konrad Zitelmann (1854–1892), German poet and novelist.

Temme, Jodocus Donatus Hubertus. See STAHL, HEINRICH.

Tempest, Jan. Contemporary mystery writer, whose pseudonyms are *Fay Chandos* and *Virginia Storm.*

Tempest, Theresa. Pseudonym of Louise Andrews Kent (1886–   ), American writer.

Tempest, Victor. See PHILIPP, ELLIOT ELIAS.

Tempka, Zygmunt. Pseudonym of Zygmunt Nowakowski (1891–   ), Polish writer.

Templar, Maurice. See GROOM, ARTHUR WILLIAM.

Temple, Dan. See NEWTON, DWIGHT BENNETT.

Temple, Paul. See MCCONNELL, JAMES DOUGLAS RUTHERFORD.

Temple, Robin. Pseudonym of Samuel Andrew Wood (1890–   ), mystery writer.

Temple-Ellis, N. A. Pseudonym of Neville Aldridge Holdaway (1894–   ), mystery writer.

Templeton, Jesse. See GOODCHILD, GEORGE.

Tendron, Marcel. See ELDER, MARC.

Tennant, Catherine. See CROZIER, KATHLEEN MURIEL EYLES.

Tennant, Kylie. Pseudonym of Kylie Tennant Rodd (1912–   ), Australian author.

Tennant, Nora Jackson. See JACKSON, NORA.

Tenneshaw, S. M. See BEAUMONT, CHARLES.

Tennyson, Charles. See TURNER, CHARLES.

Tent, Ned. See DENNETT, HERBERT VICTOR.

Tenth Earl of Bessborough, The. Pseudonym of Frederick Edward Neuflize Ponsonby (1913–   ), English author.

Terberg, Hugo. Pseudonym of Hugo Muensterberg (1863–1916), German-American writer.

Térésah. Pseudonym of Corinna Teresa Gray Ubertis (1877–   ), Italian poet and writer.

Teresa of Jesus, Saint. Religious name of Teresa Sánchez de Cepeda y Ahumada (1515–1582), Spanish mystic, better known as *St. Teresa of Avila.*

Ter-Grigorjan, Vaan. See TERJAN, VAAN.

Terhune, Mary Virginia. See HARLAND, MARION.

Terjan, Vaan. Pseudonym of Vaan Ter-Grigorjan (1885–1920), American poet.

Terni, Fausta Cialente. See CIALENTE, FAUSTA.

Terrence, Frederick J. Pseudonym of John F. Hayes (1904–   ), Canadian writer.

Terry, C. V. Occasional pseudonym of Frank Gill Slaughter (1908–   ), American writer.

Tervapää, Juhani. Pseudonym of Hella Maria Wuolijoki (1886–1954), Finnish writer of comedies.

Tesselschade. Cognomen of Maria Visscher (1594–1649), Dutch poet.

Tessier, Ernest-Maurice. See DEKOBRA, MAURICE.

Teternikov, Fëdor Kuzmich. See SOLOGUB, FËDOR.

Teutonicus. See NOTKER.

Texas Ranger. See WALLACE, JOHN.

Tey, Josephine. See MACKINTOSH, ELIZABETH.

Thackeray, William Makepeace (1811–1863). English novelist, whose pseudonyms are *Mr. Brown, George Savage Fitzboodle, Jeames, Michael Angelo Titmarsh, Théophile Wagstaff,* and *Charles James Yellowplush.*

Thames, C. H. See MARLOWE, STEPHEN.

Thanet, Octave. Pseudonym of Alice French (1850–1934), American writer.

Tharaud Brothers, Jérôme (1874–1953) and **Jean** (1877–1952). French writers and collaborators, whose real names were, respectively, Ernest and Charles. Their books were always jointly signed *Jérôme* and *Jean.*

Thayer, Tiffany (1902–   ). American mystery writer, whose pseudonyms are *John Doe* and *Elmer Ellsworth, Jr.*

Theocritus à Ganda. See HEINSIUS, DANIEL.

Theodore Prodromus. See PTOCHOPRODROMUS.

Theodorescu, Ion. See ARGHEZI, TUDOR.

Theodulus Monachus. See THOMAS MAGISTROS.

Theotokopoulos, Kyriakos. See GRECO, EL.

Thérive, André. Pseudonym of Roger Puthoste (1891–   ), French literary writer and novelist.

Thévenin, Denis. Pseudonym of Georges Duhamel (1884–1966), French writer.

Thibault, Jacques Anatole François. See FRANCE, ANATOLE.

Thibault, Maralee G. See DAVIS, MARALEE G.

Thiery, Herman. Pseudonym of Johan Daisne (1912–   ), Flemish writer.

Thijm, Karel Jan Lodewijk Alberdingk. See DEYSSEL, LODEWIJK VAN.

Thoma, Ludwig. See SCHLEMIHL, PETER.

Thomas, Andrea. See HILL, MARGARET.

Thomas, Carl H. See DOERFFLER, ALFRED.

Thomas, Carolyn. Pseudonym of Actea Duncan (1913–   ), American mystery writer.

Thomas, Cornelius Dickinson (1920–   ). American writer, whose pseudonyms are *T.N.T.* and *Neal Thomas.*

Thomas, Curtis. See KINNEY, THOMAS.

Thomas, Eugene. See GREY, DONALD.

Thomas, Gordon (1933–   ). British writer, whose pseudonyms are *Brian James* and *Robert Street.*

Thomas, H. C. See KEATING, LAWRENCE A.

Thomas, J. F. See FLEMING, THOMAS JAMES.

Thomas, Joan Gale. Pseudonym of Joan Mary Gale Thomas Robinson, contemporary English writer and illustrator of children's books.

Thomas, Lee. See FLOREN, LEE.

Thomas, Mervyn. See CURRAN, MONA ELISA.

Thomas, Murray. Pseudonym of Thomas Murray Ragg (1897–   ), mystery writer.

Thomas, Neal. See THOMAS, CORNELIUS DICKINSON.

Thomas, Philip Edward. See EASTAWAY, EDWARD.

Thomas, R. Murray. See ROBERTS, TOM.

Thomas, Ronald Wills (1910–   ). Mystery writer, whose pseudonyms are *Jeff Bogar, James Cadell,* and *Ronald Wills.*

Thomas, William. See ISLWYN.

Thomas à Kempis (c1380–1471). Dutch mystic writer, whose real name was Thomas Hemerken. The name was derived from his birthplace, Kempen, in the Rhineland.

Thomas Magistros. 13th/14th-century Byzantine scholar, also called *Theodulus Monachus.*

Thomas the Rhymer. See ERCELDOUNE, THOMAS OF.

Thomasin von Zerclaere (c1185–1238). German or North Italian writer, also known as *Thomasin de Cerclaria.*

Thompson, Augusto Goemine. See HALMAR, AUGUSTO D'.

Thompson, Eileen. Pseudonym of Eileen Thompson Panowski (1920–   ), American writer.

Thompson, Ernest. See SETON, ERNEST THOMPSON.

Thompson, George Seldon. See SELDON, GEORGE.

Thompson, Harlan H. See HOLT, STEPHEN.

Thompson, Hunter S. See OWL, SEBASTIAN.

Thompson, James H. See FREEMAN, GRAYDON LA VERNE.

Thompson, Madeline. See GREIG, MAYSIE.

Thompson, William C. L. See EDWARDS, WILLIAM BENNETT.

Thomson, George Malcolm. See MACDONALD, AENEAS.

Thomson, James. See B.V.

Thomson, Mortimer Neal. See DOESTICKS, Q. K. PHILANDER, P.B.

Thorn, Ronald Scott. Pseudonym of Ronald Wilkinson (1920–   ), British author.

Thorndike, Russell. See BUCHANAN, WILLIAM.

Thorndyke, Helen Louise. Collective pseudonym for the "Honey Bunch" series. See STRATEMEYER, EDWARD L.

Thorne, B. K. Ted. See THORNE, BLISS KIRBY.

Thorne, Bliss Kirby (1916–   ). American journalist and writer, whose pseudonyms are *B. K. Ted Thorne* (and other variations) and *Cameron Vandal.*

Thorne, Guy. Pseudonym of Cyril Arthur Edward Ranger Gull (1876–1923), mystery writer.

Thorne, Hart. See CARHART, ARTHUR HAWTHORNE.

Thorson, Delos Russell. See CHRISTIAN, KIT.

Thorson, Sara Winfree. See CHRISTIAN, KIT.

Thorstein, Eric. See MERRIL, JUDITH.

Thrasybulus. See HUET, CONRAD BUSKEN.

Thrice, Luke. Pseudonym of John Russell (1885–1956), mystery writer.

Thuong La Ong Hai (1724–1791). Vietnamese writer, whose pseudonyms are *Le Huu-Huan* and *Le Huu Traco.*

Thurley, Norgove. Pseudonym of Charles Thurley Stoneham (1895–   ), mystery writer.

Thurotte, Gui de. See CHASTELAIN DE COUCI, LE.

Tibaldi, Pellegrino (1527–1596). Italian painter and architect, also called *Pellegrino da Bologna.*

Tibbetts, William. See BRANNON, WILLIAM T.

Tibbs. See DICKENS, CHARLES JOHN HUFFAM.

Tiger, Theobald. See TUCHOLSKY, KURT.

Tillett, Dorothy Stockbridge. See STRANGE, JOHN STEPHEN.

Tiltman, Ronald Frank. See FRASER, RONALD.

Tilton, Alice. Pseudonym of Phoebe Atwood Taylor (1909–   ), American mystery writer.

Timony, Arthur N. See VAHEY, JOHN GEORGE HASLETTE.

Timrava. Pseudonym of Božena Slanciková (1867–1951), Slovak writer.

Tin. Pseudonym of Augustin Ujevic (1891–1955), Croatian poet.

Ting-ling. Pseudonym of Chiang Ping-chih (1907–   ), Chinese short-story writer.

Tinne, Dorothea. See STROVER, DOROTHEA.

Tinne, E. D. See STROVER, DOROTHEA.

Tintoretto (1518/19?–1594). Venetian painter, whose real name was Jacopo Robusti. The name was probably derived from the trade of his father, who was a silk dyer.

Tishbi, Elijah. See LEVITA, ELIJAH.

Tisi, Benvenuto. See GAROFALO, BENVENUTO DA.

Titmarsh, Michael Angelo. See THACKERAY, WILLIAM MAKEPEACE.

Tobilevich, Ivan Karpovich. See KARPENKO-KARYJ, IVAN.

Toby, Liz. Pseudonym of Betty Jane Toebe Minsky (1932–   ), American free-lance writer.

Toby, M.P. Pseudonym of Sir Henry Lucy (1845–1924), British journalist.

Tocher, E. W. Pseudonym of Denis William Johnston (1901–   ), Irish playwright.

Tod, Osma Gallinger. See GALLINGER, OSMA COUCH.

Toda Monsui. Pseudonym of Toda Takamitsu (1629–1706), Japanese poet.

Toda Takamitsu. See TODA MONSUI.

Todd, Anne Ophelia. Pseudonym of Anne Ophelia Todd Dowen (1907–   ), American writer.

Tokai Sanshi. Pseudonym of Shiba Shiro (1852–1922), Japanese novelist.

Tokitaro. See HOKUSAI.

Tokuda Matsuo. See TOKUDA SHUSEI.

Tokuda Shusei. Pseudonym of Tokuda Matsuo (1872–   ), Japanese novelist.

Tokutomi Kenjiro. See TOKUTOMI ROKA.

Tokutomi Roka. Pseudonym of Tokutomi Kenjiro (1868–1927), Japanese writer.

Tolby, Arthur. See INFIELD, GLEN BERTON.

Tolnai, Lajos. Pseudonym of Lajos Hagymássy (1837–1902), Hungarian writer.

Toman, Karel. Pseudonym of Antonin Bernasek (1877–1946), English poet.

Tomasito, don. Pseudonym of Thomas Anthony Robertson (1897–), Mexican writer.

Tomas ze Stitneho (c1333–1405). Czech religious writer, also known as *Tomas Stitny.*

Tomfool. Pseudonym of Eleanor Farjeon (1881–1965), English writer, best known for children's fantasies, verse, and plays.

Tomkinson, Constance. Pseudonym of Constance Tomkinson Weeks (1915–), Canadian-English writer.

Tomline, F. Pseudonym of Sir William Schwenck Gilbert (1836–1911), English satirist.

Tonashi. See HARRINGTON, MARK RAYMOND.

Tony. Pseudonym of Anton Bergmann (1835–1874), Flemish novelist.

Tooke, John (1736–1812). English philologist, whose original name was John Horne.

Toonder, Martin. See GROOM, ARTHUR WILLIAM.

Torbett, Harvey Douglas Louis (1921–). English writer, whose pseudonyms are *Henry Dee* and *Isis.*

Torday, Ursula. Contemporary mystery writer, whose pseudonyms are *Paula Allardyce, Charity Blackstock,* and *Lee Blackstock.*

Torga, Miguel. Pseudonym of Adolfo Correia da Rocha (1907–), Portuguese writer.

Torr, Iain. See MACKINNON, CHARLES ROY.

Torrey, Marjorie. See CHANSLOR, MARJORIE TORREY HOOD.

Torrey, Ware. See CROSBY, LEE.

Tostado, Alonso. See MADRIGAL, ALONSO DE.

Totius (1877–1953). Pseudonym of Jacob Daniel du Toit (1877–1953), Afrikaans poet.

Tournachon, Félix. See NADAR.

Tousseul, Jean. Pseudonym of Olivier Degée (1890–1944), Belgian novelist.

Tower, Stella Mary Hodgson. See WOLSELEY, FAITH.

Towne, Stuart. See RAWSON, CLAYTON.

Toyama Chuzan. Pseudonym of Toyama Masakazu (1848–1900), Japanese poet.

Toyama Masakazu. See TOYAMA CHUZAN.

Toyo. See SESSHU.

Trabia-Branciforte, Giuseppe Giovanni Lanza di. See LANZA DEL VASTO, JOSEPH JEAN.

Tracy, Louis. See HOLMES, GORDON.

Tracy, Powers. Pseudonym of Don Ward (1911–   ), American free-lance editor and writer.

Trafford, F. G. Early pseudonym of Charlotte Eliza Lawson Riddell (1832–1906), Irish novelist.

Traherne, Michael. See WATKINS-PITCHFORD, DENYS JAMES.

Traill, Peter. See MORTON, GUY MAINWARING.

Tran Khanh-Giu. See KHAI-HUNG.

Tranquilli, Secondo. See SILONE, IGNAZIO.

Tranoscius, Georgius. Latinized name of Jiri Tranovsky (1592–1637), writer of Czech and Latin poetry.

Tranovsky, Jiri. See TRANOSCIUS, GEORGIUS.

Tranter, Nigel. See TREDGOLD, NYE.

Trask, Merrill. Pseudonym of Mel Colton, contemporary mystery writer.

Trausti, Jón ("Stalwart John"). Pseudonym of Jón Gudmundur Magnusson (1873–1918), Icelandic novelist and poet.

Traver, Robert. Pseudonym of John Donaldson Voelker (1903–   ), American mystery writer and Michigan Supreme Court Justice.

Travers, Stephen. Pseudonym of Henry Garnett Radcliffe (1899–   ), British mystery writer.

Traversari, Ambrogio. See AMBROSE OF CAMALDOLI.

Travis, Gerry. See TRIMBLE, LOUIS P.

Trebizsky, Vaclav Benes. Pseudonym of Vaclav Benes (1849–1894), Czech novelist and short-story writer.

Tredez, Alain. See TREDEZ, DENISE.

Tredez, Denise (1930–   ). French writer, whose pseudonyms are *Denise Trez* and, with her husband, Alain Tredez, *Trez.*

Tredgold, Nye. Pseudonym of Nigel Tranter (1909–   ), Scottish writer.

Trefor, Eirlys. Pseudonym of Eirlys O. Williams, contemporary Welsh writer.

Tremaine, Bob. Pseudonym of R. A. Steindler (1920–   ), Austrian-American writer.

Trénité, Gijsbert Johannes Nolst. See CHARIVARIUS.

Trent, Peter. Pseudonym of Lawrence Nelson (1907–   ), mystery writer.

Trevena, John. Pseudonym of Ernest George Henham (1870–   ), English-Canadian poet and novelist.

Trevor, A. C. Pseudonym of Norman George Pulsford (1902–   ), mystery writer.

Trevor, Elleston (1920–   ). English writer, whose pseudonyms are *Mansell Black, Trevor Burgess, Adam Hall, Simon Rattray, Warwick Scott,* and *Caesar Smith.*

Trevor, Glen. Occasional pseudonym of James Hilton (1900–1954), American writer.

Trevor, Ralph. See WILMOT, JAMES REGINALD.

Trez. See TREDEZ, DENISE.

Trez, Denise. See TREDEZ, DENISE.

Tribolo, Il. Cognomen of Niccolò Pericoli (1485–1550), Italian sculptor and architect.

Tribune. See ARMSTRONG, DOUGLAS ALBERT.

Triem, Paul Ellsworth. See ELLSWORTH, PAUL.

Trilussa. Pseudonym of Carlo Alberto Salustri (1875–1954), Italian poet.

Trim. Pseudonym of Louis Fortuné Gustave Ratisbonne (1827–1900), French man of letters.

Trimble, Jacquelyn W. See WHITNEY, J. L. H.

Trimble, Louis P. (1917–   ). American free-lance writer, whose pseudonyms are *Stuart Brock* and *Gerry Travis.*

Tring, A. Stephen. See MEYNELL, LAURENCE WALTER.

Tripp, Miles. See BRETT, MICHAEL.

Tristan. Pseudonym of Édouard Joachim Corbière (1845–1875), French poet.

Tristan. Pseudonym of Sigfrid Lindström (1892–1950), Swedish writer.

Tristan L'Hermite. Pseudonym of François L'Hermite, Sieur du Solier (1601–1655), French poet and playwright.

Tromlitz, A. von. Pseudonym of Karl August Fridrich von Witzleben (1773–1839), German army officer and novelist.

Trotsky, Leon. Assumed name of Leib (or Lev) Davydovich Bronstein (1877–1940), Russian revolutionary leader and writer.

Trowbridge, John Townsend. See CREYTON, PAUL.

Troy, Simon. Pseudonym of Thurman Warriner, contemporary mystery writer.

Troyat, Henri. Pseudonym of Lev Tarassov (1911–   ), French writer.

Truinet, Charles Louis Étienne. See NUITTER.

Truman, Marcus George. See BECKETT, MARK.

Trumper, Hubert Bagster. See BAGSTER, HUBERT.

Ts'ao-yu. Pseudonym of Wan Chia-pao (1905–   ), Chinese dramatist.

Tseng Yu-ho. Pseudonym of Betty Tseng Yu-ho Ecke (1923–   ), Chinese scholar.

Tserkovski, Tsanko. See BAKALOV.

Tsubouchi Shoyo (1859–1935). Japanese writer, whose real name was Tsubouchi Yuzo. He was also known as *Shoyo.*

Tsubouchi Yuzo. See TSUBOUCHI SHOYO.

Tsuruya Inosuke. See TSURUYA NAMBOKU.

Tsuruya Namboku. Pseudonym of Tsuruya Inosuke (1755–1829), Japanese playwright.

Tucholsky, Kurt (1890–1935). German satirical writer and poet, whose pseudonyms are *Kaspar Hauser, Peter Panter, Theobald Tiger,* and *Ignaz Wrobel.*

Tucker, Caroline. Pseudonym of Jeannette Covert Nolan (1897–   ), American writer.

Tucker, Charlotte Maria. See A.L.O.E.

Tuglas, Friedebert. Pseudonym of Friedebert Mihkelson (1886–   ), Estonian novelist, short-story writer, and critic.

Tumas, Juozas. See VAIZGANTAS.

Tuohy, Frank. See TUOHY, JOHN FRANCIS.

Tuohy, John Francis. Pseudonym of Frank Tuohy (1925–   ), English scholar.

Turmair, Johannes. See AVENTINUS, JOHANNES.

Turnbull, Dora Amy Dillon (d. 1961). Mystery writer, whose pseudonyms are *Delta* and *Patricia Wentworth.*

Turner, Charles. Legally adopted name of Charles Tennyson (1808–1879), English poet, brother of Alfred Lord Tennyson.

Turner, John Victor (1900–1945). Mystery writer, whose pseudonyms are *Nicholas Brady* and *David Hume.*

Turner, Len. See FLOREN, LEE.

Turner, Peter Paul. Pseudonym of Grant Jeffery (1924–   ), Canadian financial writer.

Turngren, Annette. See HOPKINS, A. T.

Tusarova, Marie. See MAJEROVA, MARIE.

Twain, Mark. Pseudonym of Samuel Langhorne Clemens (1835–1910),

American novelist, derived from depth markings on the Mississippi River. The pseudonym was previously used by Isaiah Sellers (1802?–1864), Mississippi River steamboat pilot and contributor to the New Orleans *Daily Picayune.*

Tweedale, J. Pseudonym of Judith Brundrett Bickle, contemporary English author.

Twist, Ananias. See NUNN, WILLIAM CURTIS.

Twm O'r Nant (1738?–1810). Welsh poet, also known by his English name, *Thomas Edwards.*

Tzara, Tristan. Pseudonym of J. Rosenstok (1896–   ), French poet.

"U"

U.E.V. Pseudonym of Jacqueline van der Waals (1868–1922), Dutch poet.

Ubertini, Francesco. See BACHIACCA, IL.

Ubertis, Corinna Teresa Gray. See TÉRÉSAH.

Uccello, Paolo (1397–1475). Florentine painter. His father's name was Dono di Paolo, and under the name Paolo di Dono, he appeared in a list of young artists helping Ghiberti finish his first doors for the Baptistery in Florence. The name is derived from his fondness for painting birds (*uccèllo*="bird").

Udine, Domenico da. See LU DOMINE.

Ujevic, Augustin. See TIN.

Ukrainka, Lesya. Pseudonym of Laryssa Petrovna Kvitka (1871–1913), Ukrainian poetess.

Ulisse. Pseudonym of Davide Lajolo (1913–   ), Italian journalist and writer.

Ullah, Salamat. See SALAMATULLAH.

Ultach. Pseudonym of Joseph Campbell (1879–1944), Irish poet.

Ulyanov, Vladimir Ilich. See LENIN, N.

Uncle Esek. See SHAW, HENRY WHEELER.

Uncle Gordon. See ROE, F. GORDON.

Uncle Gus. Pseudonym of Hans Agusto Rey (1898–   ), German-American writer.

Uncle Ray. Pseudonym of Ramon Peyton Coffman (1896–   ), American author of juvenile books.

Underhill, Peter. See SODERBERG, PERCY MEASDAY.

Underwood, Michael. Pseudonym of John Michael Evelyn (1916–
), mystery writer.
Underwood, Miles. See GLASSCO, JOHN.
Unett, John. See PRESTON, JAMES.
Unger, Maurice Albert. See MUNGER, AL.
Ungern-Sternberg, Baron Alexander von. See STERNBERG, ALEXANDER
VON.
Unkoku Toyo. See SESSHU.
Unofficial Observer. See CARTER, JOHN FRANKLIN.
Unwin, David Storr. See SEVERN, DAVID.
Upton, George Putnam. See PICKLE, PEREGRINE.
Uqsor, El. Pseudonym of Dmitri Borgmann (1927–   ), German-
American writer.
Urabe Kaneyoshi. See YOSHIDA KENKO.
Urban, Sylvanus, Gent. Pseudonym of Edward Cave (1691–1754) and
later editors of *Gentleman's Magazine.*
Urbicius. See MAURICE.
Urbino, Luciano da. See LAURANA, LUCIANO.
Urell, William Francis. See FRANCIS, WILLIAM.
Uris, Auren. See PAUL, AUREN.
Urstelle, Pierre d'. Pseudonym of Jean Pierre Dorst (1924–   ),
French writer.
Uryan. Cognomen of Baba Tahir-i Hamadani, 11th-century Persian poet.
Usher, Frank (1909–   ). British writer, whose pseudonyms are
Charles Franklin and *Frank Lester.*
Usikota. Pseudonym of Carl Brinitzer (1907–   ), Russian-born writer.
Utagawa Hiroshige. See HIROSHIGE.

"V"

Vaczek, Louis. See HARDIN, PETER.
Vadianus. Latinized name of Joachim von Watt (1484–1551), Swiss
humanist and historian.
Vaga, Perino del (1501–1547). Italian painter, whose real name was
Pietro Buonaccorsi.
Vahey, John George Haslette (1881–   ). Mystery writer, whose
pseudonyms are *Henrietta Clandon, John Haslette, Anthony Lang,*

Vernon Loder, John Mowbray, Walter Proudfoot, and *Arthur N. Timony.*

Vaillant. See CHASTELLAIN, PIERRE.

Vaizgantas. Pseudonym of Juozas Tumas (1869–1933), Lithuanian novelist, short-story writer, critic, and publicist.

Vajanský, Svetozar Hurban (1847–1916). Slovak poet and novelist. He published under the name *Vajanský* first as a pseudonym and later added it to his original surname, Hurban.

Valdés, Gabriel de la Concepción. See PLÁCIDO.

Vale, Henry Edmund Theodoric. See BLEDLOW, JOHN.

Valentine. See PECHEY, ARCHIBALD THOMAS.

Valentine, David. See LUDOVICI, ANTHONY M.

Valentine, Douglas. See WILLIAMS, VALENTINE.

Valentine, Roger. Pseudonym of Donald Norman Duke (1929–   ), American writer.

Valeriano, Pierio. Latinized name of Giovanni Pietro delle Fosse (1477–1558), Italian humanist.

Valhope, Carol North. Pseudonym of Olga Marx (1894–   ), American translator and poet.

Vallette, Marguerite. See RACHILDE.

Valnay, Raoul. Pseudonym of Aimé Marie Édouard Hervé (1835–1899), French journalist.

Vamba. Pseudonym of Luigi Bertelli (1858–1920), Italian satiric writer.

Van Aken, Jeroen. See BOSCH, HIERONYMUS.

Van Ameide, Th. Pseudonym of John Hendrik Labberton (1877–1955), Dutch poet and essayist.

Van Arsdale, Wirt. Pseudonym of Martha Wirt Davis, contemporary mystery writer.

Van Atta, Winfred. See RYERSON, LOWELL.

Van Berken, Tine. Pseudonym of Anna Christina Witmond-Berkhout (1870–1899), Dutch writer.

Van Briggle, Margaret Frances Jessup. See JESSUP, FRANCES.

Van Bruggen, Jan R. L. See KLEINJAN.

Van Buren, Abigail. Pseudonym of (Mrs.) Pauline Esther Phillips (1918–   ), American advice columnist. She is the creator of the "Dear Abby" column and the twin sister of Ann Landers, also a widely syndicated advice columnist.

Van Calcar, Elise. Pseudonym of Elise Carolina Ferdinanda Van Calcar-Schiötling (1822–1909), Dutch writer.

Van Calcar-Schiötling, Elise Carolina Ferdinanda. See VAN CALCAR, ELISE.

Vance, Edgar. See AMBROSE, ERIC.

Vance, Jack. See KUTTNER, HENRY.

Vancura, Antonin. See MAHEN, JIRI.

Vandal, Cameron. See THORNE, BLISS KIRBY.

Van den Hage, J. Pseudonym of Jan Frederick Oltmons (1806–1854), Dutch novelist. The name was derived from his birthplace, The Hague.

Van der Kulk, Willem. See IEPENDAAL, WILLEM VAN.

Van der Merwe, Izak Willem. See BOERNEEF.

Van der Zant, Johan Wilhelm. See ANDREUS, HANS.

Van Deventer, Emma Murdoch. See LYNCH, LAWRENCE L.

Van Dine, S. S. Pseudonym of Willard Huntington Wright (1888–1939), American writer and critic.

Van Doesburg, Theo. Pseudonym of C. E. M. Kupper (1883–1931), Dutch poet, painter, and architect.

Van Drome, Cécile. See FRANCE, ADINE.

Van Duinkerken, Anton. Pseudonym of Willem Jan Marie Anton Asselbergs (1903–   ). Dutch poet, essayist, and literary historian. He has also used the pseudonym *Pieter Backx.*

Van Dyke, J. See EDWARDS, FREDERICK ANTHONY.

Van Dyne, Edith. See BAUM, LYMAN FRANK.

Vane, Phillips. Pseudonym of Phyllis Hambleton (1892–   ), mystery writer.

Vane, Roland. See MCKEAG, ERNEST L.

Van Eckeren, Gerard. Pseudonym of Maurits Esser (1876–1951), Dutch writer and critic.

Van Eemlandt, W. H. Pseudonym of Willem Hendrik Haasse (1889–1958), Dutch writer.

Van-Eick. See ENZINAS, FRANCISCO DE.

Vangeon, Henri. See GHÉON, HENRI.

Vann'anto. Pseudonym of Giovanni Antonio Di Giacomo (1891–1960), Italian poet.

Vanner, John. See NORTH, WILLIAM.

Vannucci, Pietro di Cristoforo di. See PERUGINO, IL.

Van Sickle, V. A. See CARHART, ARTHUR HAWTHORNE.
Van Siller, Hilda. See SILLER, VAN.
Vansittart, Jane. Pseudonym of Hilda Vansittart Moorhouse (1908–
    ), English writer.
Van Vlierden, Bernard Frans. See KEMP, BERNARD.
Van Wieren, Jan. Pseudonym of Gaston Duribreux (1903–   ), Dutch
    novelist.
Vapcarov, Nikola. Pseudonym of Nikola Jonkov (1909–1942), Bulgarian
    poet.
Varga, Judy. Pseudonym of Judit Stang (1921–   ), Canadian author
    and artist.
Varley, John Philip. Pseudonym of Langdon Elwyn Mitchell (1862–
    1935), American playwright.
Varotari, Alessandro. See PADOVANINO, IL.
Vasconcelos, Joaquim Pereira Teixera de. See PASCOAIS, TEIXEIRA DE.
Vasek, Vladimir (1862–1958). Czech poet, whose pseudonyms are *Petr
    Bezruc* and, for some of his earlier writings, *Ratibor Suk.*
Vasilevska, Ludmyla. See DNIPROVA, CHAIKA.
Vasilevskaya, Vanda. Polish author of the 1940's, also known as *Wanda
    Wassilewska.*
Vasili, Compte Paul. See ADAM, JULIETTE.
Vasilikos, Petros. Pseudonym of Kostas Chatzopulos (1868–1920), neo-
    Hellenic poet and writer.
Vasiliu, George. See BACOVIA, GEORGE.
Vaughan, Leo. Pseudonym of Kenneth Harry Lendon (1928–   ),
    Canadian scholar.
Vecchi, Omero. See FOLGORE, LUCIANO.
Vecchietto, Il ("The Lively Old Man"). Cognomen of Lorenzo di Pietro
    di Giovanni di Landi (1412?–1480), Sienese painter.
Vecchio, Il. See PALMA VECCHIO.
Vedder, John K. See GRUBER, FRANK.
Vedette. See WILLIAMS, VALENTINE.
Veer, Hendrik de. See MOBACHUS, VESALIUS.
Vega, Lope de (1562–1635). Spanish dramatic poet, whose pseudonyms
    are *El Licenciado Tomé de Burguillos* and *Gabriel Padecopeo.* His
    full name was Lope Félix de Vega Carpio.
Veigelsberg, Hugo. See IGNOTUS.
Veneziano, Domenico (1405–1461). Italian painter of Venetian birth,

also known as *Domenico da Venezia* and *Domenico di Bartolommeo da Venezia*.

Veneziano, Sebastiano. See SEBASTIANO DEL PIOMBO.

Venison, Alfred. See POUND, EZRA LOOMIS.

Venning, Michael. See RICE, CRAIG.

Vercors. Pseudonym of Jean Bruller (1902–   ), French writer and illustrator, who ran a clandestine publishing house during the German occupation. He signs his real name to his drawings and illustrations.

Veresayev, Vikenti. Pseudonym of Vikenty Vikentievich Smidovich (1867–1943), Polish-Russian writer.

Verhage, Johannes Willem Cornelis. See GREVELINGEN, H. VAN.

Vermeulen, Edward. See OOM WARDEN.

Verney, Sarah. Pseudonym of Brenda Wilmar Holloway (1908–   ), English writer.

Vernon, Olivia. See BRONTË, ANNE.

Vernor, D. See CASEWIT, CURTIS.

Veronese, Paolo (1528–1588). Italian painter, whose real name was Paolo Cagliari. The name was derived from his birthplace, Verona.

Verral, Charles Spain. See EATON, GEORGE L.

Verrocchio (or Verocchio), Andrea del (1435–1488). Florentine sculptor and painter, whose real name was Andrea di Michele Cione.

Versace, Marie Teresa Rios. See RIOS, TERE.

Verstegan, Richard. See ROWLANDS, RICHARD.

Veselin. Pseudonym of Todor Gencov Vlajkov (1865–1943), Bulgarian novelist.

Vesëly, A. Pseudonym of Nikolay Ivanovich Kochkurov (1899–   ), Soviet Russian writer.

Vestal, Stanley. Original name and pseudonym of Walter Stanley Campbell (1887–   ), American writer.

Vexillum. Pseudonym of Hubert Stewart Banner (1891–1964), English-American writer.

Vezzani, Flora. See NEMI, ORSOLA.

Viaud, Louis Marie Julien. See LOTI, PIERRE.

Vicary, Dorothy. See RICE, DOROTHY MARY.

Vicentia, Andrea di. See MANTEGNA, ANDREA.

Vicker, Angus. Pseudonym of Henry Gregor Felsen (1910–   ), American writer.

Vickers, Roy. See SPENCER, JOHN.

Vidal, Gore. See BOX, EDGAR.

Vielé, Egbert Ludovicus. See VIELÉ-GRIFFIN, FRANCIS.

Vielé-Griffin, Francis (1864–1937). American-French poet, whose original name was Egbert Ludovicus Vielé.

Vienuolis. Pseudonym of Antanas Zukauskas (1882–   ), Lithuanian novelist and playwright.

Vigg, Pelle. See ERIKSEN, ANDREAS.

Vigné, Paul. See KERHOUEL, GAÉTAN.

Vigné d'Octon. See KERHOUEL, GAÉTAN.

Vignola, Giacomo da (1507–1573). Italian architect, whose real name was Giacomo Barocchio (or Barozzi).

Viguers, Ruth Hill. See HILL, RUTH A.

Vilde, Eduard. Estonian novelist and short-story writer (1865–1933), also known as *Edward Wilde.*

Vildrac, Charles. Pseudonym of Charles Messager (1882–   ), French poet and playwright.

Vilenkin, Nikolay Maximovich. See MINSKY, N.

Villard, Henry (1835–1900). German-American journalist, whose original name was Ferdinand Heinrich Gustav Hildgard. He was editor of the New York *Evening Post* from 1881 to 1900.

Villedieu, Mme. de. Pseudonym of Marie Catherine Desjardins (1640?–1683), French writer.

Villon, François (b. 1431?). French poet. He had two aliases: *François des Loges* and *François de Montcorbier.*

Villon, Jacques (1875–1963). French cubist painter, whose real name was Gaston Duchamp. He adopted the name *Villon* in 1922. He was the brother of both Raymond Duchamp-Villon, sculptor, and Marcel Duchamp, one of the founders of Dadaism.

Vincentius, Magister. See KADLUBEC, WINCENTY.

Vining, Elizabeth Gray. See GRAY, ELIZABETH JANET.

Vinokur, Grigory. Pseudonym of Herschel Weinrauch (1905–   ), Russian-American free-lance writer.

Virginius. Pseudonym of Eugene Virginius Connett (1891–   ), American writer.

Virza, Edvarts. Pseudonym of Edvarts Lieknis (1883–1940), Latvian poet.

Visscher, Maria. See TESSELSCHADE.

Vitalis. Pseudonym of Erik Sjöberg (1794–1828), Swedish poet.

Vite, Giovanni della (1599–1663). Flemish painter and engraver, whose real name was Jan Miel (or Meel).

Vitezovic, Tomislav. See KUEHNELT-LEDDIHN, ERIK RITTER VON.

Vitringa, Annes Johan (1827–1901). Dutch satirist, whose pseudonyms are *Jan Holland* and *Jochem van Ondere*.

Vivant, M. St. See BIXBY, JEROME LEWIS.

Vivarini, Antonio. See MURANO, ANTONIO DA.

Vivian, Evelyn Charles H. See CANNELL, CHARLES.

Vivian, Francis. Pseudonym of Ernest Ashley (1906–   ), English writer.

Vivien, Renée. Pseudonym of Pauline M. Tarn (1877–1909), American-French poet.

Vizard, Stephen. Pseudonym of David Burnett Stephen James (1919–   ), British editor and writer.

Vlačić, Matthias. See FLACIUS ILLYRICUS, MATTHIAS.

Vladimirov, Ivan Egorovich. See VOLNOV, IVAN.

Vlajkov, Todor Gencov. See VESELIN.

Vlasto, John Alexander (1877–1958). Mystery writer, whose pseudonyms are *John Alexander* and *John Remenham*.

Vlcek, Bartos. See JAVOR, J.

Voelker, John Donaldson. See TRAVER, ROBERT.

Vogau, Boris Andreyevich. See PILNYAK, BORIS ANDREYEVICH.

Volder, Wiliem de. See GNAPHEUS, GUITHELMUS.

Volk, Gordon (1885–   ). Mystery writer, whose pseudonyms are *Raymond Knotts* and *Gordon Sussex*.

Volnov, Ivan. Pseudonym of Ivan Egorovich Vladimirov (1885–1931), Russian novelist.

Volpi, Giovanni Antonio. See GIANNANTONIO.

Voltaire. Assumed name of François Marie Arouet (1694–1778), French novelist, playwright, and satirist.

Volterra, Daniele da (1509–1566). Italian painter, whose real name was Daniele Ricciarelli. He was also called *Il Braccatone*.

Volterrano, Il. Cognomen of Baldassare Franceschini (1611–1689), Florentine painter.

Volyanskaya, Galina Evgenevna. See NIKOLAEVA, GALINA EVGENEVNA.

Volynsky, Akim L'novich. Pseudonym of A. L. Flekser (1863–1926), Russian essayist.

Von Almedingen, Martha Edith. See ALMEDINGEN, E. M.

Von der Clana, Heinrich. Pseudonym of Albert Maria Weiss (1844–1925), Roman Catholic theologian and writer.

von Hauenschild, Richard Georg Spiller. See WALDAU, MAX.

Von Hildebrand, Dietrich. See OTT, PETER.

Voranc, Prezihov. Pseudonym of Lovro Kuhar (1893–1950), Slovak poet and novelist.

Vovchok, Marko. Pseudonym of Maria Alexandrovna Markovich (1834–1907), Ukrainian and Russian writer.

Voyle, Mary. Pseudonym of Rosemary Manning (1911–   ), American writer.

Vrancx, Willem. Sixteenth-century Dutch poet, whose real name was Willem Elias.

Vrchlický, Jaroslav. Pseudonym of Emil Frida (1853–1912), Czech poet and playwright.

Vriendt, Frans de. See FLORIS, FRANS.

Vrijaldenhoven, Christien. See ISCHYRIUS.

Vrugt, Johanna Petronella. See BLAMAN, ANNA.

Vulliamy, Colwyn Edward. See ROLLS, ANTHONY.

Vydunas. Pseudonym of Vilius Storasta (1868–   ), Lithuanian playwright.

"W"

Waals, Jacqueline van der. See U.E.V.

Waddel, Charles Carey. See CAREY, CHARLES.

Waddell, Sam. See MAYNE, RUTHERFORD.

Wade, Bob (1920–   ). American mystery writer, whose pseudonyms, with Bill Miller, are *Whit Masterson* and *Wade Miller.*

Wade, Henry. Pseudonym of Sir Henry Lancelot Aubrey-Fletcher (1887–   ), British mystery writer.

Wade, Herbert. Pseudonym of Hugh Gregory Wales (1910–   ), American scholar.

Wade, Joanna. Pseudonym of Evelyn Domenica Berckman (1900), American-English writer.

Wade, Rosalind Herschel. See CARR, CATHARINE.

Waghorn, H. L. Pseudonym of Holloway Horn (1886–   ), mystery writer.

Wagstaff, Théophile. See THACKERAY, WILLIAM MAKEPEACE.

Wagstaffe, Launcelot. See IRVING, WASHINGTON.

Wahl, Caedmon Thomas. See FATHER CAEDMON.

Wainer, Cord. See DEWEY, THOMAS BLANCHARD.

Wakker van Zon, Petrus. See DAALBERG, BRUNO.

Walch, Jakob. German name of Jacopo de' Barbari (1440?–1516), Italian painter.

Waldau, Max. Pseudonym of Richard Georg Spiller von Hauenschild (1825–1855), German poet and novelist.

Waldmüller, Robert. Pseudonym of Édouard Duboc (1822–1910), German writer of French descent.

Waldo, David. Pseudonym of David Waldo Clarke (1907–   ), British writer.

Waldron, D'Lynn. Pseudonym of Diane Lynn Waldron-Shah (1936–   ), American writer.

Waldron, George. See BARRINGTON, GEORGE.

Waldron-Shah, Diane Lynn. See WALDRON, D'LYNN.

Wales, Hugh Gregory. See WADE, HERBERT.

Walker, Harry. Pseudonym of Hillary Waugh (1920–   ), British mystery writer.

Walker, Ira. Pseudonym of Irma Ruth Walker (1921–   ), American mystery writer.

Walker, Irma Ruth. See WALKER, IRA.

Walker, Kenneth MacFarlane. See MACFARLANE, KENNETH.

Walkerley, Rodney Lewis (1905–   ). English free-lance author and journalist, whose pseudonyms are *Athos* and *Grande Vitesse.*

Walkinshaw, Colin. Pseudonym of James Macarthur Reid (1900–   ), Scottish writer.

Wallace, Doreen. Pseudonym of Dora Eileen Agnew Wallace Rash (1897–   ), English writer.

Wallace, John. Contemporary mystery writer, whose pseudonyms are *Aintree, Gerald Grantham,* and *Texas Ranger.*

Wallace, Richard. See IND, ALLISON.

Wallengren, Axel. See FALSTAFF FAKIR.

Waller, John Francis. See SLINGSBY, JONATHAN FREKE.

Waller, Leslie. See CODY, C. S.

Waller, Max. Pseudonym of Maurice Warlomont (1860–1889), Belgian poet and novelist.

Wallis, A. S. C. Pseudonym of Adèle Sophia Cornelia von Antal (1857–1925), Dutch novelist and playwright.

Wallop, Lucille Fletcher. See FLETCHER, LUCILLE.

Walsh, James Morgan. See HILL, H. HAVERSTOCK.

Walter, Dorothy Blake (1908–   ). American free-lance writer, whose pseudonyms are *Katherine Blake, Kay Blake,* and *Katherine Ross.*

Walter, Villiam Christian. Pseudonym of Hans Christian Andersen (1805–1875), Danish fairy-tale writer, novelist, playwright, and poet.

Walter, W. E. C. Pseudonym of Virginie Loveling (1836–1923), Flemish novelist.

Walton, Francis. Pseudonym of Alfred Hodder (1866–1907), mystery writer.

Walz, Audrey. See BONNAMY, FRANCIS.

Wan Chia-pao. See TS'AO-YU.

Wang Shou-jen. See WANG YANG-MING.

Wang Wei (699–759). Chinese poet, painter, calligrapher, and musician, also called *Mo-ch'i* and *Yu-ch'eng.*

Wang Yang-ming. Pseudonym of Wang Shou-jen (d. 1528), Chinese philosopher.

Wanstall, Ken. Pseudonym of Kenneth Green-Wanstall (1918–   ), English writer.

Warborough, Martin Leach. See ALLEN, GRANT.

Ward, Artemus. Pseudonym of Charles Farrar Browne (1834–1867), American humorist.

Ward, Arthur Sarsfield. See ROHMER, MAX.

Ward, Don. See TRACY, POWERS.

Ward, Elizabeth Honor. See LESLIE, WARD S.

Ward, Janice. Pseudonym of Rachel Frieda Hartman (1920–   ), American writer.

Ward, Jonas. See ARD, WILLIAM THOMAS.

Warden, Florence. Pseudonym of Florence Alice Price James (1857–1929), American mystery writer.

Wardle, Dan. See SNOW, CHARLES HORACE.

Ward-Thomas, Evelyn Bridget Patricia Stephens (1928–   ). English author, whose pseudonyms are *Evelyn Anthony* and *Anthony Evelyn.*

Ware, Eugene Fitch. See IRONQUILL.

Warlock, Peter. Pseudonym of Philip Arnold Heseltine (1894–1930), English composer and writer.

Warlomont, Maurice. See WALLER, MAX.

Warneford, Lieut. Pseudonym of Archibald Clavering Gunter (1847–1907), mystery writer.

Warner, Frank A. Collective pseudonym for the "Bobby Blake" and "Bob Chase" series. See STRATEMEYER, EDWARD L.

Warner, Kenneth Lewis. See MOREL, DIGHTON.

Warner, Susan Bogert. See WETHERELL, ELIZABETH.

Warner, Warren, Esq., of the Inner Temple. Pseudonym of Samuel Warren (1870–1877), mystery writer.

Warren, Dave. Pseudonym of Warren Wendell Wiersbe (1929–   ), American author.

Warren, John Byrne Leicester, 3rd Baron de Tabley (1835–1895). English poet and naturalist, whose pseudonyms are *William Lancaster* and *George F. Preston.*

Warren, John Russell. See COVERACK, GILBERT.

Warren, Mary Douglas. See GREIG, MAYSIE.

Warren, Samuel. See WARNER, WARREN, ESQ., OF THE INNER TEMPLE.

Warren, Vernon. Pseudonym of George Warren Vernon Chapman (1925–   ), mystery writer.

Warriner, Cornelia. See CROCKETT, JAMES.

Warriner, Thurman. See TROY, SIMON.

Warwick, Dolores. Pseudonym of Dolores Warwick Frése (1936–   ), American author.

Warwick, Pauline. Pseudonym of Betty Evelyn Davies, contemporary mystery writer.

Wa-Sha-Quon-Asin. See GREY OWL.

Washington, Marguerite Beauchamp (1900–   ). English writer, whose pseudonyms are *Anne Beaton, Pat Beauchamp,* and *Pat Beauchamp Washington.*

Washington, Pat Beauchamp. See WASHINGTON, MARGUERITE BEAU-CHAMP.

Washington, Solomon. See GLADDEN, WASHINGTON.

Wason, Betty. Pseudonym of Elizabeth Wason Hall (1912–   ), American writer and cooking expert.

Wassersug, Joseph D. See BRADFORD, ADAM, M.D.

Wassilewska, Wanda. See VASILEVSKAYA, VANDA.

Wast, Hugo. Pseudonym of Gustavo Martínez Zuviría (1883–   ), Argentinian novelist.

Wasylewski, Stanisław. See BURY, JAN.

Watanna, Onoto. Pseudonym of Winnifred Babcock (1879–   ), American writer born in Japan.

Water, Silas. See LOOMIS, NOEL MILLER.

Waterhouse, Keith (1929–   ). British writer, whose pseudonyms, with Guy Deghy, are *Hearld Froy* and *Lee Gibb.*

Waters. See RUSSELL, WILLIAM.

Watkins, Alex. See LINKLATER, J. LANE.

Watkins, Arthur Thomas Levi. WATKYN, ARTHUR.

Watkinson, Valerie. Pseudonym of Valerie Mae Watkinson Elliston (1929–   ), Australian writer.

Watkins-Pitchford, Denys James (1905–   ). English writer, whose pseudonyms are *B.B.* and *Michael Traherne.*

Watkyn, Arthur. Pseudonym of Arthur Thomas Levi Watkins (1907–   ), British free-lance author.

Watney, John B. See ROBERTS, ANTHONY.

Watson, Frank. Pseudonym of Francis H. Ames (1900–   ), American writer.

Watson, Jane Werner (1915–   ). American writer, whose pseudonyms are *Annie North Bedford, Monica Hill,* and *Elsa Ruth Nast.*

Watson, John. See MACLAREN, IAN.

Watson, Will. See FLOREN, LEE.

Watt, Joachim von. See VADIANUS.

Waud, Elizabeth. Pseudonym of Muriel Joyce Tattersall (1931–   ), English writer of children's books.

Waugh, Hillary. See WALKER, HARRY.

Wayde, Bernard. See OLD CAP COLLIER.

Wayne, Anderson. See DRESSER, DAVIS.

Wayne, Frances. Pseudonym of Florence Wedge (1919–   ), Canadian writer.

Wayne, Joseph. See OVERHOLSER, WAYNE D.

Weale, Putnam. Pseudonym of Bertram Lenox Simpson (1877–1930), English historian and political writer.

Weary, Ogdred. See GOREY, EDWARD ST. JOHN.

Weathercock, The. Pseudonym of Lawrence B. Romaine (1900–   ), American writer.

Weaver, Bertrand. See HUNTER, PAUL.

Weaver, Ward. See MASON, FRANCIS VAN WYCK.

Webb, Charles Henry. See PAUL, JOHN.

Webb, Dorothy Anna Maria. See MARCH, JERMYN.

Webb, Jack (1920–). American mystery writer, whose pseudonyms are *John Farr* and *Tex Grady.*

Webb, Jean Francis. See HAMILL, ETHEL.

Webb, Lilian Julian. Pseudonym of Cynthia Stockley (1877–1936), Rhodesian novelist.

Webb, Richard Wilson. Contemporary mystery writer, whose pseudonyms are, with Hugh Callingham Wheeler, *Patrick Quentin* and *Jonathan Stagge*, and, with Martha Mott Kelley, then alone, then with Hugh Callingham Wheeler, *Q. Patrick.*

Webb, Ruth Enid Borlase Morris. See MORRIS, RUTH.

Webb, Spider. Pseudonym of Fred Joseph Gohman (1918–), American writer and illustrator.

Webbe, Gale Dudley. See COLE, STEPHEN.

Webster, Frank V. Collective pseudonym for the "Books for Boys" series. See STRATEMEYER, EDWARD L.

Webster, Gary. Pseudonym of Webb Black Garrison (1919–), American writer.

Webster, Jesse. See CASSILL, RONALD VERLIN.

Wedge, Florence. See WAYNE, FRANCES.

Weekes, Agnes Russell. See PRYDE, ANTHONY.

Weeks, Constance Tomkinson. See TOMKINSON, CONSTANCE.

Weill, René. See COOLUS, ROMAIN.

Weiner, Henri. See LONGSTREET, STEPHEN.

Weinrauch, Herschel. See VINOKUR, GRIGORY.

Weinstein, Sol. See PUMPERNICKEL.

Weir, John. Pseudonym of Colin John Cross (1928–), Welsh-English writer.

Weiss, Albert Maria. See VON DER CLANA, HEINRICH.

Weiss, Irving J. See FORIO, ROBERT.

Weissman, Jack. See ANDERSON, GEORGE.

Welch, Pauline. See BODENHAM, HILDA MORRIS.

Welch, Ronald. Pseudonym of Ronald Oliver Felton (1909–), Welsh-English writer.

Welcome, John. Pseudonym of John Needham Huggard (1914–), Irish writer.

Weldon, John. See MACNAMARA, BRINSLEY.

Wellesley, Lord Charles. See BRONTË, CHARLOTTE.

Wells, Carolyn. See WRIGHT, ROWLAND.

Wells, Charles Jeremiah. See HOWARD, H. L.

Wells, Herbert George. See BLISS, REGINALD.

Wells, J. Wellington. See DECAMP, LYON SPRAGUE.

Wells, June. See SWINFORD, BETTY JUNE WELLS.

Wells, Susan. Pseudonym of Doris Siegel, contemporary mystery writer.

Wen Cheng-ming (1470–1559). Chinese calligrapher, painter, essayist, and poet. He signed his works *Wen Pi* until 1518, when he adopted the name *Cheng-ming.*

Wen Pi. See WEN CHENG-MING.

Wentworth, Barbara. See PITCHER, GLADYS.

Wentworth, Patricia. See TURNBULL, DORA AMY DILLON.

Wergeland, Henrik Arnold. See SIFADDA, SIFUL.

Wermeskerke-Junius, Sophia Margaretha Cornelia van. See WOULDE, JOHANNA VAN.

Werner, E. Pseudonym of Elisabeth Bürstenbinder (1838–1918), German novelist.

Werner, Franz von. See MURAD EFENDI.

Werner, K. See CASEWIT, CURTIS.

Wertheimer, Leo. See BRUNNER, CONSTANTIN.

Wesley, Elizabeth. See MCELFRESH, ELIZABETH ADELINE.

West, Benjamin. See BICKERSTAFF, ISAAC.

West, Betty. See BOWEN, BETTY MORGAN.

West, Jerry. See STRATEMEYER, EDWARD L.

West, Keith. Pseudonym of Kenneth Westmacott Lane (1893–   ), mystery writer.

West, Mark. Pseudonym of Charles W. Runyon (1928–   ), American free-lance writer.

West, Morris Langlo. See EAST, MICHAEL.

West, Rebecca. Pseudonym of Cicily Isabel Fairfield (1892–   ), English critic and writer, derived from the character in Ibsen's *Rosmersholm.*

West, Token. See HUMPHRIES, ADELAIDE M.

West, Tom. See REACH, JAMES.

West, Ward. Pseudonym of Harold Glen (Hal) Borland (1900–   ), American writer and poet.

Westerham, S. C. Pseudonym of Cyril Argentine Alington (1872–   ), mystery writer.

Westlake, Donald E. See STARK, RICHARD.

Westland, Lynn. See JOSCELYN, ARCHIE L.

Westmacott, Mary. Occasional pseudonym of Agatha Christie (1890–
), English mystery novelist.

Weston, Allen. See HOGARTH, GRACE ALLEN, and NORTON, ALICE
MARY.

Weston, Ann. See PITCHER, GLADYS.

West-Watson, Keith Campbell. See CAMPBELL, KEITH.

Wetherell, Elizabeth. Pseudonym of Susan Bogert Warner (1819–1885),
American writer of pious stories for children.

Wetherell-Pepper, Joan Alexander. See PEPPER, JOAN.

Wetterbergh, Carl Anton. See ONKEL ADAM.

Wetzel, Friedrich Gottlob. See BONAVENTURA.

Whalley, Dorothy. See COWLIN, DOROTHY.

Wharton, Anthony. See MCALLISTER, ALISTER.

Wharton, Virginia. Pseudonym of Eleanor Eldridge Ratigan (1916–
), American author.

Wheeler, Hugh Callingham (1913–). Mystery writer, whose
pseudonyms, with Richard Wilson Webb, are *Q. Patrick, Patrick
Quentin,* and *Jonathan Stagge.*

Wheeler, Janet D. Collective pseudonym for the "Billie Bradley" series.
See STRATEMEYER, EDWARD L.

Whelpton, George Eric (1894–). French-English author, whose
pseudonyms are *Richard Lyte* and *John Parry.*

White, Dale. See PLACE, MARIAN TEMPLETON.

White, Herbert Martyn Oliver. See MARTYN, OLIVER.

White, James Dillon (1913–). English writer, whose pseudonyms
are *Felix Krull, Peto,* and *James Peto.*

White, Paul Hamilton Hume. See JUNGLE DOCTOR.

White, Ramy Allison. Collective pseudonym for the "Sunny Boy" series.
See STRATEMEYER, EDWARD L.

White, William Anthony Parker. See BOUCHER, ANTHONY.

White, William Hale. See RUTHERFORD, MARK.

White, Zita. Pseudonym of Terese Mary Zita White Denholm (1933–
), Australian writer.

Whitefield, John Humphreys. See PILIO, GERONE.

Whitehorn, Katharine. Pseudonym of Katharine Elizabeth Lyall (1928–
), English writer.

Whitehouse, Arch. Pseudonym of Arthur George Whitehouse (1895–
), English writer.
Whitehouse, Arthur George. See WHITEHOUSE, ARCH.
Whitinger, R. D. See PLACE, MARIAN TEMPLETON.
Whitney, J. L. H. Pseudonym of Jacquelyn W. Trimble (1927–   ),
American writer.
Whittlebot, Hernia. Pseudonym of Noel Coward (1899–   ), English-
Swiss playwright, author, composer, songwriter, actor, singer, direc-
tor, and producer.
Wibberley, Leonard Patrick O'Connor (1915–   ). Irish-American
writer, whose pseudonyms are *Leonard Holton* and *Patrick O'Con-
nor.*
Wichers, Herman P. Schönfeld. See BELCAMPO.
Widdemer, Mabel Cleland (1902–   ). American writer, whose
pseudonyms are *Mabel Cleland* and *Mabel Cleland Ludlum.*
Wiener, Franz. See CROISSET, FRANCIS DE.
Wiersbe, Warren Wendell. See WARREN, DAVE.
Wilcox, Harry. See DERBY, MARK.
Wilde, Edward. See VILDE, EDUARD.
Wilde, Lady Jane Francesca. See SPERANZA.
Wilde, Kathey. Pseudonym of Patricia King (1930–   ), American
writer.
Wildenvey, Herman. Pseudonym of Herman Portaas (1886–   ),
Norwegian poet, playwright, and novelist.
Wiley, Margaret L. Pseudonym of Margaret Wiley Marshall (1908–
), American scholar.
Wilkes-Hunter, Richard. Contemporary Australian writer, whose
pseudonyms are *Dean Ballard, Marc Brody, Tod Conrad, Alex
Crane, Shane Douglas, James Dunn, Peter Gordon, Kerry Mitchell,
C. M. O'Niell, Kent Sanders,* and *Alan Shulberg.*
Wilkinson, Iris. See HYDE, ROBIN.
Wilkinson, John Donald. See IRONMASTER, MAXIMUS.
Wilkinson, Lorna Hilda Kathleen. See DEANE, LORNA.
Wilkinson, Ronald. See THORN, RONALD SCOTT.
Willard, Charles. See ARMSTRONG, JOHN BYRON.
Willard, Josiah Flynt. See FLYNT, JOSIAH.
Willenhag, Wolfgang von. See BEER, JOHANN.
Willett, Brother Franciscus (1922–   ). American writer, whose

pseudonyms are *Ian Bond, Brother Jeremy Premont,* and *Brother Orrin Primm.*

Willey, Robert. Pseudonym of Willy Ley (1906–   ), German-American free-lance writer.

Williams, Beryl. See EPSTEIN, BERYL WILLIAMS.

Williams, Edward. See IOLO MORGANWG.

Williams, Edwin Alfred. See CAIRE, EDWIN DE.

Williams, Eirlys O. See TREFOR, EIRLYS.

Williams, Eliseus. See EIFION WYN.

Williams, Francis B. Pseudonym of Frances Williams Browin (1898–   ), American writer.

Williams, Joel. See JENNINGS, JOHN E., JR.

Williams, John. See PASQUIN, ANTHONY.

Williams, Jonathan Chamberlain. See CHAMBERLAIN, THEODORE.

Williams, Margaret Wetherby. See ERSKINE, MARGARET.

Williams, Pete. Pseudonym of Cliff Faulknor (1913–   ), Canadian writer.

Williams, Pete. See REACH, JAMES.

Williams, Richard. See REACH, JAMES.

Williams, Rowland. See HW'FA MON.

Williams, Tennessee (1914–   ). American playwright, whose original name was Thomas Lanier Williams.

Williams, Thomas Lanier. See WILLIAMS, TENNESSEE.

Williams, Valentine (1883–1946). Mystery writer, whose pseudonyms are *Douglas Valentine* and *Vedette.*

Williams, William (1717–1791). Welsh writer of hymns, also known as *Williams Pantycelyn.*

Williamson, Alice Muriel Livingston (1869–1933). Mystery writer, whose pseudonyms are *M. P. Revere; Teresa de Savallo, Marquesa d'Alpens; Mrs. Harcourt Williamson;* and, with Charles Norris Williamson (1859–1920), *Capt. Charles de Créspigny* and *Alice Stuyvesant.*

Williamson, Charles Norris (1859–1920). Mystery writer, whose pseudonyms, with Alice Muriel Livingston Williamson (1869–1933), are *Capt. Charles de Créspigny* and *Alice Stuyvesant.*

Williamson, Claude C. H. See HOPE, FELIX.

Williamson, Ellen Douglas. See DOUGLAS, ELLEN.

Williamson, Geoffrey. See HASTINGS, ALAN.

Williamson, Mrs. Harcourt. See WILLIAMSON, ALICE MURIEL LIVINGSTON.

Williamson, John Stewart. See STEWART, WILL.

Willis, Anthony Armstrong (1897–   ). Mystery writer, whose pseudonyms are *A.A. of Punch* and *Anthony Armstrong.*

Wills, Chester. See SNOW, CHARLES HORACE.

Wills, Ronald. See THOMAS, RONALD WILLS.

Wills, Thomas. See ARD, WILLIAM THOMAS.

Willy. Pseudonym of Henry Gauthier-Villars (1859–1932), French novelist.

Wilmot, Frank Leslie Thomson. See MAURICE, FURNLEY.

Wilmot, James Reginald (1897–   ). Mystery writer, whose pseudonyms are *Frances Stewart* and *Ralph Trevor.*

Wilson, Alexandra. See SPENCER, GEOFFREY.

Wilson, Dave. See FLOREN, LEE.

Wilson, David. Pseudonym of David Wilson MacArthur (1903–   ), Scottish free-lance author and journalist.

Wilson, J. Arbuthnot. See ALLEN, GRANT.

Wilson, John. See NORTH, CHRISTOPHER.

Wilson, John Burgess. See BURGESS, ANTHONY.

Wilson, Joyce M. See STRANGER, JOYCE.

Wilson, Lee. Pseudonym of Laura Elizabeth Lemmon (1917–   ), mystery writer.

Wilson, Mitchell A. See HOGARTH, EMMETT.

Wilson, Robert McNair. See WYNNE, ANTHONY.

Wilson, Roger Harris Lebus. See HARRIS, ROGER.

Wilson, Stanley Kidder. See PLINY THE YOUNGEST.

Wimhurst, Cecil Gordon. See BRENT, NIGEL.

Winch, Evelyn M. Pseudonym of Marie Elizabeth Agnes Winch, contemporary mystery writer.

Winch, John. See LONG, GABRIELLE MARGARET VERE.

Winch, Marie Elizabeth Agnes. See WINCH, EVELYN M.

Winchell, Prentice (1895–   ). Mystery writer, whose pseudonyms are *Jay de Bekker, Dev Collans, Spencer Dean, Stewart Sterling.*

Winchevsky, Morris (1856–1932). Lithuanian-American writer in Yiddish, whose original name was Lippe Benzion Novachovitch. In private life he used the name *Leopold Benedict* and for his writings he used the pseudonym *Ben-Nez.*

Windsor, Rex. See ARMSTRONG, DOUGLAS ALBERT.

Winfield, Arthur M. See STRATEMEYER, EDWARD L.

Winfield, Edna. See STRATEMEYER, EDWARD L.

Winfield, Leigh. Pseudonym of Norma Ione Youngberg (1896–   ), American writer.

Wing, Frances. See SCOTT, FRANCES V.

Winkler Prins, Jacob. See BRANDT, KASPAR.

Winslow, Donald. Pseudonym of Donald Atwell Zoll (1927–   ), American scholar.

Winstanley, William. See POOR ROBIN.

Winter, Bevis (1918–   ). British writer, whose pseudonyms are *Al Bocca, Peter Cagney,* and *Gordon Shayne.*

Winters, Janet Lewis. See LEWIS, JANET.

Winterton, Paul (1908–   ). English author, whose pseudonyms are *Roger Bax, Andrew Garve,* and *Paul Somers.*

Winton, John. Pseudonym of John Pratt (1931–   ), English writer.

Wireker (c1130–c1205). English satirist and monk of Christ Church, Canterbury, whose real name was Nigel de Longchamps.

Wise, Arthur. See MCARTHUR, JOHN.

Wishart, Henry. Pseudonym of Robert Henry Wishart Shepherd (1888–   ), South African writer.

Wit, Pieter de. See CANDIDO, PIETRO.

Withers, E. L. Pseudonym of George William Potter, Jr. (1930–   ), American writer.

Witmond-Berkhout, Anna Christina. See VAN BERKEN, TINE.

Witte, Glenna Finley. See FINLEY, GLENNA.

Witte, Jacob Eduard de. See HAEMSTEDE, JACOB EDUARD DE WITTE VAN.

Witte, Pieter de. See CANDIDO, PIETRO.

Wittermans, Elizabeth. See PINO, E.

Witz, Konrad (1400/10–1445/46). German painter, also known by his Latinized name, *Conradus Sapientis* ("Conrad the Wise"), and, when he moved to Basel, Switzerland, *Meister Konrat von Rotwil.*

Witzleben, Karl August Friedrich von. See TROMLITZ, A. VON.

Woden, George. Pseudonym of George Wilson Slaney (1884–   ), English-Scottish novelist.

Wodge, Dreary. See GOREY, EDWARD ST. JOHN.

Woensel, Pieter van. See BACHI, AMURATH-EFFENDI HEKIM.

Wogler, Elchanan. Pseudonym of A. Rozanski (1906–   ), Yiddish poet.

Wojciechowska, Maia. See RODMAN, MAIA.

Wolcot, John. See PINDAR, PETER.

Wolf, Frederick. See DEMPEWOLFF, RICHARD FREDERIC.

Wolf, Miriam Bredow. See BREDOW, MIRIAM.

Wolfe, Reginald. Pseudonym of Thomas Frognall Dibdin (1776–1847), English bibliographer.

Wolff-Bekker, Elisabeth. See SILVIANA.

Wolffe, Katherine. See SCOTT, MARIAN GALLAGHER.

Wolfson, Victor. See DODGE, LANGDON.

Wolseley, Faith. Pseudonym of Stella Mary Hodgson Tower (1891–   ), mystery writer.

Wolski, Marcin. See BIELSKI, MARCIN.

Wood, Clement. See DUBOIS, ALAN.

Wood, James Playsted (1905–   ). American writer, whose pseudonyms are *James S. Briavels* and *Henry Soudley.*

Wood, Kirk. See STAHL, LE ROY.

Wood, Samuel Andrew. See TEMPLE, ROBIN.

Wood, Sherry. See FREEMAN, GRAYDON LA VERNE.

Woodcott, Keith. Pseudonym of John Kilian Houston Brunner (1934–   ), English science-fiction writer.

Woodford, Jack. See WOOLFOLK, JOSIAH PITTS.

Woodrook, R. A. Pseudonym of Ranson Cowlishaw (1894–   ), English writer.

Woodruff, Philip. Pseudonym of Philip Mason (1906–   ), English writer.

Woods, Nat. See STRATEMEYER, EDWARD L.

Woods, Sara. Pseudonym of Sara Hutton Bowen-Judd (1922–   ), British-Canadian writer.

Woodward, Edward Emberlin. See GRIERSON, JANE.

Woodward, Grace Steele. See DOANE, MARION S.

Woodward, Lilian. See MARSH, JOHN.

Woolfolk, Josiah Pitts (1894–   ). Mystery writer, whose pseudonyms are *Sappho Henderson Britt, Howard Kennedy, Gordon Sayre,* and *Jack Woodford.*

Woolrich, Cornell. See HOPLEY-WOOLRICH, CORNELL GEORGE.

Woolsey, Sarah Chauncey. See COOLIDGE, SUSAN.

Worth, Nicholas. Occasional pseudonym of Walter Hines Page (1855–1918), American journalist and diplomat, used for writing novels.

Worthington-Stuart, Brian Arthur. Contemporary mystery writer, whose pseudonyms are *Peter Meredith* and *Brian Stuart.*

Worts, George Frank. See BRENT, LORING.

Woulde, Johanna van. Pseudonym of Sophia Margaretha Cornelia van Wermeskerke-Junius (1853–1904), Dutch novelist.

Wright, Amos. Pseudonym of F. Alexander Magoun (1896–   ), American writer.

Wright, Elsie N. See GRAYSON, CAPTAIN J. J.

Wright, Enid Meadowcroft. See MEADOWCROFT, ENID LaMONTE.

Wright, Judith Grovner. See BULL, LOIS.

Wright, Mary Pamela Godwin. See BAWN, MARY.

Wright, Rowland. Pseudonym of Carolyn Wells (1870–1942), English mystery writer.

Wright, Ruth. Pseudonym of Ruth Hammitt Kauffman (1883–1952), mystery writer.

Wright, Sydney Fowler. See FOWLER, SYDNEY.

Wright, Willard Huntington. See VAN DINE, S. S.

Wrobel, Ignaz. See TUCHOLSKY, KURT.

Wu, Nelson I. See LU-CH'IAO.

Wu-chi Liu. See HSIAO HSIA.

Wu Li (1632–1718). Chinese painter, also known as *Yu-shan, Mo-ching-tao-jen,* and *T'ao-chi-chu-shin.* After his conversion to Catholicism he was named *Simon Xavier,* and after his ordination, *Father Acunha.* All of his paintings are signed by his Chinese names.

Wuolijoki, Hella Maria. See TERVAPÄÄ, JUHANI.

Wurzbach, Constant. See CONSTANT, W.

Wynd, Oswald. See BLACK, GAVIN.

Wyndham, John. See HARRIS, JOHN BEYNON.

Wyndham, Lee. See HYNDMAN, JANE LEE.

Wynfrith. See BONIFACE.

Wynn, Alfred. Pseudonym of Fred Brewer (1921–   ), American writer.

Wynne, Anthony. Pseudonym of Robert McNair Wilson (1882–   ), American mystery writer.

Wynne, Brian. See GARFIELD, BRIAN WYNNE.

Wynne, Frank. See GARFIELD, BRIAN WYNNE.

Wynne-Tyson, Jon (1924–   ). English writer, whose pseudonyms are *Michel Fourest* and *Jeremy Pitt.*

Wyzewa. Pseudonym of Teodor de Wyzewski (1862–1917), Polish critic who wrote in French.

Wyzewski, Teodor de. See WYZEWA.

"X"

X. Pseudonym of Arthur Charles Fox-Davies (1871–1928), English mystery writer.

X.L. Pseudonym of Julian Osgood Field, contemporary mystery writer.

Xavier, Simon. See WU LI.

Xenius. Pseudonym of Eugenio D'Ors y Rovira (1882–1954), Spanish philosopher.

"Y"

Y.L.G. Pseudonym of Yehuda Leib Gordon (1830–1892), Russian-Hebrew novelist and poet.

Y.Y. Pseudonym of Robert Lynd (1879–1949), Irish essayist.

Yakovlev, Alexander Ivanovich. See HERZEN, ALEXANDER IVANOVICH.

Yakubovich, Peter Filippovich. See MELSHIN, L.

Yamada Bimyo (1868–1910). Japanese novelist and poet, whose real name was Yamada Taketaro. He is sometimes referred to simply as *Bimyo.*

Yamada Taketaro. See YAMADA BIMYO.

Yamaga Soko. Pseudonym of Yamaga Takasuke (1624–1685), Japanese writer.

Yamaga Takasuke. See YAMAGA SOKO.

Yamanouchi Hideo. See SATOMI.

Yamazaki Ansi. Pseudonym of Yamazaki Yoshi (1619–1682), Japanese philosopher.

Yamazaki Sokan. See SOKAN.

Yamazaki Yoshi. See YAMAZAKI ANSI.

Yambo. Pseudonym of Enrico Novelli (1875–1943), Italian novelist and journalist.

Yan, V. Soviet author of the 1940's, whose real name was Vasily Yanchevetsky.

Yanchevetsky, Vasily. See YAN, V.

Yasuhara Masaakira. See TEISHITSU.

Yates, Dornford. Pseudonym of Cecil William Mercer (1885–1960), British mystery writer.

Yates, George Worthing. See HUNT, PETER.

Yayu. Pseudonym of Yoki Tokitsura (1702–1783), Japanese haiku poet.

Yeates, Mabel. See PEREIRA, HAROLD BERTRAM.

Yehalel. Pseudonym of Judah Leib Levin (1845–1925), Hebrew poet.

Yehoash. Pseudonym of Shloime Bloomgarten (1870–1927), Yiddish poet.

Yellowplush, Charles James. See THACKERAY, WILLIAM MAKEPEACE.

Yendys, Sydney. Pseudonym of Sydney Thompson Dobell (1824–1874), English poet and critic.

Yoki Tokitsura. See YAYU.

York, Jeremy. See CREASEY, JOHN.

Yorke, Henry. See GREEN, HENRY.

Yorke, Margaret. Pseudonym of Margaret Beda Larminie Nicholson (1924–   ), English writer.

Yosa Buson. See BUSON.

Yosano Hiroshi. See TEKAN.

Yoshida Kaneyoshi. See YOSHIDA KENKO.

Yoshida Kenko. Pseudonym of Yoshida Kaneyoshi (1283–1350), Japanese writer and poet, also called *Urabe Kaneyoshi.* He took the name *Kenko* upon becoming a Buddhist monk.

Yoshimine no Munesada. See HENJO.

Yoshimura Shinshichi. See MOKUAMI.

Young, Clarence. Collective pseudonym for the "Jack Ranger," "Motor Boys," and "Racer Boys" series. See STRATEMEYER, EDWARD L.

Young, Dorothea Bennett. See BENNETT, DOROTHEA.

Young, Edward. Pseudonym of Fred Reinfeld (1912–1964), American author.

Young, Eric Brett. See LEACROFT, ERIC.

Young, Ernest A. See ROCKWOOD, HARRY.

Young, Janet Randall. See RANDALL, JANET.

Young, Percy M. See MARSHALL, PERCY.

Young, Rose. Pseudonym of Marion Rose Harris (1925–   ), British free-lance journalist.

Young, Thomas. See SMECTYMNUUS.

Youngberg, Norma Ione. See WINFIELD, LEIGH.
Younger, William Antony. See MOLE, WILLIAM.
Yoxall, Harry W. See PARTINGTON, F. H.
Yrjö-Koskinen, Yrjö Sakari. See FORSMAN, GEORG ZACHRIS.
Yuan-chang. See MEI FEI.
Yu-ch'eng. See WANG WEI.
Yusaki Saburo Kiyotsugo. See KAN'AMI KIYOTSUGO.
Yusaki Saemondayu Motokiyo. See SE'AMI MOTOKIYO.
Yu-shan. See WU LI.
Yusuf Sinan. See SEYHI.

"Z"

Z, Hasse. Pseudonym of Hans Harald Zetterström (1877–1946), Swiss humorous writer and editor.
Zako, Andon. See ÇAJUPI.
Zamorski, R. Pseudonym of Roman Zmorski (1822–1867), Polish poet.
Zampieri, Domenico. See DOMENICHINO, IL.
Zant, Johan Wilhelm van der. See ANDREUS, HANS.
Zapolska, Gabriela. See KORWIN-PIOTROWSKA, GABRIELA.
Zarnov, Audrej. Pseudonym of Frantisek Subík (1903–   ), Slovak poet.
Zbarsher, Velvel. Pseudonym of Benjamin Wolf Ehrenkranz (1819–1878?), Yiddish poet.
Zeiger, Henry A. See PETERSON, JAMES.
Żeleński, Tadeusz. See BOY.
Zemaite. Pseudonym of Julija Beniuseviciute-Zimantiene (1845–1921), Lithuanian novelist.
Zeman, Antonín. See STASEK, ANATAL.
Zeman, Kamil. See OLBRACHT, IVAN.
Zena, Remigio. Pseudonym of Gaspare Invrea (1850–1917), Italian poet and novelist.
Zendorius a Zendoriis. See BEER, JOHANN.
Zenobia, Alexandria. See BRONTË, ANNE.
Zeromski, Stefan (1864–1925). Polish writer, whose pseudonyms are *Jozef Katerla* and *Maurycy Zych.*
Zeta. Pseudonym of Vincent Zachary Cope (1881–   ), English writer.
Zetternam, Eugeen. Pseudonym of Joos-Joseph Diricksens (1826–

1855), Flemish novelist, playwright, short-story writer, essayist, and social revolutionary.

Zetterström, Hans Harald. See Z. HASSE.

Zevin, Israel Joseph. See TASHRAK.

Zillberg, Venyamin Alexandrovich. See KAVÉRIN, VENYAMIN.

Zipoli, Perlone. Anagrammatic pseudonym of Lorenzo Lippi (1606–1664), Italian poet and painter.

Zitelmann, Konrad. See TELMANN, KONRAD.

Ziya, Mehmed (1875–1924). Turkish poet, sociologist, publicist, and nationalist leader, also known as *Ziya Gökalp.*

Ziyadah, Marie (1895–1941). Syro-Egyptian essayist, whose pseudonyms are *Isis Copia* and *Mayy* ("Little Mary").

Zmaj. Pseudonym of Jovan Jovanović (1833–1904), Serbian journalist and humorous poet.

Zmichowska, Narcyza. See GABRYELLA.

Żmogas. Pseudonym of Maria Rodziewiczówna (1863–1944), Polish writer.

Zmorski, Roman. See ZAMORSKI, R.

Zoll, Donald Atwell. See WINSLOW, DONALD.

Zonik, Eleanor Dorothy. See GLASER, ELEANOR DOROTHY.

Zorzi, Giacomo. See NOVENTA, GIACOMO.

Zuccari, Anna Radius. See NEERA.

Zuccoli, Luciano. Pseudonym of Luciano von Ingenheim (1868–1929), Italian novelist.

Zucker, Dolores Mae Bolton. Contemporary American free-lance writer, whose pseudonyms are *Dee Hill* and *Devera Myles.*

Zukauskas, Antanas. See VIENUOLIS.

Zunser, Eliakim (1836–1913). Russian-American poet in Yiddish, known as *Eliakim Badchen.*

Zuviría, Gustavo Martínez. See WAST, HUGO.

Zych, Maurycy. See ZEROMSKI, STEFAN.

Zyskind, Bruno. See JASIENSKI, BRUNO.